CAN'T YOU GET ALONG WITH ANYONE?

a writer's memoir
and a tale of a lost surfer's paradise

Allan C. Weisbecker

BANDITO
BOOKS

BANDITO
BOOKS

Published in 2007 by Bandito Books
www.banditobooks.com

Cover design by Allan Weisbecker, John Benedetti and Scott Massey
Front Cover photograph by Walter Iooss. Back cover photograph by
Warwick Saint. Interior design by Peggy LeTrent and iluminada design.

ISBN: 0-9797117-0-3
ISBN 13: 978-0-9797117-0-1

Printed in the United States

contents

Young and Wild and Beautiful Once*

Odd the way a moment returns, a life-occurrence apparently lost through time's neglect, the mental resurrection the end result of a sequence of recollected images, a one-to-the-next process ruled by the arcane illogic of the subconscious, but then, unexpectedly, the procession climaxing with perfect sense -- the summoned moment as clear, flawless, and inevitable as the finale of a well-wrought tale.

I daydreamed a seascape of long ago in a foreign land, blurry but for a certain wave my old surf-chum Christopher rode upon it, which image then segued to a remote shore-side campsite the two of us shared at another faraway place, which in turn conjured a certain risk we took, a law we broke, a laugh we had at the certainty of our invincibility.

I see the logic of it now: the shared laugh, the lawlessness, the invincibility, the endeavor of wave riding in foreign lands; how they all connected and culminated in the resurrected moment, so long lost.

It was the south of France, near Biarritz, in the summer of 1970. The European surf scene was in its infancy back then. All the good surfers on the continent were foreigners, primarily Americans, Aussies, and a few South Africans. Christopher and I had made friends with a cadre of beginning but stoked French surfers who were hell-bent on staging a contest, up the coast at a little town called Hossegor, which has since become famous for its fine beach breaks. I didn't believe in surf contests in those days, still don't, but these French had been very nice to Christopher and me, had taken us into their homes and so forth, so I agreed to enter. Christopher, who felt even more negatively about contests than I did, finally acquiesced at the last minute.

Well, I won the thing, or at least that's what the judges said; aside from Christopher, there were some pretty good surfers in the finals, all serious foreign travelers. (Christopher placed third or fourth, I recall.) After the awards ceremony, Christopher and I paddled back out for a sunset session. I came in first and was walking down the beach toward the parking lot when she approached me, this exquisite young French girl whose name has been (truly) lost to me over the years. Although we had no common

---

* Written on the road in Central America in 1997.

language, we'd smiled and flirted a bit that day. Now it was dusk and the beach was deserted and the image is so clear of her sliding off her bikini top in the warm glow of that perfect light, her wide, slightly crazed eyes daring my response.

This is the resurrected moment I refer to, real and true these many years later -- as if just a heartbeat ago I'd shut my eyes on that distant beach, perhaps the better to contemplate *the simple perfection of my young life*,[*] as it was there and then.

The French girl had never been with a man before and decided to give it up to a foreign surf bum. Whether she'd picked me earlier in the day or waited to see who would win the contest, mattered not at all to me. Confronted by this vision -- part designing woman, part naughty child, part female animal possessed by some deep biological imperative -- I was suddenly and completely overcome with pure lust, mindless and unencumbered.

But how beautiful she was...

It seems incredible that she's in her fifties now -- although I'd bet a valued possession that she's still beautiful. I can imagine her in a few years, that physical beauty fading now, talking to a granddaughter, and the adolescent girl asking who her first lover was. Oh, this young American surfer, she'd say, then, smiling at her own resurrection of the moment, she'd describe the evening on the beach at Hossegor in 1970 when she threw off her bikini top and drove herself and that young surfer mad with desire. The granddaughter would laugh and scold her jokingly and then they'd hug and the grandmother would say that she was young and wild and beautiful once too.

---

[*] Italics added for my purposes here.

Writing is easy. You just stare at the blank page until your forehead bleeds.

Gene Fowler

A (Brief) Note on Veracity

The people and events described in this book are real.

What I mean by *real* in the above claim is a good question, and will be dealt with. Suffice for now to say that I haven't misrepresented anything. At least not anything important.

What I mean by *anything important* in the above claim is a good question, and will be dealt with. Suffice for now to say that this book is *nonfiction*.

What I mean by nonfiction…

And so forth.

ACW

Author's Note

First, there's something I have to get off my chest in this *writer's* memoir.

If you've ever said or even thought the words "I'm going to write a book," you may eventually do so, write a book. But if you tacked on at the end the word *someday,* as in "I'm going to write a book someday," you never will. Trust me on this. I've done the research.

Along the same lines: If you've ever said or even thought the words "*I could write a book*" – with or without the emphasis on "I" – you never will do so, write a book. This is just the way it is. It's annoying when people who've never written anything make these statements to people who actually do write. And it happens all the time, at least to me. One time this guy, in finding out I'd written a book he read, said, "I could write *three* books." I wanted to pop him then and there.

That writing is difficult is best exemplified by the Gene Fowler quote I use as the opening epigraph: *Writing is easy. You just stare at the blank page until your forehead bleeds.*

Someone could write a whole book, a good book, let's assume, about how difficult writing is and it would not come close to saying as much as Mr. Fowler does in that second sentence, and I very much hope you agree. If not, it may not work out between us.

But what's my point?

If you're one of those non-writers who has said, or has thought of saying, or is capable of saying, "I'm going to write a book someday," or "I could write a book," maybe now, knowing my attitude about these sentiments and with the imparted image of your forehead bleeding while you stare at the blank page, you'll shut the fuck up.

But I doubt it. You'll say it anyway. You and I happen to meet somewhere, you'll probably even say it to me.

In one ear and out the other is the expression that comes to mind.

Another Author's Note

Aside from the actual writing of a book, titles are tough too. In fact, I sweated over the title of this book.

Publishers consider a title to be no more than a marketing tool – point of sale and all that – so they don't much care what a customer thinks of the title once he's finished reading the book, since by then he's already bought it. A writer, on the other hand, wants the title of his book to make sense, be satisfying, after the book has been read, especially then.

It's nice when a title has a couple meanings and they both make sense. A great example of this is Jon Krakauer's *Into Thin Air,* which is about a doomed ascent of Mount Everest. What a great title. You know, "into thin air" being an expression meaning where something goes when it disappears completely, which happens in the story to some climbers. Also, the air is thin up on Mount Everest, where the climbers disappear.

I bet when Krakauer thought of that title he more or less said to himself, "Whoopee!"*

It's also good if a title asks a question that is ultimately answered by the book itself, as is the case with this book, I hope. *Can't You Get Along With Anyone?* sounds like a good title, has a familiar yet abstract ring to it, plus there's subtext about conflict, plus the You subtly challenges the reader, meaning *you,* the personal you (not the abstract, *im*personal you), asks you the question and so forth, but what if after reading the book you wonder what was the point of the title since the question was not answered satisfactorily? So you might hold off judgment as to whether you like the title until you're done, assuming you hang in.

"Can't you get along with anyone?" is the body of the email I received from my Hollywood movie-writing agent (as opposed to my book agent) in response to the email I sent her firing her. While I was sweating over the title of this book I stumbled across the email, which I had forgotten about, via a ridiculous chain of coincidences. So don't give me too much credit for

---

* Unfortunately, though, *Into Thin Air* isn't such a great title when translated to certain other languages. For example, in the language of the Ogala Sioux, the expression "thin air" refers to the situation that results when someone passes gas in a crowded teepee. Given the subject matter of Krakauer's book, the title *Into Thin Air* could be confusing in an Ogala Sioux edition.

the title, assuming you hang in and end up liking it. I'm only peripherally involved.

But the point being: As soon as I saw the email I more or less said to myself, "Whoopee!"

There's another reason for my liking the title, which has to do with my former movie-writing agent. Imagine that this book becomes a howling success, as already I do, not often but occasionally, mainly when my bad chemicals are particularly active and I need to feel better about myself, or at least my writing.* Imagine my former movie-writing agent going to a bookstore and seeing her words – the body of the email she sent me, which I believe is laden with negative subtext – all over the place, in displays in the front window, stacked up in towering pyramids on the floor, covering tables; dozens of people holding the book (with the title facing out) while waiting in the cashier line. Everywhere she looks there they are, her words: *Can't You Get Along With Anyone?*

Hold on. A good question: What's someone in the movie business doing in a bookstore?

Here's what would happen in real life Hollywood as opposed to my fantasy. Rather than go to a book store to buy this book, my former movie-writing agent would order "coverage" from one of the readers at the mega-talent agency where she works, where she pimps out writers, their talent – or lack thereof, if you get my bad-movie drift – to thieves and idiots. Coverage is sort of the Hollywood version of *Cliff Notes*. Prevents people in the movie business from having to read books – or to be in bookstores. She'd probably say to the reader down in the coverage department, "Never mind the usual crapola, just sum up what the asshole says about me."

But back to my fantasy. My former movie-writing agent would see the title of this book all over the place and realize that she is the public butt of my clever irony and likely get aggravated.

By the way, did you catch the little redundancy in the subtitle, the *A Writer's Memoir* part of it? See, a memoir is always a writer's memoir: whoever wrote it is by definition a writer since only a writer could have done that, i.e., written the fucking thing.

I didn't sweat much over this problem, though. I figured Who's going to notice?

---

* I'm sweating over this Author's Note in late May, 2006, after completion of the book but several months before publication. This is always a bad time for me, as all sorts of fears and self-doubts and even self-loathing surface regarding what I've written. Not only do I sweat but some days my forehead even hemorrhages a bit, although not as much as during the writing. So to overpower the dispiriting thoughts I fantasize about great success.

A Little Backstory

Mom and me. A strange occurrence. I say *strange* because I don't believe in this stuff.

On the night of December 12, 1978 a major turning point in my life transpired. Two, actually. The first was that I didn't die. The second was that I didn't become filthy rich. I mean filthy rich by anyone's standards.

The short version: Along with some criminal cohorts – a dozen Colombians, one Nicaraguan, plus an old surf chum – I spent some time in a lifeboat in the North Atlantic after a mammoth rogue wave spawned by hurricane force winds busted the gut of our pot-laden freighter, *Ensenada.** Along with the ship, 100,000 pounds of high grade Colombian gold buds went to the bottom that night, the cargo being worth some $30 million on the wholesale market in those days, equivalent to at least $100 million today. Some fair percentage of the money, the exact number escapes me now, was to be mine, had the voyage been successful – back in those days, when it came to money and getting filthy rich, I wasn't dickin' around. (A few years later in one of my *Miami Vice* episodes I had the bad guys weighing hundred dollar bills – U.S. paper currency weighs exactly one gram – because it was too much of a hassle to count them all. This was in fact how my partner and I tallied our ill-gotten gains when we were feeling lazy and/or were too high to deal with it.)†

But the strange occurrence between Mom and me, plus the stuff I don't believe in, came to pass a few days after the sinking, when the piratical lot of us were put ashore by the research vessel *Atlantis II* (out of Woods Hole, Massachusetts), which had plucked us from the freezing water.

Although I had a lot of phone calls to make upon our arrival on terra firma, the first person I called was Mom. Looking back, I can't explain this logically. Our ad hoc multinational syndicate – composed of our Colombian

---

*   This night is described in detail in my (first) memoir, *In Search of Captain Zero*.

†   The other touch I came up with for this episode, titled "Made For Each Other," was that I basically wrote the Don Johnson character out of it. I got a kick out of this since Donny got aggravated and Donny was someone I did not get along with.

pot lord (plus his military and government connections), a spooky Dutch industrialist, a CIA-connected Cuban, plus a certain New York mafia family which was to run the offload via the Longshoremen and Teamsters Unions – needed to know of the catastrophe somewhat more than Mom, plus I wasn't about to describe to her my current circumstance or recent events. The last thing I would do in those days was worry Mom by reminding her of my lunatic lifestyle. In fact, I called just to say, "Hi Mom, how are ya?"

"Are you all right?!" were Mom's tremulous first words upon hearing my voice.

I told her, "Sure, Mom. What's the matter?"

Mom described how she'd had a terrible nightmare three nights before, waking up from a sound sleep convinced that I was dead. Three nights before was the night of the sinking and the time Mom told me she'd awakened – around 3 AM – was approximately the time I realized the ship would founder and that the whole lot of us would surely die of exposure in the survival sea conditions. The *Atlantis II*'s appearance, literally in the nick of time as *Ensenada* was going down, was a miracle of sorts – we were far from shipping lanes (the research vessel was collecting bottom samples in that remote sea-place when the storm struck).

As I say, I don't believe in this stuff, psychic stuff, although Mom did.

How do I explain Mom's apparent awareness of my dire straights on the night of December 12, 1978?

Maybe it was enough that Mom believed.

But I suppose the real point here is that Mom and I were close. Still are. Even now.

A Little More Backstory

In the summer of 1998 when I returned from the two-year Central America journey upon which my (first) memoir, *In Search of Captain Zero*, is based, I was pretty much broke and homeless; I was living in my camper in a friend's yard at Montauk, on the end of Long Island, New York, where I'd started that journey. The emerging book was a mess. I couldn't even look at it. Mom had dropped a bomb: her breast cancer from 20 years before had resurfaced. I was exuding a sort of negativity. One way this manifested itself was that women kept saying No. They'd say No even before I asked them anything. The last time I'd had any sex was months before, in a whorehouse in Panama, and it wasn't real satisfying – I'd more or less gotten raped…

Hold on. I sort of *did* have some sex about a month after my return to the States, before I moved down to Mom's to take care of her and to try to produce a book from the mess.

… in my camper one night…

…about 30 seconds into the act, the woman says, "I got to go home." Something about her cat. Since I don't remember her name, I've come to think of this woman as Cat Woman, the fiasco that night as the Cat Woman Incident.

But being broke was worse than the Cat Woman Incident. It was terrible. I'd turned 50 on my last birthday and here I was…

Hold on. Maybe I better explain about getting semi-raped in a Panamanian whorehouse. It sort of goes to the being-broke-at-Montauk issue anyway, if indirectly.

While in Central America I did some writing and photography for a magazine called *Men's Journal*. (A self-portrait-with-my-dog appeared on the September, 1998 cover.) My most ambitious piece was an investigation into the shootout killing of a man named Max Dalton, an American expatriate living at the end of the road at the bottom of Central America, in outback Costa Rica. I met some interesting characters in the process of uncovering the truth of the killing, one being a Canadian living in a border town between Costa Rica and Panama. Called himself "The Facilitator." The guy had this thick, jagged scar running ear-to-ear across his throat.

That kind of guy. I needed the cell phone records of a corrupt Costa Rican police chief and had been told that if anyone could get those records, it was this guy. After some spooky phone calls to him – between which he did some background checking to see who I really was – The Facilitator agreed to a meeting, in a whorehouse just across the border in Panama.

So I'm sitting in this whorehouse waiting for this guy and the whores are of course hitting on me. I'm not interested. For reasons I myself don't quite understand, I've never been into whores, sexually. But I'm joking with them and we get friendly. I had my camera gear and I start taking pictures. They vamp it up. Fun. One of the whores suggests we all go into the back room for some even better pictures.

So now I'm in the back room in this Panamanian whorehouse with these four whores and they get naked and jump around on the bed and so forth and I'm shooting away. I shoot a roll, then thank them and give them some money. (I'm figuring to bill *Men's Journal* for this -- how could a magazine called *Men's Journal* object to that sort of expense?) I go to leave and the whore who'd surfaced as the alpha whore says Since I've already paid for it, don't I want to get laid? I say No thanks, not right now, and the situation immediately starts to go sour.

What do I mean, No thanks?

The alpha whore is looking at me with this expression indicating that I'm in a room with four naked women and a bed and so how could I possibly not want to get laid? Then she says Aren't we pretty enough for you? I say It's not that... What is it then? We had already gone through the Am I a fag? routine out in the bar and I'd of course vehemently denied it, so that wouldn't work. Figuring it would be indelicate to mention I'm not into whores, I say I'm just not in the mood. The alpha whore says something in Spanish along the lines of Mood, Shmood! Next thing, my clothes are coming off and these women are not fooling around.

An observation: The male member is a bizarre device. It either doesn't work at all when you really want it to, or it will work just fine in the most adverse circumstances.

But the point, and the connection to being broke at Montauk, is this: *Men's Journal* owed me expense money from the assignment, like three grand – big bucks when you're broke – but they weren't paying. Didn't say they didn't owe it, didn't complain about the whorehouse expenditure; they knew they owed it, they just would not send the money. I'd send memos, mellow reminders about the debt. At first they – this guy who was then the features editor – would come up with excuses, like the accounting department had just burned down or whatever. I forget. Then the guy ignored me. Weeks went by. I was calling the guy like every other day now. He never answered his phone so I'd leave pleading messages on his voice mail. I'm broke. Please send the money.

One day I picked up the phone, a pay phone, since I didn't actually have a phone, and called the guy. Said this on his voice mail: "Send me the money or I'll come into the city, wait outside your office on Sixth Avenue, and when you come out I'm going to beat the shit out of you."

The money arrived via FedEx the next day, along with a note of apology.

Although these incidents – my threatening the features editor of a national magazine to get money owed me after being semi-raped by an alpha whore who didn't like my attitude while I was waiting to interview a Facilitator with an ear-to-ear scar across his throat while I was investigating the murder of an American expat at the end of the road in outback Costa Rica – are probably interesting enough to be worth the words (plus they go to the title of this book, answering the question posed by it), they also act as a set up for an incident to come, in which I threaten a major Hollywood movie star, likewise to get money owed me. You'll like that one, I think.

But the real point: On top of all the sweating and forehead bleeding and firing mega-talent agency pimps, this is some wild ass job, this writing job, no?

For Lisa, who gave me what every writer needs…

PART ONE
At Age 55

CHAPTER ONE

'Where shall I begin, please, your majesty?' he asked. 'Begin at the beginning,' the king said, gravely, 'and go on till you come to the end: then stop.'

Lewis Carroll

Late winter, 2003. We're coming up on the second anniversary of Mom's death, which was in April of 2001. As I write these words – indeed, as I begin this narrative – I'm not at my home at the end of the road at the bottom of Central America, in outback Costa Rica. I'm on a certain lower Caribbean island, never mind which one – there's a great surf break here that doesn't need more surfers via my blabbing. Back in the 1990s I did a piece about the island for a popular surf magazine and not only did not name it, but I laid in misinformation as to where it is, via some subtle nonfiction deceits.

Lisa is here with me. Lisa is a woman with whom I have fallen in love, at age 55, possibly for the first time. We have a little cottage overlooking a gorgeous stretch of tropical coast. Right now (about 9 AM on a Sunday) the members of the Spiritual Baptist church up the hill are in full, melodic voice. (Back in 1995, in the shore break below us, I was baptized by the church's Spiritual Mother.) As the Baptists sing, fishermen, many of whom I know, are hand-hauling a seine net in the bay. Everywhere you look there's a postcard. Later today, the neighbor on the other side from the church will likely play *soca* music on his stereo. Soca is a form of calypso I like very much. The surf has been great since we got here a few days ago. Lisa surfs also.

As I more or less am trying to say, it's idyllic here. And you know what? I can't wait to get back to my home in Costa Rica, with Lisa, if that indeed comes to pass. That's how idyllic life is there.

That was a photo of Lisa in a bikini you looked at a moment ago. Please bear with me and take another quick glance.

Back? Holy shit, right?

I mention this stuff – plus having you look at Lisa in a bikini again – because my life appears to have worked out, which would make Mom very happy. Toward the end, Mom actively worried about me, how my life would go after she was gone. She mainly worried about me finding someone to love in this world.

As I've told Lisa, I only wish she could have met Mom.

So it appears that I've finally got what I want, after going through a lot of shit. (I'm not sure whether getting semi-raped in a Panamanian whorehouse counts as *going through shit. May*be.)

Further, I believe I've begun this narrative because of my finally having got what I want, or the appearance thereof. In other words, because of Lisa, my having fallen in love with her, at age 55, possibly for the first time.

In a narrative wherein the protagonist goes through a lot of shit, it's nice if he gets what he wants at the end. Not absolutely necessary, but nice. This is difficult in a memoir, which is a sub-genre of *nonfiction,* which is supposed to be some sort of description of real life, which this narrative is supposed to be, because real life is hardly ever like that. For example, in *In Search of Captain Zero* I went through a bunch of shit, then, at the end, pretty much just went through more shit. I mean my dog even died, for Chrissake. I had to jump through some hoops, mainly structural ones, to come up with a satisfying ending to that one.

By the way: Structure. You wanna talk about something a writer sweats over?

So I believe I want to write about my current life, how it goes now that I've got what I want and what Mom wanted for me. I say *I believe* I want to write about that because of a theory I hold.

No one knows shit about why he does anything.

This includes writing, of course. Why a writer writes anything. Sometimes I think I write to find out why I write.

CHAPTER TWO

There comes a time when every man feels the urge to spit on his hands, hoist the black flag, and start slitting throats.

H.L. Mencken

The phone rings.

Mom was out somewhere, visiting with Ellen, or shopping, or she could have been at the clinic down the street. I don't remember what I was doing either, when that call came. See, when something bad happens out of the blue your mind tends to cancel out details from just before it. Like when Mom told me on the phone that her breast cancer was back, had invaded her bones, I remember the sound of her voice, casual, as was her suggestion that I visit her in North Carolina, "maybe even stay for a while," and when she added that there was an ocean beach nearby with waves I could surf, I knew she really needed me. I remember all that like it happened a minute ago but I can't for the life of me remember precisely where I was or what I was doing when we spoke.

Same thing here. I well remember the phone call itself, even now as I write from my idyllic little Caribbean island some three years later, and two years after Mom died. The call was from New York, from Penguin Putnam, Inc., the company that was to publish my previous book, *In Search of Captain Zero*. It was my new editor. The original editor, who had acquired my manuscript for the house, had left for another job, something outside of book publishing as I recall. (In publishing jargon, I was "orphaned.") The new editor, whom I had not yet met or talked to, introduced herself, then immediately told me that my book, my manuscript, would have to be cut from its present 120,000 words to 80,000. Said this without asking how I am or anything like that first.

Before I could even respond, my writer's queasy gut flared.

I should explain about my writer's queasy gut. Sometimes when I'm writing or thinking about writing or talking about writing to someone like a movie producer or studio executive or even just to a normal non-writer – if he's saying something about writing as if he knows anything about it – I get a bad feeling, which I refer to as my writer's queasy gut. In fact, just writing this paragraph has caused a flutter of my writer's queasy gut, the full-blown version of which is like you have a swarm of terrorized centipedes down in your duodenum writhing maniacally, trying to get the fuck out.

I exaggerate only slightly.

Until this phone call, a full-blown attack of my writer's queasy gut was a rarity, especially since I'd quit writing for the movies and television, left Hollywood altogether. Since then I'd mostly just get flares and flutters of it.

So my new editor leading off our first talk with the bulletin that 40,000 words would have to be cut from my manuscript resulted in a flare of my writer's queasy gut. (A *flare* is more serious than a *flutter*, but nothing like a full-blown attack.) Imagine that the centipedes, having been snoozing, are now stirring, some of them stretching their legs, of which there are a bunch; about a hundred, I think.

"So you've gotten around to reading it," I said, referring to my manuscript. Before leaving his job at Penguin Putnam, my old editor told me that my new editor had not yet read my manuscript.

"No, not yet," my new editor said. Then this: "I don't have to read your book to know how long it should be."

The centipedes were rudely awake now, and getting edgy.

I myself was pretty much speechless. Not at the 40,000 words that according to my new editor would have to be cut, and not even that she believed she could know how long a book should be without reading it. I was speechless that she would *say* that in a first conversation with a person with whom she was about to embark upon a lengthy and in the best of scenarios potentially difficult, demanding, relationship; a *creative* relationship and all it implies.

Finally, I tentatively stuttered that William Least Heat-Moon's *Blue Highways*, which in many ways is similar to my book (my old editor had made this comparison), is close to 200,000 words and one of the most beloved works in American travel literature. "Way too long," my new editor said in the dismissive tone I would come to know well. "I would have cut it in half."

Again, I had not met this person before, nor spoken to her nor corresponded with her in any way. This was all her way of saying Hi-how-are-ya. But her comment about how she would have butchered a great book was not what goosed the centipedes to writhe maniacally. That came a minute or so later, in the context of how we'd work together.

"If we have a creative difference, we'll talk it out," I was now saying, near panic but hiding it well. (Maybe not that well, actually. Mom came home soon after the phone conversation and seeing the expression on my face, said, "My God, Allan, what happened?")

"We won't bother with any of that," my new editor said in reply to my hope that a dialogue would settle creative differences. "You'll never change my mind about anything."

You'll never change my mind about anything.

CHAPTER THREE

For what's a play without a woman in it?

William Kyd

Lisa and me. A little backstory.

When I first caught sight of Lisa in her little MG at the beach lot at Montauk, Long Island, New York, in the summer of 1998, I was so smitten that I would eventually write a poem about that moment. This in spite of my not caring much for reading poetry, let alone writing it. I was so smitten that I was also intimidated, too intimidated to say word one to her. (The Cat Woman Incident, also in the summer of 1998, preceded my first sighting of Lisa and no doubt contributed to the intimidation.)

You first see Lisa, you don't necessarily go, "My God, there's a beautiful woman," although you might. What happens, though – if you're a guy – is that some primitive area of your psyche senses you're in the presence of some sort of *ultimate female-ness.* This is not just sex appeal; it's some other level of that, as if the sex appeal spectrum had been extended solely for Lisa, in order to better define what's going on with her. Proof of this, meaning that this isn't simply my eccentric take on her, is the downside. Which is that men can't seem to *not* hit on her. It's like they can't help themselves. It's like a gravitational thing. Or maybe it's like the concept of the curvature of space.

Imagine this. Some guy sees Lisa, along with Playboy's Playmate of the Year, standing a few yards apart. The guy heads for the Playmate of the Year. But then his direction of movement veers, involuntarily, just slightly… then veers a little more… and he starts struggling with this phenomenon, wondering why he can't seem to walk a straight line… then next thing he's forgotten about the Playmate of the Year and finds himself saying "Hi there!" to my girlfriend.

For guys, space itself is curved in Lisa's direction.

This is tiring for both of us and aggravating for me. I come in from surfing, for example, there's generally some guy hitting on her on the beach, some guy who knows good and goddamn well she's with me. One time here on this little Caribbean island I got so tired of this bullshit that when I paddled ashore and saw a guy doing his routine on the sand by her – this guy knew good and goddamn well Lisa was with me – I was going to just flat pop him then and there. He must've caught a vibe; when he saw me coming he got up and beat cheeks for higher ground.

But again, you first see Lisa, you don't necessarily go, "My God, there's a beautiful woman," although you might.

CHAPTER FOUR

Writing is pretty crummy on the nerves.

Paul Theroux

Before I press on about my relationship with my previous book's editor, I have to explain about a writer's rights, such as they are.* The basic deal a writer has regarding editing is that the writer has final say about changes. He can refuse to make certain changes, or any changes. His word is law. Sounds good and right, right? The book is the writer's vision, all that. Okay, but here's the catch: The publisher can, at any time, change its mind about publishing the book at all. Can even demand that the writer's advance be returned. Ouch. Sort of takes the pizzazz out of the first clause, no? In fact, what this clause does is pretty much say this about the first clause: Fuhgedaboudit.

Keeping the above in mind, also keep in mind that my only connection to this giant, faceless corporation, Penguin Putnam, Inc., that was contractually obligated to publish my book – if it felt like it – was this mega-maniacal editor. She personally had control of my book. I have to repeat something because it's vital: She didn't acquire the book. Which means she had virtually nothing at stake, professionally or personally. She may not even have liked the material. (Plus, she may have had horns growing out of the top of her head.) At any time she could have gone into one of her weekly meetings and said, "You know that book I was assigned? Well, it's not working out. The writer is impossible, won't agree to edits. The book is not going to be publishable. Let's demand our money back and drop it from the list."

And you know what? Odds are they would have done it, dropped my book, without further ado. There were about 60 books on Tarcher's (the Penguin Putnam imprint that published me) spring 2001 list; these were busy people. Although mine would turn out to be among the top three or

---

* Not counting best-selling hacks like, say, John Grisham or Dan Brown, who can dictate their own rights via their contract terms, in spite their not giving a flying fuck about their sentences. I mean in their books, not their contracts. I bet they give a flying fuck about the sentences in their contracts.

four sellers of that list, no one knew that at the time. (As of this writing it's the number two best seller from that list, after a self-help book entitled *Who Moved My Cheese?*.)* I was a nobody, having only produced a weird little cult book back in the mid 1980s (*Cosmic Banditos*, Random House). That I'd written a bunch of television and feature film scripts probably counted against me, if it counted at all.

The possibility that my book would be dropped was on my mind from the moment my new, assigned editor uttered that first whiz-bang zinger, "I don't have to read your book to know how long it should be."

For a year I lived in a constant state of fear.

I did make a critical error in judgment, a big mistake, right at the beginning and which I'll describe, because it surely exacerbated coming events. It also amounted to an object (abject, too) lesson in the creative process; why writing is so difficult; why writers sweat so much; why their foreheads may even bleed. Why that blank page is so terrifying. Why at this very moment I should be too paralyzed with self-doubt to write the next word.

As I say, my new editor was assigned to me near the beginning of the editing process. Thing was, the original editor – the one who acquired my book, who *liked* my book – had already started editing before he left the company; he'd got to around manuscript page 60. I was not sure if my new editor was aware of this work, but early on we had a conversation, the gist of which was that she maintained that editing is a science, with certain principals written in stone (although I never figured out what they were); no gray areas; this is right, this is wrong kind of thing. "You'll never change my mind about anything" certainly makes sense in this context.

So we're at the very beginning of the edit; our relationship had not yet completely deteriorated. Some disagreements had come up; no surprise there. Although "You'll never change my mind about anything" hovered over me like an ion-bloated thunderhead, I tried my best to explain my point of view regarding edits I disagreed with – predictably, I never got anywhere. Out of curiosity, but also thinking to buttress my points, I went back over the first editor's edit of those first 60 pages. It was a revelation.

There was virtually no correlation between the two editors' edits. In fact, in three places my first editor had made margin notes like "Good!" or "I like it!" or "Yes!" In two of the three cases, my new editor not only didn't say anything positive but *she edited out* the passages previously extolled. For example, early on (page 9 in the book) I describe my friend Chris's ability to see positives in horrific situations, like a mortar barrage in Vietnam. I point out how the drawback is that while "he's dwelling on some preposterous

---

*   If you bought and then actually read a self-help book entitled *Who Moved My Cheese?* it's best you put this book down and forget about it. It's unlikely to work out between us.

silver lining in an outright horrific cloud, a means of extrication from the situation may get overlooked." The next line pays off the idea expressed, and also sets up events to come: "I know this to be the case from unnerving personal experience."

The first editor saw fit to circle this line and write "Yes!" in the margin. His replacement, my new editor, deleted the line and wrote in the margin, "This is looping." Looping. What the fuck is that? was my initial reaction. Although my editor would use this "looping" concept all over the place as a justification for cutting stuff, I never got a comprehensible definition out of her. Something to do with hinting at future narrative events, which apparently is bad. When I asked her what was the difference between looping and legitimate foreshadowing (a.k.a. a *set up*) my editor talked for a bit without saying anything, then changed the subject.

I don't know about you and I don't know about the "science" of editing and I still don't know exactly what "looping" is or why it's bad, but I like the line, "I know this to be the case from unnerving personal experience." It's in the book and the book is better for it. In other words, I refused to cut the line. Every time I did this, refused an edit, I knew my book was getting closer to being dropped from publication, out of spite.

So I sometimes caved and agreed to edits I considered bad.

Fear.

Another incident; I think it's worth the words.

We were near the end of the editing process; the manuscript was about to go to galleys. In theory, this should have been a relief. Light at the end of the tunnel. The worst should have been over by then, all the "You'll never change my mind about anything" crises and conflicts dealt with, a reduction of the amplitude of my writer's queasy gut. But in point of fact my editor had not yet hit her stride, crisis and conflict-wise. She hadn't even come off the starting blocks. She was still on the infield, stretching and loosening up.

This current incident had to do with a sentence in my memoir that I decided to delete as we went to galleys. It comes pretty far along in the narrative, after my journey south in search of my missing old buddy. I'm deep down in Central America, reflecting on my career as a Hollywood screen and TV writer. The sentence I wanted to delete was this: "I'd alienated half the people I worked with."

My reason for deleting the line had nothing to do with not wanting to look bad or anything like that. Throughout the book I own up to all sorts of fears and insecurities and character flaws. The more the merrier was my view of that sort of thing. In fact, that was why I'd written the line to begin with. The more the merrier. The problem with the line, though, was that it wasn't true; I had not alienated half the people I'd worked with. I *did* alienate some people out in Hollywood, more than a couple, but not *half* the ones I worked with. And, anyway, the people I alienated were almost all studio executives (plus a dimwit producer here and there), which, in my view, don't count.

On the surface, the deletion of the line should have pleased my editor, since she was crazed to cut stuff. Why was she crazed to cut stuff? Goes back to her original assertion – made before she read the manuscript – that the book should come in at 80,000 words; that 40,000 words would have to be cut. That, plus "You'll never change my mind about anything." See, the book was still over 100,000 words. (It would *stay* over 100,000 words, in case you're wondering.) So, again, she was crazed to cut stuff.

But as I sat there in Mom's house looking at that line...

I'd alienated half the people I'd worked with...

...I had a premonition, along with a brief but intense flaring of my writer's queasy gut.

Not only did I delete the line, I completely obliterated it. In ink, not pencil, which is what you're supposed to use. Here's what the line looked like when I was done with it:

██

I also wrote "delete" in the margin, with a little arrow pointing to where the line used to be. I may have also written in the margin, "This line should not be in the galleys when you print them." I forget.

In any case, overkill. Bordering on the ridiculous.

Right: The line was still there, in the galleys. If you can get hold of an ARC (Advance Reading Copy) of *In Search of Captain Zero* – a paperback version of the book made from the galleys to send to critics and PR people – you'll see it's there. It's not in the actual store-sold book. I made sure of that by sending a personal note to the typesetter and to the copy editor, as well as deleting the line again in the galleys.[*]

True or not, "I'd alienated half the people I worked with" sounded good to my editor, since it was evidence that I was an asshole, maybe even

---

[*] Some genuine paranoia raised its funky head shortly after I got my box of ARCs. An ARC just sort of fell open and it was to the page with the sentence I'd deleted and which my editor had put back in. I immediately assumed my editor had conspired with the printer to manufacture the ARCs so this would happen. Wild-eyed, I started tossing ARCs around the room to see what page they would fall open to. My fear was unfounded, but I'll tell you, I was crazed about this for a few days. I'd suddenly and without warning toss an ARC onto the floor then drop to my hands and knees and squint at the page it fell open to. Never again fell open to the offending page. Okay. Good. One less thing.

a lunatic. Which was evidence that *she* was just fine, mentally. So she'd stetted that line before my book went to galleys. She'd outright fucked with *my* words, with *my* book, for *personal* reasons.

Although this drove me nuts, I kept my trap shut (except to my agent, who did nothing).

Fear.

An example of fear, and of some caving-in I did and of which I'm ashamed: When I submitted my Acknowledgements I thanked my editor profusely for her help. I was hoping that for ego reasons she would soften up on me, or at least not drop the book from publication. (For a related reason I also thanked my then-book agent, at whom I was pissed off as well.) After a quick glance to see that it was in the finished book, I've never once looked at the Acknowledgements in the back of *In Search of Captain Zero*.

A side issue, call it a Meanwhile: When in 2002 *Zero* was poised to come out in paperback I informed my editor that I wanted the Acknowledgements page deleted (for obvious reasons). She of course left it in, to aggravate me. Point being: Now, with the publication of *this* book, anyone wanting to know my editor's actual name can do so very easily via a glance at *Zero's* last page, rather than having to jump through any Googling hoops or some such. There's a great expression that applies here, to my editor: *Hoisted by her own petard.**

Anyway, every time I came across a bad edit, I had to take into consideration that my standing firm in not accepting it would be some sort of last straw to this person who flat out told me she would never change her mind about anything. Do you have any idea of the anxiety this caused me? I'm talking a high-amplitude, near-constant writer's queasy gut. For a year.

Before I circle back – *loop* back – to my big mistake I'll give you one more example of what I was up against, maybe persuade you that my anxiety and near constant stomach ache were justified. A couple months down the road from my big mistake I came across a particular error on my editor's part. This one was so small and so clear cut that I only brought it up to her in passing. On page 179 I refer to a certain North African beach as "that" North African beach. My editor changed "that" to "a", the reason being that since no North African beach had yet been mentioned, "a" was the proper indefinite article.

Not only had "that" North African beach been mentioned several times,

---

* In case you're not familiar with it, *hoisted by one's own petard* pretty much means *to outsmart oneself*. The derivation of the expression is this: *Petard* is a French noun which refers to a certain type of bomb or loud firework, but in English usage means *the act of breaking wind*. Picture being (literally) *hoisted* in this manner – the rush of insight that results when you connect the image with the intended meaning, *to outsmart oneself*, is a howler, no? Don't you love language?

there was a whole chapter about it. She had forgotten. Not wanting to provoke her, I summoned my meekest tone and tentatively reminded her about the chapter. There was this pause. It went on and on: the conflicting forces of Truth, Justice and the American Way and "You'll never change my mind about anything" were battling it out in her psyche. Then my editor said this, and I wrote it down: "You can *choose* to think I made a mistake, but I don't see it that way. If *I* didn't remember that chapter, it's likely that readers won't either." There was another pause. (Actually, you yourself might want to pause here, to absorb this quote.) Then in a tone that I can only describe as ominous in portent she said this: "It's your book. Do whatever you *want*."

It occurred to me then and there that my book might not see the light of publication because I'd refused to change "that" to "a".

My big mistake. I sent my new editor the previous editor's edit of the first 60 pages, pointing out that his edits had nothing in common with hers, and wasn't this proof that editing is a subjective process, not a science?

I know: What an idiot I was to think that this unequivocal example of my editor having her head up her ass would do anything but enrage her. Her arrogance turned into a full-blown blood feud (albeit a one-sided one, since, with the cancellation clause hanging over me, I was severely outgunned) that lasted through the rest of the edit and then evolved into outright sabotage of my book upon publication.

But at least my worst fear was not realized. The book eventually did get published.*

---

* My theory as to why my editor let the book be published is this: She realized that it was a good book and wanted her name associated with it. I know. That theory has a self-serving ring and is therefore suspect. So how about this one: My shameful toadying in the Acknowledgments worked.

CHAPTER FIVE

The imagination of a boy is healthy, and the mature imagination of a man is healthy; but there is a space of life in between, in which the soul is in ferment, the character undecided, the way of life uncertain.

John Keats

My father died while I was taking care of Mom, struggling with my memoir, with my demented editor, and, by the way, not getting laid. (I hadn't gotten laid since either the Cat Woman Incident or the Panamanian Whorehouse Incident, depending on how you define *getting laid*.)*

I talk about my father twice in *In Search of Captain Zero,* plus up front just after the dedication (which is For Mom) I quote from a poem he wrote, over an old black & white photo of him looking like a god. Then, right at the beginning of the text I describe a camping trip to the end of the road place called Montauk, on Long Island, New York, with my father when I was nine years old. I make the point that my father was responsible for my love of the sea, which in turn led me to surfing, which in turn changed everything.

I worshiped my father. I wanted to be just like him.

In *Zero's* epilogue I visit my father, who lived in New York just a couple of blocks from where I grew up, and whom I hadn't seen in several years. I describe how he'd become a recluse, living with thirty cats in a filthy house with instruments of torture and primitive warfare hanging all over the place. In a quiet, still-able-to-function way, he'd gone insane.

The way I found out my father had died was that the local police came knocking at Mom's door late one night – this was early January, 2000 – and told me. They'd tracked me down via my North Carolina driver's license. When I'd last visited my father – this was the time described in *Zero's* epilogue – I'd given his next door neighbor my phone number at Mom's in case anything happened. But the neighbor had lost it. He did remember that I was living in North Carolina. He told the police up there and they

---

* In the strictest, no holds barred sense of *getting laid*, it's possible that neither of these incidents count, which is a depressing notion.

called the North Carolina police.

The way anyone ever knew that my father had died was that the mailman noticed he wasn't collecting his mail. The detective with whom I spoke when I went up to deal with all this told me that my father had likely died on New Year's Eve – the day before the turn of the millennium. When they broke in, the detective told me, the police found my father on the living room floor. Sprawled in the filth, I added mentally.

The detective started to go on about the circumstances of my father's death but I sensed where he was going and stopped him. I didn't want to hear it. I didn't want to hear how after a few days the cats had become crazed with hunger and had got to him. I didn't want to hear about the autopsy, which, I suspected, would say that my father had had a stroke; he'd had a couple of minor ones before. I didn't want to hear this, or the details of exactly how long the mail had been piling up, because it all might mean that my father had lain there paralyzed for days before he died and the cats had got to him while he was still alive.

My father kept everything; kept everything he ever bought, collected, was given; every photo he ever took (he was a serious amateur photographer for a few years) or was taken of him or anyone he knew; there were dozens of photo albums stacked up or lying around the house. He kept everything he ever wrote (he was a writer with a column at one time); everything I ever wrote since I was a kid-writer; postcards I'd sent from far-flung places while I was on surf trips or smuggling runs. Everything about the family going back 100 years right up to the present – there in the filth and clutter on the floor next to where my father died in the living room was the Christmas card I'd just sent him, although it was unopened.

My father's house was big, four-stories, four bedrooms, and was so crammed with junk that I had to break down one of the bedroom doors to get in; a pile of boxes of junk had toppled over in there and fallen against the door. I was greatly affected by some of the stuff I found; all kinds of memories came rushing back. For example, at the bottom of a box of framed newspaper articles about the defunct family business I came across an old letter, four pages on paper that with the years had become brown and thin like parchment. Handwritten, beautifully so, almost like calligraphy, it looked like it should have been in a glass case at the Smithsonian. Thing was, though, there was so much stuff and at this point I was so tired and distraught that I almost didn't read the letter; I almost tossed it aside. What prompted me to read it was the date at the top, the year, 1948, which was the year I was born.

As I read, I got a strange feeling, a classic déjà vu, I suppose, although I hadn't actually seen the letter before. The letter was written by a man whose name was unfamiliar to me. He was writing from Nairobi, Kenya. Africa. 1948. Africa was still… Africa. The prose was wonderful. Simple sentences, yet very strong, vivid imagery. The writer was describing his life in Africa as a hunter, a white hunter, as the description used to go.

The tone of the letter was intimate, as if the writer and my father had been very close. Here and there, for emphasis, the writer would insert my father's name, Allan, the same as mine, which heightened the peculiar feeling I was experiencing.

The first specific recollection that surfaced as I was reading the letter was this: I was checking out a book from my old high school library. I was not yet in high school, though; I was much younger, seven or eight. The book was titled *Hunter,* and I remembered that the author's name was actually that, Hunter, John Hunter, I think. He was a white hunter in Africa. The book was his memoir.

The next thing as I sat there in the clutter of my father's house with this old letter in front of me was that I realized that I had read this book, *Hunter,* many times. I recalled checking it out of the library again and again. If you're old enough, you might remember that there used to be a 3 x 5 card tucked in the jacket of library books. When you checked out a book, you'd sign the card, which the librarian would then file, so she'd know who had the book. As I was reading this letter from Kenya, Africa, 1948, I got a mental picture of the 3 x 5 card that went with *Hunter.* Stacked up on the thin blue lines on the card were my signatures, in my childish scrawl. A dozen at least. Just mine. No one else had checked out the book.

Then I remembered that for some period of time when I was a kid I was obsessed with becoming a white hunter in Africa.

As I sat there with this old letter, something buried even deeper down surfaced. A story my father had told me when I was about ten years old. When my father was fighting in North Africa in World War II, he and a buddy made plans to come back to Africa when the war was over. To the real Africa, equatorial East Africa, to become white hunters. They corresponded when they came home, got specific about where they would go and how much money they'd need to get started as white hunters, and so forth. Then, in 1946, just as everything was coming together, my father met my mother. Fell in love. What my father told me when I was about ten years old, and which I was just now remembering, was that when he asked my mother to marry him, if she said No he was going to Africa with his war buddy, as planned.

She said Yes.

A part of me wishes she hadn't said Yes and that my father had gone to Africa. This notwithstanding that I would then never have been born. See, had this come to pass my father might still be alive. Or he might have died in some heroic way instead of on his living room floor in the filth, his body desecrated by his goddamn cats.

As life went, my father and mother were divorced in 1971 while I was in North Africa, surfing and smuggling hashish.

CHAPTER SIX

What I like in a good author is not what he says, but what he whispers.

Logan Pearsall Smith

I don't know if they still do, but one of the C-SPAN channels used to run *Book TV* every weekend. (I don't know if they still do because C-SPAN doesn't reach my home at the end of the road at the bottom of Central America or this Caribbean island.) Forty-eight hours straight of interviews with authors and publishing people. Some of it was terrific, some really boring; writers (myself included) are often terrible public speakers. Mom and I used to tune in, maybe learn something, find out about a good book. Sometimes we'd just let it play in the background all weekend, except Sundays during football season. Mom was a big pro football fan, God bless her, especially regarding the New York Giants.

One weekend in the midst of the *In Search of Captain Zero* editing process I fell asleep with the TV on. Late that night I awoke, or semi-awoke, to find a frightening image suspended before me in ghostly glow. My editor. Her face. (I'll spare you my admittedly biased perception of her looks.) I'd had nightmares of this sort before but this one persisted even as my head cleared. Then I realized that the image was real, more or less. *Book TV* on C-SPAN. My editor was a participant in a panel discussion about the publishing business. The moderator was introducing her, giving her resumé, listing books she'd worked on and so forth. I reached for the remote device but my finger froze over the power button. As with actual nightmares I've had, I was fascinated as well as horrified. Before I knew it my name was mentioned, right there on the tube. The moderator was saying that my editor was "currently working with surfer/photojournalist Allan Weisbecker, author of *Cosmic Banditos.*" It was weird, hearing this stuff.

The *Book TV* discussion began and eventually got around to the working relationship between writers and editors. As it turned out, my editor had actually written a book, which I didn't know at the time. Someone asked my editor how the editing had gone on it; an interesting question, in theory, she herself being an editor and all. (The *Book TV* folks didn't know just *how* interesting, as I did.) Here was her answer: "When I handed it in, it [her book] was perfect. It was flawless."

The audience and panel immediately cracked up; a huge laugh. My editor had brought down the house with that one.

Here's the thing, and if you look at the tape you'll see: *She wasn't joking.**

You must understand something. In the context of producing a book, taking it from raw manuscript to store shelf, my editor's words are in another realm from "I don't need to read your book to know how long it should be," or even "You'll never change my mind about anything." (Let's not forget what she would have done to *Blue Highways*.) Another realm of over-the-top, maybe pathological arrogance. The *Book TV* audience, which was virtually all people in the publishing business, had immediately cracked up because they could not believe anyone would say that and not be joking.

It was a wonderful moment for me. I almost woke Mom up to tell her what happened. She knew very well about my problems with my editor, which by that time had become downright Kafka-esque; and Mom knew of my occasional doubts about myself and how I was handling the situation. Although Mom's cancer was by now advanced and she was constantly in some degree of discomfort, it was my pain in giving birth to my book that was her main source of concern. (I tried to hide the extent of my anxiety but Mom saw right through me.)†

Next morning, I told Mom about my editor's *Book TV* moment, her blurt, and we celebrated. It was a vindication. It was objective, verifiable proof that *I* wasn't nuts. It also proved that my editor did say those other nutso things, if you think about it. I mean given this quote, it would be surprising if she hadn't said them, no?

I'll subject you to another of the volumes of her beauts because it applies in the context of her *Book TV* blurt: "When I'm editing a manuscript and I find a page I haven't marked up, I feel like I didn't do my job." Not exactly music to a writer's ears, but my point is this: When she's editing someone

* I've archived the video clip on this book's adjunct website (not aweisbecker.com).**
    ** I have on my site material backing up virtually all the events as described in this narrative. I'll provide you the URL later. For reasons of momentum and gradual disclosure (the bedrock principle of storytelling), I'd prefer that you wait until you're finished reading (assuming you hang in) before checking up on me. Suffice for now to repeat that I haven't misrepresented anything, at least not anything important, and I can and do prove it.

† Mom hung in there for many weeks longer than the most optimistic doctors said she would. Knowing what I went through with my book, she wanted to see it, to hold it in her hands, so she hung in. I vividly remember the look of pride/relief/joy on her face (and how bright her eyes were!) when the box arrived and I opened it and handed her a copy.

else, every page needs slashing and burning. When she writes a book, it not only does not need *any* editing, but it's *perfect. Flawless.*

Here's the title of the book my editor wrote: *Surviving Your First Year of Marriage.*

It's almost a publishing cliché that the writer-editor relationship is akin to a marriage. And as I say, my "relationship" with my editor lasted almost precisely one year.

The main secret to surviving your first year of marriage, according to my editor, is this: An openness to communication.

You'll never change my mind about anything.

I couldn't make up this shit. I don't have the imagination.

CHAPTER SEVEN

Publishers are those who, not being able to find any honest occupation, become the brokers of literature, live on our works, steal our manuscripts, falsify them, and sell them.

Voltaire

In July, 2000 I submitted the following Author's Note to Tarcher with the final draft of my *In Search of Captain Zero* manuscript:

Author's Note

I've used a fictitious name for the old friend I went looking for in Central America. I did this partially to protect my friend's privacy, and partially because I put him in some backstory situations from which in reality he was absent. The motive here was to impart a sense of narrative unity to the chaos of my life, and to that of my friend as well. In a sense, and I say this without guile, I was attempting to make the story truer than it otherwise would have been. To put it another way: I was trying to make the truth, as I see it, comprehensible.

Long-past events were described to the best of my recollection, although I do not claim to have transcribed specific conversations verbatim. Dialog was often recreated with the goal of imparting the flavor of the situations and events depicted.

There were a few changes in chronology and occasionally scenes and characters were combined. This was done for the sake of brevity, clarity, rhythm and pizzazz.

Upon receiving this, my demented editor in effect went ape-shit, although on a certain level I believe she was pleased as punch. I believe she was pleased as punch while simultaneously going ape-shit because she would use the above Author's Note to scare me. I mean scare the living *shit* out of me. She would use my Author's Note to suspend publication of my book. This in spite of the fact that my admissions were old news to her, and in spite of the fact that all nonfiction writers use the devices I admit to – these nonfiction deceits – to one extent or another, usually more than I do in *Zero*.

Memoirs are especially notorious for this. And look at history books – which are used to mold the minds of our children. Christ. Don't get me started.

The difference between me and most of the other nonfiction writers on the planet was that I desired to own up to the use of these devices, these deceits.

My demented editor would teach me a thing or two for wanting to own up. She gets together with the Tarcher corporate lawyer and he completely rewrites my Author's Note. I've searched everywhere for the lawyer's version and have been unable to find it. Not that I'd reproduce it here, but I would quote from it to show you how horribly it was written, crafted. Rampant grammar and punctuation errors. I mean it was borderline illiterate.

But worse than being borderline illiterate, the Author's Note as written by this lawyer would have severely damaged my book, maybe ruined it. See, what he did was reveal explicitly the devices, the nonfiction deceits, I used to make the truth as I see it comprehensible. In other words, he blew the whistle in detail on the backstory tales my friend was absent from and the changes in chronology and character-combining. Defined them specifically.

This whistle blowing would in effect become the ending of my book. And it would be like saying, "Remember that part of the book you love so much? Hah! What a sucker you are for believing *that* crapola!"

Readers would have fucking *hated* me. By keeping it non-specific, as in my version, they could fill in the blanks, or, more likely, not fill in the blanks, themselves. Would it still have hurt the book? Sure, with some readers, mainly those few who didn't really like the book to begin with. I was willing to accept that, for the sake of veracity. (As I first submitted it, the Author's Note was titled "A Note on Veracity.")

You may be thinking this: But, asshole, the lawyer was just trying to be completely honest. What's the problem? Hypocrite!

To which I ask this: You ever hear of a lawyer who was "just trying to be completely honest"?

Christ. Please.

So I'm confronted by this horrendous, borderline illiterate Author's Note – written as if by me, although not one word was mine. I call my editor and, mustering the non-confrontational tone that, due to my fear, I always used with her, ask why she'd had my Author's Note rewritten.

"Legal reasons," is her response. Says Penguin Putnam, Inc. (Tarcher imprint) doesn't want to give my old friend from the book the idea of suing.

What? Give him the *idea* of suing? My writer's queasy cut is flaring here.

"Call our lawyer," she says when I say I don't understand, and then she hangs up on me. Probably. I think she hung up on me. She often did this. I forget in this case.

Before calling the lawyer, I contact a half dozen people I know in the publishing biz; former editors, other writers, plus my Hollywood attorney, Steven. They all say the same thing, which I already know from simple logic: the above reason for the new Author's Note is nonsensical. Balderdash. A complete crock of shit.

I call the Tarcher lawyer but he's unavailable and for a few days he doesn't return my call.

Meanwhile my editor informs me that the production of my book has been suspended, for legal reasons. They're afraid my old friend will sue. This based on my Author's Note, which, keep in mind, no one has seen except my editor and the Tarcher lawyer. (This is an example of what I mean by *Kafka-esque*.)

But wait! I have good news! A development that will put all this crapola to rest! A legal release is on the way from my old friend from the book. Tarcher requested a release weeks before but due to communication problems – down in the wilds of Central America, my old friend had no phone, no mailing address – I was unable to get it together until now. "A legal release!" I can hardly contain my glee in blurting the news to the Tarcher lawyer when I finally get through to him. "We can go back to my Author's Note!"

"If the book does get published, we'll use my version," the lawyer says, and I can tell he's pleased as punch at having said that.

"I don't understand," I respond, my writer's queasy gut in full bloom. "A possible lawsuit is now a non-issue."

The lawyer tells me that my editor has decided to run his version of the Author's Note whether it's legally necessary or not. Keep in mind that it was never legally necessary to begin with, and keep in mind that his version of the Author's Note would severely damage my book, maybe ruin it.

"Her decision, huh?" I say, referring to my demented editor.

"That's right."

"No legal issues involved."

"That's right."

It is now clearly defined where all this is coming from, although I already suspected it. My editor is trying to sabotage my book. Or, at the very least, she is trying to scare the living *shit* out of me.

In the end, no Author's Note about veracity ran; not mine, not the lawyer's. I assume that my demented editor realized that the lawyer's Author's Note actually being in print in a book of which she was the editor would have reflected poorly on her. Someone, everyone, at her company would have asked, "How did *that* get included?" She couldn't have blamed it on me: I'd written letters to everyone at Tarcher, including the head of the imprint, pleading for reason. Even had a lawyer friend of mine put my correspondences on his letterhead, for some legal pizzazz.

So after being suspended for specious reasons, my book did go back into production. But my editor had nevertheless succeeded in her goal. She had scared the living *shit* out of me.

Are you outraged by my editor's behavior, not only regarding the Author's Note but over all? Just a little bit outraged? I realize that I'm not describing The Holocaust here, but I am implying the same sort of root mentality that led to it. The root mentality that is a necessary condition for bad behavior of any kind.

What root mentality is that?

A lack of self-reflection.

Since "lack of self-reflection" is unwieldy and refers to something that isn't, let's go to a word that I believe means the same thing.

Denial.

Let's define the word as I use it. Hey, let's look it up.

Denial, according to *Webster's New Universal Unabridged Dictionary*, definition #4, is "a refusal to receive, believe, accept, or embrace; as, a *denial* of the faith or the truth."

"Denial of the truth." Since you can't define a word using the word itself, let's rearrange *Webster's* so it comes out this way: *Denial*: "A refusal to accept the truth." Never mind that we might be tempted here to look up "truth." You get the idea.

Hold on. Listen to this: I tried looking up *self-reflection* to see how close the definition (of a lack thereof) is to *denial*. Guess what? *Self-reflection* isn't listed. *Webster's New Universal Unabridged Dictionary* weighs about a hundred fucking pounds – it's a major hassle to haul it around with me – and what do I find out? Right: Even *Webster's New Universal Unabridged Dictionary* lacks self-reflection. According to *Webster's New Universal Unabridged Dictionary* there is nothing between *self-recording* and *self-regard*.

While I was at it with self-reflection, inspired, I riffled over to where *nonfiction* should have been, figuring to find out what it is I'm doing with this book I'm writing, since it's nonfiction. It isn't. I mean it isn't listed. According to *Webster's New Universal Unabridged Dictionary* there's nothing between *nonfeasance* and *nonfilterable.*[*]

Another question: Is the world – with the collusion of the wordsmiths at *Webster's New Universal Unabridged Dictionary* – actively trying to drive me insane, or is it more of a passive attempt?

An oh-by-the-way kind of thing.

---

[*] Not only that, but according to my computer's Word spell-check feature, *nonfilterable* isn't even an actual word. It appears on my screen with a wavy red line under it. The word *nonfiction* does not appear with a wavy red line under it. This is a further example of what I'm talking about here, I think.

CHAPTER EIGHT

All kings is mostly rapscallions.

Mark Twain

During the Author's Note debacle, in one of my panic-stricken letters to the Tarcher lawyer (cc'd to everyone) I pointed out that the deceits I used in *In Search of Captain Zero* are commonplace in the nonfiction genre, memoirs especially. As an example I mentioned Frank McCourt's Pulitzer Prize winning memoir, *Angela's Ashes*. I said it was well-known that McCourt played fast and loose with the facts of his life. This was a bit of a stretch, I admit it. I *had* heard something, but could not remember what exactly or where I heard it. But I was nevertheless able to say this because I was sure that McCourt had played fast and loose with the facts of his life. Here's how I was sure, plus some other stuff that's on my mind.

In the spring of 2000, a few months before the Author's Note debacle, Mom and I are watching *Book TV*. Frank McCourt is on. McCourt is great on *Book TV*. Reading from his new memoir *'Tis*, McCourt has them rolling in the aisles. Everyone loves the guy, including Mom, sitting with me in her living room.

McCourt is perfect, downright Capra-esque. He looks more like a character Jimmy Stewart would play than any of the characters Stewart did play. Irish slum kid to inner city schoolteacher to Pulitzer prize-winning author, and a favorite on the talk-show circuit. Bright, genuine, charming, modest, without guile. His is a Cinderella story of the best and most hopeful sort, especially if you happen to be a writer.

But as he reads along in *'Tis* and the *Book TV* audience is rolling in the aisles and Mom is all bright-eyed and on the edge of her seat, I'm beset by a flutter of my writer's queasy gut. The passage he's reading from *'Tis* is too funny. It's like a well-wrought scene from a screenplay, a fast-paced, good-hearted light comedy with an underlying serious theme and just enough believable slapstick. Downright Capra-esque, come to think of it.

Life isn't like that, is what I'm thinking. I look over at Mom and say something to the effect that life isn't like that.

Mom wants to know what I mean.

I tell Mom that the incident from McCourt's book never happened. Maybe something like that happened, maybe not, but in any event it did not happen the way he wrote it. Not even close, I'd bet.

Mom gets angry, which is unheard of.

Sorry, Mom, I say, but he's lying.

Now Mom's really mad. I've called this wonderful man a liar.

I tell Mom that I'm not passing judgment on McCourt, God knows I'm not. I tell her I lie in *my* memoir and she knows that. She remembers when I made the breakthrough and decided I could lie about certain things. I'd gone through some terrible conflicts about this. And Mom herself advised me not to worry so much and to write it any way I saw fit. It's just a book, is what Mom said.

McCourt has to pause in his reading for the laughter to die down.

Mom is still angry with me.

McCourt finishes his reading from *'Tis* to wild applause. And it's deserved; he's an excellent writer, a creative one: he made up a wonderful little story, the one he just read. Now it's question and answer time. McCourt is completely at ease, a natural. He's self-effacing and quick and funny as hell.

Someone asks McCourt why he doesn't use quotes around the dialog in *Angela's Ashes*.

Now I'm thinking this: Don't disappoint me, Frank.

Frank disappoints me. Guileless and charming as ever, McCourt says something to the effect that quotations marks are a relatively new convention, hardly a hundred years old, and therefore he'd decided...

Mom, I say, as McCourt goes on about the history of quotation marks, the reason he doesn't use quotes around the dialog in *Angela's Ashes* is because in the book he's claiming to remember verbatim conversations that, in some cases, took place 50 years ago. Quotes would have made it more obvious how unbelievable that is.

Mom looks at me and she knows I'm right.

I'm sorry, Mom, I say, but now he's *really* lying. His really lying now is what disappoints me. I don't like the guy anymore.

Mom is still thinking about the passage from *'Tis*, how much she enjoyed it. But it *could* have happened! Mom says.*

Mom just couldn't let go.

A question: Why didn't McCourt answer the quotation mark question

---

* Come to think of it, Mom hit the nonfiction nail on the head here. *But it could have happened* is one of the keys to nonfiction. You fuck up with *but it could have happened* and you lose your reader immediately.**

   ** As you may have noticed, I sometimes use quotation marks in reproducing dialog, sometimes not. I only use quotation marks when, via notes or tape recordings or because my recollection is so vivid, I'm sure the words spoken are exact, or very close.

truthfully?

I'm going to surprise you here, I think.

Technically, McCourt *did* answer the question truthfully.

What?

By *truthfully* I mean he believed his answer. Had McCourt been hooked up to a polygraph (and assuming polygraphs work) I'd bet the needle would not have budged while he blabbed about quotation marks being a relatively new convention and so forth.

Denial. When you're in denial you can say pretty much anything without lying, since lying is *knowingly* misrepresenting something.

I know this is the case because of my own denial. I have come to accept the lies I tell in my first memoir as being non-lies, as being the truth. The exception being moments like this one, right now as I write. Right now I'm not living in denial regarding the lies I tell in my first memoir; I'm self-reflecting. But odds are, later today or maybe tomorrow, I'll be back to my old denial tricks. Self-reflection will be defenestrated.*

Which prompts me to ask: Is it okay to live like this?

Sure. I mean what's the big deal?

I dunno...

'Tis is just a book! *Angela's Ashes* is just a book! *In Search of Captain Zero* is just a book!

What about history books, which mold the minds of our children?

Still just books!

Remember George Orwell's *1984*?

What about it?!

It's a book about denial, right? The whole world, everybody, living in denial. Denial here meaning "A refusal to accept the truth."

So what?!

I'll tell you so what: Orwell was an *optimist*.

1984 could never happen! It's 2003, two decades later and that stuff hasn't happened!

I know it hasn't happened. What's really going on is worse, way worse, because as it turns out you don't need to go to the brutal totalitarian lengths of *1984* to get the whole world, everybody, to live in denial. You just gotta *ease* them into it.

How do you *ease* them into it?

You can start by giving Pulitzer Prizes to authors who won't admit why they don't use quotation marks. Reward them with wild applause after

---

* According to *Webster's New Universal Unabridged Dictionary*, *defenestration* is "the state of being thrown out a window." Bet you didn't know that. And why should you? It's a stupid, useless, pretentious word, for all intents and purposes unusable in speech or in writing. So how come it's in *Webster's New Universal Unabridged Dictionary* whereas *nonfiction* and *self-reflection* are not? This is my point in using this word here.

they read in public their nonfiction that never happened and that fooled my dying mom.

What the fuck am I talking about?! It's just a goddamn book! What am I, jealous because McCourt's books sell better than my self-indulgent crapola? I'd no doubt feel different if *I* won the Pulitzer Prize! Hah! Fat chance of that!

Maybe so, but you want to talk about denial? What it leads to? Just one example that comes to mind: In 1998 Bill Clinton fired Tomahawk missiles into the city of Khartoum in Sudan, blowing up the Al Shifa pharmaceutical plant, which intelligence had claimed was making chemical weapons. Turned out the intelligence was wrong; the pharmaceutical plant was not making chemical weapons. It was making... pharmaceuticals. Typhoid and cholera and tuberculosis vaccines and the like. It's against a myriad of international laws and treaties, plus the U.N. Charter and Geneva Conventions – all of which were solemnly signed by the United States[*] – to send missiles (flying bombs) into a civilian building because you *think* chemical weapons are being made there. Or for any other reason. (Attempting to distract the world from blowjobs by White House interns would seem to apply here.) Otherwise lunatics like Osama bin Laden (or whoever was behind 9/11) could also send flying bombs into civilian buildings then say they thought something bad was going on in those buildings and face no repercussions.

Estimates are that *tens of thousands* of human beings, virtually all civilians and largely children, died as a direct result of being deprived of the vaccines and the like produced by the plant – Sudan is too poor a country to buy medicines from foreign sources. (These deaths don't count the human beings killed outright by the flying bombs.) And most of those deaths were from terrible diseases; agonizing deaths. Clearly, by any legal (or reasonable) definition of the word, Bill Clinton murdered those people.

George W. Bush says Arabs hate us because of our freedom and because our women wear blue jeans. Maybe so, but I suspect that at least *some* of them hate us because we send flying bombs into their civilian buildings and in so doing kill tens of thousands of innocent human beings.

As I say, regarding everyone living in denial, Orwell was an optimist.[†]

---

[*] When the United States signs an international treaty it becomes U.S. law, i.e.: "the supreme law of the land," to be exact.

[†] Where's the denial? Right now odds are that you're shaking your head and thinking something to the extent of "that's different." Meaning that you refuse to accept that Bill Clinton is a mass murderer, and on a larger scale than the 9/11 attacks (which, keep in mind, occurred three years after the Sudan incident). Even if/when you go to the adjunct website and read the inarguable facts of the matter, plus the treaties signed by the U.S. and that are hence the supreme laws of the land, odds are you'll still say something like "that's different." That's denial.[**]

    [**] Another example of denial, and I'll phrase it as a question for Bill Clinton (the pure-hearted liberal whom Al Franken so loves): Hey Bill, when you found out that the intelligence about what was going on at the pharmaceutical plant was faulty, why didn't you at least send those poor bastards the medicine you deprived them of? Am I out of line in asking this? A simple Yes or No will do.

But let's lighten up, have some fun with denial. Who needs this political shit, right? You could be reading a book that makes you feel all warm and fuzzy and comfortable. You could be reading a book that alleges that the world *makes sense*.

Some fun. At least from my point of view.

"When I handed it in it was perfect. It was flawless."

Remember where that came from? Right: My editor. Talking about the book *she* wrote.

Here's a sentence from her book, page 78, second paragraph, lead sentence: "Let's examine the couple's relationship with both your mother and your father, starting with Mom."

I don't know what she's talking about here. What "couple" is she referring to in the first clause? Sounds like some other couple, not the couple you are a part of. Based on context, however, I believe she is referring to the latter – the couple you are a part of. The sentence doesn't say that, though, does it?

The first rule of writing: Clarity. Say what you mean.[*]

Here's another sentence from the book my editor wrote: "Many women truly feel that their mothers prefer their husband's company to that of their own flesh-and-blood." When she says "their husband's company," to whom is she referring? Could be the woman's husband, meaning the woman who is part of a couple, and I'm pretty sure that was her intent. But she could be referring to the mother's husband – the woman's father (or stepfather), not the woman's husband. Again, clarity is lacking here.

And what's with "truly" as modifier to "feel"? Either you feel something or you don't. If she really wants to support "feel," the proper adverb is "strongly." But even this would be a mistake. *Avoid needless words.*[†]

---

[*] An exception to the Clarity Rule is Cormac McCarthy. Once in a while he'll have a sentence that no matter how many times I read it, I don't know what the fuck he's talking about. Somehow (and please don't ask me to explain) this is part of the pleasure of reading the guy.

[†] This is from *The Elements of Style*, by William Strunk and E.B. White, a wonderful little book that, should you read it and pay attention while doing so, your writing will improve immediately. (Again, Cormac McCarthy is an exception here. His reading *The Elements of Style* might actually fuck up his writing, if he paid attention.)

Yes. Lose the adverb in the above sentence.[*]

Further, to whom is my editor referring with the phrase "flesh-and-blood"? To the woman as part of a couple, sure; as daughter. But "flesh-and-blood" also refers to any close blood relative, not just the daughter. So the phrase is vague, although not terribly so. You could leave it in. If you leave it in, though, it should be written "flesh and blood," without the hyphens between the words. That's proper English usage. (In the spirit of this meticulously researched and backed-up nonfiction book, I've archived on the adjunct website the rules of hyphen-usage. Since I use quite a few hyphens here [including one in the previous sentence] my demented editor will no doubt spend many hours [perhaps days] finding errors I myself have no doubt made. To which I say to her: I'm looking forward to hearing from you!)

I found a bunch of looping in the book my editor wrote, too.

One more thing. The second sentence I quote follows the first directly in the text; that's why I singled the two of them out. I had to make choices and I had a lot to chose from: Bad sentences are all over the place in the book my editor wrote, the book that is *perfect* and *flawless*. I chose these sentences because they are joined together like dimwitted Siamese twins.

That was fun, wasn't it? Sure was for me.

---

[*]   Months after writing this chapter I read Stephen King's memoir, *On Writing*. King's view of adverbs is that they "are not your friend." Later, adverb-crazed, he goes on to opine that "The road to hell is paved with adverbs." Whoa! ‡‡

   ‡‡   To my great relief, King says in *On Writing* that he'll sometimes come across a McCarthy sentence and not understand what the fuck McCarthy is talking about either.‡‡‡

      ‡‡‡   Here's my take on Cormac McCarthy: Imagine Louis L'amour at the typewriter with Elmore Leonard pacing behind him and yelling what to write, after they've been up for four days whacked on acid and bourbon, reading aloud some early Hemingway (for laughs), and both having just read *The Elements of Style*, too, but only one of them having paid attention while doing so (it doesn't matter which one), and meanwhile their thesaurus is not of the English language, plus the period key on the typewriter only sporadically works. (I mean all this is in a good way.)

CHAPTER NINE

There goes another novel.

Honoré de Balzac, referring to ejaculation

Here on this idyllic little Caribbean island I've started making a list of women I've had sex with, including a few details about how it went. Anecdotes, some sordid, some not. Mostly sordid. Here's one.

In the late 1980s, producer Steve Friedman (*The Last Picture Show, Slap Shot,* among others) and I were working with actor Jon Voight on a screenplay of mine that Steve had optioned and that Jon loved and wanted to star in. I was living on the oceanfront at Venice Beach, California, just down the boulevard from Hollywood itself. I'd made money writing, had a Porsche. A bachelor on the hunt, big shot Hollywood screenwriter. A real jerk. I get a date with this aspiring actress who lives in the next building. We go out for dinner then I bring her back to my apartment. It's touch and go, me wanting to touch, she wanting to go. Phone rings. I let the machine pick up. It's Jon Voight; you can't mistake that voice. "Hi, Allan, it's Jon. Read the new draft. Allan... you're the real thing." Click. (I remember this verbatim because the timing was so good in terms of my immediate agenda.)

No more touch and go. It was all over but the moaning in my apartment on Venice Beach.

Here's something about comedy/humor/whatever you want to call it, of which I hope there will be some in this narrative: The root of it is almost always obsession, someone's obsession. A desire that gets out of hand. A good example is the movie *There's Something About Mary.* Holy shit, what a funny movie. Based, of course, on everyone's obsession with this beautiful woman, Mary. Or *A Fish Called Wanda,* in which each character has his own oddball obsession. (The image of my demented editor spending red-eyed days combing this book for hyphen-mistakes comes to mind.)

With obsession as the root of humor it almost doesn't matter what the obsession is, only that you believe; believe in the sense that the character believes. My first book, *Cosmic Banditos,* is a good example. In it, the protagonist – a mentally unbalanced guy strongly based on me – becomes obsessed with quantum physics. Which sets off a chain of events that alters the lives of everyone he comes into contact with. It's a very funny book.

The other thing about comedic obsessions is that the obsessed sap is unsuccessful in dealing with his obsession. This was the case with me when I got back from Central America in 1998 and then while I was living with Mom. I was obsessed with sex, with getting laid, and was unsuccessful in dealing with it – nothing I would do had the result I expected and hoped for.[*]

My making a list of women I've had sex with is an offshoot of my obsession from back then, I think, and which has surfaced again. It's surfaced again because of another little sexual fiasco, like the Cat Woman Incident, this one having to do with Lisa. Hold on. *Little* fiasco? Forget little. Were I to put a title to this one, it'd be "The Horror."

Some backstory. Lisa and I have been together for a total of 57 days, meaning 57 nights, actually. Meaning since we started having sex. Once we started we pretty much never stopped. One reason for this is that Lisa and I have known each other for five years and were attracted to each other that whole time, although we didn't do anything about it. So the pressure had been building for a long time.

For about the first 40 days/nights we had sex an average of once per 24 hour period. (The average would be higher except we had a couple sick days, plus one day when Lisa had to "rest.") A fairly high but not outlandish frequency. The first explosion of passion, all that. But lately we've been having sex on average twice per 24 hour period, maybe more. This is not counting "take fives", which is a concept Lisa came up with. Means that if one of us says "Let's take five," we drop whatever we're doing and have five minutes' worth of sex. Or more than five minutes' worth. According to Lisa, there are no hard and fast rules to take fives, notwithstanding that it sounds like there are. I mean, five minutes should be five minutes, no?

So, counting take fives, we're now having sex at least three times per 24 hour period. Even since The Horror. Hold on. *Especially* since The Horror. Not only that, but since the beginning the sex itself has gradually improved in quality. Started out great, even the very first time, then moved on to better than great. An example of how it got better than great is that during the sex we had for the three days immediately after The Horror I didn't have an orgasm. We had all kinds of sex, all over the place – once surreptitiously in public view – plus several take fives per 24 hour period,

---

[*] Screenwriting guru Robert McKee coined the term "gap," referring to the gap "between expectation and result" a character goes through in a properly wrought tale. This is equally applicable in drama and comedy. In the latter I like to think of the gap concept as The Banana Peel Effect. (Say there's a puddle you keep stepping into in front of your house, then one day you remember it's there and you outsmart that fucking puddle, jump to the side, and… right… a banana peel awaits – a touch being that you yourself were eating a banana the day before, when you last stepped into the puddle, creating a little rush of insight about the chain of causation of the fiasco, who was at the bottom of it.)

and I didn't have an orgasm. If this doesn't sound like great sex, let alone better than great, hang in with me and I'll explain.

I love making love to Lisa so much that I don't need to have an orgasm. I don't *want* to. I don't want to because I don't want to have that period of time right afterwards wherein I don't want to make love to her any more.

Women may think they know about this period of time after a guy has an orgasm but they don't. If they did know about it, *really* know about it, they probably would never have sex with us.

There's a great scene in Stanley Kubrick's *Doctor Strangelove*. (With the possible exception of *Tootsie*, *Doctor Strangelove* is the funniest movie of all time. Oh, and *Some Like It Hot* is up there.) The Sterling Hayden character, who is in the process of ending the world, is telling Peter Sellers (in one of his multiple roles) about when he first became aware of the international communist conspiracy to sap our bodily fluids. "It was during the physical act of love, Mandrake," he says. "A profound sense of fatigue, of loss of essence."

A profound sense of fatigue, of loss of essence.

Yes, that's it! In *Doctor Strangelove* this guy-moment-after-orgasm would ultimately result in the end of life on earth. For me, it results in a moment wherein I don't want to make love to Lisa any more.

The origin of this guy-moment-after-orgasm is an evolutionary one, I'm quite sure, going back to our early ancestors. Once a guy planted his seed, there was no reason to hang in there any longer. His reproductive job was over, immediately, as soon as he went boom. So, evolutionarily speaking, as soon as he went boom he was either up and off to kill his next mastodon, or asleep, in order to rest up to kill his next mastodon. A result of this was that the first thing that came into his mind, immediately after an orgasm (and immediately after a profound sense of fatigue, of loss of essence) but before he actually got up or went to sleep, was something about killing his next mastodon. Where he might find it, how he might kill it. Something like that.

I myself don't actually think about mastodons after having an orgasm, by the way. What I do think about after having an orgasm is this. I mean literally this, this narrative, this book I'm writing. Or whatever I happen to be writing at the time. I go from some degree of passion and desire and animal lust (with Lisa all three are off the scale) to a profound sense of fatigue, of loss of essence, then quickly to the pondering of something about whatever I happen to be writing at that time. So with Lisa I avoid having an orgasm.* Even though I wouldn't actually get up and leave – or

---

* How I do this – avoid having an orgasm – is unimportant, at least for the purposes of this book. Trust me that I don't do mathematical figuring in my head, like I did when I was younger. Suffice to say that I've broken on through to the other side, orgasm-wise.

even want to – I don't want to be thinking about what I'm writing while we're in bed together, let alone mastodons.

An offshoot of my avoidance of having an orgasm with Lisa is that when I eventually do have one, it's a doozey. Or even a double doozey. The third day after The Horror, for example, after not having had an orgasm for those three days, I had a double orgasm. I went boom, and then a couple minutes later went **BOOM.**

At this point you may be thinking – you *should* be thinking – that this isn't bad for a 55-year-old guy who has been on the sexual sidelines a while: The Cat Woman period, my time taking care of Mom, and so forth. I read somewhere that women tend to hit the peak of sexual desire at around 40. Lisa is 39, so with her all this screwing makes sense. Guys, according to this same article, hit the peak at about 19 and commence a decline from there.

So what's up with me?

Please pay attention here, because I'm trying to connect a lot of stuff, tie up loose ends, including the What's up with me? question, and then get on with the actual The Horror itself.

The Jon Voight-getting-laid-at-Venice-Beach anecdote occurred to me immediately after the double doozey orgasm I just mentioned, while I was lying there with Lisa, cuddling or whatnot, and pretending to be concentrating on her when actually I was working on my mental list of women I've had sex with, which I'd already started, and which I figured would somehow fit into this narrative. By the way, this goes to one reason the process of writing is so scary. I mean I have a double doozey orgasm – go boom and then go **BOOM** – and what results? You're subjected to an anecdote involving the actor Jon Voight that happened years ago.

What kind of shit is that?

Another thing. Lately it's been Lisa who calls it quits, sexually. Sort of rolls over and makes it clear we're done for now. Can't go on. Sated. A curious reversal of the usual, wherein the guy rolls over and goes to sleep (or gets up to go kill a mastodon). Not that Lisa actually goes to sleep, not right away. She'll want to cuddle, like guys pretend they want to after they have an orgasm. (She'll also formally thank me for my efforts. Say, "Thank you very much," or the like. I find this very endearing.)

But how about this business with Lisa, our increased screwing frequency over time and my dearth of going boom? Point being that this stuff has never happened before. I mean I haven't always been a Sex God, as Lisa has so kindly started referring to me these days, these post The Horror Days.[*] Which goes to the What's up with me? question. What's up with me is that with Lisa I actually *am* in love for the first time. No more *possibly.*

This is it, the love of my life.

With my revelation that with Lisa this is it, the love of my life, we're now all set up. Here we go. I mean with the actual The Horror itself. It's about time, no?

About a week ago, just a minute or two prior to The Horror, Lisa rolled over, formally thanked me for my efforts, then said, and I'm talking breathlessly here, "That was... otherworldly."

Oh. Another thing women don't understand is how good a guy feels on the level of being a guy when a woman rolls over and says something like, "That was... otherworldly." As if he'd just killed a mastodon, choked it to death with his bare hands.

So Lisa had just rolled over and said, "That was... otherworldly," and I was feeling like I just choked a mastodon to death with my bare hands. I couldn't leave well enough alone, though – if there's a tragic flaw involved in this fiasco, this is it – so while we were after-glowing I started asking Lisa stuff about her sexual history. I'd done this before. Has to do with intimacy, honesty, that two people are so intimate and honest with each other that they will tell each other anything. Pretty soon I asked her this: "What was the best week of your life, sexually?"

To this Lisa said, quickly and with a wistful smile, "That's easy."

I too smiled. It'd been about a week since my full-blown Sex God act had kicked in. Remember that during that week it was always Lisa who would roll over, sated, formally thank me for my efforts, then say something along the lines of "That was... otherworldly."

"It was 1989," Lisa said with a throaty laugh, referring to the best week of her life, sexually.

In 1989 I hadn't yet met Lisa.

"In Boston."

Lisa and I had never been in Boston together.

"This guy and I got snowed in at a hotel..."

I have a feeling that what you're thinking right now will depend on your gender. If you're a guy you're probably thinking something like, "Yeah, The Horror is a perfect description of this." If you're a woman, something more like, "So what's the big deal?" Or, possibly, "What did you expect, asshole?"

---

[*] I'm thinking of writing another book that will divulge my Sex God secret, i.e., how I avoid having an orgasm for as long as I want. In fact, the title would be *The Secret of a Sex God.* It would likely be a howling success, no? By the way, this is the real reason why I don't divulge how I do it here, in this book. In other words, if I blow my Sex God wad here, I've blown the *The Secret of a Sex God* book.

Lisa didn't go into any gory details about her week with The Boston Snow Storm Guy. She's not like that. She did mention that he was in the movie business and would eventually be an important figure in the production of *Magnolia*. Although of relative insignificance, this little detail didn't help matters, since *Magnolia* is a successful feature film starring Tom Cruise, and the only feature film I was an important figure on (sole screen credit) is a catastrophe with Loretta Swit, which shall remain nameless.

Keep in mind I hadn't had an orgasm and theoretically should have been ready to go again at the drop of a hat, or the drop of anything. Well, The Horror having taken place, I *wasn't* ready to go again at the drop of a hat, or the drop of anything, and I immediately started worrying that this condition would be permanent, if you get my drift.

Another thing women don't understand is how fragile the male member is. I mean all a guy has to do is have a miniscule, *microscopic* thought *way* in the back of his mind that there just might *possibly* be a problem, and wham, the next thing you know, no more booms.

Just writing about no more booms right now is making me nervous.

Making matters still worse was that I couldn't say anything. Because of certain other things that had recently happened in our relationship, I'd been harping on the point of honesty. That there could be no secrets between us. That was number one. No secrets. Honesty. I couldn't keep my stupid trap shut on this.

So what could I say?

I let Lisa finish her story about The Boston Snow Storm Guy. (I would eventually shorten this, start thinking of him as The Snow Storm Guy, then finally just The Snowman.) I started to tell Lisa about a woman named Maria, with whom I was going to claim that I had had the best week of *my* life, sexually. The truth was that the best week of *my* life, sexually, had just occurred, with Lisa. But under the circumstances no way was I going to admit to that. Being a nonfiction writer, I was well-trained to diddle with facts a little. Or a lot.

I hardly got a word out about Maria when Lisa said, "I don't want to hear it."

Trying to keep my voice calm, I said, "Whaddya mean, 'You don't want to hear it?'"

"I've told you I don't want to hear about the other women in your life."

This was true. Lisa had made this plain a couple of times. If asked, she didn't mind talking about her sexual history, but if I started in she'd stop me.

"This is not fair!" I screamed. Mentally. In reality, I didn't say a word. I just lay there, pretending everything was just fucking great.

"I love you, Allan," Lisa said a little while later, then sighed and went to sleep.

I couldn't sleep so I started making the list of women I've had sex with.

One of them wasn't the aspiring actress who appeared in the Jon Voight-getting-laid-at-Venice Beach anecdote. Not yet. Again, I would think of her three days later, after my double doozey orgasm.

Aside from obsession, another thing about comedy/humor/whatever is that it generally is based on some sort of pain, usually the pain other people cause.

Come to think of it, the same could be said of tragedy.

Obsession and pain. There you have it.

CHAPTER TEN

If my books had been any worse I would not have been invited to Hollywood, and if they had been any better I would not have come.

Raymond Chandler

When Advance Reading Copies (ARCs) of *In Search of Captain Zero* came out in early 2001, my movie-writing agent – whom I would later fire and whose response to that is the title of this book – gave one to a producer she represented, who liked it a lot. The producer called my agent saying she wanted to option the book.

I was wary.

Why was I wary?

Because there was a catch-22, based on the fact that there is no movie in *In Search of Captain Zero*. (My favorite catch-22 is the old Groucho Marx line, "I wouldn't belong to any club that would have me as a member.") Here the catch-22 was more or less this: *No one who wants to make a movie out of my book is smart enough to get it done.*

So I was wary.

But the movie producer had a trump card to play in persuading me to let her option my book. The trump card was Sean Penn. She'd made a documentary that Sean had narrated. Sean's manager had read my book and really liked it, thought it would make a terrific movie, she said. Sean hadn't read the book yet but wanted to co-produce it and maybe star in it. (If you find it surprising that a Hollywood star would want to produce and maybe star in a movie made from a book he hadn't read, I can only chuckle at your ignorance of how Hollywood *is*.) Said she knew a director who wanted to direct it – the guy who directed the documentary Sean had narrated.

Given that there is no movie in my book, and given that all these people wanted to make a movie out of it anyway, I was thinking that there are a lot of dumb people in Hollywood. But I already knew that, from personal experience. From *unnerving personal experience*, if you get my demented-editor drift.* So I waffled out of wariness, out of fear of getting involved with a lot of dumb people.

The producer sensed my wariness. She of course had no idea of the *reason* for my wariness. I mean I didn't *tell* her that there was no movie in my book, or that I assumed she was dumb. Hey, *I'm* not dumb. But having sensed my wariness, the producer had Sean Penn call me. On a certain level it was a strange conversation, since Sean and I were discussing making a movie out of a book that he had not read.

That Sean had not read my book was never outright dealt with during our phone conversation. The closest we came was when – in response to one of my desperate ideas on how to make a movie out of a book wherein there is no movie – Sean said, "I'm missing a little information here."

Although I was wary, I was also human. I pictured Sean Penn up there on the silver screen, playing me. I also pictured the money. Although the option offer was small, a couple grand, if the producer could get studio backing the movie deal would be up in six figures whether the movie got made or not. And I knew that since there were so many dumb people in Hollywood, studio backing was not out of the question; far from it. I mean look at the movies that *do* get made. I mean who knew.

I let the producer and Sean Penn option my book.

---

* A note to my demented editor: Since I'm using "demented editor" as an adjective (a compound one, modifying "drift"), a hyphen is called for between "demented" and "editor". (See the Hyphen Usage section of the adjunct website).

CHAPTER ELEVEN

The Greeks had a word for it.

Zoë Akins

Part of the life Lisa is giving up to come live with me at the end of the road at the bottom of Central America is her career, although she's out of work right now due to the economy. Lisa was, or is, a high-powered businessperson. In fact, she was, or is, so high-powered that I don't really understand what it is, or was, that she did, or does.

During Lisa's second trip to be with me in Costa Rica – this was a couple of months ago as I write from this little Caribbean island – I made a deal to buy six acres of land near my home. The price I was to pay was very low, a quarter of the real, current value. How this came about had to do with being at the right place at the right time. The connections I'd made during my years in Costa Rica and my books and movie deals having made me a minor celebrity amongst the expat contingent may have played a role also.

The way I arranged it was that I would finalize the land deal with the lawyers in San José the day before I put Lisa on the plane to go back home. We had not yet broached the subject of her giving up her old life to come live with me.

Lisa came with me to the lawyers' offices to sit in on the deal. The lawyers were Costa Rican, three Latin men. Being Latin men, they gave Lisa the Latin-man-once-over when I introduced her, then puffed up in their three-piece suits, made their voices deeper, adjusted their jewelry, and strutted with added flamboyance as we went to sit down. One, a pompous little fuck I already wanted to strangle for other reasons, positioned himself so he had an unobstructed view of Lisa's long, excruciatingly shapely bare legs. So with these Latin lawyers, Lisa's *ultimate femaleness* was in full force and then some. They commenced lawyering away, trying to impress Lisa with how much they knew that she couldn't possibly, when Lisa's high-powered businessperson persona kicked in.

"Excuse me, Mauricio," she said – Mauricio being the pompous little fuck I wanted to strangle – "but there's something in the contract I don't quite understand." Then she proceeded to show Mauricio and everybody else how far Mauricio's head was up his ass.

"Oh, yes, yes, yes, I see what you mean," Mauricio mumbled, and there was a lot of paper rustling and throat clearing, not only from Mauricio but from my lawyer, who had missed the fuck-up in the contract too. And so it went from there. Lisa pretty much took charge of the negotiations. I just sat back and grinned.

The next day I popped the question to Lisa about coming to live with me.

CHAPTER TWELVE

Context is all. And a relatively pure heart. Relatively pure –
for if you had a pure heart you wouldn't be in the book-writing
business in the first place.

Robert Penn Warren

Last week just before The Horror took place here on this little Caribbean
island I got an email from the movie studio that wound up backing the *In
Search of Captain Zero* movie deal. As things go in Hollywood, and as I more
or less predicted back in 2001, the producer who optioned the book was
able to find a studio to put up the money to make a movie out of my book,
even though there is no movie in my book. One reason for this, I think,
was that the studio head who decided to shell out the cash hadn't read the
book. If this sounds somehow both odd and familiar – and it would be odd
(or flat nuts) in a similar situation in any other business – the familiar part
is likely due to Sean Penn having co-optioned the book without reading it
either.

And the deal *was* up there in six figures. I'm rolling in loot. Mostly
because I insisted on writing the screenplay. Screenplays are where the
money is. You think I cared that there is no movie in my book when I
insisted on writing the screenplay to my book, given that screenplays are
where the money is?

Ha!

But to sum up: Two of the main people who wanted to make a movie out
of my book hadn't read it, and, meanwhile, another important person, the
one writing the screenplay, me, knew there was no movie in my book.

To knock off an old song title: Hooray for Hollywood!

A digression to a related matter, a Meanwhile: Nonfiction writers, of
which I am one at this moment, routinely lie like slugs in their narratives.
Often they'll lie like slugs about facts, which, as you already know, I
sometimes do. Sometimes lying about facts is okay, sometimes not. But
what's never okay is to lie in subtext, purposely cause the reader to have a
rush of insight about the workings of the world which the writer knows to
be false. Lying in subtext is a *sin*. Writers who do this, of which there are a

bunch, will rot in Writer Hell. My theory is that this worse case lying-in-writing scenario is invariably caused by the same condition that causes bad behavior of any sort: a failure in self-reflection.[*]

If you're going to write a book (but not *someday*): The key to writing, good writing, is self-reflection. In a sense, it's a writer's job, his *only* job. Take that to the bank and put it in an interest-bearing account.[†]

I know a writer, mostly a Hollywood writer, who, when he looks in the mirror, does not realize that there is little more than a lying, treacherous shitball motherfucker staring back at him. So even when he's looking in the mirror there is no self-reflection. The guy is a pretty good writer, but only in that he knows how to string words together. Other than that, he's a shitball writer. No self-reflection.

But what does all this have to do with movie deals and making a movie from a book wherein there is no movie?

My going on about demented editors and people I've fired and am pissed off at and shitball motherfuckers in general raises a question about *my* character. I'll phrase the question like this: What sort of potentially cynical and greedy shitball motherfucker would let his book be optioned and accept a ton of money, like 200 grand, to adapt it to the screen if he knows there is no movie in the book? I use the qualifier *potentially* (which is an adverb, possibly on the road to hell) here because the status of this hypothetical person (based on me) as a cynical and greedy shitball motherfucker is pending.

So this is the question, and it's a good one, no? I mean possibly humorous catch-22s aside...

No one who wants to make a movie out of my book is smart enough to get it done.

By way of answering the question, in essence defending myself against a serious charge – and plus maybe against the most serious charge there is regarding self-reflection, or lack thereof, which is hypocrisy – here's how the deal went down...

But first for perspective I want you to imagine something. Imagine that a bunch of lawyers and MBAs get together and buy a hospital. One day they're sitting around and an MBA or lawyer says, "You know, I've always wanted to try my hand at brain surgery." Another MBA or lawyer nods, saying that when he was a freshman at college he was thinking of going to medical school. "Hey..." he says, "we own the hospital. We can do what we

---

[*] My view is that lying about facts is *sometimes* "okay" when the writer's sole motive is to keep the story moving, or to foster unity (symmetry), or to *ease* the narrative onto another subject (a segue), with no deceitful implications about how the world works.

[†] Aside from self-reflecting in his work, a writer has to keep the reader wanting to know What Happens Next. So, regarding only jobs, writers actually have two.

want. Let's go down to the operating room and give it a shot!"

This is Hollywood in a nutshell, when producers and studio executives, MBAs and lawyers, insert themselves into the creative process, the storytelling process. They just can't help themselves. It makes them feel like they're actually *doing* something -- aside from making phone calls and getting coverage instead of reading anything. They also do it because they *can*. Hey, they own the hospital.

Enough perspective. Defending myself against these serious charges. The deal. How it went down.

By July of 2001, two months after Mom died, the producer, along with Sean Penn as co-producer, had found a studio that was interested in the *Zero* project -- an executive at the studio plus his yes-man had actually read the book. A meeting was set up to discuss a possible development deal. Development deals are deals wherein the first money the studio coughs up goes to the screenwriter, plus expenses and an up front fee for the producers. Then, if the screenplay passes muster, the movie gets made – assuming a few miracles transpire. If the miracles transpire and the movie gets made, everyone gets a lot more money.

The meeting was to be at breakfast at the Four Seasons Hotel in L.A. In attendance were the producer, the director ('attached' to the deal), the studio head, the executive who had read the book, his yes-man, plus Sean Penn, plus me. I say the meeting *was to be* at breakfast because it pretty much ended up being at lunch due to Sean Penn being a couple hours late. This notwithstanding that he was staying at the Four Seasons, meaning he didn't have far to go to get to the meeting. Traffic was not a problem.

"You know Sean," the producer said to me as we waited and waited in the lobby, along with the director. Although I had talked with Sean on the phone about making a movie out of my book – the conversation wherein he said he was "missing a little information here" – I didn't actually know him. But okay. The producer reiterated that I was going to enjoy working with him, meaning in the writing of the screenplay, in the process of which I had been assured that Sean gets involved early.

I'm looking forward to it, I said, as we waited.

Eventually Sean steps out of the elevator and says Hi to the producer and the director, whom he knows, then he and I shake and say Hi, then, by way of apology for his tardiness, Sean says he had "a pharmaceutical night." We all laugh.

We join the studio people in the dining room.

Everyone says Hi to everyone else. Sean and the studio head are old pals. Sean repeats his de facto apology about his pharmaceutical night and we all laugh. Sean sits down and lights up a cigarette. By this time I could use one myself, but I can't bring myself to do it, what with the No Smoking signs and people eating nearby.

Allan smokes too, the producer says to Sean. You two are going to get along great. We all laugh, although I'm wishing she hadn't said that. I'm embarrassed about smoking.

There's chit-chat about some party Sean went to the previous night, who was there and so forth, then the meeting gets underway. You must remember that no deal has yet been struck with the studio. The only money I'd got was a couple grand for a year-and-a-half option on my book. So big bucks were hanging in the air for yours truly that morning (maybe it was afternoon by now) at the Four Seasons Hotel in West L.A. – in Hollywood, actually, the state of mind Hollywood.

Cutting through the politics and the personal relationships and the compliments about how great my book is and other bullshit, what this meeting is, is an audition, my audition, as screenwriter.

So I've got the floor. I'm hoping I'll be "good in a room" as the Hollywood expression goes, and which I used to be back in my old Hollywood days. So I start in on how to make a movie out of my book but my rhythm is broken by a waiter who comes over and asks Sean not to smoke. An ashtray is secured and Sean eventually puts out his cigarette. I try to inhale the last wisp of the fucking thing.

All right. Here we go.

In a sense my pitch of how to make a movie out of my book is of the *I have good news and I have bad news* sort. The bad news, I say, is that there is no movie in my book.

Hold on. I don't exactly phrase it this way, as I will much later when the deal turns into a full-blown fiasco. Here's how I do phrase it: My book does not provide an actual story, I say, due to a lack of real conflict between the two main characters. I then point out that conflict is what a story is built upon. In essence, conflict (plus the turning points it creates) is what a story *is*. But we all know this, I say. I'm being disingenuous since – possibly apart from Sean Penn (pharmaceutical night or no) – I know that no one here knows this, although they all nod.

The book works, I go on (trying to avoid sounding too didactic), because of the narrative voice, which defines the book's principal conflicts as internal – internal conflicts are not directly translatable to the screen. Further, I say, the book ending hinges on an internal turning point and is likewise not translatable to the screen. In other words, we have no ending.

I then point out something else I claim we all know, which is that in storytelling, especially screen storytelling, endings are very important. In fact (and here I quote screenwriter William Goldman), endings are *everything*. No ending, no story.

What the book provides, I say, is a premise, a good one, and I'm not being disingenuous here. I really feel that way. The premise: *A middle-aged surfer gives up his straight life to search for an old friend and ex-partner in crime from their younger days, who is missing in Central America.*

That's pretty much all the book provides, I reiterate. So: They're contemplating coughing up a couple hundred grand plus a producer's fee (plus overhead and interest) for one sentence. To distract them all from this implication I quickly ramble on, saying that the narrative will have to be reinvented. That's the word I use. *Reinvented.* I also work in the fact that my book is nonfiction, meaning some sort of portrayal of real life, and real life, almost by definition, is not dramatic. Real life is a pain in the ass that way, making a movie out of it.

Everyone agrees to all this, including Sean Penn, via a nod, although, aside from his pharmaceutical night, he's missing a little information here. But okay. That everyone agrees is a relief. It's a relief because not only do I want the money, I want to write this screenplay. I want to reinvent my book.

See if you concur: With everyone's agreement that the book lacks an actual story and that the narrative will have to be reinvented and that they're coughing up a couple hundred grand for one sentence, they are in effect also agreeing with my catch-22, notwithstanding that they don't realize it.

More defensiveness on my part: Was it my responsibility to *outright* define my catch-22? I didn't – and still don't – think so. I'm trying to let myself off the cynical and greedy shitball motherfucker hook here. I admit that.

Back to the meeting. I then go on to outline the conflicts I concocted that will provide the turning points necessary to build an actual story around my premise. Now, I say, regarding the ending, which the book does not provide, what I want to do is create a mythical kind of *The Endless Summer* meets *Apocalypse Now* finish. I know better than to use *Heart of Darkness*, the novel upon which *Apocalypse Now* is based, in my Hollywood short-handing, figuring that no one else in the room has read, or even knows about, Joseph Conrad's book.

Not only does everyone like my concocted turning points that will provide the necessary conflicts, plus the idea of *The Endless Summer* meeting *Apocalypse Now*, but the studio head, (who, again, hasn't read the book) says this, and I remember his words exactly because I will repeat them minutes later when the producer and I are alone, and then again on the phone to my then-agent, whose response to my later firing her is the title to this book. He says, "I want to stop you right here, Allan." He pauses. He has everyone's undivided attention. "I just want to say that you have this deal right now, if you want it."

Not only has the studio head not noticed my implied catch-22, but he apparently is sufficiently impressed by not noticing it, if you get my drift, to offer me the deal then and there, no further ado or blabbing or being good in a room on my part necessary. So it's agreed: Everyone's people will be in touch with everyone else's people to work out the legal details.

Sean adjourns to the patio and lights up. The producer, the director and I join him. I light up. We chit-chat for a bit and the producer reiterates how Sean and I are going to enjoy working together.

I'm looking forward to it, I say.

So this was in July of 2001 and now it's March of 2003. I'm on a little Caribbean island with Lisa, the woman with whom I've fallen in love at age 55. The Horror will soon take place and, meanwhile, I've received an email from the studio from the above meeting, the outfit that's paying me to adapt my book for the screen. The email includes the studio's "notes" on how I should rewrite my last submitted draft of the screenplay.

As a result of this email I've decided to go into the tank.

Go into the tank is a boxing expression. It means a boxer is going to throw a fight. Lose on purpose. In this case, *go into the tank* means I'm planning on writing a piece of shit screenplay. Write a bunch of utter crapola and do it on purpose.

Why would I do this?

Hang in and I'll get around to that, but first some other stuff, including stuff with Lisa that makes The Horror look like a day at the beach.*

---

* Since I'm hinting at future narrative events, this chapter ending is an example of looping, which I'm doing all over the place. I love looping! Hey, I'm becoming an "I loop, therefore I am" sort of writer. To put it another way: To my demented editor, assuming she is reading this right now: Take your looping and shove it up your ass.

CHAPTER THIRTEEN

I'm a Hollywood writer; so I put on a sports jacket and take off my brain.

Ben Hecht

More Hollywood stuff, this regarding my first book, *Cosmic Banditos*, a goofball novel about The Meaning of Life wherein the protagonist is an unbalanced guy strongly based on me.

There's a movie deal for *Cosmic Banditos* too. The actor John Cusack has optioned that book. Here on this little Caribbean island I got an email from Cusack's company, New Crime Productions, saying he wants me to adapt that book for the screen. I got that email within a few days of the one from the movie studio for which I'm writing the screenplay to *In Search of Captain Zero*.

I've got movie deals up the wazoo.

If you're one of those sad souls who is fascinated by movie stars and who has kept reading this book solely to find out which major movie star I physically threatened, why, and what happened when I did so, I have something to disclose: It was John Cusack I physically threatened. If you don't remember that I physically threatened a movie star – it was mentioned a long time ago – good for you. In a sense I respect you for it.

The *Cosmic Banditos* saga is a good one, with plenty of bizarre Hollywood doings. The bizarre Hollywood doings are best summed up by the fact that I physically threatened John Cusack and now he wants to hire me.

How did that work?

I'll soon get around to that, but first: My having fired my movie writing agent means that Steven, my Hollywood attorney, will handle the *Banditos* contract negotiations. At first I thought this would save me money since I would not have to cough up the 10% commission agents get for making a couple of phone calls. However, Steven informed me that since he will be acting as my agent as well as my attorney, *he* will get the 10%. I came within a hair's breadth of firing him on the spot for this bullshit, but decided to wait on that, since it would mean I'd have no one left to handle my affairs in the States.

An important point is that I myself put the *Cosmic Banditos* deal together in the first place, minus only the contract details. Putting the deal together in the first place is 90% of an agent's job. So, in theory, I should get to keep 90% of the 10% Steven wants. When I mentioned this to Steven, he said, "That's different," then changed the subject.

We'll see how it goes with Steven, but I'll tell you, my finger is quivering on the firing-someone-else trigger.

At the time of the original *Cosmic Banditos* option deal, which was back in the spring of 2001, two other writers – a *writing team,* as the Hollywood expression goes – were hired to write the screenplay. How did they do? I'll put it this way: If they were a football team instead of a writing team, the goddamn New York Jets could have kicked their ass. They wrote The Worst Screenplay in the History of the World. But more about that to come. I'll fucking *loop* back to it.

Still more Hollywood stuff. In order to keep my fee down, Cusack's company is calling it "a rewrite." A rewrite of The Worst Screenplay in the History of the World. Since it's The Worst Screenplay in the History of the World I will not in any way be referring to it in my work. Cusack's people have agreed to this, i.e., that I should not refer to it in my work. (They have more or less agreed that the first screenplay is The Worst Screenplay in the History of the World.) So how could it then be a rewrite? When I queried everyone involved on this matter they all said the same thing: "That's different." Then they all changed the subject.

Anyway, all kinds of things will be up in the air when I leave this little Caribbean Island and return to my home at the end of the road at the bottom of Central America, aside from how it goes with Lisa.

I'm supposed to be writing the screenplay to my first memoir, *In Search of Captain Zero,* a book wherein there is no movie, and for which I'm being paid a ton of money, and in the writing of which I intend to go into the tank, i.e., purposefully come up with a bunch of utter crapola.

I'm also about to be hired to write the screenplay to my other book, which was optioned by another major Hollywood star, one whom I physically threatened. (Did I mention that I have doubts about whether there's a movie in *that* book?)

And yet I'm not writing either screenplay. I'm writing this book, for which there is no guarantee that I'll be paid anything, or even that it will be published at all. Not only that but – in case you haven't figured it out – as soon as word about this book gets out, my writing career will likely be over.

Who is going to want to come near me after this?

Unless, of course, this book becomes a howling success. If this book becomes a howling success, I'll basically be able to do what I want, including answering thorny questions with the words, "That's different."

I gotta say it again: On top of all the sweating and forehead bleeding and firing mega-talent-agency pimps, plus queasy guts, this is some wild-ass job, this writing job, no?

CHAPTER FOURTEEN

I went out there [to Hollywood] for a thousand a week, and I worked Monday, and I got fired Wednesday. The guy that hired me was out of town Tuesday.

Nelson Algren

By way of Hollywood backstory:

John Cusack Makes Quantum Leap in New Movie
January 10, 2001 1:55 am EST
By **Claude Brodesser**

HOLLYWOOD (Variety) – **John Cusack**, last in theaters with "High Fidelity," has committed to star in and produce "Cosmic Banditos."

Based on the soon to be republished novel by **A.C. Weisbecker**, "Banditos" follows the adventures of some Colombian marijuana smugglers on the lam in the jungle – one of them an American expatriate who would be played by Cusack. The tome will be republished in March by the New American Library trade imprint.

The book will be adapted for the screen by "Sid and Nancy" scribe **Abbe Wool** and **Jimmy Fishman**, the producer of 1999's "Desperate But Not Serious."

"It's just really original," said Cusack, adding, "It deals with quantum mechanics in a gonzo, gung-ho sort of way."

The picture concerns what Fishman, a former solid-state physicist turned producer-screenwriter, calls a group of smugglers "whose chaotic and random lives are suddenly given meaning by the laws of subatomic physics." The expatriate has what Fishman calls "a quantum epiphany" about how their lives are governed by particles.

Cusack said he first became interested in physics while shooting the 1989 picture "Fat Man and Little Boy" in the New Mexico desert when he was 21. The film allowed him to spend time discussing the Manhattan Project and the Los Alamos labs with numerous physicists consulting on the picture.

"Those first atomic physicists were real cowboys," he explained,

"like mystics, only they dealt with numbers instead of language."
The project will be developed by New York-based independent
producer **The Shooting Gallery**.

Know how I found out that this major star intended to produce and
star in a movie version of my book? (Keep in mind that the article is from
January, 2001, two years before the email from Cusack offering me the
adaptation.) A friend read the above *Variety* piece and emailed it to me,
several days after publication. Then the Hollywood writer I refer to as a
shitball motherfucker called to say he saw Cusack on TV, talking about
how great the book is and how he was going to make a movie from it. The
shitball motherfucker was trying to sound all rosy and happy for me but I
could imagine his green-with-envy complexion and forced grin – imagine
a seasick jackass chewing on a swarm of yellow jackets. See, he already
knew about the *Captain Zero* movie deal, Sean Penn wanting to play me.
Now with Cusack joining the ranks of movie stars wanting to play me,
we're talking about an envious shitball motherfucker here.

But the point being: Does the above strike you as odd? Like maybe I should
have known about the deal before it appeared in the trade publications,
and Cusack himself blabbed about it on the tube?

Here's how it went: Around June, 2000, the guy mentioned in the above
article, Jim Fishman, calls me and then my agent (my New York book agent,
not my Hollywood movie agent) about optioning the book. Fishman says
he's a buddy of John Cusack, who loves the book, and maybe he could get
Cusack involved in the future, but he doesn't have a lot to spend on an
option, blah blah. I say, Okay, why not, and Fishman coughs up $1,500 for
a year option. A clause in the contract states that if Fishman makes a deal
with a third party – any third party – he'd immediately owe me another
$15,000.

Months go by. It's now January of 2001 and I've haven't heard anything
from Fishman. Suddenly and without warning, according to the above
article and the interviews Cusack has done on the tube, deals have now
been struck (by Fishman) with three third parties: screenwriter Abbe
Wool, the production company called The Shooting Gallery, and Cusack
himself.

To repeat: No one, not Fishman nor Cusack nor The Shooting Gallery
notified me about the deals. If you're thinking that this is incredibly rude,
and completely unprofessional, you're absolutely right. It's out there, even
by Hollywood standards. But you know what? You ain't seen nothin' yet.

So my agent (my book agent) makes a flurry of phone calls to the people
involved. Nobody will take her calls or return them. How could this be?
They owe me money, the fifteen grand, that's how. I know: By the standards

of the movie biz, chump change – although it isn't chump change to me. Plus I'm pissed off at the insult, the lack of respect. Not surprised, just pissed off.

January goes by, then February, then we're well into March and still no money. I call Fishman myself, whom I already talked to once, about the adaptation he and Woole are doing. Fishman tells me to call The Shooting Gallery about the money. Okay, I say, figuring to play his game for the moment. I do remind him about our contract, which has no assign-the-debt clause. In other words, he owes me the money, not The Shooting Gallery. From his response, I can't tell if Fishman is simply a moron or if he's stonewalling me, trying to make me believe there's something wrong with me in expecting him to live up to our agreement. Anyway, although he admits that there's no assign-the-debt clause in our contract, he still insists – without logic or explanation – that he no longer owes me the money and that I should deal with The Shooting Gallery. Talk to Amy at The Shooting Gallery, Fishman says.

So I call this Amy, one Amy Nickin, a lawyer at The Shooting Gallery. Nickin chit-chats a streak, saying how much everyone at The Shooting Gallery loves my book and respects the material and how it's going to make a helluva movie and so forth.

I go along with this until I can't stand it anymore and ask, Where's the money?

Oh, *that*, Nickin says. No problem. Says they'll pay me in 30 days. Can't pay me right now because The Shooting Gallery is merging with some big company and has a cash flow problem. Just be patient and I'll get my money. To this I ask Nickin if they're telling, say, the electric company that The Shooting Gallery has a cash flow problem and that the light bill can't be paid but they'll get their money if they're patient. Or if her own paycheck is being held up.

Nickin, of course, says That's different.

I surprise her here, I think, given my query about the electric company and her salary check, which queries had sarcastic subtext, although my tone was pleasant. I say, Don't worry about it. I tell her that Fishman owes me the money anyway, not her company.

She tells me that Fishman doesn't have the money either.

I know a rip off coming when I see it, from my old smuggling days. There is now no question in my mind that Fishman and The Shooting Gallery have no intention of paying me the 15k. But why would they do this, rip me off for a measly 15k when the movie will cost millions?

I have a theory. Based upon the conversation about the adaptation I already had with Fishman, I'm thinking that there is zero chance that the screenplay being written by Fishman and Woole will be shootable. In other words, there will be no movie, no millions spent. This is obvious to everyone involved, I figure, especially to The Shooting Gallery, which is stalling payment after being nearly three months late to begin with. (The Shooting Gallery probably agreed with Fishman to shoulder the 15k debt, but that had nothing to do with me; that was between them and Fishman.) Cusack himself, I'm figuring, doesn't give a shit about me getting paid or not getting paid – there's no way he's made himself liable for any outlay. He's free-riding it on this, as movie stars do, based on Hollywood entitlement, as with Sean Penn and my other book.

Why do I figure the screenplay is unshootable? During our conversation about the adaptation Fishman informed me that "one change" was being made from the book to the screen story. What change is that? I wanted to know, and yes, my writer's queasy gut was already flaring.

The change was that they made José, the Full Blown Bandito, the Cosmic Bandito of the title, a woman...

If you happened to have read the book, and if you happened to be dead right now, you'd be spinning in your grave. And while spinning in your grave you'd maybe be concocting variations of catch-22s about dumb people and movies not getting made. But I have to assume you haven't read the book. So imagine this. Imagine that *Butch Cassidy and the Sundance Kid* was originally a book. Imagine that a movie producer options the book and then tells the author that he loves and respects the book, and the one change they're making is that Butch is going to be a babe.

Now try to imagine how the movie would go... instead of one of the classic buddy movies of all time... instead of that great scene at the end when Butch and Sundance are all shot up and about to be slaughtered by a thousand Bolivian soldiers and they're arguing about where they're going next... instead of that climactic scene now imagine they have a lover's spat about... about that time Sundance was insensitive when Butch was PMS-ing. (Butch would be the babe, I figure, since a babe who robs banks is going to be... well... butch.)

Hearing the above about José now being a woman, I was too astounded to respond. All I managed as a stalling tactic while I regrouped was a query about what the babe full blown bandito was now named.

Still José, Fishman said.

I don't understand. José is now a woman but she's still named José?

Yes! Fishman said. As if this is some sort of subtle stroke of genius. A *touch*.

Maybe Fishman was also comparing the scenario to *Butch Cassidy* and figured that if Butch could still be called Butch if Butch was a babe, he should call José José even if José was now a babe.

Or maybe he kept the name José out of respect for the material.

Boy, I'd like to read the screenplay, I said. I was curious, in the morbid sense. (Right: It would turn out to be The Worst Screenplay in the History of the World.)

Sure, Fishman said, but first he wants to give it to The Shooting Gallery, see what they think, and then give it to Cusack. My theory at the time was that Fishman gave the screenplay to The Shooting Gallery and The Shooting Gallery wanted to save 15k by ripping off the author of the original material, me, since the screenplay was unshootable.

As it will turn out, I gave The Shooting Gallery too much credit by assuming they even realized the screenplay was unshootable. As it will turn out, the reason The Shooting Gallery intended to rip me off was less subtle and imaginative, albeit sleazier.

After talking with The Shooting Gallery's lawyer, Amy Nickin, the lying slug, I call Fishman back and get right to the point. I tell him if I don't get the money by the next day I'll come out to L.A. and deal with the problem in person. I add that since I don't like dealing with lawyers – or even being in close physical proximity to the shitball motherfuckers, even Steven, my Hollywood one – I have no intention of *suing* him. I then muster a tone best described as…. *demented…* and say that I'm *really* looking forward to meeting him, if he gets my drift. Thinking about the *Men's Journal* guy's reaction to this sort of thing, I'm figuring a FedEx-ed check will arrive the next day.

Fishman tells me Great and that he's looking forward to meeting me and lunch will be on him. I swear to God that's what he said. I have it right here in my contemporaneous notes.

I don't want to fly out to L.A., I'm thinking, especially with Mom so sick and all. Plus, beating up Fishman would probably not get the job done; I'd just get in trouble, or maybe get myself beat up. The guy didn't sound tough, but who knew? The thing about dumb people is that sometimes they'll surprise you. All that unused brain power can surface in weird, unexpected ways.

So I ponder my options.

Who should I turn my attention towards?

Why not Cusack?

So I call his company, New Crime Productions, and speak to the executive in charge of the deal. To my chagrin, she's very nice, seems really genuine and concerned when she tells me that she understands my frustration at not getting paid, and at finding out about all the deals that had been struck through articles in *Variety* and calls from envious shitball motherfucker Hollywood writers, words to that effect.

Before she can get *too* nice and genuine and concerned – which would cause me to lose heart in my mission – I muster a tirade to the effect that

I'm coming out to L.A. to look up her boss Cusack and confront him for the money since it was he who blabbed all over the TV and to the Hollywood trade papers that he had control of my book and was now a producer on the project along with the dumb-ass Fishman and since producers are responsible for seeing that writers get paid I don't care who my contract is with so I'm coming to L.A. and I'm *really* pissed off. I may have worked in my outrage over my Full Blown Bandito José character now being a woman who is somehow still named José. If I didn't, I should have.

An added plus here is that the main source of humor in *Cosmic Banditos* is that the narrator is pretty much out of his mind (if not outright demented); he is the drug–addled perpetrator of rampant criminality, blatant and unapologetic nihilism and all around chaos and destruction. And keep in mind that the narrator is based on me. This is all anyone involved in the deal really knows about me. I haven't yet met any of them.

In the wake of my mustered tirade the woman executive is *still* nice and genuine and concerned so I do what I have to before I lose heart and apologize for my ranting hostility. I hang up.

I wait to see What Happens Next.

It's spectacular.

The phone will not stop ringing.

First my then-literary agent calls wanting to know if I'm crazy or what and then Amy Nickin, the lying slug of an attorney for The Shooting Gallery, calls, all irate that I'm "behaving unprofessionally." Fishman calls saying... I don't remember; I have no notes or recollections on the call. Maybe something about our upcoming lunch, whether I have any dietary preferences.

The phone keeps ringing, various Hollywoodites wanting to know if I'm crazy and accusing me of unprofessionalism and so forth. Sitting by the kitchen phone at Mom's house in North Carolina, I'm rather enjoying all the fuss and dismay.

Mom is toward the end of her life during all this; she will die in a few weeks, in late April. She's weak but still lucid. She says she's worried about me threatening people but has faith that I know what I'm doing. I tell Mom not to worry, that I do know what I'm doing, and that the situation and how I'm handling it is the usual with Hollywood deals. This isn't strictly true, of course. I say it to un-worry Mom.

Late that same night Cusack himself calls, wakes me up. He's affable, chit-chats a bit, asks how Mom is; I've made no secret that I'm taking care of her in her illness. (The image of a demented writer taking care of his dying Mom may be a source of further worry about what I'm capable of -- I think Jeffrey Dahmer loved his Mom, too.) He seems genuine, mentioning something about his own Mom. Then he gets to the point, says he didn't know about my treatment by Fishman and The Shooting Gallery. He's off promoting his latest movie and out of that loop. He doesn't blame me a bit for my behavior and promises that my money is forthcoming, and soon. Says he'll be personally responsible for the payment.

Okay, I say. Great. Thank you. I definitely believe him on all this. I didn't threaten the guy because I figured he directly had anything to do with the problem; I just figured it would work. I tell him this and we laugh. I even apologize if I've upset anyone other than Nickin or Fishman, although in my opinion I haven't upset Fishman since Fishman apparently doesn't realize that I *have* threatened anyone. Fishman isn't the brightest bulb on the Hollywood marquee, I say, words to that effect. Cusack laughs, but with a little edge to it; I'm talking about his producing partner here. But our conversation winds down naturally and quite cordially.

The guy's all right, I'm thinking. Provisionally. I wait to see if the money shows up.

The check arrives by FedEx the next day. Issued by The Shooting Gallery.

But one last thing. I wait to see if the check clears.

It does.

As I say, I was wrong in my theory that The Shooting Gallery was refusing to pay me because they knew the movie was not going to get made (due to the script being unshootable), and they were trying to save the 15k. They *were* trying to save the 15k but for a different reason.

I monitored the situation to see What Would Happen Next.

Less than a month later The Shooting Gallery went belly up. Chapter 11. Poof. Gone.

Remember Amy Nickin's promise that I'd get my money in 30 days?

Right: They had no intention whatever of paying me before running for the bankruptcy hills.

But why *did* they pay me?

Because everyone involved in the company figured they'd soon enough be back working in Hollywood (maybe they'd immediately start another company fresh and debt free) and therefore did not want to alienate John Cusack, who no doubt made an irate call to them, demanding that I be paid.

I was crazy and unprofessional but I got my money.

Mom loved it that all this worked out. She even saw the humor in it, my threatening a movie star and so forth. But she worried, too. She worried about all the problems I was having with people, like my demented *Zero* editor, who by now had cut off communications with me, partially due to treachery on the part of my then-book agent.

But the main thing Mom worried about was that I'd find someone to love in this world.

CHAPTER FIFTEEN

When God hands you a gift, he also hands you a whip; and the
whip is intended solely for self-flagellation.

Truman Capote

Today as I write is March 17, 2003. A big day for world affairs. George W. Bush, the shitball motherfucker who wasn't elected President of the United States, is going on television tonight to tell the world that he is going to attack that other shitball motherfucker, Saddam Hussein, within 48 hours, if Saddam doesn't get out of Iraq. But that's not what's on my mind right now; I only mention it because in the future when you are reading this you might remember where you were today, March 17, 2003, which gives us an historical perspective.

So no. The impending war is not what's on my mind right now. What's on my mind right now is *really* important. Which is that Lisa left this Caribbean island earlier today to go back to the United States for a couple weeks. She is going back there to close down her old life; among other things to move out of her Manhattan apartment and tell her parents and her brother Marc and her friends that she is leaving permanently; that she is going to live in Costa Rica, to a place far to the south in that country, to a little piece of paradise at the end of the road in a province called Pavones, which is Spanish for Big Turkeys. To live there with me.

You may remember that when Lisa came to visit me in Costa Rica the second time, which was a couple of months ago, she sat in on the negotiations involving land I was buying. She pointed out a fuck up in the contract, embarrassed the Costa Rican lawyers, took over the meeting and so forth. As of that meeting we had not broached the possibility of living together in Costa Rica.

But the next morning, over our eggs and toast at the hotel just before she left for the airport, I asked Lisa if she'd like to go in as my partner on the land deal. Lisa looked up from her plate and we had a... a moment. A silent moment, just with our eyes. What my eyes said, without a word being spoken, was this: "I love you, Lisa, and want you to come live with me in Costa Rica."

And Lisa's eyes in return said, "I love you too, Allan, and very much want to come live with you in Costa Rica."

But here's What Happened Next: Lisa spent that very night with her ex-boyfriend at her Manhattan apartment and then told him that she was coming back to him. At the same time she sent me an email saying that of all the things I had to worry about the one thing I didn't have to worry about was her, Lisa herself. When I sensed something wasn't right and begged her to please stop turning off her cell phone because it made me nervous not being able to contact her, Lisa said that she was sorry and that she "gets it" (she emailed saying the same thing, putting quotes around the words) and would not do that again. Then when she was supposed to be at a girlfriend's at Montauk and I queried her as to why she had turned her cell phone off again after promising not to, she said she'd left her charger in the city and had to do that to save the battery. As it turned out she was with her ex-boyfriend, in bed.

Going back further, to her first trip to be with me in Costa Rica, which was back in December: Within days of her return to the United States around Christmas Lisa had got back with her ex-boyfriend then too – whom she had told me she left – screwing him and so forth, meanwhile lying to me about where she was and why she'd turned her cell phone off. All in all, the cheating and lying, which was continuous, spanned an eight-week period. I found out all this the day before I flew to this island to be with Lisa.

A few days after our uneasy reunion here, and referring to her cheating and lying, Lisa said this: "There are worse things a person could do to another person in a relationship."

To sum up: With Lisa, I may be in love with someone deficient in self-reflection. Someone who is *dishonest*.

This is my worst nightmare.

CHAPTER SIXTEEN

The writer has a grudge against society, which he documents with
accounts of unsatisfying sex, unrealized ambitions, unmitigated
loneliness, and a sense of local and global distress.

Renata Adler

War rages in Iraq.

I was watching a CNN news conference – which was beamed into space from the other side of the earth then back down to this little island – and some media people were asking an American general about the recent attempt by the United States military to kill Saddam Hussein by dropping a bomb on a restaurant in a Baghdad suburb. Intelligence reports indicated that Saddam may have been having lunch there.

"We were trying to 'cut the head off the serpent,'" the general said. Unfortunately, he went on, Saddam was not having lunch at the restaurant at the time the bomb was dropped on it. There were apparently some civilian casualties, "collateral damage." The media people asked a few questions about how the intelligence was gathered and about where Saddam might really be. No one asked whether or not dropping a bomb on a civilian restaurant, and in so doing killing folks who happen to be eating there, is a war crime, or how the general might react if the Iraqi military dropped a bomb on a civilian restaurant George W. Bush might have been having lunch in. There was subtext here, not so much in the bomb-dropping but in the failure of the media to ask these questions about it, but that's not what's on my mind right now. What's on my mind right now is *really* important.

Yesterday morning I tried calling Lisa in the United States and her cell phone was off, as it was continually last winter when she was screwing her ex and lying about it. I waited a while then redialed. Still off. Then Lisa finally called me and said it had been off because it was a new phone and wasn't taking a charge – this in spite of the fact that the phone had taken a charge and worked fine the day before. Said she would immediately go back to the store and exchange the phone for one that worked and call me back. While I was waiting for Lisa to call back I was calculating the odds that a brand new cell phone would work fine then the next day suddenly be defective. Conversely, what were the odds that Lisa would be lying, given her past behavior upon returning to the United States, especially regarding her cell phone being off. I was also remembering that the last time she had had a charger problem – when she said she left it in the city – it wasn't that at all. She'd been with her ex-boyfriend at Montauk, in bed.

Lisa called back and said that the charger worked after all, which made me think that she too had been calculating the odds of a new phone working fine then being defective, and decided to change her story. When the guy at the store plugged it in, she said, it suddenly took a charge fine, like it did two days ago. "I can't explain it," was her explanation.

Now, today, as I write these words, Lisa is at a weekend psychotherapy symposium in upstate New York with her best friend Vanessa, *or so she says*. The purpose of the symposium, Lisa says, is to help people get in touch with themselves. Lisa said this without irony, by the way.

Here's how I'm going to find out the truth about where Lisa is and what she's doing: If Lisa is lying, if she's back screwing her ex-boyfriend, say, rather than trying to get in touch with herself in upstate New York, Vanessa will not be nearby. So I figure if Lisa cannot put Vanessa on the phone she is doing something bad, screwing her ex-boyfriend again, most likely.

The one time I got through to Lisa – the one time her cell phone wasn't turned off – I asked to speak to Vanessa. Lisa said she'd try to find Vanessa but wasn't making any promises since she hadn't seen Vanessa for a while at the symposium. This didn't sound right since they'd gone there together. Also, her voice got breezy when she told me this. Back in January and February, when Lisa was screwing her ex-boyfriend, her voice would get breezy when she was lying about where she was and what she was doing.

From where I sit waiting to find out if Lisa is doing something bad, I can hear soca music and laughter coming from a local bar down the street where, last week before she left the island, Lisa did something inappropriate with another man and which upset me and embarrassed me.

Because of the revelation about her screwing around with her ex-boyfriend after both times she'd visited me in Costa Rica and then lying about it, and because men can't seem to not hit on her, soon after Lisa arrived on this island I asked her not only to not flirt with other men, but to even avoid giving the impression of flirting. At least for a while, until the stress backed off. Lisa said she understood and promised.

A matter of a few days later, and along with another couple we knew well from Montauk, Lisa and I were at the local bar down the street having sundowners. The four of us were standing outside on a little grassy area by the road, with soca music playing from inside the bar, as it is now. It was early, the sun was still up, and we were the only people there, aside from two or three local guys inside the bar. A beautiful evening, Lisa and I holding hands outside on the grass next to our friends from back home.

One of the local guys came out of the bar and strutted over and asked Lisa to dance. I have to describe this guy. If you've been to Caribbean islands, you'll be familiar with his type. One of those Caribbean local guys – yes, a black guy – who thinks he can take your woman if he wants. Or, even if it doesn't work out that way, he figures to aggravate you by giving it a try, and what are you gonna do about it? It's a territorial thing, a dominance thing, a racial thing, an ignorant thing.

His move was an insult to me as a man and to Lisa as a woman. I was just about to take control, say No thanks, we're fine here, but Lisa beat me to it, dropping my hand and giving me her drink and saying Sure, and then she commenced to gyrate with this guy right in front of me. Lisa, as mentioned, is slim and very sexy and she was all dolled up and she really got into it with this guy; the two of them put on a show.

At first I was more embarrassed than anything, as were our friends. We all just stood there with our drinks – me with Lisa's drink as well – staring at the ground as this went on and on in front of the bar.

Eventually, the local dropped to his knees in front of Lisa and started moving toward her, shucking and jiving and grinning salaciously. Rather than backing off at this added rudeness, Lisa danced closer, pushed him over playfully, and continued to gyrate above him.

Having had it with this, I walked over and said to Lisa, "That's enough."

Lisa, who was tipsy, didn't argue, seemed to sober up. I led her across the grass, and not wanting to cause a scene in front of my friends or this local or his friends grinning from the bar doorway, kept my voice down, saying, "That wasn't cool, Lisa. In fact, it was humiliating."

Lisa nodded, saying, "You're right. I'm sorry."

I'm not going to hassle her, I was thinking, but I reminded her about the promise not to even give the *impression* of flirting with other men. "Listen," I said, "With… everything…"

Lisa interrupted, repeating that she was sorry, and repeated the promise she would not even give the impression of flirting with other men.

Now, as war rages in Iraq, and as Americans, of which I am one, are dropping bombs on civilian restaurants to cut off the head off the serpent, I wonder if Lisa will keep that promise, plus other promises, with me a couple thousand miles away, the one promise already having been broken right in front of me at the local bar down the street. This aside from the cheating and lying, which Lisa says is not the worst thing a person can do to another person in a relationship.

I wait to see What Happens Next.

CHAPTER SEVENTEEN

In the act of loving you arm another person against you.

Anonymous

Two hours later. One of the things I did during the past two hours was make some calls to Montauk. I found out that Lisa is not at Montauk, but that her ex-boyfriend is. I have spies there and it's a small town and our affair is a major scandal. Her ex-boyfriend, whom she left for me (or whom she says she left for me) is, was, sort of a friend of mine; more like a long-time acquaintance. I may have neglected to mention this.

So wherever Lisa really is, she is not with her ex-boyfriend. This was a relief, but only temporarily. My mind is in overdrive as to what may be going on. I have a theory. Best way to explain it is to bring you back to this Caribbean island, to when Lisa was still here.

We decided to take a trip around the island. I know this island very well. Aside from having come here to surf for 20 years, I've done a couple magazine articles on it, including one for *Men's Journal* – this was before I threatened the guy there, of course.

After a night at a little guesthouse on the windward side, Lisa and I drove the winding coast road to the next village for breakfast. Meanwhile, I hatched a plan. The plan had to do with The Horror, the snowstorm in Boston, the guy from that. The Snowman. The guy responsible for the best week, sexually, of Lisa's life. I was still thinking about him now and then. Or a lot. Or constantly. Depends on how you define these concepts.

Remember when I wanted to describe to Lisa the best week of *my* life, sexually, how I was going to lie like a slug and say it was with someone else, a woman named Maria? And how Lisa didn't want to hear it? Since then I'd been working in references to Maria. I wouldn't get very far before Lisa would say, "I don't want to hear it," but with dogged determination I made some progress.

By the way, one time when Lisa wanted to stop me in one of my sex stories she phrased it thus: "I don't want to hear about any of the three hundred women you've had sex with." This gave me pause. The actual number is half that. Hold on. Less than half that, considerably less. Christ, why am I lying to *you* about this? The number is 118, according to my still-in-progress list. I may have, am hoping I have, forgotten a few.* I've been especially hoping this since Lisa's estimate of 300. But what does it mean that Lisa figures I've had sex with more than twice as many women as is the case? Is this good, in that she figures a Sex God like me ought to have had sex with 300 women? Or bad, in that I haven't lived up to her expectations?

I did manage to tell in its entirety one story about a woman I'd had sex with, before Lisa could say, "I don't want to hear it." I did this by going in through the back door, so to speak, disguising the real nature of the tale until it was too late. This is the secret here. You wait for an opening, act innocent, then go in through the back door. I'll tell you the short version. With Lisa, going in through the back door made the tale a long and winding road, not to mix metaphors.

When I was a marijuana smuggler back in the 1970s I had a lot of money, ridiculously so. One time I was in New York City staying at an ostentatious suite at the U.N. Plaza. I had the hots for this girl who lived in New Jersey, two hours away. (Okay, I admit it – an "exotic dancer.") One night I called her and suggested she come into the city. Said I'd send my limo. Aside from my Learjet waiting on the runway across the river at Teterboro, I always had a limo outside the hotel. She said it was too late; it'd take too long to get there. I asked if there was an airport nearby. She said not really. I asked if there were any open spaces nearby. She said she lived near a high school where there was a football field. I told her to be on the 50-yard line in half an hour. I called a helicopter pilot I knew and had him go get her. Landing a helicopter on a football field is extremely illegal, so I had to pay him something like a thousand bucks extra to do it; this was in 1970s dollars, remember. So that was how I got laid that night.

Lisa let me finish this story even when she sensed where I was going with it, mainly because she was laughing too hard to stop me. She found it hysterical that a guy would go to those lengths to get laid. Said it was a perfect example of how guys – me being the archetypical guy – "were obsessed with sex and with screwing as many women as possible." To which I reminded her that it was almost always she who would say "Let's take five" and so who was she to accuse me of being obsessed with sex? To which Lisa replied, "That's different," then changed the subject. Pissed me off.

Anyway, Lisa and I were approaching this village after our night at

---

* I made the dubious decision to include Cat Woman in my total, to get the number up. In my own defense, I did not include the Panamanian alpha whore who semi-raped me. This was because, technically speaking, I'd paid her for the sex. In my view, you pay a woman for sex, she shouldn't count in any list you might make of women you've had sex with – even if the woman you paid for sex ends up semi-raping you.

a little guesthouse and I hatched a plan to work in my story about the fictitious best week of my life, sexually – with the woman named Maria.

Lisa had met Maria on this Caribbean island in the fall of 2000 when she came down with her boyfriend (now her ex-boyfriend, although the "ex" part seems uncertain at best). I was on the island with Maria. (Mom was still well enough to be on her own for a couple weeks, plus friends like Ellen helped out in my absence). The four of us would hang out together. Maria is a local, born and raised on the island, although she is Caucasian; the vast majority of islanders are black. This makes Maria exotic, what with the cultural differences and her West Indian accent and so forth. Maria is also very attractive, very sexy. In fact, she exudes female-ness, although not ultimate female-ness like Lisa does. This is okay, though, since Lisa doesn't know she exudes ultimate female-ness. If she knew it, she wouldn't exude it anymore. That's the way that works.

So via my aborted storytelling Lisa knew that it had been Maria with whom I'd supposedly had the best week of my life, sexually. The other detail I'd managed to slip in was that the week had involved a trip around the island. This was true, which was good: lies work best if they are wrapped around some truth. In our trip around the island, Maria and I stayed at a hotel in the village Lisa and I were now approaching. The crux of the plan I hatched was that Lisa and I would have breakfast at that hotel.

Lisa noticed the hotel rates, which were on the menu, and remarked how expensive the place was. This was the opening I'd been waiting for. I said that I had stayed there once, for a whole week, but only had to pay half price, the locals-only price.

Lisa asked how I'd managed that.

I said that I paid the locals-only price because I'd been there with a local.

Boom. Lisa should have immediately had a rush of insight. She should have realized that I'd had the best week of my life, sexually, at the very place we were now in, with Maria. Right upstairs over our heads in one of the rooms. Never mind that that wasn't the case. I mean although it was a great week, sexually, it was not the best. But you already know that.

Look. If Lisa and I had been in Boston, at a hotel there, and if Lisa were to say, "By the way, this is the hotel where I had the best week of my life, sexually," I'd get weird. I'd react in some way.

Lisa nodded absently and continued to chow down. No reaction.

I wasn't going to let this alone. Thinking back, it's possible that my idea of a trip around the island may actually have been subconsciously motivated by my desire to expound in more depth about the fictitious best week of my life, sexually. It's possible. (Possible, but who knows? *No one knows shit about why he does anything.*) If true, then I'd gone to great lengths with no payoff.

So I waited a bit then brought up The Snowman. I edged the conversation around so it didn't come out of the blue. I asked Lisa how it was possible that this guy had been responsible for the best week of her life, sexually, when I – according to Lisa herself – was a full-blown Sex God with whom she had just had a week of spectacular, *otherworldly* even, sex.

This question had been on my mind now and then – or a lot, or constantly, depending on how you define these concepts – but I'd never had the courage to blurt it out. I was probably afraid of what the answer might be.

Lisa didn't respond right away so I rambled on, trying to keep my voice casual, reminding her how lately it was she who would call it quits, sexually, how she'd roll over and say something like, "That was… otherworldly." I was about to say, "I mean what more can I do?" but Lisa interrupted, saying, "You can't compare the two." The two meaning The Snowman and me, I assumed.

"What do you mean 'You can't compare the two?'"

To which Lisa replied, "There was a… lack of commitment with him... I don't know…I didn't love him like I do you." She shook her head, saying she wasn't explaining this right, then went on about what was going on with her life at the time, but I wasn't really listening.

So that was it. A lack of commitment with The Snowman.

Thing was, Lisa had already told me that one reason sex with me was so spectacular was because she loved me. Yet the best week of her life, sexually, had been with The Snowman, whom she didn't love.

This didn't jibe.

Which brings me back to my theory of what Lisa is doing if she isn't actually at a psychotherapy symposium in upper New York State with her best friend Vanessa, supposedly trying to get in touch with herself.

But first I need to disclose a couple things. Toward the end of her relationship with her ex-boyfriend, the two had drifted apart sexually, which, Lisa said, was very frustrating for her. Also, toward the end Lisa would often stay in Manhattan, where she had her own apartment. Keep in mind that Lisa exudes ultimate female-ness. In other words, she is a very sensual woman. Plus guys can't help hitting on her.

Do you see where I'm going with this?

Sometime during the waning months of her relationship with her ex-boyfriend, Lisa met someone while she was in Manhattan. Let's call him The Cityman. She still loved her ex-boyfriend, but since the relationship was waning and since they had drifted apart sexually, Lisa was vulnerable and took up with The Cityman. She did not love him, was not committed to him, so the sex was spectacular, as it had been with his predecessor, The Snowman. She kept The Cityman a secret from her boyfriend, of course, maybe from everyone except Vanessa, who helped her with alibis when needed.

The Cityman, like The Snowman before him, was Lisa's fuckbuddy.

Then Lisa came to Costa Rica and fell in love with me but when she returned home she was loathe to give up her fuckbuddy, The Cityman, since she finds sex with a fuckbuddy to be more spectacular than with a guy she loves, even if he's a Sex God.

When Lisa told The Cityman that she was moving down to Costa Rica, he was disappointed but not devastated, since he and Lisa were not in love, not committed. So he said, casually, "How about a last fling?"

Maybe a weekend somewhere while Lisa was closing down her life in the United States. (It was March so maybe they'd even get snowed in.) Hence the alibi of the weekend at the psychotherapy symposium with her best friend Vanessa.

One more thing. When I last talked to Lisa – at the supposed psychotherapy symposium a little while ago – as part of her get-angry-at-me-for-not-trusting-her routine, Lisa said this, sarcastically: "What do you think I'm doing, fucking some guy?" This was interesting, since the issue between us was whether she'd gotten back with her ex-boyfriend yet again. I knew her ex-boyfriend was not at the psychotherapy symposium in upper New York State – assuming there was one – but *Lisa didn't know I knew that*. So why didn't she say, "What do you think I'm doing, fucking my ex-boyfriend?"

See what I mean?

The existence of The Cityman would explain everything.

CHAPTER EIGHTEEN

Literature should not disappear up its own asshole, so to speak.
Kurt Vonnegut

Vanessa was there. Lisa called and put her on the phone. While we made small talk I was listening to the background chatter, which was considerable. There was no question that they were at a psychotherapy symposium. There was even no question that the people there were trying to get in touch with themselves. I heard some guy say this: "Blah blah blah... try to get in touch with myself... blah blah blah."

There is no The Cityman. Lisa has not been cheating and lying again. I know because I'm writing this from the point of view of two days after the phone call with Vanessa, after I uncovered some other exculpatory information. I didn't really need any more exculpatory information, though, since my suspicions, the house of cards of it collapsed when Lisa put Vanessa on the phone.

What's been going on here?

Have you ever heard the expression, "A little information is a dangerous thing"?

Let's assume this expression is true, because it is true.

Then how dangerous is a little information supplied by a lovesick fool?

I've gone to great if unintentional lengths to prove I'm a lovesick fool, right? Or maybe you weren't paying attention. Maybe you merely found my obsession and pain humorous (or annoying). Maybe you missed what was really going on.

I sure did.

Allow me to suggest something: You don't know anything about Lisa. This notwithstanding that everything I told you about Lisa's behavior is the truth, in that I wasn't misrepresenting anything; I wasn't lying.

There is war in Iraq as I write these words. Not long ago George W. Bush, the shitball motherfucker who was not elected President of the United States, gave a speech explaining why we are going to war. One issue he raised was Saddam Hussein's use of poison gas on other nations and on his own people. And it was true. Saddam *did* use poison gas on other nations and on his own people. The shitball motherfucker – our shitball motherfucker – wasn't lying.

But what the shitball motherfucker neglected to mention was that when Saddam was using poison gas on other nations and his own people *he was our ally*. He was our ally and we were sending him military aid, including the helicopters with which he dropped the poison gas. We were directly helping him to use poison gas on other nations and on his own people. Not only that, but it was George W. Bush's daddy – the original shitball motherfucker – who was either Vice President or President at that time and who was sending Saddam this military aid, meanwhile knowing the terrible things Saddam Hussein would do with it.

This represents what's known as a *lie by omission*.

It's a whopper, isn't it?

I've been doing the same thing with my tale of Lisa's and my relationship, with my suspicions. Inadvertently, but still, I've been doing it. In other words, like the shitball motherfucker who wasn't elected President of the United States, I left out some stuff.

One reason you leave out stuff is that you can't put *everything* in your fucking narrative. Or in a speech about why you're going to attack some other shitball motherfucker. But there are other reasons. (Not wanting your daddy to be tried and convicted of aiding and abetting genocide, for example.) Remember at the end of the last chapter I said that Lisa should have said, "What do you think I'm doing, fucking my ex-boyfriend?" instead of what she did say, which was, "What do you think I'm doing, fucking some guy?"

This was all true, i.e., *I wasn't lying*, but what I failed to mention was that while Lisa was in Manhattan and I couldn't reach her via her cell phone, I also made inquiries at Montauk, as I did two days ago. Found out that Lisa and her ex-boyfriend were not together then either. And I failed to mention that I told Lisa that I checked on this. So she probably was remembering that and assumed I wasn't suspicious about her ex-boyfriend anymore.

Hey, I can't put everything in this fucking narrative.

Remember the moment wherein Lisa and I had the eye contact that said those nice things about love and I asked if Lisa would go in as my partner on the land deal? I then described how Lisa spent that very night with her ex-boyfriend. What I neglected to mention was that her ex-boyfriend was waiting for her in front of her Manhattan apartment when she got in from the airport. Waylaid her. She had no intention of seeing him upon her return from being with me.

I can't put everything in this fucking narrative.

And Lisa did tell her ex-boyfriend that she would get back with him, but that was after this exhausting night with the guy – who has always known how to push her buttons – wherein she was too emotionally drained to think clearly. And I failed to mention that within hours she called him and cancelled the idea of getting back with him.

I can't put everything in this fucking narrative.

These lies by omission are whoppers, but there are others that are not whoppers, smaller lies by omission, that taken individually don't mean much, but en masse constitute the biggest whopper of all, which is that I failed to properly define why I love Lisa in the first place, I mean aside from her ultimate female-ness, all that sexy stuff and how smart she is and so forth. All the things about her that tell me that at heart she is a good and honest person.

When I told you Lisa went back with her ex-boyfriend, a man she'd been with for five years, did you maybe wonder what kind of loyalties and dependencies – healthy or not – may have been lingering and that may have caused her to do that? Did you wonder *anything* about that relationship, how it ended, what were the emotional issues involved? Or were you too busy being amused (or annoyed) by my obsession and pain?

But what about Lisa's godawful comment about cheating and lying: "There are worse things a person could do to another person in a relationship"?

Have you ever said something stupid that you really didn't mean, maybe while you were distraught and being defensive?

When I told you that Lisa had got back with her ex-boyfriend after her first visit to Costa Rica, did you wonder what sort of commitment Lisa and I had made during that visit? Here's what sort of commitment: None. At least on my part. "Let's do this again sometime," was pretty much my parting endearment.

Right: I must've figured I can't put everything in my fucking narrative.

While I was watching CNN a few days ago some toady of the shitball motherfucker who wasn't elected President of the United States came on and said that the destruction of oil wells by the Iraqis would constitute a war crime. Hey, last I heard, the destruction of resources – the spoils of war – by an invaded country in a conflict was pretty much standard war procedure. Apparently the shitball motherfucker who wasn't elected President of the United States has decided to rewrite the book on what constitutes a war crime. Fuck with the oil and we'll hang you by your balls.[*]

---

[*] What *is* a war crime, according to the Geneva Conventions and other international treaties solemnly signed by the United States (and are therefore supreme laws of the land), is the bombing and sabotaging of civilian infrastructure, like water purification plants, which the United States has been doing since the first Gulf War. Iraqi civilian deaths due to lack of potable water are estimated to be in the tens of thousands. But hey, *do not fuck with the oil.*

What's really going on here (aside from Orwell's optimism)? Right: *The war in Iraq is about oil.*

Notice how a couple of times I use one long paragraph to inventory Lisa's transgressions? And how I repeat the words "cheating and lying" in close proximity to Lisa's name? I call this device a Downhill Paragraph, because it gains momentum as it goes, with no pauses to take a breath and maybe think about what's really going on, and what with the cheating and lying juxtaposed to Lisa's name, at the end you're all wild-eyed and ready to shout, "What a cheating, lying bitch that Lisa is!"

But, hey, with those paragraphs, *I wasn't lying.*

Trust me on something. A clever nonfiction writer with an agenda (conscious or not) can make you believe just about anything, without lying. But here's the unusual part, for us, here: Not only was I not lying, I wasn't misrepresenting anything in any sense.

What?

I've been writing from the point of view of uncertainty. Aside from you, I myself didn't know What Happens Next with respect to Lisa being my worst nightmare – what kind of human being she really is.

Had I written all this from the point of view of later, of knowing the truth – that Vanessa was at the psychotherapy symposium and that Lisa was innocent of more cheating and lying – then I would have been misrepresenting, lying, in every sense. I would have been manipulating you in ways that are unconscionable; trying to get you to believe one thing when I know the truth is another.

Had I done that then I should rot in Writer Hell.

But I didn't know the truth. I was writing from the point of view of a lovesick fool who obviously wanted to believe the worst.

Point being: The state of mind of the writer as he writes is a vital element in assessing what's really going on in the world of a nonfiction narrative.

Odds are that you, like me, were oblivious to what was really going on.

What was really going on?

Almost nothing about Lisa as a human being.

A little about you, the collective you, but also maybe the personal you. *You.*

A bit about me. Hold on. Maybe a lot about me. About how fucked up I am in my sudden neediness -- the extremes in thought and behavior that resulted from it.

You wanna talk about a lack of self-reflection?

What *has* been going on, I *think*, is a whole lot about the literary genre known as nonfiction, of which this book is an example (even though *nonfiction* is a non-word, according to my mammoth *Webster's New Universal Unabridged Dictionary*).

Nonfiction. A load of horseshit is what it is.

PART TWO
Big Turkeys

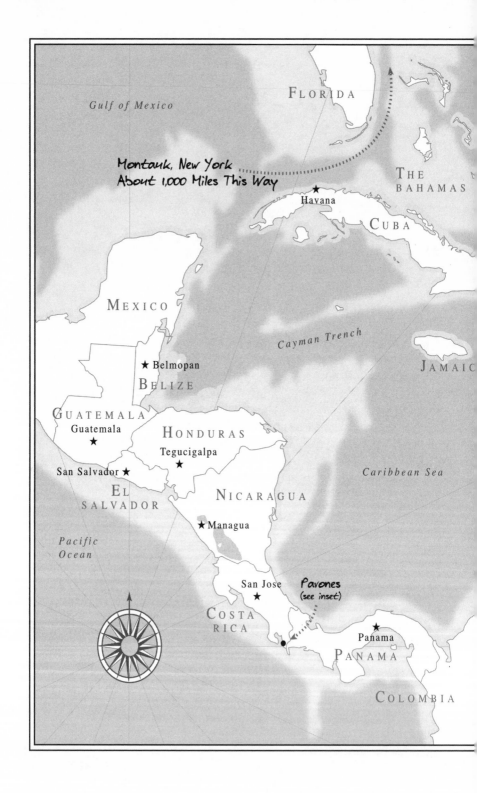

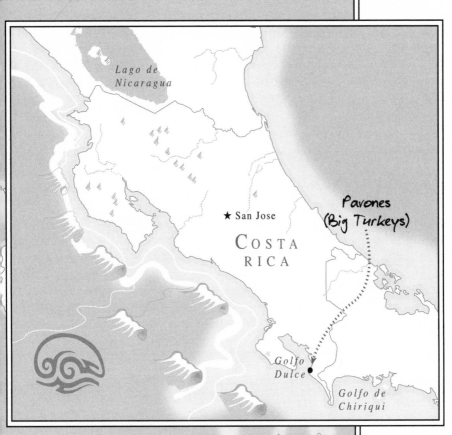

Pavones
(Big Turkeys)

★ San Jose

COSTA
RICA

*Lago de
Nicaragua*

*Golfo
Dulce*

*Golfo de
Chiriqui*

Caribbean Island Somewhere Over Here

★
Caracas

VENEZUELA

GUYANA

0 Kilometers   300

0 Miles   300

CHAPTER ONE

You shall judge a man by his foes as well as by his friends.
Joseph Conrad

December 11, 2003

Allan Weisbecker
Arriba del Rio Higuito
Pavones, Costa Rica

Enclosure: *In Search of Captain Zero* by Allan Weisbecker (the author of this letter)

Ms. Robin Morritz
Consul General
U.S. Embassy
Caja 920-1200
San José, Costa Rica

Dear Consul,

I'm writing you because I have a story to tell, and as my representative in this foreign country I need you to be the first to hear it.

I've been threatened and by putting on the record the prediction that something bad is going to happen to me before it does so, I'm hoping for a measure of protection, even if only retroactive.

If you turn to page 321 of *In Search of Captain Zero* (the book is basically the story of how I came to be here), you'll find that I was at Pavones in 1997-98; I left (returning in 2001) partially because of death threats I received while investigating the shootout killing of an American here (for *Men's Journal* magazine), during the height of the squatter problem. That American was Max Dalton, a name I suspect you are familiar with. I'm enclosing an article I wrote about my investigation, titled "A Night at the Cantina" – it only tells a tiny part of the story.

It would be natural to assume that the death threats I received in '98 were from the squatters. True but not the whole story. One threat on my life was from a fellow North American, an expat living in Pavones. His name is Derek Logan.* I was made aware of the threat by a confidential Tico source, one whose information I found to be totally reliable.

Logan was not involved directly in the killing of Max Dalton. His problem with my investigation was that I was uncovering the history of the land conflict here. Logan has a lot to hide in this regard. If you read the enclosed article, you'll come across the name Danny Fowlie, who is now in prison in the United States. Logan did not want his past relationship with Fowlie made public. Logan harbors other dirty little secrets as well, a couple of which I'll get to.

In the article I also mention the U.S. Embassy, and my "intelligence sharing." The reason I informed the Embassy of the information I uncovered in the Dalton matter (this is in 1998, remember) was similar to the reason I was contacting you now: if something had happened to me, or if I'm forced to defend myself with physical violence, I wanted certain things on the record. If you are able to contact the U.S. Consul of that time, Ian Brownlee, he will verify what I'm saying here. Ian would tell you that – for example – I provided him the OIJ [the Costa Rican FBI] Report on the Dalton killing, a document that was "officially" unavailable, even through the U.S. Intelligence sources and their connections. It was explosive to say the least and – along with other information I provided – was no doubt largely responsible for the U.S. congressional resolution censuring Costa Rica for their mishandling of the Dalton matter.

When I returned to Pavones in 2001, Logan was still here. Our relationship was edgy, as you can imagine; we pretty much avoided each other. (We both surf, so our encounters were mainly in the water.)

Then, on Thursday, November 27th I was surfing and Logan paddled up to me and commenced a strident tirade about my website (www.aweisbecker.com). He took exception to the fact that I was writing about Pavones. I send out a newsletter every couple of weeks, which is very popular – I have 7,000 subscribers.

I told Logan to mind his own business. To which he said, "You are a persona non grata." When I inquired as to what that meant, he replied, "I'm going to run you out of town."

There were witnesses to this exchange, other surfers who live here. Under conditions of anonymity, I believe they would be willing to verify my account. Why anonymity? Because Logan has the

---

* A name change. As with the few other name changes in this book, it is not related to the veracity of events depicted.

community of Pavones – expats and Ticos alike – cowed. Logan is *feared*.

I had heard "I'll run you out of town" before, in September, when he said he'd do as much to an expat friend of mine, Al Bollinger, whom Logan didn't like. Al has since left Pavones.

I'll tell you another story, one that comes under the heading of "common knowledge" here. I also confirmed the story via a Costa Rican who worked for Logan. In the mid 90s, Logan took a dislike to an American expat here know as Mountain Mike. Logan's problem with Mike was over an issue of trespass – Mike, who lives the campesino life, was foraging on property that Logan "owns." (I put quotes around "owns" because the land most likely came to be in Logan's possession illegally.)

A few days later Mike was in jail on a trumped-up drug charge (as a Bahai, Mike does not go near drugs). Logan had paid the OIJ to set Mike up. As I say, I confirmed this via one of Logan's former employees.

This incident – plus many others – is why Logan is feared here.

Back to my story. As I say, the incident in the water took place Thursday, November 27th. "I'm going to run you out of town," etc.

The following Monday the local police showed up at my property and shut down a small building project I was involved in – a *casita* for my caretaker.

This sort of thing is Logan's modus operandi. And I strongly suspect that there is more to come. Which, again, is why I'm writing to you now. If I'm set up on a trumped up charge or any violence occurs, I want you to know about it ahead of time, and who will have been responsible. This is a measure of protection. I hope you will help me on this, simply by filing this letter.

And aside from my problem with Logan, I believe you should be aware of the fact that you have this type of person operating under your jurisdiction.

In any event, please file this letter and remember what I've said. If something bad happens to me here – including physical violence and possibly my reaction to it – Derek Logan is responsible.

Yours truly,

Allan Weisbecker

CHAPTER TWO

When you leave your typewriter... the rats come pouring through.

Charles Bukowski

Mid-December, 2003, Pavones, Costa Rica.

Been eight months since I wrote the words, *Nonfiction. A load of horseshit is what it is.* Which is the way Part One of this book ended, or ends -- depending on your view of tense, the definition having to do with time, not stress. During these many months, apart from some emails and letters to U.S. consuls, I didn't write anything.

This morning: I got up figuring to write at around 4 AM. Fired up the coffeemaker, brushed my teeth and then moved my bowels while the coffee perked. Went back into the bedroom for my reading glasses and took a moment to look at Lisa while she slept. Then I searched for and found the special insulated coffee cup Mom got me for writing (no dumb jokes on it, God bless her). Added sugar first then milk then poured the coffee then 60 seconds in the microwave to get it really hot. Still in the nude so far. Put on my shorts, no shirt, then up the stairs to the office here and sat down. Lit up a cigarette while booting up, then popped a codeine tablet, which will help me feel normal. First sip of coffee now.

So far the familiar routine from when I used to write. I would then immediately have gone to this Word file and reviewed yesterday's work, which is a stalling tactic to avoid staring at a blank page. Couldn't do this since I didn't write yesterday, plus this file didn't exist yet, so I stared for a bit at my screensaver, which is a photograph of me surfing the wave on the Caribbean Island of The Horror fame.

The photograph appeared in *Surfer* magazine a year or so ago, as part of a profile they did on me. Here's what they put on the mag's cover as a point of sale device: ***Smuggler's Blues: Allan Weisbecker's Incredible Ride.***

Aside from the *Surfer* profile, of the half dozen other magazine and newspaper profiles done on me over the past couple years, I was to some degree unrecognizable to myself in all but the one I basically wrote myself. In which I came off well: smart, literate, funny, candid, adventurous, a helluva guy, meanwhile self-effacing, plus spontaneous. I worked especially hard to pull off the latter.

The guy who did the *Surfer* profile came down here to the paradise at the end of the road at the bottom of Central America, to this place called Pavones, Spanish for Big Turkeys, and stayed with me for a week; we surfed together and got friendly. When he returned to the States he went to the studio that's financing the *In Search of Captain Zero* movie project to see if he could replace me as screenwriter if and when I get fired. I find this amusing, some sort of goofy, backdoor comment on the state of surfing these days, how it's gone the way of everything else after being pretty interesting sociologically for a while. By which I mean that everyone figures he can write a screenplay, even surfers now. (Right: Including me.)

Here's some news for you: Screenplay writing is not so easy, in spite of screenplays being mostly white space. Or maybe screenplay writing is not so easy *because* screenplays are mostly white space. Or maybe both. Yes, *in spite of* and *because of*.

Which reminds me. During the past eight months, during which I didn't write anything, I wrote my third draft of the screenplay to *In Search of Captain Zero*. See, I don't really count this as writing, since it was whoring. To put it another way: Done just for the money. (As I said I would in Part One, I went into the tank.) As a writer – as with lists I make of women I've had sex with – it doesn't count if the sole motivation on someone's part is money. Even if there's somehow a semi-rape involved.

What else did I do during all that time?

I read a lot. I read books about the creation of the cosmos and books about the lies we've been told by the people who run this sorry ass world. A few novels. One of the novels I read was *Ahab's Wife*, by Sena Jeter Naslund, a yarn that exists in some sort of parallel literary universe to *Moby-Dick*. *Ahab's Wife* is a great book, in my opinion. I figure a book is great if I reread sentences just to hear them in my mind – while at the same time crazed to keep reading on to find out What Happens Next – and then get discouraged that I'm not able to write like that. When this happens I tell myself Yeah, but she couldn't write what *I* write. This doesn't work, so what I'll then maybe do is dig out one of the emails or letters I've gotten that says *In Search of Captain Zero* changed someone's life. Or one that says *Cosmic Banditos* made someone laugh until he cried, words to that effect. I mean try writing a book that changes someone's life or makes him laugh until he cries.

You could write a book. *Someday.*

All else fails, as a last resort I might compare one of my book's Amazon. com sales ranking with that of a great book like *Ahab's Wife* and find that – according to marketing theory – my book is half as good. Which is impressive, trust me.

See, Amazon.com's book sales ranking amounts to a Best Seller List that goes beyond the top ten that appear in, say, *The New York Times* Best Seller List. In fact, Amazon.com's de facto Best Seller List lists *millions* of titles. (Holy shit, there are a lot of books out there!) This is useful for authors who don't make the *New York Times* or any other best seller list, because their books don't sell very many, relatively, yet they want to know how their books are selling. Authors of this description, of which I am one, can't just call their publisher to find out how their books are selling because the publisher doesn't know offhand and doesn't care, so they're not going to look it up. In my case, no one at my publisher would take or return my call anyway, and certainly wouldn't look up anything for me under any circumstances. Nor would my ex-literary, or book, agent, whom I fired for treachery. (So you don't get confused: It was my movie agent, not book agent, whom I fired and whose response is the title of this book. The firing of my book agent didn't result in any titles, subtitles, or even a footnote. Only this parenthetical mention.)

Theoretically, at some point the Amazon.com list segues from a Best Seller List to a Worst Seller List. I'm not sure where this occurs numerically. It's another spectrum kind of thing, as with Lisa and sex appeal, although I'm not so sure about that theory now. Not that Lisa has gotten less sexy...

In Search of Captain Zero has an average ranking of about 4,000 these days. This may sound discouraging but it's not. For example, *Ahab's Wife*, upon initial publication in 1999, made a bunch of real, actual Best Seller Lists, including the *New York Times* list. A few days ago I checked *Ahab's Wife's* Amazon.com sales ranking. It's now two thousand and something. So my book is currently selling about half as well as this former National Bestseller. As I say, this is impressive.

In case you're wondering (and I hope you are because it would mean you're paying attention): *In Search of Captain Zero* was first published in the spring of 2001 – almost two years after *Ahab's Wife*. So *Ahab's Wife* has had more time to slip in the ranking.

Good point.

Somewhere in Part One I mention a writer I know, whom I refer to as a shitball motherfucker due to his lack of self-reflection even when he's looking in the mirror. I refer to the guy this way because of all the petty jealousies and even outright treacheries he's directed toward me over the years. He mostly writes for Hollywood, but he's also written a book. Once in a while, usually when I'm feeling particularly low, I'll check its Amazon. com sales ranking – it's always way up there in the hundreds of thousands, meaning hundreds of thousands of books are selling better than his book, rather than only about four thousand, as with my book, *In Search of Captain*

Zero. (*Cosmic Banditos* is hovering around 8,000, which isn't all that bad either.) This makes me grin or sometimes actually cackle with glee.

Another thing. One of Amazon.com's many devices to get you to buy books is reader reviews. Readers get to be critics. As part of this, readers give books between one and five stars; little yellow five-pointed jobs. Both my books average 5 stars, based on a total of 80-something reader reviews, about 40 for each. This means almost everyone gave them 5 stars, the highest rating. *Ahab's Wife* only averages 4 stars – plus a tiny bit of the tine on the fifth star.

Extrapolating: These days I'm capable of going to great and convoluted lengths to feel better about myself, or at least my writing.

Sometimes I outsmart myself, though – hoist myself by my own petard. While I was at it, so to speak, with *Ahab's Wife*, I looked up *Moby-Dick's* sales ranking. I wrote it down. On that day it was 788,765. For a brief moment I felt some sort of weird conglomeration of exhilaration and dismay. The reason for the exhilaration is self evident; not so for the dismay. Possibly something to do with Melville being dead, or dead for so long. A bit of the old doom-driven dread: I myself will be dead soon enough, and then remain that way for all of eternity. Or maybe my dismay was based on the hopelessly awful taste of the reading public, meaning you – the collective you, not you personally. I know: On some weird level *Moby-Dick* has had well over a hundred years to slip in sales ranking, so the above number is misleading. Also, a writer capable of producing *Moby-Dick* would likely be above concerns like Amazon.com sales ranking – which I, obviously, am not. This thought may have been involved in my dismay. It's hard to say. *No one knows shit about why he does anything.* Add *or feels anything* to that.

The last book I read was Stephen King's memoir, *On Writing.* Finished it last night, as a matter of fact. A good book. Not great, but definitely good. In my opinion, one of the few howlingly successful commercial writers who deserves all that success is Stephen King.

You know what? Who am I to imply that other best selling authors don't deserve their success? Christ, talk about a lack of self-reflection. They all deserve it. Even John Grisham and Dan Brown. Maybe especially them. I mean who knows what they go through when they sit down to write. So never mind the Grisham/Brown insult in Part One.

In *On Writing* King says that the worse thing a writer can do is stop writing in the midst of a book, which, obviously, I have done in spades. You stop in the midst, you lose all kinds of stuff, King says. Momentum, of course. Big Mo. But worse than losing Big Mo, you lose touch with your characters.

There is no question that King is right. Over the last eight months I *have* pretty much lost touch with my characters. Especially my main character.

I've lost touch with my own self.

Having just last night finished *On Writing* accounts for me starting up again after eight months of not writing anything (except writing that is whoring). At this moment I don't know whether to thank Stephen King or figure out a way to fuck him up. Point being, though, is that my starting up writing again is Stephen King's doing. I'm only peripherally involved.

Here's how I came to read *On Writing*: Day before yesterday I was rummaging through my *bodega* (a sort of strong room that most houses in Costa Rica have), looking for a couple of things. One was a drill bit I needed to hang a surfboard on my bathroom wall. The other was a box of double ought buckshot that I knew was in there somewhere. The last time I saw the buckshot was back in June, when I loaded my shotgun to go out looking for someone, a fellow North American, a fellow surfer. Rich is his name. My intention was to blow a few holes in Rich's Jeep while he watched. My current need for the ammunition is based on my having been threatened by a nutcase who also lives here at the paradise at the end of the road at the bottom of Central America called Big Turkeys. Another fellow North American surfer.

Right. The nutcase in the letter to the U.S. consul here in Costa Rica, which letter I saw fit to make a chapter all on its own. I wrote and sent that a few days ago. You may have noticed that I didn't ask much of the consul, just to file the letter. There's good reason for that. See, I've had some experience with the U.S. State Department here (foreign embassies are under the aegis of the State Department). During my investigation into the murder of American expatriate Max Dalton the bastards directly put my life at risk, for political reasons. Which means my letter may have been a mistake, rather than merely useless. We'll see.

Aside from my own government being capable of putting my life at risk for political reasons, there is no real police presence for many miles around, and what presence there is, is on the dole from the nutcase who's threatened me, this guy Logan. Point being: Around here you pretty much have to deal with threats from nutcases yourself. Although since the incident with Rich my shotgun has been loaded at all times, I wanted extra ammo on hand.

Having found the drill bit and then while reaching for the buckshot way in the back I came across a pile of books I'd shipped down and which I figured I'd get around to reading. My eye happened to fall upon *On Writing* – it was sticking out a little from the others. I read it in a couple sittings; as I say, I finished it last night and as a result starting writing again.

It wasn't that King's book inspired me, not exactly. See, King says he writes a minimum of 2,000 words a day, every day, 24/7. This means that that in the past eight months, during which time I wrote nothing, King wrote about half a million words. Thinking about this made me feel so discouraged and crummy that I felt I had no choice but to start writing again.

In case you don't know: In 1999, while taking a walk up in Maine where he lives, King was run down by a van driven by some shitball motherfucker who has since died. (Good.) Busted King up real bad, just about killed him. He stopped writing. Had to ease his way back. Said it was tough. The past eight months represent my version of getting hit by a van. I'm at this moment easing my way back. Doing some "throat clearing," as my writer friend Lesley would say.

By the way, towards the end of Part One I basically accuse you of having your head up your ass for thinking negative thoughts about Lisa. As with the Grisham/Brown insult: Never mind.

I do stick by my last sentence, the one about nonfiction being a load of horseshit. More than ever.

CHAPTER THREE

To be a writer you need to see things as they are, and to see things
as they are you need a certain basic innocence.

Tobias Wolff

I first came to this paradise at the end of the road called Pavones, Big
Turkeys, in June, 1997, just after the events described in my (first) memoir,
In Search of Captain Zero. Here's my description of my arrival, as written in
my journal, and which I wrote quickly and with a minimum of after-the-
fact rewriting, as I recall. It flowed. And in this case the first person present
tense is not just a device aimed at instilling a sense of You Are There
immediacy. I really did write it, most of it, as I imply, i.e., that morning as
it happened.

I'm watching through my camper's open door as the first wave
of a stacked-up set wraps in from the south and charges across
the seascape in the dreamy glow of first light. The wave churns
its way through the inside shallows, then rushes over the beach
in front of my campsite, which was dry a few hours ago at low
water. I thought I'd be safe here from inundation, but still the wave
comes, up and over the sloping dirt berm separating beach from
jungle; then it sloshes under my hammock, rousing my dog Shiner
and chasing her inland from her nest there. In its final throes now,
the dying wave gurgles under my doorstep and then suddenly
all earthly traces of it are gone. It's a fierce expiration I have
witnessed.

I sip my coffee and consider my options as the rest of the set,
wave by wave, probes my position, each successive incursion
reaching a yard or so further inland than the one preceding it,
until the last wave disappears under the Ford's front bumper with
a crackle and a hiss. The groundswell has been on the rise since I
ran out of road in my travels here yesterday afternoon and is rising
still; and the full moon high tide has another hour of flood before it
peaks and begins its withdrawal.

In all prudence, a move to higher ground would seem to be
called for. But since when in my life have I conducted myself

prudently? No, I'll ride out the rising tide, make a stand. I need not fear the water, or so I've been told.

I seem to be attracted to end-of-the-road places. Montauk – my home on the last left on Long Island before the lighthouse – was at road's end. So was the Punta Lobo campground up in Baja, at which I tarried for so long last year. Back on the Caribbean side where I found my vanished old friend Christopher, a.k.a Captain Zero, some three months ago: the end of the road. And this wilderness I have come to on the Pacific, the road likewise ends here. So for the second time I have come to the bottom of coastal Central America.

Perhaps my attraction to these sorts of locales lies in their feel of voluntary isolation, inaccessibility and seclusion. The sense that one is unlikely to be disturbed by some fool asking directions to somewhere else – people do not pass through end-of-the-road places. There is also the sense that the civilized world has been tilted and given a shake, with the result that those individuals with the most tenuous grasp on what is considered normalcy have slid down the resulting figurative slope and collected at the bottom, from where there is nowhere left to go, and where are formed enclaves and subcultures rooted in extremes.

And often, I've found, waves will be encountered at end-of-the-road places. Yes, there is a wave here all right. A point wave steeped in both speed and stamina, a rare combination on this planet. With a sizable long period south swell like the one still building out my back door, spawned by some far distant Southern Ocean tempest, the wave here is so fast and so long as to be almost hallucinogenic. A miracle of a wave.

Not much here, in terms of the works of modern man. There is a cantina just down the shore from my campsite in the bush, looking out upon the middle part of this long, long wave, and by which charged a horseman on the beach yesterday, wild hair flying and a surfstick tucked under his arm. And there is a little fish camp further along, around the point from the cantina.

A long, fast point wave. A cantina and a fish camp. Horsemen carrying surfboards. The end of the road. Everything about this place suits me. I believe I'll stay for a while.

I stayed for a year, during which time I did the investigation into the Max Dalton killing for *Men's Journal*. As described in my letter to the U.S. Consul General, one result of my investigation was a death threat towards me, issued by this guy Logan, the North American nutcase who now figures to run me out of town. Plus I believe that the squatter who murdered Max, Gerardo Mora is his name, had designs on murdering me for what I'd uncovered in my investigation.

But there was another, more important, reason for leaving when I did. Mom's breast cancer from the 1980s had resurfaced. I had to go back to the States and see her. As it turned out, I would move in and take care of her for two years. During this time I struggled with *Zero*, writing and rewriting; I'd get an agent and eventually a publisher, Penguin Putnam (Tarcher imprint), who assigned me my demented editor when the original editor left the company. All that stuff.

I would return to Costa Rica in early September, 2001, a few days before 9/11. My intention was to build a house and settle, which I did.

For me to do this, Mom had to die first.

Mom died at home on the night of April 28, 2001. I was with her constantly toward the end; I'd taken to sleeping on a mattress pad next to her bed. She had been mostly unconscious for a couple of days prior to the 28th. She'd come around for brief periods and talk to me, sometimes lucidly, sometimes not. When she was lucid she'd squeeze my hand or stroke it gently; when not, she'd withdraw her hand if I picked it up. She'd even turn away if I touched her face. I was not hurt by this behavior. I assumed that in facing death she sometimes just needed to be alone.

Aside from being at her side, my main duty toward the end was to administer liquid morphine orally via an eyedropper and to keep her lips and mouth moist; being mostly unconscious she was unable to take liquids. She was on an intravenous drip that was tended by me and by a hospice nurse who came by every day. By coincidence, the nurse was the wife of a guy I'd gotten friendly with while surfing at a local beach. Although Mom died late at night, this lady came over immediately when I called and quietly held my hand while I sobbed and sobbed. A special person. I wish I could remember her name now.

My father had died a year and four months prior to Mom dying.

I have no brothers or sisters, just an uncle I'm not close to, Mom's brother, who lives out in Colorado; I have a cousin to whom I don't speak much. That's it for family. Upon making a list and analyzing it, I realized that of my other relationships there was no one I couldn't do without, permanently if it came to that. I actually did this, made a list of people, and then one by one crossed them off. (My writer friend Lesley was the exception but she lived in England anyway.)

At the time Mom died, my writing career was what it was. By which I mean that *Zero* was done, in print, along with the reissue of *Cosmic Banditos*. Penguin Putnam was doing absolutely nothing to promote either book. Less than nothing, actually; my demented *Zero* editor had formally cut off communication with me and – in loose collusion with my then-agent, who had female-bonded with her – was well into her sabotage behavior, which I could do nothing about. So my presence stateside was unnecessary. The movie deals for both books were coming together so I'd have money. I could write the screenplays from wherever I was.

Point of all this being that after Mom died there was nothing preventing me from moving down to the paradise at the end of the road at the bottom of Central America known as Pavones, Big Turkeys.

CHAPTER FOUR

Women are like tricks by sleight of hand,
Which, to admire, we should not understand.

William Congreve

Some stuff that's on my mind, piling up over the past eight months, that when taken all together along with other stuff you'll hear about is my version of getting hit by a van; stuff that swims in my head in a random way, a structure-less way, often during my after-writing throes, which are especially severe after whoring in my writing, or thinking about that sort of writing; or, if I'm not writing anything, when I'm thinking about not writing anything. In other words, I can be beset by my after-writing throes even if I haven't actually been writing.

I should describe my after-writing throes. Best I can do is to refer once again to *Doctor Strangelove* – the Sterling Hayden character's psychological response to the physical act of love, which resulted in his rush of insight about the international communist conspiracy to sap our bodily fluids, the rush of insight that would eventually result in the end of life on earth, via The Doomsday Machine.

A profound sense of fatigue, of loss of essence.

It's particularly distressing when a bout of after-writing throes coincides with an attack of my writer's queasy gut. I mean who needs a bunch of centipedes writhing maniacally in your duodenum on top of profound fatigue and essence-loss?

Christ.

Okay. The getting-hit-by-a-van stuff, a taste of it.

This fall Lisa and I were watching Monday Night Football and a female sportscaster was interviewing a player, while surrounded by more players.

"I bet she gets laid a lot," Lisa said.

To which I said, "Maybe she's married or in love."

Lisa let out a snort of pure derision and said, "Yeah, *right.*"

I turned and looked at her in shock, my shock being at the vehemence of her snort of pure derision at the possibility that marriage or love would stop the female sportscaster from getting laid with a lot of football players.

When I got upset, Lisa said that she'd meant the snort of derision at the possibility that the female sportscaster was married or in love. When I asked her why a pretty, thirty-something woman wouldn't be married or in love, Lisa said that you can't take little random comments a person makes and inject some sort of malevolent meaning into them, especially given the lack of perspective of thinking about the random comments during after-writing throes, and, further, this lack of perspective can then spill over into regular life, meaning when you're not experiencing after-writing throes. She went on and on along these lines, getting angry as she did so, until I apologized for my lack of perspective.

One time Lisa and I were watching CNN and a promo came on telling us to stay tuned for a special on infidelity. Lisa immediately picked up the remote – it would not be hyperbole to say she grabbed it – and changed the channel.

Lisa got angry when I brought this up a couple days later after a bad bout of after-writing throes, Lisa saying it was an example of my irrational suspicions. Christ, she said, she just wasn't in the mood for that show. Get a grip on yourself, Allan, she said.

Infidelity. Sometimes during my after-writing throes I'll read to distract myself from them. Once I was reading a book that Lisa had read before me, a novel entitled *Love Warps the Mind a Little*, in which a major theme is infidelity. Lisa had underlined a few passages, presumably because they meant something to her. Here's one: "<u>Female baboons copulate with all the males of their troop except their sons.</u>" Another concept worthy of underlining was how with infidelity, with cheating on your mate, you get to "<u>reinvent yourself.</u>"

When I told her the underlined passages made me uneasy since they rationalize either promiscuity or infidelity, Lisa said that she found animal behavior interesting, which I didn't know she did. She told me she didn't remember why she had underlined the other one, about reinventing yourself. Then, the next day, she remembered that her ex-husband had cheated on her once and had explained that he was reinventing himself.

She was thinking of him, and of men in general, Lisa said.

Men in general. Lisa keeps a journal, most of which is on her laptop. Last spring, after I found out about her screwing around with her ex-boyfriend and then lying about it, I peeked at the journal while she was walking the dogs. In one section she analyzes herself sexually. Says that Buddhists would refer to her as a "yang-like woman." She goes on to write that this means a woman who perceives sex the way a man does.

I told Lisa that for her to perceive sex the way a man does is upsetting, a paralyzing thought even. My after-writing throes were likewise involved in my coming to this conclusion, I think. As Lisa has pointed out, after-writing throes are not the best time to think about things rationally, like what's a paralyzing thought and what isn't.

Thing is, though, one time when she was tipsy and voluble Lisa told me that the first thing she thinks of when she meets a man is whether she'd like to have sex with him. Went on to say that a Yes or No actually goes off in her head.

This *is* a paralyzing thought, isn't it? *I* perceive sex the way a man does, I think, and Yeses and Noes don't go off in my head when I first meet a woman. When I mentioned this to Lisa she said she hadn't meant that *literally*. When I asked how she *had* meant it, if not literally, she shook her head and left the room, saying There you go again.

During my after-writing throes I tend to connect Lisa perceiving sex the way a man does and Yeses and Noes going off in her head with something she said and which I've told you about. It was during one of my many attempts to tell Lisa about women I've had sex with; this was soon after The Horror. The time I'd chartered a helicopter to pick up a woman I wanted to have sex with. As you might remember, after laughing her ass off Lisa said my chartering a helicopter to get laid was a perfect example of how men are "obsessed with sex and screwing as many women as possible." I took that to mean that that's the way Lisa figures men perceive sex. And she perceives sex the way a man does, according to her own journal. Therefore Lisa is obsessed with sex and screwing as many *men* as possible, since Lisa is not particularly interested in women sexually, I don't think. Maybe a little bit.

Lisa hit the roof at my mention of this connective logic, and pointed out that if my having snooped in her journal makes me miserable, during my after-writing throes or any other time, I deserve it, for violating her privacy.

One time Lisa and I were having sex and I said, "Sometimes I imagine you with another man." Right there, immediately, out of the blue, Lisa had an orgasm, a big one – Lisa doesn't *always* have orgasms. Lisa did not deny that my comment precipitated her orgasm, or that this was the first and only time a comment on my part while we were having sex (dirty talk) turned her on to the extent of precipitating an orgasm, let alone a big one.

When I told her that a physiological response like a big orgasm at the mention of sex with another man is a paralyzing thought, Lisa got angry and said that "all bets are off in bed" and, anyway, wasn't I trying to turn her on? And if so, what am I complaining about?

I don't know if my after-writing throes were involved in the matter of Lisa's big orgasm at the mention of sex with another man, but at some point I did experience a profound sense of fatigue, followed by a loss of essence.

CHAPTER FIVE

If you haven't got anything good to say about anyone, come sit by me.

Alice Roosevelt Longworth

My thinking last summer (2003) when I stopped working on this book and while I was in the process of getting hit by a van was this: Having finished Part One, I'd take a getting-hit-by-a-van break and bang out my whoring draft of the *In Search of Captain Zero* screenplay, which I did, going into the tank while doing so. Meanwhile, I'd send out Part One of this, get a new literary (book) agent, since I had fired my old one for treachery during the editing phase of *Zero*.

The new agent would sell *Can't You Get Along With Anyone?* as "a work in progress." I'd come back to the writing all raring to go. I have two books in stores, both in their 4th paperback printing (*Zero* was still in hardback too), both making money. Both have "legs," as the expression goes. I have movie deals. Hey, Sean Penn and John Cusack both want to play me. I'm being interviewed and profiled, doing my own promotion. I found the German house that bought the rights to *Zero*. *Banditos* has sold to nine foreign markets, the last being the Turks, of all people. I put that deal together too. Point being that agents should be clamoring to rep my sorry ass. In theory.

So I send Part One to my Hollywood attorney, Steven, figuring he'll send it to agents. Steven knows everyone, or can get to them via the doing lunch grapevine. Steven reads Part One, tells me it's not publishable. Since I'm not famous, he says, no one will care about my life and times and problems with people. Won't send Part One to any agents.

Okay, only slightly depressing. Steven's a fucking *lawyer*, what does he know? That I didn't see what was really going on is a perfect example of my denial regarding stuff I should know better about. I merely figured Steven had his head up his ass, not that there was anything duplicitous afoot.

But within days of this development I get a call from the producer who, along with Sean Penn and the studio, optioned *In Search of Captain Zero* for the movies. She's threatening a lawsuit, talking about restraining orders.

Turns out that Steven told her about the book I was writing, this book, what I wrote about her and about the other people involved in the deal. He may have even sent her the manuscript.

Think about that.

No one who wants to make a movie out of my book is smart enough to get it done.

And, if you flip back and look, there's plenty more where that came from.

Steven also spilled the beans to my ex-Hollywood movie-writing agent (as opposed to my book agent), whom I fired for her behavior during the *Zero* movie deal (as opposed to the book deal), and whose email response to that is the title of this book. Among other details, he no doubt told her where the title of this book came from.

Word quickly reaches me through multiple sources that I am persona non grata in Hollywood. One agent, a major one who works in a big talent agency, a guy who surfs and who read and loved *Zero* and hinted that he'd like to represent me, will now not return my calls – a major disappointment, since anyone in Hollywood who *reads* is unusual (let alone one who surfs), and is to be sought after and treasured.

Meanwhile, the deal to write the screen adaptation of *Cosmic Banditos* is mired, tied up in the contract stage, Steven says. Tied up in the contract stage? Odds are that Cusack's people, directly or indirectly through Steven were informed of my writing about *that* deal as well, and are in the process of backing out. In other words, they will not hire me after all, fearing that I'll expose *their* shortcomings.

I must repeat: This is my attorney who did this, a contractual associate (for over 20 years) who legally and ethically should not do anything to harm the interests of his client, me.

As if this isn't enough, during the conversation wherein Steven informs me that the book you are now reading is un-publishable, I ask him to get "my" draft of the *Zero* screenplay to Sean Penn (the draft immediately preceding the whoring draft wherein I went into the tank). As I say, Steven knows everyone, or can get to them; he could no doubt get my draft to Sean Penn.

Before I press on, it gets weirder. I mean weirder if you're not familiar with how Hollywood works, how the people there think, if you can call it that.

Last spring (2003), three or so months before Steven got treacherous on me and before I got hit by the multi-faceted van, I sent the producer my second-to-last contractual draft of the screenplay. The one before I went into the tank as a reaction to the notes from the studio. I like this draft a lot – I like the way I reinvented my book.

The producer read the draft and called to say it's brilliant. It's so brilliant, in fact, that before she called to say it's brilliant she gave it to another writer she works with and trusts to see if it's as brilliant as she thinks it is. The other writer read it and agreed that Yes, it's as brilliant as she thinks it is. According to the other writer, I'm "the real thing."* Another line of hers I can put quotes around because I remember the exact words: "You gave the studio exactly what you said you would."

Also: I'm her "little genius."

She sent the studio the draft and expected to hear from them soon.

A note regarding geography, chronology, and state of mind. I had the above conversation here in paradise at the end of the road at the bottom of Central America, getting my sorry ass ready to go meet Lisa on the Caribbean island where The Horror would soon take place. Down on the beach with my cell phone in my ear, sitting on a piece of driftwood with my dog Fang (short for Jack London's *White Fang*, my favorite book from childhood), who was just a puppy at the time, wandering around nearby. Looking out at the pristine waters of El Golfo Dulce, The Sweet Gulf, perfect waves rolling in. Although I was pleased as punch at hearing that my draft is brilliant and that I'm the real thing and a genius who gave the studio exactly what he said he would, I felt a subtle stirring in my gut listening to the producer go on. In retrospect, I believe the stirring was a flutter of my writer's queasy gut. Or maybe I'm projecting this because I *should* have felt a flutter. In any event, the queasy gut flutter, assuming I had it, was based on the producer having to ask someone else for his opinion of the draft before actually voicing her opinion to me. But still, my draft is brilliant and I'm the real thing and her little genius who gave the studio exactly what he said he would.

According to the producer, my agent whose email response to my later firing her is the title of this book, and who also was the producer's agent,† agreed with the other writer regarding my draft's brilliance and so forth. So that's two people's opinions the producer had to hear before she voiced her opinion to me. Hold on. The producer's boyfriend also read my draft (and agreed with the other two opinions). So that's three opinions she needed before voicing hers to me, not two. This was all a bad sign, even though the three other people thought the draft was brilliant and so forth.

---

* If this sounds familiar, Jon Voight also labeled me thus. For some reason, this "real thing" accolade is a favorite in Hollywood. Possibly they got it from that old Coca-Cola commercial and it just stuck.

† If it sounds a little iffy, conflict of interest-wise, that my agent was also the producer's agent: My attorney Steven was also the producer's attorney and the director's attorney as well. *Not only that:* Steven and my agent used to be a guy-gal couple. So in a sense there was some incest, on top of the conflict of interest. In other words, I *really* should have seen Steven's treachery regarding his big mouth and this book coming.

You may be wondering where the director is at this point, and what he thought of the draft, its possible brilliance and so forth. Maybe you're not wondering that, on second thought. But I was. So I asked the producer. He hasn't read it yet, she said. This is another bad sign, since the director had told me that the *Zero* project was number one on his list of priorities. But letting the mounting bad signs go for the moment, I asked the producer if Sean Penn had read the draft. I mean everybody else she knows had, apparently, except the director. No, the producer said. He didn't have a copy. She's going to let the studio send it to him.

Still another bad sign. A doozey of a bad sign, as it would turn out.

A matter of days later I was on the phone in a San José hotel room, finding out that Lisa had been screwing her ex-boyfriend then lying about it. So, all fucked up over this development, I went to the Caribbean island where The Horror would soon take place (and where I started this narrative). As mentioned in Part One, while there I got the email from the producer saying that the studio executive read my draft - this email resulted in my going into the tank. One reason I decided to go into the tank was the producer saying in the email that my draft was "not the draft we were expecting." Important for our purposes is that she now included herself in this assessment of my draft. My draft was no longer brilliant. I was no longer the real thing and her little genius who gave the studio exactly what he said he would.

My response to this email was terse. I didn't bother reminding the producer that she completely flip-flopped on her opinion of the draft based on someone else's opinion, or that in pure force of numbers it was either four-to-one or three-to-two or three-to-one in favor of my draft still being brilliant and me still being the real thing and a genius who gave the studio exactly what he said he would. (The numbers depending on how you now view her original opinion, whether you count *that* opinion, or her flip-flop opinion, or cancel her opinions altogether due to lack of consistency – this last one seems most reasonable, no?) I just wanted to know when Sean Penn was going to read the draft. I wanted *his* opinion. By now the flutter of my writer's queasy gut, assuming I'd originally had it, had bloomed into my full-blown writer's queasy gut.

The producer emailed back saying that the decision had been made not to give the draft to Sean Penn. The draft was "not ready" for him to read. I emailed reminding her that in talking me into the original option deal she'd assured me that Sean "gets involved early in the script stage." Since I already wrote two drafts of the screenplay and was now about to launch myself into the third, we were way past any reasonable interpretation of the concept "early in the script stage."

I have her reply here in front of me as I write. Rather than quoting it, I'll sum it up. The email is words to the effect of "That's different."

Back to the conversation with Steven that occurred three months after the above nonsense. After he tells me that the book you are now reading is un-publishable and therefore he will not send it to any agents, Steven tells me he will not try to get my draft to Sean Penn because, "Sean Penn is just a stoned-out actor who doesn't read anything." I can frame Steven's words in quotes because I wrote them down, figuring they would come in handy someday.

To sum up, in case you're confused by all this convoluted Hollywood shit: Aside from the Cusack/*Cosmic Banditos* deal likely going into the toilet and the unlikelihood that Sean Penn will ever read my once-brilliant draft, I'm persona non grata in Hollywood, plus in the publishing business, aside from my similar status with a guy down here at the paradise known as Big Turkeys, this nutcase Logan who figures to run me out of town.

And then there's Lisa, the love of my life.

CHAPTER SIX

In love, assurances are practically an announcement of their opposite.

Elias Canetti

The love of my life.

Early last May (2003), a month or so after The Horror, Lisa went back to the States to finish up some personal and financial matters she didn't get around to before (a lot of time was wasted trying to get in touch with herself at the psychotherapy symposium back in March), see her Mom, Fran, and her brother, Marc, put stuff in storage in Montauk, deal with some loose ends. She'd go alone, we decided. I'd stay here at Pavones, Big Turkeys, and supervise the project we'd started on the land we're partners in.

We'd had some rough moments since she came down to live with me but they'd pretty much been smoothed out. Sort of smoothed out. More or less. Up-and-down, up-and-down, up-and-down kind of thing.

Notwithstanding the smoothing out, the ups that followed the downs, I was concerned about her trip north: the rental house she'd be in at Montauk was about a quarter mile from her ex-boyfriend's, with whom she screwed around then lied about it multiple times last winter.

So Lisa is at Montauk and I'm still down here. First full day she's back there she calls and says her old landline phone number is on, reactivated to ring at the rental house. Says she'll be there after 7 PM. I call at 7:30. No answer. I call at 8. No answer. I call about every half hour for the rest of the night. No answer.

One of the chores for the previous day was to go over to her ex-boyfriend's house to collect some belongings and to deal with money he owes her. And then she's out all night, apparently. I'm of course remembering that each time Lisa went back to Montauk (except maybe, apparently, the last time) she ended up in bed with the guy.

As it turned out, there was an innocent reason for her not answering her phone. I *think*. But: WhatamInuts? Was what I was thinking, notwithstanding the apparently innocent explanation for the non-phone answering.

I gotta get up there. Like right the fuck now.

Getting from the end of the road at the bottom of Central America all the way to the little fishing village at the end of the road on Long Island is a major production. Borderline-impassable roads, river crossings on ferries that sometimes sink or break down, puddle jumpers to San José that periodically crash into the sides of mountains, then connecting flights to the States. Plus I have to find someone to house sit, take care of the dogs, and pay our workers. The guy I get to do this is named Rich, by the way. Right: The guy I went looking for with the shotgun, and whose Jeep I was going to blow a few holes in while he watched. I'll try to circle back, *loop* back, to that at some point, explain what happened.

Somehow, within 36 hours I'm back up north Stateside. Lisa meets me at Kennedy Airport. A passionate reunion, in spite of our only having been apart for three days. I tell Lisa that I do trust her, although I admit that I rushed up to the States because I was nervous about her being so near her old boyfriend. Lisa is very understanding. I reiterate that I trust her, and have forgiven her for her transgressions with her ex-boyfriend. And I mean it. We have otherworldly sex. Lisa thanks me for my efforts. I'm so in love it's ridiculous.

A couple days of bliss at Montauk.

During the couple days of bliss Lisa makes arrangements for a dinner at which I would meet her family, minus her father, who has disappeared. He has a habit of doing this, Lisa tells me. Just up and disappears, for days, sometimes longer.

I'm a little nervous about the dinner. No one in Lisa's family is happy about her moving to Central America to live with some guy they know nothing about, except that he's a writer or something. They don't even know that I'm a former criminal. None of them has read *Zero*, which amounts to a confession to all sorts of misbehavior.

Lisa is of Italian extraction, barely one generation removed from Sicily, a small town there. Which reminds me. One of my favorite movie lines of all time is from *The Godfather,* when Michael Corleone is in exile in a small town in Sicily. He asks his Sicilian bodyguard where all the young men are.

"They are all dead from vendettas," the bodyguard says. I *love* that line.

So we have this dinner date with Lisa's Sicilian family that I'm nervous about. It's for Friday, the next day after our couple of days of bliss. The bliss is about to come to a crashing finale.

I have to go see Lisa's ex-boyfriend. I owe him that. Although we were never what you would call *friends*, I've known him for twenty or so years. The morning of the dinner date, Friday, I call and say I'm coming over, if that's all right.

Yeah, okay, he says.

I walk over to his house, a quarter mile away. Nice house on Lake

Montauk. A fine, clear spring day. I'm wearing ten-dollar sneakers, the old Keds brand, which I didn't know was still around, and which I bought more for reasons of nostalgia than the low price. Within a hundred yards they raise blisters on my heels so I take them off and go the rest of the way barefoot. So much for footwear nostalgia.

Lisa's ex-boyfriend opens the door, I come in, put down the Keds, then hold out my hand for a shake. He turns and walks away. He's agitated, paces around. I'm thinking maybe he's going to get violent, so I prepare myself for that. Finally we both sit down, on opposite sides of his living room table.

The conversation is actually mostly a monologue, him talking, me nodding or shrugging or just sitting there. I'm a scumbag. He goes on along these lines for quite a while. He and Lisa would have worked it out, he says, if it hadn't been for me, the scumbag. I nod, although I know this is a delusion, notwithstanding that Lisa got back together with him twice since she's been with me.

Lisa has a violent temper, he says. Comes up with some anecdotes about her violent temper, like the time she attacked him with a knife. I occasionally have a violent temper too, I'm thinking, although shotguns are more my style. A match made in heaven.

Now he's reliving the previous fall, when Lisa came down to visit me the first time, right after Thanksgiving. "Said she was going to Costa Rica on a *surf trip*," he says, launching some spittle in disgust. "She told me there was nothing going on between you two and that she just needed a break. She *swore* that there was nothing going on. For weeks." Lisa had told me of the surf trip deception – this lie to her ex-boyfriend bothered me at the time but I'd let it slide – but she also told me she'd left the guy, her ex, and he knew this. If what her ex is now saying is true, Lisa lied to me last fall, aside from lying to him.

"Nothing *had* been going on," I say in response to his assertion that Lisa had lied about nothing going on between us, although my comeback is somewhat disingenuous. Hold on. It's bullshit. Christ, why am I lying to *you* about this?

"I mean nothing physical had happened between us." This is true. What is also true is that when Lisa first came down to visit me the two of us were so crazed with pent-up lust that we nearly consummated our four year-long non-affair during the taxi ride from the San José airport to our hotel, the Balmoral. As Lisa's ex-boyfriend is repeating something about how they would have worked it out if not for my treachery I almost smile, remembering that when the taxi driver asked if he could stop at a gas station to take a leak – he was having bladder problems, he said – Lisa screamed, "No, get us to the goddamn hotel!" Point being that although nothing physical had happened between us before she came to visit me, we were far from innocent.

More warnings from Lisa's ex-boyfriend about Lisa but now I'm back in the hotel room in San José reliving our lust consummation. She's a flirt, he's saying, especially if she's been drinking. One time when they were at a party Lisa had a few drinks and disappeared with some guy for an hour. I'm meanwhile back to being distracted by Lisa's having apparently lied to both of us: the lie to him about nothing going on between herself and me, and the lie to me about having left him.

Up and pacing and rambling now, Lisa's ex-boyfriend starts in again about what a scumbag I am for stealing his woman, given that we've been friends for so long. I don't correct him on the *friends* assertion. We've been *acquaintances*, not friends.

"You'd been sleeping on the couch for like six months," I say instead, using some information Lisa provided me. This gives him contemplative pause. He gropes unsuccessfully for a comeback. I fill in the silence by asking rhetorically what kind of relationship is that?

"We would have worked it out," he eventually repeats.

"Lisa loves me and I love her," I say, getting to the heart of the matter.

Yeah, well, around last Thanksgiving Lisa had two one-night stands in the city, he says. I nod. In other words, a couple days before she gets on the plane to come see me she's balling guys at random. Right. Lisa's ex-boyfriend is getting desperate, lying outright to turn me against Lisa.

At about this point I stifle a yawn. I just want to get out of there. I mean now that I'm sure there will be no physical violence, I'm just bored.

Lisa's ex-boyfriend claims yet again that they would have worked it out if it hadn't been for me.

I, the scumbag, finally get out of there.

Lisa is on the rental house deck reading when I get back. She's a little tense as she asks how it went. I kiss her and tell her it went okay, except that I got bored. She seems relieved. We have a Take Five that lasts for about an hour. It would be our last take five for many days, not counting when I banged Lisa out of anger later that night. I came as quickly as possible so as not to satisfy her. So technically, it probably *was* a take five. Or a take three-and-a-half.

Around sundown we're on our way to the dinner date with Lisa's family, at an Italian restaurant about two hours away, Lisa driving. I'm talkative, rambling on about this and that to submerge my nervousness about meeting Lisa's family. Apropos of nothing I bring up my talk with Lisa's ex-boyfriend, telling Lisa how desperate he was in trying to turn me against her, although I don't mention his claim that she said she just needed a break when she'd told me the two of them had *broken up*. "He said some really nasty things about you," I say, and look at Lisa. She nods but doesn't say anything; she's very tense. Something occurs to me.

"He claimed you had two one-night stands just before you came down to see me the first time," I say. "Thanksgiving."

Lisa doesn't say anything, won't look at me.

I'm still looking at her.

The seconds tick by.

"I'm sorry, Allan."

I'm too dumbstruck to say anything.

"Except it wasn't two, it was only one, and wasn't Thanksgiving." She pauses here. "It was New Year's Eve."

New Year's Eve was a few days after she'd gotten back from being with me for three weeks. Three blissful, sexually and otherwise, weeks. And it was soon after New Year's Eve that she started screwing her ex-boyfriend again, and then lying about it.

"A guy I met at a party."

I'm still unable to say anything. I can't even look at her. My mind is somehow blank and racing simultaneously.

New Year's Eve. I'd gone to a party at the local cantina but came home early to call Lisa. To tell her how much I already missed her after just a few days, and that I wanted her to come back to Costa Rica to be with me as soon as possible. I'm recalling that I left a message on her voice mail saying this stuff.

As we tool on through the Hamptons toward the dinner date with Lisa's family, I recall that I had to leave the message on her voice mail because her cell phone had been turned off again.

CHAPTER SEVEN

An absolutely necessary part of a writer's equipment is the ability to stand up under punishment, both the punishment the world hands out and the punishment he inflicts upon himself.

Irwin Shaw

I pretty much know in detail what Lisa was up to on New Year's Eve, 2002. I made her tell me everything. I grilled her. This is the way I am, a glutton for misery in my need to know *everything*.

There was another reason for the intensity of my grilling. See, back in March when I found out about Lisa fuckfesting with her ex-boyfriend I asked her several times if she was hiding anything else. I even asked her if she'd been with any *other* men – aside from her ex-boyfriend – since she came to visit me and our relationship began. She assured me that there were no other men; she was telling me everything. There were no more lies. I made her look me in the eye when she said this. The exchange occurred on the Caribbean island of The Horror fame, a few days before she humiliated me by dancing with the local guy in front of the bar.

So based on The New Year's Eve Guy revelation, I now knew that Lisa is capable of lying and not telling me everything even when she looks me in the eye and tells me there are no more lies and she's telling me everything.

Remember The Cityman? The guy I was worried about in Part One? The possible fuckbuddy? I came to the conclusion that there was no such guy after making both you and I think there probably was? After The New Year's Eve Guy revelation, I flip-flopped back to worrying that there was such a guy. Maybe it wasn't just a one-night stand. Maybe The New Year's Eve Guy was/is in fact The Cityman.

Lisa assures me that this is not the case – this is back in May, remember, at Montauk – that she never saw The New Year's Eve Guy again after that night. Looks me in the eye and swears that now she really is telling me everything.

I grill Lisa. If she's still not telling me everything I'll eventually catch her in the details, I figure. I've already noticed that she tends to talk too much when she's lying. Then she forgets what she said and fucks up and contradicts herself. Plus her voice gets breezy.

And I do nail her on some stuff.

Like regarding the message I left on her cell phone on New Year's Eve, saying how much I missed her and so forth. I ask her when she got that voice mail message. She already told me that The New Year's Eve Guy had stayed over at her apartment until the next morning. He took a shower and left.

Lisa tells me that she got my message that afternoon, meaning New Year's Day. Problem, though, is that in another grilling she told me that her brother Marc had called her early New Year's morning and had left a message, which she got just a few minutes after he left it when she turned her cell phone back on; this was while The New Year's Eve Guy was in the shower. Since I left my message the night before, it was on her voice mail before her brother's message. She therefore must've got it early that morning, while The New Year's Eve Guy was in the shower, not that afternoon. (The message her brother left was to verify that Lisa didn't fuck the guy she met the night before [the New Year's Eve Guy], whom her brother knows from business deals, presumably because it would be embarrassing that his sister would do that, fuck a guy she just met. When he got out of the shower, Lisa told the New Year's Eve Guy to lie to her brother and say they hadn't fucked. Then Lisa called her brother to assure him that no, she didn't fuck the guy. The lies were really piling up, no?)

Lisa didn't want me to know that The New Year's Eve Guy was right there in her apartment when she listened to my syrupy and lonely and depressed message from paradise asking her come to back and be with me. So she lied. She lied after swearing for the second time that the lying was over. And looking me in the eye as she did so. So now that's three times she's lied after swearing not to lie ever again. That I know of.

Then there was the condom question. My grilling involved several well-orchestrated stages in which I asked seemingly innocent questions that set up the real question I'll ask later. I'd more or less perfected this technique during my Max Dalton murder investigation at Pavones in 1998, when everybody was lying about everything. Here's how it went with Lisa:

Did you use a condom?

Yes.

Whose idea was it to use a condom?

His, actually.

How did that work? I mean when was it decided that you two would use a condom?

One thing led… we'd gotten… naked and then it was decided.

Who supplied it?

He went out to get one.

You were both naked and he got dressed and went out?

Yes.

You'd both been drinking and it was like two in the morning and freezing out and he got dressed and went out for a condom?

Yes.

He must've been really worried about catching something.

Lisa's response here is inaudible.

Never mind. Oh. I forgot to ask you where this guy lived.

Over on the West Side.

All the way cross-town from you?

Yes.

Okay.

A couple days later:

While he was out getting the condom, what did you do?

Nothing. Waited.

By yourself, obviously.

Yes.

Did you think of me?

I don't remember, Allan.

Sorry…

That's all right.

At this point I touch Lisa in a way indicating that this is difficult for me too – and it surely is, in spite of the calculation behind each query and gesture.

While the guy was out getting a condom you had time to think about maybe changing your mind about having sex with him.

Yes, I guess I did.

How long were you by yourself, thinking about stuff?

Not long.

How long? Can you estimate?

Ten minutes.

Okay.

The next day I resume with this:

Can you imagine someone lying about whether they used a condom?

No. Why would they lie?

Okay.

Later that day I pay off the earlier grillings:

Just before he went out to get the condom, did he ask you anything?

No. He just went out.

He lives over on the West Side, right?

Yes.

He couldn't have known your neighborhood very well then.

No, I guess not.

He didn't ask you where he might buy a condom?

No... he... As I said, he just went out.

We've established that by now it's at least two AM.

Yes.

New Year's Day.

... Yes.

He just went out and found a condom store open at that hour on New Year's day?

...I told you that, Allan.

You already told me he didn't ask you anything before he went out, so he didn't ask where he might find a store open at that hour on New Year's Day, right? And since he lived all the way across town he couldn't have known the neighborhood well, right?

It... didn't occur to us that there would be a problem.

Two AM on New Year's Day and it didn't occur to you there might not be stores open?

He went out and came back with condoms, Allan.

Okay...

I don't see your point.

Where might he have found a store open?

Lexington Avenue probably.

You're on Park Avenue so that's a cross-town block, a long block.

Yes.

You told me yesterday that he was gone ten minutes.

...Maybe he was gone longer.

He couldn't've walked much more than over to Lexington and maybe then a block or at most two uptown or downtown and still had time to buy condoms, and get back in ten minutes.

...Maybe he was gone longer.

You know your neighborhood. What store within a couple blocks might've been open on New Year's Day at two in the morning that carries condoms?

...Maybe he was gone longer!

Is there such a store?

What's the point of all this?

The point is I think when I asked you if you used a condom you lied when you said yes.

I told you what happened!

You couldn't even admit the possibility that someone might lie about whether they used a condom while screwing around on the one they

129

supposedly love.

We did use a condom!

I mean Christ, Lisa.

That's basically how the condom grilling went. I've pared it down, but one aspect I cut that bears separate mention was when Lisa said The New Year's Eve Guy came back with condoms, plural. I asked her how many they'd needed. Two, she said. They'd needed the second one when they woke up next morning. Then the guy hit the shower. Here is where I got to make the point that when Lisa was listening to my syrupy and lonely and depressed voice mail message from Big Turkeys – which she'd got that morning, *not* later that afternoon – she was still sweating and heaving from banging her one-night stand again.

This naturally segued to my asking how the sex was; I opined that it must have been okay if they did it again in the morning. I was asking for it here, I know, like when I'd asked her about the best week of her life, sexually. As I say, I'm a glutton for misery when it comes to my need to know everything.

Lisa, to her credit – I *think* to her credit – didn't hold back on this one. The sex was top notch, she said, words to that effect. The guy knew what he was doing, knew how to please a woman and so forth. Plus, since the sex was uncommitted, Lisa was feeling loose and randy. Right: "Uncommitted" also was the way she'd described the sex with The Snowman – the best sex ever. In fact, when Lisa owned up to the sex with her ex-boyfriend – which occurred a few days after the New Year's Eve Guy – she volunteered that that sex, too, was top notch, because she and her ex were now "uncommitted."

And yes, she'd had orgasms with the New Year's Eve Guy, which she doesn't always have.

Anyone else know about this? I wanted to know, aside from her ex-boyfriend, who spilled it to me.

Yes, Lisa said. Vanessa. Lisa bragged to her friend Vanessa about that night, how she'd picked up the guy and how he looked like a "younger Marlon Brando" and how great the sex was.

Vanessa's a friend of mine also. Thanks for the heads up on this, Vanessa.

It occurs to me that reliving events in writing about them you can get as pissed off and miserable as when you lived them originally. Even more so, as you tend to dig deeper and see more implications in the writing process.

It also occurs to me that there are two people sitting here at my desk: The me-as-a-writer who dispassionately writes away, and the me-as-a-person who is reading what the me-as-a-writer wrote away at, and is squirming and anguish-ridden about it. "It" meaning what he learned about himself by virtue of having written... it.

I press on.

A couple days after The New Year's Eve Guy revelation, I constructed a chart of Lisa's sexual partners for December 2002 through February, 2003 and left it where she'd come across it in the rental house in Montauk. (1) Me. (2) The New Year's Eve Guy. (3) Her ex-boyfriend. (4) Me. (5) Her ex-boyfriend. (6) Me. This was how it read. And remember, these were *known* sexual partners. (Had I had the relevant maps – Montauk, Manhattan, Costa Rica – I would have used them as an addendum, with circles and arrows.)

Later that day I told Lisa that what bothered me most about all this was not so much the fuckfest with her ex, or the one-night (plus the morning) fuckfest with the New Year's Eve Guy, but the combination of the two fuckfests. I told her I was worried she had a dark side and that maybe she thought this dark side was just a quirk or something, and that's how she lived with it.

I don't have a dark side or any quirks, Lisa said.

During this time at Montauk in May I called my writer friend Lesley. Lesley is my dear old friend. Lesley is the kind of friend you may not talk to very often but when you do it's an immediate, intimate connection, as always. You can tell her anything, ask her anything and you'll get a real, truthful, insightful response. There are no hidden agendas. Lesley is not an ex-girlfriend. Ex-girlfriends can never become dear old friends in this sense, because with ex-girlfriends there are always hidden agendas lurking. Trust me on this. I've done the research.

Lesley and Mom were tight. A couple of weeks before Mom died Mom asked me to get Lesley on the phone, in London where she lives with her husband Tom and their daughter Nora. They talked for a long time in spite of Mom's weak condition. From the bits and pieces of the conversation I overheard, they mostly talked about me. Like Mom, Lesley was worried about me, my happiness. She hoped I'd find someone to love.

So I càll Lesley in London and tell her the latest about Lisa, starting with an account of The Horror and about her screwing around with her ex-boyfriend and lying about it for weeks then about The New Year's Eve Guy and my fear that he's also The Cityman and how the condom grilling went and how the chart of Lisa's sexual partners for December 2002 through February 2003 reads and how I'm trying to get to the bottom of it all and I mention dark side possibilities and quirks and then I circle back to how Lisa humiliated me on the island of The Horror fame by dancing with the local guy right after her promise not to even give the impression of flirting with other men, and so forth. It takes a while. Lesley listens patiently, not saying much. She has one real question, she says, when I'm finished.

Okay, I say. Fire away.

As preamble to her one real question Lesley asks me if in spite of our problems I'm sure I love Lisa and want to stay with her.

I say Yes, I'm sure.

Lesley's one real question is regarding my grillings and detective work: *Are you out of your fucking mind?*

CHAPTER EIGHT

Writing is putting one's obsessions in order.

Jean Grenier

December 24, 2003. Christmas Eve at the end of the road, at Big Turkeys. Somewhere around 8 AM.

Lisa has just left, went down the dirt road to deliver fresh-baked pizzas to some Tico (Costa Rican) neighbors; Christmas presents. The Ticos love Lisa. She is kind and generous without being condescending and has amazed everyone away with how fast she's learned Spanish. You'd be surprised at the number of North Americans who live down here and haven't bothered to learn Spanish. One guy has been here twelve years and knows three words: *Chicas, cervesas* and *cigarros*. Girls, beer and cigarettes.

At the same time that she's liked by everyone, especially Ticos, Lisa doesn't take any shit from anyone, including Ticos. Maybe especially Ticos. For example, last week we were surfing in front of the cantina and this Tico kid snaked her on two waves in a row – no doubt figuring she's a woman, a gringa at that, so what's she going to do about it? What she did about it was paddle over to him and yell in his face, "Que eres, un maricon que necisita robar olas de una mujer?!"

What are you, a fag that has to steal waves from a woman?

She bellowed this out so everyone in the water heard it. I was on the beach 50 yards away and I heard it. Now the tables were turned: What was the kid going to do about it, given that Lisa's a woman, a gringa at that? What he did was paddle away through the derisive laughter in the lineup looking completely hang-dog and then not snake Lisa anymore.

Thing is, although Lisa's ballsy, guy-type attitude in the water is humorous and even endearing, there is a very definite down side to it; a down side that almost ended our relationship.

Back in June, less than a month after I found out about The New Year's Eve Guy, Lisa and I were surfing in front of the cantina and I noticed Lisa and some other surfer, a guy, were sitting together down the way in the lineup. At first I didn't think much of this; the guy no doubt paddled over to give her a try. Guys can't help themselves with her and so forth. But a half hour later, they were still at it. They'd catch waves then wind up sitting together again after paddling back out, blabbing about whatever.

The etiquette with this sort of thing is simple. When a woman with a mate gets hit on in the water (which is what was going on, no question) she soon makes it clear she's with someone – a casual reference to "my husband" or "my boyfriend" is usually sufficient – then subtly paddles away or, more often, after catching a wave will go to a different spot in the lineup. Women know how to blow off guys no matter the situation. I've done the research on this one too.

Not so here. It was clear they were "surfing together."

Then Lisa or the guy caught a wave and went in and the other followed; I didn't see who went in first.

Now they were sitting together on the cantina seawall. I was upset, worried. I paddled in, showered at the cantina and went and sat a few feet away from Lisa, who was deep in conversation with this guy; he was good-looking, mid-thirties or so. Lisa didn't acknowledge my presence; her back was toward me. This went on for like a half hour and then I was really worried. Not angry. Worried. Maybe a little angry, but mostly worried. Finally, trying to keep it casual, I said, "Can we go home now?"

"Can we come back?" Lisa replied, quickly, with an impatient edge, not looking at me. I was too dumbfounded to respond. I just got up and walked to the car. After a bit, Lisa followed.

As would become a motif in incidents like this, I didn't say anything, although for the rest of that day and that night my mind was in overdrive on Lisa's behavior. Especially that edgy, "Can we come back?" query at the end. As if I were an inconvenience.

I believe my silence here, and in the many situations that would follow, was based on fear. Fear of not only a blowup, but of what Lisa would say about her behavior. I was afraid she'd lie, say that her behavior with this guy didn't mean anything or was harmless, words to that effect. I didn't want to hear any more lies, nor did I want to bring up the past, which I was trying to put behind us. And, of course, denial was there too. If I didn't acknowledge this, maybe it would go away.

It did not go away.

The next day the scenario repeated itself. We paddled out, got separated in the course of picking our waves, and then suddenly the same guy was there, he and Lisa surfing together, sitting rail-to-rail talking in the lulls. For an hour. They paddled in together and sat on the seawall.

Now I was *frightened*. I paddled in immediately and sat on the wall behind Lisa, whose back was again to me. This went on, like the day before, and I was not only frightened but curious – in the morbid sense – to see how far this would go.

I was also thinking that this was... borderline insane. I had just a few weeks ago found out about her cheating and lying about it with her ex-boyfriend and then, three weeks ago, about her New Year's Eve one-night-plus-the-next-morning-stand, plus her deceit over that, and had elicited her second promise not to even give the impression of flirting with other men. This based on her inappropriate behavior with the local on the Caribbean island of The Horror fame. (And let's not forget The Horror itself.)

Finally, I heard Lisa say something about the land we were selling adjacent to our house and the guy said something back that I didn't catch. Lisa turned to me and after two days of not acknowledging me, finally introduced me to the guy, then said, "He's interested in land. Can he come up to the house?"

Now she's inviting him to our house.

I was too nonplussed to come up with an excuse to say no – to show my fear and anger would have been a further humiliation – so the guy came to the house, supposedly to look at our land. As I would find out later and as I already suspected, the guy had no interest in buying land. He was interested in fucking Lisa, my girlfriend. Even though he knew she was living with me, he figured he'd give it a shot, what with Lisa's behavior, the signals she was broadcasting and so forth.

That night I told Lisa she would have to leave. Pack up her stuff and go. Told her that if she's capable of behavior like that after the shit she'd put me through, she's capable of a lot worse, which I didn't need in my life. Lisa didn't deny the inappropriateness of her flirtation, or that it was a flirtation. She apologized, cried, apologized some more, cried some more, said I was the love of her life and she couldn't bear to lose me and would never do anything like that again. Never.

I caved.

She could stay.

A couple weeks later I saw Lisa engage in another flirtation with another surfer, on the beach. It was brief, but blatant, one of those wordless come-ons women do. Five minutes later when I calmly asked her not to do that, flirt, reminding her of her various promises, she denied having done it.

The next morning I woke up at first light after a fitful sleep, Lisa asleep next to me, a notebook by her pillow; her journal, one of her hand-written ones. I moved it closer and in the faint gloaming read her entry. She'd written about the incident, referring to it as "Allan's imaginings on the beach."

In other words, the incident never happened. I imagined it.

Weeks later in a letter to her mother she had me read – no snooping – Lisa admitted to the flirtation behavior on the beach, excusing herself by saying, "Maybe I just couldn't help myself."[*] When she had me read the letter she forgot that she had previously denied the flirtation.

So Lisa lied when she denied the incident five minutes after it happened, and she was also lying in her private journal when she wrote that I imagined it. In other words, she was lying to herself. Or possibly she knew exactly what she was doing and wrote how I'd imagined the incident figuring I'd see her journal by her pillow and read it and then doubt what I had seen. There's a word for this–trying to make someone doubt their own eyes– taken from the title of a classic movie with Ingrid Bergman and Charles Boyer. *Gaslight*. The Boyer character tries to make his wife, Bergman, think she's going insane.

I'm not sure which possibility is worse, that Lisa was lying to herself in her journal or that she was attempting to gaslight me. It's a toss up.

Soon after this incident there was another blatant flirtation, and one morning just after it, during my after-writing throes, I was thinking about this narrative–or maybe I was thinking about my sorry-ass life and times (or maybe I was thinking about how I often get mixed up as to which one I'm thinking about at any given moment, meaning my sorry-ass life and times or this narrative)–and something occurred to me. Remember that stuff about Lisa's *ultimate femaleness*? Which was supposed to explain why guys can't help themselves in hitting on her? I even made up a little piece of business about how space itself is curved in Lisa's direction? What occurred to me was that that is bullshit. The reason guys can't help themselves from hitting on her is that Lisa gives off signals that she's available. She does this even if I'm right there. Women of course can do this in an eye blink. Literally.

So that stuff about Lisa's *ultimate femaleness*? Never mind.

---

[*] In the letter to her mother, Lisa also describes her two-day flirtation with the first surfer, admitting it was "beyond the pale" and "in another realm."

CHAPTER NINE

I hope you have not been leading a double life, pretending to be wicked and being good all the time. That would be hypocrisy.
Oscar Wilde

The other thing Lisa is doing this Christmas Eve morning is visit Gerardo Mora's house to help Gerardo's wife, Mayela, make tortillas for Christmas dinner. If the name Gerardo Mora sounds familiar, Mora is notable in that he is the man who murdered Max Dalton back in November of 1997; I believe he was considering murdering me for what I'd uncovered about him in my investigation. So, again, it wasn't just the other North American, Logan the Nutcase, who had it in for me back then.

Lisa says she's going to ask Mayela to help her with her Spanish lessons, make some sort of continuing arrangement. Mayela is notable in her own right as having put a knife to Max Dalton's throat and telling him he was a dead man three days before Max was murdered. She'd also been part of a squatter mob that roughed up landowner Billy Clayton at the gate to his Sawmill property. An oft-repeated story: in the 1990s, while presidential candidate José Figueras was giving a speech, Mayela jumped up on the podium and attacked him.

And the Moras' son, Esteban, is cut from the same mold as mom and dad. Although it was his father who actually shot and killed Max Dalton, Esteban has bragged that he participated directly in the slaying; he also has a well-established rep as a drug dealer, con man and all around miscreant. (There's another son, David, but I've only met him briefly and don't know much about him.)

I have reasons for staying on surface-friendly terms with the Moras, which I've explained to Lisa – and which I'll get to in this narrative – but Lisa's overt friendship with these people is disconcerting. I'll have to sit down with her about this matter.

But my point for now is that I'm not completely sure that Lisa is actually going to do nothing more than deliver pizzas and collaborate on tortilla baking with a murderous family. It's possible that she's fuckfesting with someone here at Pavones – a sort of tropical Snowman or Cityman incarnation – and is going to see him. There have been signals to this effect, the most blatant being Lisa's frequent solo trips to Golfito, some of which were unnecessary, one particular proposed trip absurdly so: not being able to get online one morning at home, Lisa claimed she had to go to Golfito to use the Internet café to retrieve a friend's phone number from her Yahoo email account. This meant an all-day drive over bad roads to retrieve a phone number that she could have easily got via a call to a third party in the States; or, indeed, an hour or so wait for our Internet cell connection to come back up would accomplish the same. In any event, when I asked what was the emergency in calling her friend, Lisa shrugged and said something strange: "I gave it a shot."

When a moment later I asked her what she meant by *I gave it a shot* Lisa put on a confused face and denied having said that. Well, she said it, just seconds before. She said *I gave it a shot* and it was in reference to her absurd reason to go to Golfito. It was like she was thinking *I gave it a shot* and it just leaked out of her mouth.

At my request, Lisa didn't go to Golfito that day.

One time Lisa took one of my little codeine pills. As when she's drunk or sleepy, codeine makes her talkative and spontaneous. She asked me what one thing about myself I would change, if I could. I said I'd make myself more self-reflective.

"How about you, Lisa?"

"I wish I'd think before I speak," she replied.

Lisa's response was a classic blurt. Her wish that she'd think before speaking accidentally referred to voicing the wish itself, since if she had, at that moment, been thinking before speaking she would not have said she wished she'd think before speaking.

To put it another way: In voicing this wish, Lisa was admitting that she reveals things she'd rather not, which is an admission she would never make, except by not thinking before speaking.

See what I mean?

CHAPTER TEN

There is only one thing that can kill movies and that is education.

Will Rogers

There's a character in this *In Search of Captain Zero* movie deal confederacy of dunces* that I've so far only mentioned in passing, but who deserves more words: the director of record on this project.

As mentioned back in Part One, this fellow directed a documentary that Sean Penn narrated and that the producer who originally approached me about optioning my book had produced. As part of the producer's pitch – sensing my wariness about letting her have the option – she sent me a cassette of the documentary, a history of the skateboard subculture in America. The movie was supposed to be an indication of how brilliant the director was. I watched it with Mom down in North Carolina – this was in early 2001, a few months before Mom died. It was good, if a bit long; it had a certain pizzazz. Thing was, though, about halfway through I noticed something that gave me contemplative pause regarding the director's brilliance: almost all the footage, certainly the pizzazz-rife footage, was archival, from the early days of skateboarding and surfing in Venice, California. In fact, the director himself was a character in the movie; he was a kid for most of it. It was obvious that he hadn't shot or directed this stuff. By the end I realized that the director had only "directed" the interviews with the now-aging characters from the archival footage, which was maybe 10% of the movie. All he had directed was talking heads.

Also, documentaries are not principally a director's medium to begin with. Although there are lots of fine lines and blurry distinctions in the implications of who-did-what based on credit given (as there are in feature films), documentaries are primarily an editor's medium, depending on who develops the final structure – the order in which the images are presented. In a feature film the structure is defined by the screenplay, i.e., the writer,

---

* I suspect I use the title to John Kennedy O'Toole's book here because suicidal authors are on my mind these days

but in documentaries this is not necessarily the case. What often happens is that the producer and/or director will dump a mountain of raw footage in front of the editor and say, "Find the movie."

So the movie Mom and I watched really indicated nothing about the director's ability to conceive of and execute a filmed narrative. That no one at the studio noticed this before hiring this "hot new" director should have completely, formally, tipped me that my catch-22 regarding the whole bunch of them was not only on the money but an understatement.* So here we have still more Hollywood nonsense. Imagine watching a *Larry King Live* and saying, "The guy who shot that is a fucking genius! Let's get him to direct our next star-studded feature!"

But direct evidence that the director was not only not the genius he was purported to be but an outright dimwit was forthcoming. Not only a dimwit, but a rude and discourteous and unprofessional dimwit.

In September of 2002, more than two months after I handed in my "first draft" of the *Zero* screenplay, I went up to Hollywood for a meeting with all involved (minus Sean Penn): the producer, the director, the studio executives. They flew me up from Pavones (first class, as the Writer's Guild demands) and put me in a hotel on Venice Beach, just a few blocks from my old beach pad from the late 80s and early 90s (where the getting-laid-at-Venice Beach-Jon-Voigt anecdote took place, my asshole-screenwriter-with-a-Porsche days).

Before our meeting with the studio the producer and director came over to my hotel for a strategy sit-down. Having struggled for months to come up with a draft that worked, I expected us to go over the work in order to solve the problems I myself knew were there, and which I'd told them about.

I'd been sending the script pages as I wrote them, a practice frowned upon by the Writer's Guild; since the producer/director/studio can send notes on changes during the writing of a draft, the writer may in effect end up writing two (or more) drafts for the price of one. I didn't mind this – my main concern, my only concern, was to "give the studio exactly what I said I would." I just wanted to make this deal work, and see the movie made. And I was getting nothing but accolades in return for the pages sent, at least from the producer. The director was largely silent, only occasionally making minor suggestions, none having to do with the essence of the story, i.e., the conflicts that define the turning points of the narrative, which had been agreed to by everyone at that breakfast meeting at the Four Seasons. I'd further refined them in detailed memos sent weekly. In Hollywood,

---

* That the director won an award at the Sundance Film Festival is proof that even folks who theoretically should know better (so called "independent" filmmakers) in fact have their heads up their asses just as far as the rest of them.

silence is taken as a sign of approval.

In meetings such as this one, the purpose of which is to analyze the screenplay in detail, everyone brings his own copy, which is invariably marked up in the margins and blank facing pages. My assumption was that since I'd gotten nothing but accolades for the pages sent, we'd concentrate on the problems I myself had seen in the story, and on minor issues such as the specifics of dialog.* In fact, since the two had read the screenplay over the months of its writing, I did not expect any surprises at all. I was wrong, of course, as I so often am in expecting Hollywood stuff to proceed in a rational, efficient, professional manner. I was wrong big time.

The first surprise was that neither the producer nor the director brought a copy of my screenplay. A bad sign on top of a surprise. The second surprise and bad sign was the producer saying this: "This isn't the screenplay we thought we'd get." If this sounds familiar, if you recall the producer saying this before, I'm not reproducing the previously mentioned instance; that instance (months later while I was on the phone on the beach here at Pavones) was the second time she'd used the pronoun "we" in referring to an "unexpected screenplay" after she'd been reading it as I wrote it.

And both times she used the words "unexpected screenplay" she'd been sending me accolades about the work as she read it.

As it turned out, the producer had not been passing my pages along to the studio. They had recently been given the draft in its entirety, however, which they'd read. Hold on. *One* of them (at the studio) had read it, the executive who had been at the breakfast meeting at the Four Seasons and who had approved my approach to conflicts and turning points. The studio head, of course, hadn't read it, nor my book; I'm quite certain he never reads anything. "They" decided they didn't like it, in spite of there being no surprises in it; all the major story events had been approved at the breakfast meeting.

You wanna talk about a writer's queasy gut?

But it gets better. Since neither the producer nor the director could point out where I'd gone wrong in my draft – or, for that matter, how what I'd written was different now that it was bound together with a title page – they started in on how I'd over-written stage direction. Stage direction is when you describe action: "Sam Spade picks up the gun and checks to see if it's loaded" kind of stuff. Overwriting means you've got stuff in there that can't make it to the screen: "Sam Spade picks up the gun and checks to

---

* Contrary to popular perception, dialog is one of the least important aspects of a screenplay. Much more important are the *events* – the turning points. Even if the events involve dialog – and they very often do – the words spoken are the means to the events, not the events themselves. There's a story about Alfred Hitchcock that is instructive here. When asked how a particular screenplay was coming, he replied, "The screenplay is finished. We just have to add the dialog."

see if it's loaded, unaware that he would never get to use it." The last clause might work in a novel, but it should not be in a screenplay since there's no way to translate "unaware that he would never get to use it" to the screen.

And it was true. I *had* overwritten my stage direction, although not as blatantly as the above example. My overwriting was more of the flowery prose sort, as in, say, going on too long about how beautiful a sunset is. I had already told them I'd correct the problem. That should have been that, end of problem, for this reason: Regarding *story*, the specific wording of stage direction is irrelevant. What *happens* is what counts.

But they just would not stop. Had to point out each and every bit of description I'd overwritten. Thing was, even with this nitpicking they often had their heads up their asses. Near the beginning of the story, for example, I have the two main characters at age 17 sitting on a fence at the back of a drive-in watching the movie *The Endless Summer* and reciting Bruce Brown's narration by rote. I add by way of description, "They've seen *The Endless Summer* 20 times." The director said to cut that line since it wouldn't make it to the screen. While that was technically true, I replied, the line gives the actors something to work with – it explains why the two kids know the narration by heart, gives a feel for what's going on.

The director shook his head in disgust at my ignorance and insisted that the line should be cut. (If you're already wondering *what the fuck is with this guy*, all I can say – via a little looping [call it a loopette] – is *you ain't seen nothin' yet*.)

Here I had an idea. Upon arriving at Hollywood I'd asked the producer if she had any good screenplays lying around, something I could read. I love reading good screenplays – believe me, they are tough to find. She did, one called *Fever Pitch*, by Lowell Ganz and Babaloo Mandel, maybe the best writing team currently working in Hollywood. The story was about baseball, or, rather, baseball fans; it follows the hopes and dashed dreams of a group of rabid Boston Red Sox fans, via the travails of another losing Sox season.[*] A terrific screenplay, funny and poignant and superbly crafted. The screenplay was there on the table; I'd breezed through it the night before. I held it up.

"Wonderful screenplay, right?" I said.

The two agreed vociferously.

"Maybe the best writing team working today, right?"

The two agreed vociferously.

---

[*] I can only imagine Lowell and Babaloo's horror when the Sox came back to win eight straight in the 2004 playoffs/World Series to take it all, effectively destroying their story's premise. (Months later *Fever Pitch* was released: The boys had solved the problem by rewriting the screenplay, now setting it during that miraculous season, *using* the Sox's incredible comeback as the crux of the ending. A smart move, all they could do, really, but the ending didn't have the same melancholy yet uplifting pizzazz as the original.)

"No problems with the writing, the stage direction?"

They had no problems with the writing, the stage direction.

I flipped the screenplay open to a random page. Near the top was a description of an establishing shot of the crowd at Fenway Park on opening day. I read aloud: "It's opening day and the Sox haven't broken any hearts yet."

The two nodded approvingly. For some reason they didn't see where I was going with this. Which was here: "How do you put 'they haven't broken any hearts yet' on the screen?"

Here the director not only shook his head at my ignorance but let out a scornful blast of air. As I pictured myself strangling him, I repeated my query:

"How do you put 'they haven't broken any hearts yet' on the screen?"

The director wouldn't stop shaking his fucking head, that dumb baseball cap on it, which I suspect made him feel more like Ron Howard, a *real* director, one who often wears a baseball cap. (A lot of directors, real and otherwise, wear baseball caps. I have a theory to explain this phenomenon, but now's not the time.)

"I suppose in shooting this crowd scene the director could bellow through his bullhorn to 20,000 people, 'Remember that the Sox haven't broken your hearts yet!... And... Action!'"

Still the head shaking.

You know, I said, and the image of my hands around the guy's neck lingered, screenplays are written to be read. Sometimes lines like "They haven't broken any hearts yet" and "They've seen *The Endless Summer* 20 times" are there solely to make them readable. And in the case of my line, it actually does have a purpose.

The producer, who was marginally less of a dimwit than the director, was aware that I was right. We have some ideas, she said, in order to change the subject, then suggested that the director describe "that scene you thought of."

The guy's eyes lit up (at least he'd stopped shaking his head) as he described a scene in Mexico wherein the main character (me) gets a sea urchin spine in his foot and uses his own piss to extract it (urine supposedly helps dissolve urchin spines). That was it, the scene he thought up. Had nothing to do with advancing the story or anything else, but he loved it.

Here I made a mistake. I humored him. Although I knew no such scene would make it into a screenplay I'd write, I suggested that maybe – in order for the scene to have an actual purpose – our guy is with a bunch of local fishermen and is short of urine. So the fishermen pass a cup, piss in it; he uses their urine to get the spine out. Although this is dumb too, at least this dumbness could result in our guy bonding with the locals, and if well executed the scene might be marginally humorous. Truth is, it doesn't matter whether my version had any merit. The instructive aspect of this piece of business is in the director's reaction: More head shaking at my ignorance, along with an even more explosive snort of derision.

"What?" I wanted to know as the strangulation image resurfaced, now with some added stage direction about veins popping on his forehead (which *could* be put up on the screen).

"An actor would never let *someone else* piss on his foot!"

This is what he said, verbatim (hence the quotes). Hold on. I gotta ask you something, and it's important because it goes to the veracity of this narrative: Do you think I could *make up* this shit, a line like that? Okay. Good.

In the larger sense, anecdotal stuff like the above does not equal truth, in this case meaning how Hollywood *is*. Maybe most Hollywood people are actually smart and creative and I've either been unlucky or am exaggerating to make my Can't-I-Get-Along-With-Anyone point; trying to say "It's not me! It's everyone else!" When it actually is me.

In my twenty-some-odd years and thirty-some-odd Hollywood projects, at least two-thirds (I'm being conservative) of the people I've been subjected to were of this caliber; small bore intellects. Fucking BB guns.

For now, just one more example, one that reflects not only dimwittedness, but the life's work, i.e., the only real goal, the *raison d'etre*, of Hollywood folks, which is this: *To avoid looking foolish*. Or, failing in the avoidance of looking foolish, which they invariably do, this: *Cultivating and maintaining the denial that they in fact do look foolish*.

Early on in my career, before my comeuppance (the phone stopped ringing), I was offered one assignment after another, based on my first original screenplay, which Michael Mann had optioned, and then my quickly getting a movie into production with an Oscar-winning producer (but before that turkey came out). And, God help me, I took 'em. Hey, 75 grand for three month's work (in early-to-mid 1980's dollars). So what if the studio-supplied ideas behind these projects were dumb or even un-writeable? Who cares? What, me worry?*

One such assignment was to write a Richard Pryor vehicle – this was pre-cocaine-self-immolation/pre-multiple-sclerosis and Pryor was a very hot property. The premise I was shouldered with doesn't matter – it was no dumber than the rest – but I did a decent job with the first draft. I was dealing with the actual head of the studio (now defunct), which is unusual; an underling exec is usually the go-between with the writer. The guy loved

---

* Even I had my limits, however. One assignment I turned down was based on a studio executive's idea that a great white shark befriends a young boy. The great white is severely misunderstood; in the end the boy saves his buddy from the evil shark hunters. Sort of a cold-blooded *Free Willy*. The exec's solution to the problem of how to make this believable was the following: "We just have to make the shark... you know... fuzzy..."

my writing samples, liked me and liked my first draft. I was optimistic that the movie would fly. The studio head called me in to go over the draft prior to my doing revisions. His notes were minor, which was a relief. One little problem involved the Pryor character calling CIA headquarters in Langley, Virginia. I had the operator at CIA answering "CIA, how can I direct your call?"

The studio head turned to this page, shook his head at my ignorance, and said that the CIA doesn't answer the phone like that.

I said I thought it pretty much did.

More head shaking. Didn't you see *Three Days of the Condor*?

I said that I had.

The studio head said when Robert Redford called the CIA, they answered with a code of some sort.

That was different, I said. Redford was calling a CIA covert operation H.Q. Here we're calling headquarters at Langley.

As often happened in my Hollywood life, the idiot I was meeting with would not stop with the head shaking and frowning at my ignorance of how things are. (At least he wasn't wearing a baseball cap.) Here I made another big mistake, one that may have cost me getting a movie made, a Richard Pryor vehicle at that, which would have quadrupled my base assignment pay and led to a higher-end Porsche and more getting-laid anecdotes. Instead of agreeing with him and making the wrong, dumb ass, nonsensical but minor dialog change he wanted (which would have been corrected later anyway, after the movie was a "go")… instead of letting him feel harmlessly useful, out of pure self-destructiveness I suggested we call CIA headquarters at Langley and find out for ourselves.

Here I got the snort of derision, plus this: You think their phone number is *listed*?

I said that I thought it was.

The studio head put his assistant on the speakerphone and told her to get us CIA headquarters at Langley, Virginia. He smirked and sat back, eyes bright, waiting for vindication. Waiting for an example of why he was the head of a studio and I was a lowly screenwriter. A matter of seconds later – after information spouted the CIA's number in Langley, no problem – an operator's voice boomed over the box, "CIA, how can I direct your call?"

The studio head's head bobbed in astonishment. He looked at his watch and said he had another meeting he was late for.

I had fucked with the studio head's raison d'etre. His denial.

My screenplay suddenly had fatal flaws.

I never saw the guy again.*

---

* Later, through a friendly secretary at the studio, I managed to secure coverage of my first draft – the half-dozen underling executives' written reaction to it. They all loved it as much as the studio head initially did. No one actually told me what the sudden fatal flaws were.

CHAPTER ELEVEN

Oh God! I could be bounded in a nutshell, and count myself a
king of infinite space, were it not that I have bad dreams.
William Shakespeare

Back in August Lisa had her passport stolen. We were coming back from
a Stateside trip and had just arrived at the San José airport. We took a taxi
to the hotel, first stopping at a bus depot to drop off our heavier luggage.
A company at the depot called Tracopa would transport our stuff down to
Pavones, which would save us money; the puddle jumper we were to fly
home on charges big bucks for excessive baggage.

At Tracopa, Lisa's passport plus some other stuff was stolen out of our
taxi while we were dealing with the luggage. As of a month later, she hadn't
replaced her passport with a new one. She was legally in-country based on
a copy of the old one, plus the police report of the theft. But come October it
was time to go to the U.S. embassy in San José and deal with the problem.

Lisa and I had got friendly with some female pro surfers we met at a
surf contest, one being a big fan of *Zero*. A half-dozen of them came down
to surf our home breaks and we got even friendlier. A fun bunch, terrific
surfers.

When the women left to fly back to the States, Lisa caught a ride with
them up to San José to get a new passport; this would take a few days,
with the traveling and paperwork and so forth. Given, well, everything,
I was edgy about Lisa being alone in San José after the surfer girls flew
out. Lisa's behavior with other men, her apparent inability to refrain from
blatant flirting right in front of me was a source of anguish, although I
rarely voiced it out of fear of blowups and lies. I no longer had the heart
for hardcore grillings. I'd largely put behind us the screwing around she'd
done with her ex-boyfriend, and the New Year's Eve one-night-plus-the-
next-morning stand; the lying after swearing that the lies were over was
tougher to deal with.

The morning of her San José trip, I was driving Lisa to the *cabina* where
the pro-female surfers were staying and pulled over and told her I needed
to talk about something. Without bringing up specifics I told her I was

edgy about her trip, about her being in San José alone.

Lisa nodded, said she understood.

I'm going to ask you one favor.

Yes.

Keep your cell phone on and within reach.

Yes, sure, of course.

Okay, good. Thank you.

The first night after the surfer girls left I couldn't reach Lisa on the cell phone. It just rang until the voice mail came on. I couldn't reach her for more than three hours.

I was meanwhile thinking about her behavior with other men while I'm right there and wondering how it goes when I'm not right there. I was thinking about the signals of availability Lisa gives off, as opposed to ultimate femaleness.

Lisa calls sometime after 8:30 while I'm downstairs and didn't hear the phone ring. She leaves a message detailing her night, all the things she did and what she had for dinner and how it's raining and how she figures I'm watching Monday Night Football and so forth. Her tone is so breezy and cheerful and so much like the tone she uses when she's lying that it literally makes me nauseous.

I call back and I'm angry, demanding to know why she didn't answer her phone. She tells me that earlier in the day she'd dumped her purse on the hotel room bed and the cell phone slid under the pillow, so she didn't know she didn't have it in her purse when she went out again.

Try to imagine it. Or, better yet, duplicate it. Try to dump a cell phone from a purse onto a bed and have it end up under the pillow. Pretty much can't be done.

The rest of the night doesn't go well. I'm thinking Lisa may have someone in her room, so I call periodically and have her say out loud "There's no scumbag in my room," words to that effect.

There's no scumbag in my room.

Louder, Lisa.

No, I won't.

Fuck you then with your cell phone bullshit.

I'm not with anyone!

Then say it!

No!

She's back two days later and things don't go well.

I'm angry.

She's angry.

I calm down. I apologize for being over-the-top. I let some time pass. We go surfing. I ask about that night again, about the cell phone, why she'd gone out without it. These are not hardcore grillings like before. I'm trying a different tack. Key is to be casual and make it look like you're really interested in a different aspect of the person's story; you act innocent and then go in through the back door; a similar technique to when you're trying to recount the best sexual week of your life, fictitiously speaking. Or when you're investigating the murder of an American expatriate for a national magazine.

Now when she dumped out her purse the phone fell onto the floor and slid under the bed.

I thought it went under the pillow.

No, now she's remembering what really happened.

Then she hadn't dumped all the contents of her purse on the bed, she'd dumped them on the floor. Try picturing a woman dumping all the contents of her purse onto a linoleum floor.

Then she didn't dump out her purse until after she got back to the room that night. The cell had now fallen out of her purse when she simply put the purse on the bed earlier that day.

The changes in the cell phone's timeline, trajectory and final destination would take place over several days, and, again, were not based on hardcore grilling, as with, say, the New Year's Eve condom story. Though well orchestrated, my interrogations were casual and through the back door.

The second day after her return from San José, Lisa was describing her movements during the time she didn't have the cell phone with her. She'd gone to a watch repair shop to get a battery for my mother's watch, which I'd given her, but the place was closed, then she went to dinner…

"…then I went back to the watch place and got the battery… by this time it was about eight o'clock… then we went to the bookstore… I mean I went to the bookstore… then…"

What? What was that?

What was what?

You said "we" went to the bookstore. Who were you with?

I was alone.

You said "we went to the bookstore."

Lisa denied that the "we" slip meant anything.

I need to ask you something here, and please be honest with yourself – try your best to self-reflect.

First: Are you in love? I'm not talking about run of the mill love, love you may have felt before. I'm talking about *the love of your life* kind of love. And imagine that this kind of love has been a long time coming; you're no kid anymore. It's not that you're desperate because of your age, no, not at all. You've been content being single, living a solitary life. And hey, you've had fun with the opposite sex.

Further, in spite of some problems, maybe serious ones, you've decided that with this person *this really is it*.

Okay. Now try to put yourself in my place. It appears that Lisa was lying about why she didn't have her cell phone with her that night, or why she wasn't answering it. And it appears that – with the "we" slip – she was with someone.

The question: Should that have been it? Should I have ejected Lisa from my life then and there, based on these appearances?

CHAPTER TWELVE

...what seemed paradise is mere scenery, a curtain that, lifting,
reveals pitchforks and fire.

Truman Capote

The last few days here at Big Turkeys have been one goddamn thing after another, with no segues.* Starting with the relatively small stuff,† let's look at the day before yesterday, that morning.

But first: When you're as depressed as I've been lately, you don't want to deal with other human beings. Aside from whatever chemical imbalances you might have, other human beings are the main cause of your depression to begin with, so you know in some deep and soulful way that your interacting with them is only going to worsen matters.

An example of someone I've put off interacting with is Logan the Nutcase, who figures to run me out of town, although we did have a confrontation a couple of weeks ago. I'd just found out that he'd gone to the mayor of the town that supposedly governs this area, Golfito, and told him I was illegally selling land here – which I'm not. The mayor of Golfito is about as corrupt as they come – even considering that this is Central America, the end of the road at that – and, like the local police, is on the dole from Logan, so I could very well have major problems looming. I don't have my official Costa Rican residency yet, for example, and could be thrown out of the country at any time. (After more than two months I have not heard back from the U.S. Consul in San José regarding the letter I sent her.)

I confronted Logan in the garage of a house he's building just down the dirt road from me. Told him he's fucking with the wrong guy in my case

---

* Some wag once described life as "just one damn thing after another." In other words, no segues. This dearth of segues, it seems to me, is a major difference between real life and narrative descriptions thereof, i.e., nonfiction. Nonfiction writers therefore cherish segues, covet them, and will, if necessary, lie like slugs to fashion them if facts are not cooperating.**
    ** When a legitimate segue occurs in my real life I usually go, "Holy shit, a segue!"

† There's a former best selling self-help book wherein the author claims via the title that you shouldn't sweat the small stuff. Okay. I agree. The title goes on to claim that "It's all small stuff." Yeah, well, I have news for the asshole on that one.

(he's fucked with literally everyone here) and, paraphrasing another great line from *The Godfather* movies, added that *if lightning strikes my house* I will personally come after him.

In retrospect, this may have been a mistake.

So there's that.

Regarding my aversion to interacting with other human beings: Lisa is taking care of me these days, which is not easy, trust me. For one thing, she's my buffer, my defense, my Maginot Line, between me and other human beings. Someone comes over to the house, she deals with it. She usually makes the run into Golfito or to the Panamanian Frontier to buy things and do other stuff; this way I don't have to be around the large groups of people found in these places. Except during my really dark moments, like my after-writing throes, I've put out of my mind (so to speak) the possibility that Lisa volunteers these solo missions so she can have a fuckfest with some tropical Snowman (or Cityman) incarnation while she's away.

So on the morning in question, the one-goddamn-thing–after-another morning, Lisa goes into Golfito to take care of some business and to buy me some more codeine, leaving me alone here.* Which means that regarding other people – having to deal with them – I'm defense-less, buffer-less, Maginot line-less. It's around 9 AM. I've been up since about 2 AM working on this narrative; writing something out of sequence, I think. I'm downstairs on the bed, semi-conscious, wallowing in my after-writing throes, and the dogs go wild out front. This usually means someone's at the gate. I cover my head with a pillow, figuring to weather it. Whoever it is will eventually go away, I figure, and leave me to wallow in peace. Not so. The racket goes on and on and then on some more. I start worrying that whatever is going on has something to do with Logan the Nutcase. Then I start worrying about the dogs, which I've been doing a lot of lately. Worrying that someone will poison them by throwing spiked meat over the fence. Part of the reason for this worry is that my old pup, Shiner, died here of suspicious causes back in 1998, during my investigation of the killing of Max Dalton.

So I get up, pull on my shorts – my after-writing throes are best experienced naked, I've found – and hoof it out to the gate, blinking in the harsh morning sunlight. I'm somehow at once alert for trouble and mindlessly shit-brained.

Guy out there at the gate. A Tico who looks familiar... right. The wood guy. Wants money. Here's why the wood guy wants money: a few days ago he heard that Lisa and I were looking for some 4 x 4s for the house we're building on one of our lots. So the next day he came up to the project and

---

* I've tried all the Prozac-type antidepressants. They do ease the depression. Problem is, they replace it with a deep sense of existential dread.

dumped off some crapola 4 x 4s. Just flung them on the ground and left. I even saw him do it from here, looking out the office window as I was working. Now he's back wanting his money. This is often the way Ticos do business with gringos here. Just dump off some crapola then come back later and demand money. I guess they figure since the crapola they dumped has been sitting there in your possession for some period of time, it's too late, it's yours now.

I don't want his crapola 4 x 4s, I say. He starts to get *bravo* with me. I use the Spanish here because it has some nuances. *Aggressive* is the English word that comes closest. Meanwhile the dogs are going even more nuts, snarling and barking at the wood guy on the other side of the gate. Five full-blown dogs and six puppies (Lisa having adopted a mama dog and her litter), the latter pitching in as best they can with their little yelps. I have to be careful here because of the poisoning possibility; the wood guy might come back and throw spiked meat over the fence. So I'm polite, even though what I really want to do is tell the shitball motherfucker to go fuck himself. Look, I tell him, I'm sick with *la grippe* – my after-writing throes *are* sort of like *la grippe* – and can't talk now. I walk away. He yells that he'll be back for his money.

I'm on the bed again. No more than ten minutes later there's another dog-racket. I try the pillow thing. Same result. Whoever it is won't go away. I pull my shorts back on and so forth.

Guy out there at the gate. A Tico who looks familiar... right. One of the guys who works for a neighbor, a Swede named Hans. The Tico wants money. Here's his story: Hans owes him money so Hans told him to get it from me since, Hans claims, I owe Hans money. Well, I don't owe Hans money. In fact, Hans owes *me* money. In the interest of making a long story short – or at least the attempt thereof – just trust me on this. Hans is trying to not pay this guy via me, using money that I don't owe Hans and that the guy now expects from me. In any event, you don't do things this way, expect someone to pay someone else because of a whole other debt, even if the debt existed. I tell the guy words to this effect. He gets *bravo* with me. I tell him i'm sick with *la grippe* and can't talk now. I go back to bed.

So now I've dealt with the wood guy and then my neighbor Hans's attempt to con me with the Tico he owes money to. I'm in bed again, stripped naked again and in the throes.

Right: The dogs.

Guy out there at the gate. A Tico. One of our workers this time. Flaco. Good kid; I like Flaco. Flaco and I have bonded: One night just before Christmas, Flaco was about to step through the door to his little rancho down the hill and zap, a terciopelo – the deadliest of the Central American vipers – nailed him on his right foot. His big brothers Roman and William rushed Flaco up here. We had to get him to Comte, where there is a clinic that stocks the anti-venom. Comte is forty-five minutes away on a very bad road; potholes like tiger pits, moguls that if you take them at more than 10 mph you catch air. Plus it was raining hard that night. So add really bad visibility and deep mud to the image.

I made it in 18 minutes.

The doctor who injected Flaco with the anti-venom figured we were in time, just. So Flaco and I bonded based on the likelihood that I saved Flaco's life. Plus Lisa and I gave Flaco a surfboard for Christmas to offset the week he spent in the hospital with his foot looking like a purple soccer ball; now he won't have to wait around to borrow a board from his brother William after the wind has come up and blown out the surf.

So I don't mind so much that Flaco has interrupted my after-writing throes. I mean not like the first two, anyway. But Flaco is the bearer of gloomy tidings, as it turns out.

Before leaving for Golfito that morning, Lisa told Flaco to go over to a Tico neighbor's property and cut down the banana trees that were obscuring our view of El Golfo Dulce, The Sweet Gulf. The neighbor's wife, Flaco is now telling me, told Flaco that he could not go onto the property and cut the banana trees. This pisses me off: when I originally bought my house lot back in 2001, my Tico neighbor immediately planted a score or so banana tree seedlings on a little strip of land right in front, where my plateau drops sharply off toward the beach. He did this to obscure my view; I'd have to pay him to cut the trees when they grew up. As if to add to the humor of this welcome-to-the-neighborhood gesture, the day after he planted the banana tree seedlings the guy came over looking for work in the building of my house. The guy is a squatter, by the way. He invaded the adjacent property while the North American who owns it wasn't looking.

Notwithstanding these neighborly quirks, I gave the squatter a job and started negotiating for the cutting of the banana trees. First he wanted $1,000. I laughed at him. Banana trees here are literally weeds; they're everywhere. But as my house got built and the banana trees grew, I wasn't laughing anymore. I ended up paying $500 to cut down his banana trees, which, by the way, were shitty banana trees – their bananas were tiny little dried-up jobs, the size of your shriveled penis after surfing in cold water. I insisted on a written guarantee that no more banana trees or any other kind of trees were to be grown in my view, either by him or by God, ever. "By God" meaning seeds that may come to be there and sprout by natural means. I all but added a clause that forbade him from *standing* in my view. I had about 75 people witness the contract.

Now his wife is saying that the new banana trees can't be cut unless I pay again. The deal I have is with her husband, not with her, she says, and her husband isn't around anymore – he's on the run from the police for drug dealing. Which is why I didn't have to fire him for the banana tree extortion.

All right, fuck this. I grab the machete from Flaco and hurdle the fence like that shitball motherfucker O.J. Simpson from his old Hertz commercials. In about 2.3 seconds banana tree leaves and debris are flying like when Johnny Depp was sculpting hedges in *Edward Scissorhands*, not to mix popular culture allusions too much.

Although trespassing – let alone hacking away at someone's vegetation – is a serious crime in this country, neither the wife nor her three sons say a word as their banana trees topple. Maybe it's the look in my eye.

This was my day a couple of days ago when Lisa went to Golfito and wasn't here as my buffer. Something I'm just remembering now, as I write: Lisa got back really late from Golfito after not getting much done, which worried me. But I put the worry out of my mind (so to speak) then, and I will do so again now.

The above is the small stuff in the recent one-goddamn-thing-after-another arena. The stuff that is not small stuff – no matter the title of dumb-ass-former-best-selling self-help books – has to do with Logan the Nutcase.

Once again the old *I have good news and I have bad news* bit comes to mind. The good news/bad news is supporting evidence of a provisional theory of mine:

In my narratives as opposed to my life, everything works out for the best.

So the news is good news for this narrative, bad news for my life. To put it another way, in case you're not getting the drift: The news is good for you, meaning as a reader, bad for me, meaning as a person. The me-as-a-writer is somewhere in the middle on this good news/bad news issue, hovering in some sort of twilight zone, since although me-as-a-writer loves good news for this narrative, me-as-writer and me-as-person are very close; we're tight. Hence the me-as-a-writer has mixed feelings regarding the news.

Usually when someone says they have good news and bad news, they ask, "Which do you want to hear first, the good news or the bad news?" Here it doesn't matter, since the good news and the bad news are one and the same. The status of the news, whether it be good or bad, depends on the point of view taken, as above.

Here we go with the good news/bad news: Logan the Nutcase is possibly considering hiring someone to murder me, if he hasn't already done so.

This is good news for this narrative in that the essence of all stories, no matter the genre or medium, is... what?

The answer – which I've mentioned in the context of screenwriting (the meeting with Sean Penn et al at the Four Seasons in L.A.) but applies in any sort of storytelling – is *conflict*. Not only that, but as a story moves along you gotta… what? What do you gotta do?

Escalate the conflict.

If you don't escalate the conflict the story peters out; you lose momentum. Big Mo.* I mean how would it work if I told you Logan the Nutcase has maybe hired someone to murder me, then later informed you that he sent a couple cops up to my property to hassle me about a permit for the construction of my caretaker's little house? (I have told you the latter via my letter to the U.S. Consul.) Coming after the murder-for-hire bulletin, it'd be, Oh-hum, who cares, right? You might actually yawn while reading. Or, worse, you might get aggravated and *stop* reading, even permanently – God forbid – which is my worst nightmare, aside from being in love with someone who is *dishonest*.

It occurs to me that my provisional theory that *In my narratives as opposed to my life, everything works out for the best* is likely to break down at some point. For example, say the conflict keeps escalating until Logan the Nutcase does in fact have me murdered. Be dramatic, no? But then what are we left with? Not much, I would submit. The narrative would peter out *toute de suite.* Hey, talk about the *I can't put everything in this fucking narrative* excuse. You know, since I'd be too dead to write about it. We'd lose Big Mo (both kinds, actually) in a big way.

Your response might be that I therefore better murder Logan the Nutcase before he murders me. That'd be cool. I mean narratively. And assuming you're on my side in all this.

Here's the problem with that story turn: This stuff is really happening, pretty much. In other words, this book is *nonfiction*, whatever that means. Are you keeping this in mind? Or are you reading along like this was another… I gotta say it… John Grisham or Dan Brown yarn? You know, something *made up*, a fabrication, and one with crummy sentences to boot.

So I murder Logan the Nutcase, or have him murdered, you think I'm going to tell you about it? Right: Another catch-22, like the *No one who wants to make a movie out of my book is smart enough to get it done* one.

To sum up: Assuming the conflict keeps escalating – which it must if this is to be a well-wrought narrative – what happens? He murders me – boom! – you don't hear about it. Or I murder him – boom! – and likewise you don't hear about it.

I can't win. You can't win.

We're on thin ice here, no?

But let's press on anyway, you and me.

---

* There are two kinds of Big Mo: Writer Big Mo, which refers to the writer's word output as he writes, and Reader Big Mo, which is what keeps the reader reading the stuff the writer wrote. It's my theory that the two types of Big Mo are unrelated. In other words, the writer can have all kinds of Big Mo while he's writing, while the reader – later of course – might not give a shit about what the writer wrote, due to a dearth of Reader Big Mo.

CHAPTER THIRTEEN

How often have I said to you that when you have eliminated the impossible, whatever remains, however improbable, *must be the truth?*

Sir Arthur Conan Doyle

Here's how I found out that Logan the Nutcase is possibly considering hiring someone to murder me, if he hasn't already done so.

Yesterday morning – also while wallowing on the bed in my after-writing throes, come to think of it – I heard either an ATV or a motorcycle roaring up our dirt road from the main dirt road down below. I sensed it stopping at our gate. The dogs went nuts, ran out to the gate barking and snarling, then quieted right down. From this I deduced it was Clay out there. Clay has an ATV. Clay is a dog person and our dogs know and like him. Which is why they quieted down.

Lisa comes into the bedroom and asks if she should get rid of Clay, tell him I'm sick with *la grippe*, our M.O. when I'm in one of my agoraphobic states, due to after-writing throes or if my bad chemicals are particularly active.

I tell Lisa no, I'll handle it, even though I'd rather be left alone to wallow. One reason I decide to handle Clay is that I like the guy, with reservations. Another is that he knows a lot of stuff about Logan the Nutcase and I'm figuring to subtly grill him.

Clay. Background. Clay has been here at Pavones for many years, longer than almost any of the local expats, as he himself will tell you, whether you want to hear it or not. For Clay, how long an expat has been here is a major issue. The longer you've been here, the cooler you are; a oneupmanship* device. Gives you all sorts of privileges and a priori dispensations, especially in the surf lineup – who gets first choice of waves and so forth. (Clay has a

---

* Having no idea how to write this word (I thought maybe there were dashes and/or spaces somewhere), I referred to *Webster's New Universal Unabridged Dictionary*. NOT FUCKING THERE. Oneupmanship, with or without dashes and/or spaces, is definitely a word, no? So where is it? One more incident like this – a word that should be in *Webster's New Universal Unabridged Dictionary* but isn't – I'm going to defenestrate the fucking thing.

convoluted mathematical formula meant to define how long an expat has actually *been here*. It's based not only on your original arrival date, but on the number of times you've been back to the States [or wherever] during your expat residence, and how long you stayed away before your return. Too many Stateside trips or too long a stay during one of those trips and you're back to square one – you're a new guy all over again, meaning you lose your privileges and a priori dispensations. If there's any doubt in a one-to-one confrontation over this issue, the tiebreaker is this: If you don't have a return ticket to the States and the other guy does, you get the nod. If you both have return tickets, you get the nod if your ticket originates here and the other guy's originates Stateside. All else being equal in the tiebreaker, an ad hoc panel is formed to judge who tears it up better in the surf. The panel usually consists of one – Clay himself. With predictable tiebreaker results, when Clay is one of the disputees, which he invariably is.)

Clay is an ex-pro surfer, getting older now, late forties, but he still tears it up out there. This is another source of pride for him, of one-upmanship,[*] and which I buy more readily than his who's-been-here-longer routine. The latter can get tiresome, although I understand and identify with Clay's underlying motives, which are no doubt related to self-image, to his wanting to feel better about himself. I mean look at the convoluted lengths *I* go to – Amazon.com sales ranking and how many little yellow stars my books rate and so forth – to feel better about *myself*. Who am I to judge Clay on this one?

Clay drinks a lot and does various drugs, but mostly he drinks. And when he does so, he'll talk; he'll go on and on. My idea that morning when Clay roared up on his ATV was to exploit all of the aforementioned Clay-traits so he'd spill some beans about Logan the Nutcase – Clay also prides himself on knowing everyone's business. First I'd ask him if he wanted a cup of coffee, knowing he'd insist I spike it with a big dollop of rum. The rum and caffeine would loosen his tongue. Then I'd stroke him about how he's been here longer than almost anyone (as a Meanwhile, I'd mention how he still tears it up in the surf). I'd work in Logan the Nutcase in the who's-been-here-longer context. Since the two of them arrived here at about the same time (going on 15 years ago), this sore point would produce a measure of hostility towards, and disdain for, Logan the Nutcase, a Clay-condition I knew would be ripe for bean spillage.

All this took time and patience and a lot of rum-spiked coffee; I almost failed in my mission anyway. A couple hours after his arrival, Clay was back out at the gate, unsteadily mounting his ATV, having revealed nothing

---

[*] I finally figured out that it's spelled *one-upmanship* via my Word Spell Check by trying all the variations until there was no wavy red line under it.

about Logan I didn't already know. Then almost as an afterthought, Clay said this, regarding my conflict with Logan, which Clay already knew about: "Careful with the fucker. He tried to put a hit on Billy Clayton."

This perked my sorry ass up, but knowing how to handle Clay, I affected disdain. "Yeah, right," I said. "Who told you *that* piece of bullshit?"

"Nobody *told me*, dude," Clay retorted. "I was there when the deal almost went down." I use quotes here because those were Clay's exact words. I'll give you the rest mostly as description, for the sake of brevity and clarity – Clay continued to ramble all over the place.

First, a bit more backstory. Throughout most of the decade of the 1990s and right up until last year, Logan was embroiled in a land dispute here with an expat named Billy Clayton. Clayton had control of a 14-acre oceanfront parcel known as The Sawmill, the plum of Pavones. Logan was crazed to make The Sawmill parcel a part of his growing empire, which was mostly land formerly owned by Danny Fowlie. (If this name sounds familiar, it was mentioned in my letter to the U.S. Consul, and how Fowlie is the Underground Empire insider and mythical founder of Pavones, now in prison in the United States.)

But nothing worked. Copious bribes to high officials in Golfito, harassment by the local and federal police, threats and intimidation, you name it, Logan tried it. Clayton hung in there, kept control of the parcel. Logan was obsessed with The Sawmill property. Picture a two-bit Hitler unable to get his hands on the Sudetenland.

Then, in the late 90's, a guy, Ron, blows into town. Ron, like many of the expats who wind up here at Pavones, has "a history." Ron is an ex-mercenary, right out of *Soldier of Fortune* magazine. I mean the real thing, unlike, I'm sure, 90% of the magazine's readership, guys with unresolved dick-size issues or the like. About my age, mid-50s, Ron came to Costa Rica to retire from his former career. Whether he's actively on the run from someone, the law or worse, is unclear. Ron denies it but that of course doesn't mean anything.

According to Clay, in 1999 Logan approached Ron to solve the land dispute by murdering Clayton. A hit for hire. Notwithstanding Ron's theoretical retirement, Ron agreed he'd do the job as long as the money was right. It was here that the deal went sour. Logan would not cough up enough money. The highest he would go was $8,000. Not enough. So that was that.

I believed Clay, for various reasons. The details, the mention of a specific amount of money, the way the subject came up. Although Clay is given to bullshitting at the drop of a sombrero, the story rang true.

You may be wondering something. Why would Ron and Logan conspire to kill someone in front of a third party – Clay? Conspiring to commit murder is illegal, even here at the end of the road at the bottom of Central America. The last thing you need is a potential witness listening in. A good question, no? Well, it's actually not a good question.

Rather than explaining why this is actually not a good question, I'll give you an explanatory example. Recently a friend of mine, Kim – I do have friends here – had his home invaded by thieves who assaulted Kim's son. The head thief was caught but by immigration, not the police; he was a Panamanian illegally in the country. Immigration was holding him temporarily; they were merely going to deport him, not knowing he was wanted for the home invasion and assault. When Kim contacted the police saying that they could find and arrest the head thief over at immigration, the police told him that the paperwork was too much of a hassle, and why didn't Kim just kill the head thief? They even supplied Kim with the head thief's home address. Point being: In an environment like this, who cares who's listening in while you're conspiring to commit murder?

Although I believed Clay's story, I wanted to confirm it via another source before making an actual move based on the story, whatever that move might be. The only other person who could confirm the story – aside from Logan – was Ron himself. I was optimistic about getting confirmation from Ron, since he and I had previously bonded based on an unfortunate circumstance in Ron's life.

Ron arrived in Costa Rica with a briefcase full of cash, some $250,000, which, if properly invested, would provide him with income to live out his days. But Ron made a mistake here, a doozey. He invested the whole bundle with a San José outfit that paid 3% per month on money you gave them. If this sounds fishy – 15 times normal bank interest – it of course was, although the company had been in business for some 20 years and boasted it had never missed an interest payment to any of its investors in all that time. This may have been true but the shit was about to hit the fan big-time, thanks to the shitball motherfucker who wasn't elected president of the United States. And I'll tell you what: I saw this coming and warned my friends who had invested with this outfit to withdraw their money and run for the hills.

Bush, aside from making a mockery of the U.S. Constitution's Bill of Rights with his 1984-esque Patriot Act, decided to fuck with other countries' internal affairs as well. (Christ, what an understatement.) He bullied Costa Rica into shutting down the aforementioned investment outfit, using the rationale that maybe they were supplying money to terrorists. So Ron, along with hundreds of other retired expats living in Costa Rica, lost not only his income but his principal as well in the resulting fiasco. Ron lost everything.

Ron, mid-50s and having already been through some shit in his life, found himself destitute in a foreign country, a Third World one at that. Here's where our bonding comes in. This was about a year ago, in late 2002.

One day after Ron lost everything I was on my way home from a surf session and spotted Ron walking along the dirt road out of here with a cloth sack over his shoulder. I'd heard he was leaving to look for work up north. By God, he was a sad sight. He'd sold everything he had for eating money, even his knapsack; hence the cloth sack, in which were all his remaining earthly possessions.

I drove on by him, waving weakly – we were merely acquaintances at the time – then a hundred or so yards further on I stopped the car and thought about things. Among the things I thought about was something to the effect of *there but for the grace of God go I.*

When Ron caught up to me I called him over. Said I was sorry to hear about his troubles. I handed him 10,000 colones (about $25), which was all I had on me. For a long moment neither of us said anything as Ron stood by my car window and we looked at each other. There was something about the situation – the dusty dirt road so far from our common country of origin, Ron's sad cloth sack, our similar histories as outlaws, my monetary gesture – that affected us both, deeply. I wanted to say something else but the truth is I got choked up. Ron did too. I saw it.

So Ron left to look for work. This was months ago. I hadn't seen him nor heard word of him since. Listen: the very day of the scene with Clay – and with me needing confirmation of Clay's story – Ron showed up again. I ran into him at the cantina, like an hour after the scene with Clay. If this story were fiction, if I were *making it up,* rather than whatever it is and whatever I'm doing, I would never write it this way, with a coincidence like Ron showing up at the moment I needed him. But there you have it.

At our reunion at the cantina Ron wanted to talk about that moment we shared on the road. It had been on his mind constantly since he left, he said. He told me that that moment helped him get through the toughest time of his life. He couldn't explain it, he said. That was all right. I knew what he meant.

Ron and I had a beer, then I put my cards on the cantina bar, told him of my conflict with Logan. Then, without mentioning Clay, I said I heard Logan had offered Ron money to kill Billy Clayton. I asked him if he would confirm that. Without hesitation, Ron confirmed everything; he even offered that Clay had been there for the meeting. There was one difference, though, and it didn't surprise me. Ron said his turning down the hit hadn't been a question of money, of the $8,000 not being enough. Ron said he just didn't like Logan, didn't want anything to do with him, or with killing someone Logan didn't like. He used the money issue as a way to refuse the job.

"The fucker is evil," is how Ron summed up his view of Logan. Keep in mind that Ron has seen some shit in his life; he's seen his share of bad people.

Is it enough that Logan conspired to put a hit on someone else for me to believe he'll do the same to me? Let's keep in mind a few other things. During my Max Dalton investigation in 1998, Logan issued a death threat towards me (recounted in my letter to the U.S. consul). And at that time I had no direct interest in his affairs. I was merely digging around on the Dalton killing and the land conflict here that led to it. While it's true that I peripherally uncovered some minor shit about Logan, there was little reason for him to feel threatened. Yet, to quote my source at the time, "Derek Logan wants you dead."

A related matter. When I cornered Logan in his garage and told him *if lightning strikes my house* and so forth, I also told him that it was a mistake for a guy like him to threaten a *writer*. I said it like that, with emphasis. I also told him that the Costa Rican legislature was looking into his relationship with Danny Fowlie. This news visibly alarmed Logan, and with good reason. Fowlie was currently doing a long stretch on the RICO Act (conducting a continuing criminal enterprise); the same statute they use to put away mafia dons. Although there will be more on Fowlie to come, suffice to say that I already possessed – via my Max Dalton murder investigation – a lot of damaging information on Logan's relationship with Fowlie, information Logan desperately wanted kept hidden. (As it was, just recently Logan had adamantly denied to *The Tico Times* knowing Fowlie at all.) I also had spoken with an associate of Logan's who claimed Logan was a cocaine dealer in the States – a bombshell, given Logan's current pose as defender of law and order at Pavones. Further, the fact that I had the information about the Costa Rican legislature and he did not told Logan that I was on his case and had some serious sources of my own.

Whether or not my thinly-veiled threat that I might very well write about him was a mistake on my part is moot; it's a done deal. Point being: it's not merely his well-known paranoia that might force Logan's hand, cause him to do me harm; this narrative itself is proof of that. But is there more going on here than Logan's fear that I'll write about him? My theory is yes, most definitely. I believe Logan sees me as a threat on a deeper level than exposure of his illegal activities: I'm a threat to his self-image. I'm a threat to his *denial*.

In my (first) memoir, *In Search of Captain Zero*, I categorize the types of expats who have come down south, based on their motivation for being here. One such type is the Big Fish in a Little Pond type. I'll quote: "Types who, for psychological (or pathological) reasons have sought a simplified social hierarchy in which they are dominant figures, a status not possible in the more intensely competitive world stateside."

This is Logan the Nutcase to a T. This little piece of paradise is just what the doctor ordered for a Big Fish in a Little Pond type. The lack of any real rule of law, for example: into this vacuum, Logan has inserted himself; in his view, he *is* the law here.* By confronting him on his own property and issuing threats, I *challenged his authority*, his dominion, meanwhile exposing his cowardice – he reacted fearfully rather than returning my aggression.

There is nothing, no one, as dangerous as a coward exposed, not when he has the wherewithal to exact retribution without putting himself at personal risk. Plus I surf better than he does. Don't laugh; this is also a possible factor, in terms of the threat I pose to Logan's view of himself. Why? Because surfing is what Pavones is all about. It's why we're all here, even Logan. I surf rings around the asshole.

In my letter to the U.S. Consul I describe my original confrontation with Logan in the surf lineup. I left something out, assuming it would be incomprehensible to the Consul; I trust that, my having the time here to explain, you'll get it. When Logan paddled over and told me that he didn't like my website, I responded that I didn't care what he thought of my website. To which he replied that he doesn't mind me surfing here, but…

But hold on.

He doesn't *mind* me surfing here?

Here's what that's like: Picture you're a homesteader, a farmer, in the old west. You've given up your life back East to move to an unspoiled environment far from civilization in which to live in peace with your family. Farming is your life. One day a guy rides up, the owner of the vast tract of land surrounding your little homestead. Behind him ride the sheriff and his deputies, who are obviously in his employ, and who are the only law for a hundred miles. This guy sits his horse, scanning your little piece of property, the crops you've planted. Then he says this:

I don't *mind* you farming here, but…

Right. That guy is eventually going to try to run you out of town, or, failing that, try to kill you. Guaran-fucking-teed. *Shane*-like, the conflict is going to escalate.

I will not be run out of town.

---

* There are so many examples of Logan considering himself the law here that it's dispiriting to even begin to make a list, so I won't. The incident wherein he set up my friend Mountain Mike on a bogus drug bust is just the tip of the iceberg.

It's late afternoon now. Having weathered the after-writing throes following today's work, I returned here to the office to finish this chapter, which will be followed by a Part break, which will then be followed by my Max Dalton Investigation from 1998, resurrected here to give you the background of certain conflicts and fiascos that continue on to this day at Big Turkeys; in the process, you may figure out a few things about me. Deep character. Or lack thereof. We'll see.

I'm tired. I'm so tired that my bad chemicals are a non-issue. It's as if my blood-pumping apparatus is too all-in to hoist them against gravity up to my cranial area, where they do their best work.

I'm going to write just one more sentence today after this paragraph then go downstairs and open a bottle of Chilean red wine and sit with Lisa out on the porch after the dogs are fed and watch the sun go down over The Sweet Gulf while the howler monkeys bellow in the bush out back. Here's the sentence, the last one I'll write today:

Although I hide it from Lisa as best I can, I have this sense of impending doom.

But I will press on.

Okay, two sentences, not one. Three now. No, four.

And so forth.

PART THREE
The Max Dalton
Murder Investigation*

---

* Written in the spring of 1998 for *Men's Journal*, this is the long version, which I intended to expand into a book.

BACKSTORY

Back in 1974 Danny Fowlie had it all. Well, almost. Danny was a very wealthy man, a spectacularly successful *contrabandista*, his specialty being multi-ton loads of marijuana driven, flown or boated north from Mexico, plus freighters-full of Thai sticks. Aside from his flotilla of yachts and miscreant-manned fishing boats, his private aircraft, innumerable big-boy toys and trinkets, personal extravagances and priceless artifacts from primitive cultures worldwide, he owned, or would soon own, a multimillion dollar farm in Riverside, California, a ranch in Baja, Mexico, plus fugitive financier Robert Vesco's splendiferous, heavily-fortified compound in San José, Costa Rica; and Danny, toting a suitcaseful of *gringo* green, was poised to possess the one thing he did not have, but wanted most – his own private piece of paradise, a far-flung Shangri-La which he would benignly rule, and share with his entourage of spooky hipster-savant cronies and hangers-on, plus assorted living legends of the surfing subculture.

Apocryphal or not, my favorite discovery story (there are a few) goes as follows: One day, while on a scouting mission by air out of the old Costa Rican banana port of Golfito, Danny overflew a remote tract of land at the mouth of El Golfo Dulce in far southern Costa Rica near the political technicality of the Panamanian frontier. Unreachable except by boat or horseback along the unsullied, palm-girded beach, the tableau below him appeared to be exactly what he was looking for. Riffling, clear water rivers snaked down from the high reaches of the inland rainforest (wherein still lived stone age aboriginals) onto a fecund littoral plain that would be ideal for the growing of food crops and the grazing of livestock. The inshore waters, Danny knew, given the coast's isolated location at the mouth of the broad, unpolluted "Sweet Gulf", would be teeming with fish.

But there was something else down below along that shoreline that day and it riveted Danny's attention and no doubt made him blink in disbelief, heart racing. He no doubt told his pilot to circle back and descend for a closer look. And it would be hard to imagine Danny not – at some point as he stared wild-eyed out the side window of his plane, nose pressed against the glass – hooting in unbridled glee as the implications of what he saw settled in.

The wave Danny discovered that day would become legend in the surfing world; a wave that wrapped along the shore from the jagged, rocky point at the mouth of El Rio Claro in the province known as Pavones then peeled endlessly into the bay, a rocket left slide ride-able for nearly *one mile* on good days.

Danny Fowlie did not do anything in a small manner. Using the official and clandestine sources he'd cultivated, he bought the whole shebang, over 6,000 acres, including much of 12 miles of stunning beach front. By barge and tugboat Danny hauled in heavy equipment, building materials and generators, along with foodstuffs to sustain his crew of Costa Rican laborers and imported agronomists, veterinarians, oceanographers and engineers, until the farms and fishing boats he envisioned could start producing and make the community he foresaw self-sustaining. Danny cut roads, at first only within his kingdom, demurring on the idea of a direct connection with the outside world; bridges soon spanned the plethora of rivers and streams descending from the inland rainforest; the deep seaside bush was cleared for a private airstrip; schools and churches were built; farms sprang up, overseen by experts in soil and crop management. Danny built what he dubbed The Clubhouse on the property known as The Sawmill, a three-story manse a couple of kilometers down the coast from The Point, and which overlooked its own perfect wave.

And another thing Danny built was the cantina, a private watering hole overlooking the point wave at Rio Claro, where he could kick back with his surf buddies and Underground Empire sidekicks and exult in what he had created.

Yes, Danny, build it, build Dannyland… and they will come.

"You gotta picture what it was like back in the beginning," my Long Island surfbuddy Dave Ferraro told me. Dave and his brother Ben had come to Pavones in the late 1970s, at the beginning of the Fowlie era.

"We'd sit in the cantina after riding these perfect waves on this wild, stunning piece of coast," Dave went on, grabbing my arm, so jazzed at the memory, "and here comes a couple of Danny's vaqueros on horseback, they'd ride right up to the bar and order a brew, a cold one if the generator was working. Wide-brimmed straw sombreros, lariats, six shooters, bandoleers stuffed with bullets... picture it! I mean it was the frontier, man, almost inaccessible, an adventure just getting there... with no authorities... you could do what you wanted. My friend, your imagination could go wild in a place like that..."

And all was well in Dannyland in those early years, indeed, for a full decade, until 1985, when *el excremento* hit *el ventilador* with a vengence, and the imaginations of a lot of people went wild. And a lot of people did what they wanted.

FLASHPOINTS

1985, Pavones, Costa Rica. Danny Fowlie becomes a fugitive from United States justice, having been hounded by U.S. law enforcement agencies for years.

1985 is also the year the United Fruit Company pulls out of nearby Golfito when demands of the Cuban and Eastern Block-backed communist labor movement makes continued business untenable. With thousands of jobs lost in the area, the local communists need another focus for their agitation, and to give their idle campesino minions something to do. And by what must have appeared as a miraculous coincidence, that focus suddenly lay waiting just a few miles to the south at Pavones where, due to the influx of surfers, real estate values are skyrocketing. With *el dueño* himself, Grandee Danny, on the run in Mexico, communist organizers calculate that Dannyland is up for grabs: Over the Easter holiday known as Semana Santa, several hundred squatters are bused and trucked to Pavones in a large scale, unlawful invasion of the area. The Costa Rican government, fearing political fallout from the left, does nothing.

The squatter wars have begun.

April, 1985, Pavones. Former Nixon financial advisor and current Fowlie lieutenant Norman Leblanc orchestrates a mass *desolojo* (eviction) of that first mammoth wave of communist-organized squatters. Within weeks the squatters are back in full force. The Costa Rican government does nothing.

October, 1988, Pavones. The Sawmill property – Dannyland's most valuable beachfront parcel – is overrun and taken by armed squatters. Four buildings are burned to the ground, including the Sawmill itself, which smolders for weeks. A protracted gun battle ensues, the invaders failing to take the adjoining property, which is defended by Costa Rican Carlos Lobo and *norte* Owen Handy.

April, 1991, Pavones. As part of a mob advancing on *norte* surfer Peter Noeldecken's property adjacent to The Point, campesino Hugo Vargas is mortally wounded by Noeldecken's caretaker. In retaliation, three *norte* houses are burned down and the cantina is surrounded by an enraged throng, waving machetes and calling for blood.

Also in 1991, 72-year old American expatriate rancher Max Dalton buys an oceanfront parcel of heavily-squatted Dannyland some five miles north of the cantina. Max's personal war with the squatters has begun.

November, 1992, Golfito, Costa Rica. The Golfito Municipal Building is overrun and occupied for four days by a gang of squatters who are unhappy with the Municipality's handling of the Pavones land dispute. The San José government, still fearing political fallout, does nothing about the armed takeover of a government agency.

November 13th, 1997, Pavones. Max Dalton is mortally wounded in a wild west style shootout while trying to round up squatter cattle that had trespassed onto his pastureland. A squatter leader is briefly detained for questioning then released.

November 20, 1997, Washington, DC. Senate Foreign Relations Committee Chairman Jesse Helms issues a strongly worded letter to Costa Rican president José Figueres, demanding a full investigation of the Max Dalton killing. The OIJ (Costa Rica's equivalent to the FBI) report on the incident smacks of a cover up.

Novemebr 26, 1997, Washington, DC. The State Department issues a travel advisory, warning U.S. citizens to avoid the Pavones area, due to "roving bands of squatters... acting with impunity," and cautioning further that evacuation of the area may be necessary if Costa Rican authorities continue to ignore the problem.

December 15, 1997, Pavones. American landowner James Pospychala, along with a cadre of local police sent to protect him, is driven from his property by a stone throwing, machete brandishing mob of squatters. A few days later his house is burned to the ground.

January 12, 1998, Washington, DC. Senator Jesse Helms urges the Inter-American Development Bank (IDB) to hold back on a proposed $70 million loan to Costa Rica, until "concrete progress" is made in resolving the Max Dalton case and the land conflict in Pavones.

A NIGHT AT THE CANTINA

January 21, 1998

"All our lives are in danger," the basso *gringo* voice says when Billy Clayton hands me the cell phone at the cantina bar at some point between dinner and my third Pilsen. Billy wishes me happy birthday and sets me up with a rum shooter on the house, but I'm too distracted by the bizarre phone greeting to thank him.

"Who is this?" I inquire.

"I'd rather not say," the phone voice says.

"Where are you?"

"Nearby... but not... too near."

"How did you get this number?"

"The embassy."

There being no land line to Pavones, I left the cantina cell number with the embassy people up in San José in case... just in case.

"What do you mean `our lives are in danger'?" I want to know. Then, recalling that this bulletin is pretty much old news: "I mean, specifically?"

"Listen..." the lowered voice says, *basso* verging on *profundo* now. "If you want the real story about what happened to Max Dalton... follow the money."

Wait a minute, I'm thinking. I've heard this dialog before... while munching popcorn in a multiplex somewhere. I suppress a giggle. I mean, come on.

"Five point two million dollars from Union Europa for the southern zone."

"Huh?" Follow the money.

"At least a million dollars to Gerardo Mora and his precarista movement." Mora is the local squatter – *precarista* – leader who was present at the shootout that killed Max and Alvaro Aguilar, and who was briefly detained as a suspect in the crime.

"Look," I say, still racking my brain for the name of the goddamn movie.

"Why don't we get together sometime?" But the line has gone dead.

Billy Clayton is leaning over the radio by the register, trying to catch the news from San José maybe; I can hear staticy Spanish over the bar noise. A stateside story broke today, I hear. Bill Clinton in hot water again, something about some salacious doings with a White House intern. Maybe Clayton cares, but I have my own intrigues to deal with here and now, plus this 21st day of January, 1998, is my goddamn Big Five-Oh, a potentially stress-producing benchmark, especially for someone whose life is... well, is what it is. And this week-long flat spell – a result of some mid summer doldrums in the Southern Ocean – isn't helping.

The phone call.

My thought is that the call was a prank. The fact that I'm investigating the killing of Max Dalton for *Men's Journal* magazine is common knowledge in this remote little gobbet of paradise, and although all the *norte* expatriate residents knew and liked Max, a certain blackly comic slant prevails, and naturally so; it helps take the edge off the chronic uncertainty of the *precarista* situation. Plus that deep, gravelly voice could've been disguised... plus the goofball movie allusion...

All the President's Men. Right.

The question is, which one of my motley crew of compadres slunk off to make the call?

I scan the cantina to see who's missing from my birthday festivities. Clay has a cell phone up at his Punta Banco hideaway and is something of a demented jokester, but he's currently two barstools down in besotted conversation with Mountain Mike. The two are reminiscing about Clay's terciopela encounter a couple of years ago in the bush at Altamira. I've heard the story before. Clay's leg had turned plum-purple right up to his groin from the snake's bite, and Mountain Mike, with input from an Indian *bruja*, had concocted a tea from roots and tree bark that counteracted the venom. Still, Clay had spent three days in a hutch in the hills, racked by convulsions, while *la bruja* tended him.

No, wasn't Clay.

Alex? Alex hasn't moved from his usual corner stool, nor has he apparently missed a beat in his rap about the seraphic inter-dimensional beings he occasionally converses with, especially after a rip-roaring surf session has sufficiently heightened his metaphysical percipience. According to Alex's cosmology, flitting around the earthly firmament are vibrational traces of the consciousness of past dwellers of any given space, and these "mindbits of bros past" will interact with the inter-dimensional beings, as well as with the consciousnesses of current space-dwellers. Something like that.

Tonight the unlikely victim of Alex's ramblings is Carlos Lobo, Danny Fowlie's former right hand man from back in the day, variously described as a "one man army", "crazier than a drunk Hawaiian", "a sufferer of Post Traumatic Stress Disorder" (from the year he spent holed up in his house, defending it against continuous *precarista* snipering, drive-by shootings, bomb-throwings and ground assaults), and – by my buddies, Erik and Joachim – as "the straightest, most loyal man in Pavones."

Carlos? Carlos speaks not a word of English. No, wasn't Carlos.

Erik and Joachim? The caller had mentioned the embassy as the source of the cantina phone number. Erik and Joachim know about my embassy visit, my intelligence sharing with the State Department, but they're here also; I've just had dinner with them. Who else knows about my embassy visit? No one. No one I know of.

Whoever made the call knows.

How about Logan, Derek Logan, locally known as "the fool on the hill" (for the elevated location of his command post/domicile) or, simply, "the nutcase," who has already made it known that my meddling presence in *his* bailiwick pleases him not a bit? Logan never, ever, sets foot in the cantina. Billy Clayton's cantina.

Shit.

I hope it wasn't Logan.

Now I'm thinking the call was probably not a prank... I'm thinking that the Union Europa tidbit was too out of left field for the conversation not to have been the real thing... Union Europa. Some sort of international banking crew. Follow the money...

Gerardo Mora. The voice had mentioned Mora as the beneficiary of Union Europa's munificence. Nobody around here jokes about Gerardo Mora.

No, definitely not a prank. But it still could've been someone I know, a Pavones *norte* who somehow found out about my embassy visit and wanted me to have the information... but did not want to involve himself in the Dalton matter, probably out of fear of retribution from Mora.

Erik and Joachim have warned me about what might happen if Mora learns how much I've uncovered about the day Max took a bullet in his chest. Further cautioned that if Mora and his men come for me, it will be from the river side of my house (which is primitive and except for the *bodega*, or strong room, cannot be locked). Suggested that I sleep in my camper, which is parked in the yard, because these men most likely won't think of that, and that I should keep the Browning 9mm Erik lent me within reach at all times.

And of all the players actively involved in the land conflict in Pavones, it's Erik and Joachim – with their dead of night retaliations against the most militant of the squatters during the two-year period in the mid-90s when the land war here last reached flash point – that I should listen to in matters of personal safety.

Erik and Joachim: the two in camo and blackface roaring down the rutted dirt track between Pavones and Pilon in their stripped vintage Land Cruiser, quivered-out surf racks tagging them as warrior/waveriders, on moonless nights their headlights and million-candlepower spot the only illumination for 20 ks on this wild, lawless coast (no electricity back then). The two scanning the dense, ink black bush of potential fields of fire, popping off rounds from their AK and sawed off twelve to let the Down South world know that of the remaining *norte* landowners who hadn't been driven off by *precarista* intimidation and outright violence, there were a couple left who were out there ready to rock and roll, maybe kick some ass of their own.

Surely, these guys know whereof they speak. So I have taken certain precautions, although I still sleep in my upstairs sanctum overlooking El Rio Claro.

Billy Clayton sets up fresh Pilsens as Alex sidles over, wishing me a "Happy birthday, dude." I hand the phone back to Billy, who has abandoned the radio and is now eyeing me as if to ask who the caller was. Had he not been the one who handed me the phone in the first place, Billy would have been my first choice as to the caller's identity. With the possible exception of Erik and Joachim (hard to say one name without the other – a Rosencrantz & Gildenstern kind of thing), he is the most knowledgeable of the resident *nortes* regarding the various intrigues of the land conflict here, albeit the most skittish.

Billy's problems started on the morning of September 16, 1991, when Costa Rican Hugo Vargas was gunned down, the first death in the squatter wars. A fired up mob had stormed a *norte* surfer's oceanfront property just south of El Rio Claro and the panic-stricken caretaker had opened fire with a buckshot-loaded scattergun. Vargas had been killed on the spot, another campesino severely wounded, gut shot. Billy had run the gauntlet of enraged squatters in his van to rescue the caretaker and his family; then, that night, after the cantina had been surrounded by a machete-brandishing mob, Clayton fled Pavones, hiding under a tarp in the back of a truck. He would not be able to return for a year.

"Look, we'd all been warned that a gringo was gonna get bush-whacked," Billy told me a couple weeks ago over a Pilsen at the cantina, after claiming the Dalton killing was a setup. "It was just a matter of who. There was a hit list... Max was on it... I was on it."

"Who warned you?" I'd wanted to know, but Billy stood up suddenly and turned seaward, shaking his head as if he'd already said too much. The wave in front of the cantina that day was shoulder high and Billy and I watched a hot local kid named Meco rocket by as a distant thunderhead morphed surreal and vaguely angry, spouting veined lightning in the liquid gold over the distant Osa Peninsula.

"On a certain level..." Billy muttered, and I was not sure whether he was addressing me or simply having a thought that had inadvertently found voice. "...it was the wave here that killed Max."

So true. Without that miracle of a wave roaring in from the southern latitudes, none of this would be here, not the settlement, the farms, the fish camp, the school, the churches, the roads and bridges (such as they are), the cantina itself. Nor the people, the expat *nortes* who have settled here looking for their own little piece of paradise. And nor would the squatters, the *precaristas*, be here, looking to take it from them.

And, certainly, absent that wave nor would I be here, contentedly settled in after well over a year of wandering the coast between Tijuana and the Panamanian frontier.

"Don't worry about it, bro. Probably just another harmless whacko," Alex says after I run down the basics of the clandestine phone call, although I omitted the vital detail of the caller's mention of the embassy. "We got our share of whackos around here."

I have to smile at that. Much as I like the guy, Alex himself has been known to evidence some peculiar thought processes, even aside from his goofball cosmology. He'll expound at length on his deep involvement in the postmodern peace and brotherly love movement, then, with nary a connective, suddenly be discoursing on the merits of the Chinese version of the AK-47 assault rifle and the design subtleties that make it less likely jam up in adverse bush conditions on full automatic, while the inferior Czech model will likely fail. That, or the artistry involved in constructing a pipe bomb with a uni-directional blast locus, and how to position the device to blow a big enough hole in an inch-thick bank vault to reach through to grab the goodies.

All this while looking like a fugitive from the rock band Kiss. Alex is in fact not a *gringo*, but a Mexican national, although his English is flawless. A former Tijuana gangbanger, Alex escaped the perils of that dead end through the surfing life; he ducked south to Pavones some five years ago, toting a hollowed out surfboard packed with cash to buy land with and an assortment of weaponry with which to defend that land.

When I pointed out the possible inconsistency implied in his commitment to pacifism while simultaneously surrounding himself with the tools of warfare, Alex frowned at my failure to see the larger picture. "We *are* all bros, bro," he replied, "but if a bro fucks with you, you got to be ready to wax his gnarly ass, post haste."

The cantina is starting to cook as representatives of the various Pavones factions materialize from the surrounding bush and attach themselves to cerveza bottles and plastic cup rum shooters. Wenste and his cabal of *precas*-at-the-point are outside by the seawall, Wenste looking as mean-drunk as usual under his straw sombrero; he's probably packing weaponry under his tattered *guayabera*. Luis, another squatter, albeit of considerably mellower disposition than Wenste, and a buddy of mine – he's nicknamed me Malo, Bad, which I admit I kind of like – wishes me *feliz cumpleanos* and insists on buying me another Pilsen, although by now I've made the move to cane juice.

El Gitano (the Gypsy) is cross-eyed drunk and running amok at the bar with the money I gave him this morning. A.k.a. El Brujo (The Sorcercer), Mal Ojo (Evil Eye), El Gitano is a binge-type alcoholic, self-professed dabbler in the occult and accused child molester. I've hired him as my link to the *precarista* movement. Everyone, *nortes* and Ticos alike, has warned me about him, saying he'll turn on me in a heartbeat. But it was El Gitano's introduction to Gerardo Mora that was my first breakthrough in the Max Dalton investigation. El Gitano, of course, is a *preca* himself.

Maybe half the cantina crowd tonight is of the *preca* persuasion, ranging in mien from mellow to not-so-mellow to outright nasty. Gerardo Mora himself is perhaps conspicuous by his absence: he and his crew keep to their own territory just up the road at Langostino. Nevertheless, the vibrational mix is edgy, with some former and even current enemies occupying adjacent bar stools.

The cantina, being the only watering hole within many miles, is de facto neutral territory; those who enter here have an unspoken agreement to temporarily put aside their quarrels. Still, with the nearest real police presence a good two hours away (if the road in is passable and the bridges intact), the so-far lack of outright bloodshed (fist fights are common) is in my view something of a miracle. I can't help but wonder, however, how Billy Clayton – a human lightning rod in the land conflict here – feels as he serves *malvados* who not so long ago waved machetes in his face and threatened to dice his *gringo* ass into fish chum, and who just might be sitting at the bar, *his* bar, planning his demise.

Alex has wandered off so I return to my table, join Erik and Joachim.

German expat Joachim Gerlach is a former European stunt driver, occasional jewel thief and all-around international scammer whose connections run the gamut from the Israeli Mossad to the most vicious criminal organization on the planet, the Bulgarian mafia. His partner, Erik Reinhold, is a Dutchman who came to Pavones "because of an Arab with a knife..." The story gets better from there, its upshot being that the fellow's knife was no match for Erik's gun.

After spending a year in prison, and seduced by his buddy Joachim's idyllic accolades of the down south surfing life, Erik arrived innocently wide-eyed and ready to unwind in the lineup, but within days found himself armed to the teeth at a dead-of-night bridge blockade, looking to bushwhack the squatters who stole Joachim's $30,000 grubstake.

Having committed themselves to fight the *precas* on their own terms, Erik and Joachim's lives got nothing but crazier from that night on. I've become tight with the pair over the seven months since the battered old rig I call La Casita Viajera first rumbled down the dirt track to road's end, the search for my long-missing old friend, Christopher, a.k.a. Captain Zero, having come to its disorienting denouement. With respect to the Dalton matter, they have in fact become my confidants. Although I have other friends amongst the Pavones expats, it's these guys I trust, and, I believe, vice versa. And trust is everything down here.

I tell the boys about the phone call, the cryptic missive from my down south Deep Throat. Erik, who is the more sanguine of the two, smiles at the spy-vs-spy theatricality of the affair. Joachim does not. "Listen, my friend," he says in his light German accent. "This is a box of snakes you're dealing with."

"The Union Europa connection is interesting," Erik muses, ever more analytical than his volatile partner and brother in arms. "Maybe it's not just the Dutch who are financing Mora." The fact that his countrymen, through their embassy, have been funding the squatter movement is a sore point with Erik, especially since Max's death. He and Joachim were close to Max, had for a time acted as his bodyguards.

"I'll ask Mora about Union Europa," I say. "I have another meeting with him in a couple days." Between his leftist diatribes and mendacious punditry on the history of the Pavones land conflict, Mora has been letting a lot of vital information slip, especially if I'm careful in directing the drift of our talks.

"Listen to me," Joachim says, leaning forward, voice lowered. "You're going to go up to the bush at Langostino one too many times. And it won't be messy, like what they did to Max. It will be just poof! – hey, where's Allan?"

"I don't think they'd actually kill him," Erik opines. Over the past couple of weeks Erik has been vacillating with regard to the degree of possible peril I'm subjecting myself to in my relationship with Gerardo Mora.

The two argue the point in what sounds like a conglomeration of Dutch and German. It gets heated. Finally, I request that they maybe include me in the discussion by reverting to English, since it's the possible future of my ass they're debating. But they simply shut up, Erik sighing, Joachim red-faced.

"If he's careful, he'll be all right," Erik says, blithely sipping his rum and looking around, bored with the conversation now.

"Hey, man. Happy birthday," Joachim says, hoisting his rum.

I return his grin. That's right. The Big Five-Oh.

I look around at the cantina crowd, something out of early Peckinpah as updated by Tarantino. If I'm thinking a candle-festooned cake is about to be wheeled in followed by this lot breaking into the birthday song, well, I've got another think coming. No, Dorothy, you're not in... well, even in Baja anymore.

If Alex's notion that we leave vibrational traces behind us in our earthly travels is correct, surely the cantina – this ramshackle wrinkle in space-time – would be bubbling the ether tonight. Whose phantasmal vibes are even now pulsating through the celebratory continuum of my Big Five-Oh, colliding with those of this oddball mix of multinational vagabonds and terror-bent locals? Who that has come before is now missing?

Max is gone, of course, shot down on his own land that drizzly November day and left to die while a *precarista* mob taunted him.

Gone from paradise.

And how about Owen Handy, the Vietnam vet brought to Pavones in the late 1980s to teach weapons and hand-to-hand combat techniques to those *nortes* who hadn't already been driven off by *preca* violence? Although Handy's courage in battling the most violent of the squatters is undeniable (he'd stood his ground in full-blown firefights in which automatic weapons were used against him), the pressure of living in a guerrilla war environment had eventually driven him over the edge. He'd psychologically survived the trauma of Vietnam but the pressures he had been subjected to in Pavones precipitated a descent into greed and drug addiction.

Gone from paradise.

Or the Right Reverend Loren Pogue, the *gringo* expat whose fiduciary schemes ran the gamut from hilariously in-your-face land swindles to cocaine trafficking to the black-market baby business, and who boozily oversaw his nutso enterprises from his banana port brothel. (His business card proclaimed him the proprietor of a local home for unwed mothers.) Perhaps best known locally for having shot an unarmed *precarista* in 1989, the Reverend is currently serving a 27 year sentence in a stateside prison for... well, you name it.

Likewise gone, gone from paradise.

Or how about Winfred Zigan, who, like some Bob Hope From Hell, would catch and eat assorted cantina bugs (the bigger and crunchier, the creepy-crawlier the better) to entertain the beer-guzzling expat troops on bleak and womanless post-surf session nights? Winfred fled Pavones in 1992, not because he'd recently been shot in the head in a squatter-related tiff (a mere crease of the scalp), but from disgust when completion of the dirt track from Golfito began to afford easier access to Pavones for the multitudes Up North. In Winfred's view, the squatter wars were a minor nuisance. That which, well, bugged him, was his perception that Pavones was getting civilized – notwithstanding the fact that electricity had still not yet arrived at the still barely-accessible end-of-the-road hamlet.

Winfred elected to beat cheeks further south (the natural direction of vanishment), but since the road ends here, his escape was by sea. Rumor has it that he is now the lord and master of his own otherwise uninhabited island somewhere off the coast of Panama, his battlements no doubt directed seaward, protecting the sanctity of his own private perfect wave. (Winfred would approve of the State Department travel advisory urging U.S. citizens to avoid the Pavones area, for how it has kept the surf lineup uncluttered with those uncommitted, here-on-a-two-week-surf-vacation lightweights he so detests.)

No, not gone from paradise. On the contrary, Winfred has only dug in deeper.

How about the itinerant Aussie who was strung up here in the cantina for some now-forgotten, surf-related faux pas back in the early 80s? Bound and gagged, noose tautly rising from his outstretched neck to an overhead rafter, he'd been left teetering on a bar stool while the boys hoisted brews and staggered around, occasionally bumping him to test his balance. He'd eventually been cut down, patted on the behind and informed he could go now.

Definitely gone from paradise is that discourteous Aussie, but what sort of jagged, get-me-the-fuck-out-of-here vibrational traces linger?

Just one more, and I save the best for last.

Long gone from paradise is Danny Fowlie, to his new home stateside at the Terminal Island Federal Penitentiary.

Danny. The Waterman Who Would Be King.

The Investigation

1

Today, March 21, is the equinox of this year, 1998, one of two days (the other being September 21) when the sun "crosses the line" as the nautical expression goes, meaning that at local noon the sun is directly overhead at the equator. (On those two days, a line drawn from the center of the sun will intersect the earth's axis at a right angle.) A result of this fleeting alignment of the sun and earth is that at latitudes far enough from the poles that the sun rises and sets, the day and the night are of equal length for that one rotation of the earth. Near the poles, where the sun stays under the horizon for the equinoctial 24 hours of "day/night" (there being no meaningful distinction), the overall ambient brightness of the sky remains constant while the sun does its 360 degree revolution below the rim of the world. Darkness and light are hence in equilibrium on the equinox, everywhere on earth. It is, in a sense, a day of balance. Of symmetry.

The March equinox is also an important astronomical event to the expatriate surfers of Pavones, as it marks the end of the meteorological doldrums of the austral summer and hence the dearth of groundswell-producing storms between Tierra Del Fuego and New Zealand. Although the December through March season has seen fairly consistent surf, it's been primarily in the shoulder-high class.

The swell this equinoctial morning off the tiny hamlet of Pilon – a six kilometer jounce north of the break in front of the cantina – is clearly on the rise; the healthy multi-wave sets are a solid head high, with occasional boomers half again as big. Sizable though it is, the wave today is even-tempered and forgiving, ideal for my preferred longboard toes-to-the-nose style of wave riding.

As I bob solo in the lineup, there is a geographical perspective at work, another sort of symmetry. Although I cannot see it for the dense copse of palms that lines the most pristine shoreline I've ever come across – not a human soul nor a work of man visible as far as the eye can see – just a few hundred yards to the east is the spot where Max Dalton took a bullet in his chest back in November, then lay gasping and crying out for help for maybe a half hour while the squatter mob which had surrounded him jeered and threatened those few neighbors who would help; and if my coterie of informants is to be believed, Gerardo Mora, with help from his son, Esteban, stuck the butt of a machete down the old man's throat to exacerbate his agony and hasten his demise.

About a mile due north of my location in the lineup of the near-perfect surf I'm riding, in the deep bush beyond the luminous sweep of deserted beach in an area called Langostino, lives Mora himself along with his hellion wife Mayela and their two sons; their isolated thatched hutch is situated on one of the many tracts of land Danny Fowlie bought so many years ago with his ill-gotten gains. Langostino is the stronghold of the most militant of the squatters, Mora their unquestioned master.

The outcome of my three months of digging into the killing of Max Dalton is that I now know most of the truth about what happened that day, November 13, 1997, and why. Although the information I've uncovered was derived from a variety of sources, including documents procured through clandestine and/or illegal means, much of what I've learned resulted from the trust I've gained from Gerardo Mora's friends and enemies, some of whom put their lives at risk in speaking to me.

I've also come to know the truth through many hours spent with Mora, the man himself, in that rough-hewn shanty in the bush.

2

Mayela Mora didn't trust me, that was plain enough from her darting looks as she made coffee on the woodstove at my first sit-down with Mora back in January, two weeks prior to my 50th birthday. I recalled the of-repeated story of how she had jumped onto the podium and tried to throttle then presidential candidate José Figueras while he was giving a campaign speech; how she'd slapped Billy Clayton around at the gate to Billy's Sawmill property while Gerardo and the boys chanted for Billy's demise; and, according to rumor (later verified by a document I uncovered), how she'd put a knife to Max Dalton's throat and told Max he was a dead man on November 10th, three days before he was gunned down. Short, compact, tightly wound like a coiled spring, Mayela Mora was not the usual diffident down south campesina *dueña de la casa*.

But Mora himself, at 40 prematurely gray, tall, gaunt, with a direct, penetrating gaze, was affable enough as he answered my initial questions concerning the genesis of the land conflict in Pavones. I'd heard most of it already, if with a *norte* spin.

"Danny Fowlie was a narcotraficante," Mora was saying through El Gitano – who had introduced me to Mora as an independent journalist

181

come to tell the squatters' side of the land conflict story – after some political puffery, including the quote from Oscar Arias Sanchez about "no land without campesinos, no campesinos without land." "And therefore Fowlie's property is subject to liberation by the people, for the benefit of the people."

Mayela plunked coffee down in front of me, along with a bowl of sugar. No spoon. Chilly, narrow eyes. I thanked her.

"Was Fowlie ever convicted of a crime in Costa Rica?" I asked Gerardo, already knowing the answer, as Mayela stalked off.

"No, not convicted. No."

"Arrested?"

"...No."

"Was the source of his money ever investigated here?"

"...No."

"You're taking the word of a foreign court then." A gringo court at that, I was thinking.

"Danny Fowlie abandoned his land in 1985, when he went to Mexico," Mora said, abandoning his initial rationale relating to Danny's criminal enterprises. "Abandoned land is subject to seizure by the people."

As I well knew, Fowlie's property had never been abandoned, not by any stretch, even after Danny went on the run. And those *nortes* who had left were in fact driven off, violently, by Mora and his ilk. But I kept these thoughts to myself, let Mora go on about Costa Rica's squatter laws, which give campesinos the right to live on and work land in disuse and, eventually, allow them to gain legal title.

Yeah, I was thinking, having already done some homework, gain title "after 10 years of uncontested, peaceful residency." Given that the last ten years had seen nearly continuous *desolojos* (court-directed evictions) – squatters legally removed then, after having signed agreements never to return to Pavones, immediately doing so, to start it all over again... Uncontested residency? And given that the last ten years had seen nearly continuous squatter intimidation and violence in the form of fence cuttings, livestock thefts and mutilations, bombings, dead of night burn-outs, drive-by-shootings, machete wielding mobs and, sporadically, full-blown shooting wars... Peaceful residency?

Notwithstanding my friendships with the nonbelligerent of their kind, there isn't a squatter within 50 miles of here that has a legal right to anything, was what I was thinking, but "There have been *nortes* or local caretakers living on Fowlie's land since he left, right?" was all I said, questioningly, meekly even, not wanting to get too Socratic in my initial sit-down with Gerardo Mora. "I mean people who bought Fowlie's land or were given power to administrate it," I added, feigning confusion.

"Narcotraficantes," Mora replied, returning to his previous argument – which he'd dropped when I'd pointed out its essential weakness – thus completing the disputative circle. Narcotraficantes. Everyone is a narcotraficante. Problem is, there's not a whit of evidence to support the claim that a single Pavones resident is currently diddling any down south drug-related statutes. But I just nodded, took notes.

"Have you ever seen this?" I asked toward the end of that first sit-down, extracting a three-page document from my knapsack.

Mora picked up the papers, scanned them with narrowed eyes; he shook his head. "Max Dalton's land lease/purchase agreement with one of Fowlie's corporations," I said. I reached over and indicated a notated passage. "It expired last May." Mora blinked at the implications, read on. Read the other notated clause that proved that Max had entered into the agreement knowing full well that squatters were already on the land, had been for several years; they had not invaded it later, as was claimed in the embassy press releases, which also implied that Max owned the disputed land rather than leased it.

I figured that with the brouhaha over Max's death threatening to turn into a major international incident, any evidence, however indirect, that his land situation was legally shaky would be important to Gerardo Mora. And I was right; Mora was delighted with the document.

"Listen, Gerardo," I said. "I'm here to get the truth, no matter where that takes me." El Gitano relayed my words, grinning, leaning forward, digging it. "You help me, I'll help you."

Mora looked down at the document I had given him then bored into me with those eyes, dark, intense, unblinking eyes. He reached across the table and grasped my hand in a thumbs-up shake of brotherhood.

January 22, Washington, DC. The State Department, seeking to pressure the Costa Rican government to issue its findings on the Max Dalton case, extends the travel warning, urging U.S. citizens to avoid the Pavones area.

3

"Still here, huh?"

I'm maybe an hour into my equinoctial surf session when the hostile *gringo* voice brings me up short, informing me that I'm no longer solo. Lurking distractedly on the outside with the rising swell boosted by a flood tide, I hadn't noticed the fellow paddling out. And although his query was vague – "here" could refer to the here and now of the surf lineup or here on planet earth – I know he means here in Pavones.

"Sure, why not?"

"You got a serious rumor problem, Mister Journalist or whatever you are." A hoisted brow, a smirk. "That's why not."

I scan the inside, then the beach. The fellow has stroked out alone, which I should have expected. With the exception of his woman – a stunning earth mother *mestiza* – I've never seen him in the company of others, either in the water or on land, nor in my total of ten months in Pavones have I ever had occasion to speak to him, mostly due his aloofness, or elusiveness, a trait I've experienced before in certain types of longtime expats between Tijuana and Panama. But his rep, as they say, has preceded him. A hermetic Pavones resident going back to the Fowlie era, now subsistence farming in the bush and known to have pro-squatter leanings, I'd heard stories about the fellow, his past associations, his present doings. I'll not describe him further, nor divulge his name, for such is his wish. (I've altered some details in my descriptions of him.) Suffice to say that both ends of the old aphorism, "Two types come here, the Wanted and the unwanted" apply to him.

"The thing you have going for you is that it's unlikely anyone around here wants another dead *gringo* littering the landscape." The hoisted brow again, and a grim grin. "Still..."

"How well did you know Max?" I want to know. Enough of the gloom and doom; I've heard the fellow and Max had had a tumultuous relationship.

And indeed: "Max and I disagreed on things."

"Such as?"

A pause as he contemplates me askance, one eye alert to the outside. "Such as you don't come to a place like this and evict people from the land they've been living on for years, take a chain saw to the rancho they've raised their kids in, then torch the rubble and destroy their crops." He turns and levels his gaze at the sea horizon. "Shit like that tends to create bad blood, sabes?"

I've heard the stories about Max's extremism, his hidebound refusals to compromise or negotiate, but...

...my companion is staring at me now, and I don't care for the look in his eye. "You need some straightening out, motherfucker, if you're going to write about this place, and get it right." But damn, the fellow is suddenly hot, all tensed up and sinewy. *Cálmate, hombre.*

"I like your style, your nose-riding in particular," he says after a brief silence, suddenly the laid back, solicitous surf chum. A set looms and we stroke for the outside. "Not many longboarders around here. It's good to see."

As it turns out, this is why the fellow has decided to talk to me. He likes my nose-riding. Well, nutso or not, *lo que trabaja*, whatever works. It's the down south way.

But remembering the wild-man gleam in his eye a moment ago, and aware of his rep as a martial arts master, I give him his choice of waves.

4

Juanito (not his real name) was edgy that afternoon back in late January when I'd asked about the squatter cattle, how they had gotten onto Max's property. Sitting in his scrap lumber and driftwood shack near El Rio Claro, Juanito fidgeted at my query, looked away. His wife Maria nursed their new baby from the dim recesses of the tiny hovel and fixed Juanito with a warning glare.

Since cantina proprietor Billy Clayton told me about a squatter hit list, I had confirmed through three other sources that word had indeed leaked to the *norte* contingent about a coming ambush. In fact, there had been two warnings, the first a month before Max's death, which listed the names of the six possible *norte* victims, all of whom owned squatted land. As Billy had said, he and Max were on that list. Then, two weeks later – and two weeks before the killings – word came that the target would not be Billy. But since the other four *nortes* were all currently in the States, Max was obviously it, by default if not logical design.

"I called Max and told him to be extra careful," a *norte* who wishes to remain anonymous told me. "But Max had been threatened and physically attacked so many times that I think he just shrugged it off. I couldn't get through to him about the seriousness of the situation."

Sitting with Juanito that afternoon, my question about how the cattle had wound up on Max's pastureland hung in the sweltry air between us like the smoke from Maria's wood-burning cook stove, a palpable presence. Since the trespassing livestock had been the precipitator of the shootout that followed, we both knew the answer was key. If the confrontation had indeed been a setup, then the squatter (and the OIJ – the Judicial Police) version that the cattle had gotten away from a young boy who was tending them and that Mora, Aguilar (the squatter who was killed in the shootout, supposedly by Max) and the half dozen or so other squatters who had accosted Max were merely trying to help the boy, was specious. And although Juanito had not been on-scene that day, he knew well several of the squatters involved.

He knew what happened that day and I knew that he knew.

And notwithstanding the fact that Juanito was a squatter himself and had had confrontations with the *norte* who owned the land upon which his family lived, he was angry about the killing of Max Dalton. And afraid that local *nortes*, many of whom he knew and liked (I'd been friendly with Juanito since the previous June), would think that all squatters were violent and lawless.

Juanito's answer was very slow in coming; he was in fact agonizing over it. But when it came it was direct and unflinching. "The cattle were driven onto Max's land," he said, although it took my asking for *otras palabras*, other words, to understand, since I hadn't brought El Gitano along. Juanito didn't like, nor did he trust, El Gitano.

"Entonces la confrontación fue planeado," I said. Then the confrontation was planned.

"Si, fue planeado."

Maria rose suddenly and stood by the cook stove staring at Juanito, her eyes wide with fear. Then she bolted from the shack carrying the baby.

"Ella tiene miedo," Juanito said. She's afraid.

"Y quien la planeó?" Who planned it? I knew I was pushing it, but Juanito did not hesitate.

"Gerardo Mora."

Then Juanito told me that Mora would kill us both if he knew what we were talking about. I nodded, saying "Yo lo sé," I know, adding that Mora would never find out.

Juanito was leaning forward, his forearms resting on his knees, staring down at the hardpan earthen floor. He began shaking his head slowly with his lips pressed together in a tight horizontal line.

February 18, 1998, San José, Costa Rica. The Costa Rican Judicial Police (OIJ) unofficially reiterate that the evidence supports the squatter account of the shoot out which claims that Max Dalton and Alvaro Aguilar killed each other in an accidental encounter that escalated to deadly violence.

5

"It happened very quickly," Gerardo Mora was telling me through El Gitano at our third sit-down in the bush at Langostino in late January. "We were trying to help the boy who lost his cows when Max runs up, draws his gun and says `someone's going to die today.'"

I of course already knew via Juanito that the squatters had driven the cows onto Max's property in order to provoke a confrontation. (I had by now confirmed this through two other sources.) But I just nodded, took notes.

Mora stood up, directing me to do so also. He took a half step back. "Max and I were about this far apart" – seven, eight feet – "when Max started shooting, once at the ground, then once at me." He held up his hand, indicating the now-healed chunk that had been taken out of the end of his right forefinger. "Then Alvaro (Aguilar, the squatter killed in the shootout), who was over there (indicates a support post of the house about

25 feet away), shot Max to defend me. Max returned fire with two shots. They both went down." Mora shrugged, as if that was that.

I nodded again, feigning satisfaction with the account, although I had some serious problems with it already: Max had fired at Mora from a distance of about eight feet (cut that to five feet, counting his extended gun hand) and essentially missed, then put two rounds in the X-ring on a target 25 feet away. (Aguilar had been hit in the shoulder and a kill shot to the head.) And Max did it after having been shot full in the chest.

Also, according to four people who had been in the area that day and heard the gunfire, there had only been three shots fired, not five. And those three shots were accounted for by the three wounds sustained by Max and Aguilar.

So how had Mora taken a bullet in his hand?

At the end of that sit-down Mora reciprocated my sharing of the documents and information I'd been uncovering – much of which he claimed was vital to his cause – by giving me the OIJ Police Report on the Max Dalton/Alvaro Aguilar case. An absolutely secret document, un-releasable to anyone, let alone the press, until the investigation was deemed "complete" – which, I would come to realize, might actually be never. (In Costa Rica, gag orders with respect to on-going police investigations are automatic and strictly enforced.) The U.S. Embassy's chief spook, when I gave him a copy, would be positively drooling. That Gerardo Mora, the prime suspect in the killings, had a copy of this classified document was indicative of the far-reaching power of the man.

The report turned out to be a nightmare, on a couple of levels; to get through, for one. Two inches thick and in Spanish, it would take El Gitano and me a week for the first run through. Although El Gitano was competent with verbal translations, his literary skills, or lack of them, along with the torrid daily heat of the worst drought in local memory, drove me up the wall.

The report was also a nightmare on the level of police work, sort of José Jimenez meets Inspector Clouseau. But, finally, it would go beyond loopy incompetence into another area altogether.

6

"Esperaban por un documento," Juanito was telling me as we walked the seaside dirt track that Danny built, skirting the land that Danny bought and Juanito had subsequently invaded and where his family now lived. He'd met me 100 or so yards from his shack so his wife Maria would not know of our talk. Maria was deathly afraid of fellow squatter Gerardo Mora.

"They were waiting for a document," Juanito had said, referring to Mora and his inner circle, a half dozen or so heavyweight Langostino and Pilon squatters.

"And what would they do when they got the document?" I asked in my broken Spanish. Once again, at Juanito's insistance, I'd come alone, without El Gitano.

"Matarian Max Dalton." They would kill Max Dalton.

The document Mora had been waiting for came on November 1st, two weeks before the killings. A one-page letter from Golfito Municipality executive Jimmy Cubillo, giving the squatters an oceanfront piece of land on which to build an icehouse. Problem was that the land was already occupied, and according to the laws of Costa Rica, legally, by Max Dalton. And Cubillo well knew this.

As Cubillo himself would later admit – apologizing for "making a mistake" – the letter was completely invalid; it was in fact an archetypical example of the rampant corruption and squatter leanings in the municipality that oversees land rights in Pavones. But, invalid or not, it represented for Gerardo Mora a toehold on Max Dalton's land. A toehold that just might stick, if Max were out of the picture.

7

Two squatter kids have joined us in the surf lineup, although they're sitting way inside, where the wave in front of Max's ranchland walls and charges after a long, rolling, cutback-rich outside section.

After months of taciturn silence my new *norte* surfbuddy can't seem to keep his trap shut, and is now going on about Danny Fowlie, his altruism, his paternal concerns for the well-being of the local populace and its culture; how the campesinos, including some currently militant squatters, reciprocated that respect and to this day defend him, canonize him, even as they denounce his notorious criminal associations and enterprises as rationalization for their own land-grab designs.

"It wasn't the squatters who betrayed Danny, my friend," he says, "who looted his holdings. It was his so-called friends and associates and the granola-munching hypocrites who followed."

I nod, wanting to interject an affirmative but he's on a roll now, reciting a list of current *norte* residents who bought squatted chunks of Dannyland dirt cheap then sought to increase the value of their purchases through evictions of squatter families who had been occupying the land for years; guys who claim to be here for the wave and the paradisiacal habitat, asserting their concerns for keeping out development, while accruing land holdings far beyond reasonable personal needs, in many cases perpetrating blatant, money-driven malfeasances.

"The squatters took their cue from their greed and just followed suit. And why not? It's their fucking country."

And he still isn't finished, is now going on about Billy Clayton's plan to build a golf course complex on his oceanfront Sawmill property while at the same time asserting that Pavones should remain pristine, but I'm distracted by the set bearing down on us from the south, wrapping eastward now toward the rock reef; perfectly stacked, tapering walls. My companion is aware of the looming lines and is daring me with a look to abandon his proximity mid-tirade. The first couple of waves pass under us unmolested, tops feathering silently then vaporizing with a faint hiss as the wave face pitches forward just inside.

"Check out some of the *nortes* you've been hanging with, opportunists like Clayton," he says over the boom-and-grumble white noise that is the music of surfing. "And the king of them all, Derek Logan."

It was Gerardo Mora himself who perhaps best summed up the overall perception of Derek Logan by those involved in the land conflict in Pavones, both *norte* and Tico: "Derek Logan es el hombre mas peligroso en Pavones." Derek Logan is the most dangerous man in Pavones. Indeed, I had a personal interest in the matter of Logan. His reply when I first requested of him a formal interview regarding the land conflict in Pavones was this: "IF YOU WRITE ANYTHING ABOUT ME I'LL SUE YOUR FUCKING ASS!" His outburst was so booming and crazed that heads turned the whole quarter-mile length of the lineup (we were surfing at the time). An absurd threat, if only in the jurisdictional sense. My compadre Joachim, who was sitting his board close by, and I shared a good laugh after Logan paddled off in a huff, his glistening, sunblock-smeared face twisted in cartoonish malice. The humor, however, did a fast fade two weeks later when El Gitano informed me that, according to a friend of his who worked for Logan, "Derek Logan wants you dead."

Indeed, the embattled Billy Clayton, no question, fears Logan, his moneyed political power, his use of the OIJ for his own personal ends, even more than he does Mora and his terror tactics.

"And your buddy Clayton," my companion goes on as another glassy wall passes us by, exploding on the inside. "He ever mention how he and his Texas investors stole the cantina from Danny?"

"But it's not quite that simple," I counter, knowing the story, or rather the several different versions of it, but I'm too distracted to elaborate: there look to be two waves remaining in the set and I definitely, absolutely, want one.

"And Max was no better than any of them." Veins are popping again, that feral gleam. "You ever get a look at the purchase option in his land/

lease contract?"

I'm impressed that this bush-living wild man, this surfy survivalist, is privy to a piece of paperwork even Gerardo Mora with his far-reaching connections had been ignorant of. The buyout clause enabled Max to purchase the land at a fraction of its real worth if (and only if) he was able to rid it of the squatters who had been there for several years prior to his entering into the agreement. The bottom line was that Max could increase the value of his ranch many-fold by ridding it of squatters. Conversely, if he failed to do so, he was legally liable to lose the land altogether. The provision was undoubtedly a source of Max's intractable refusal to negotiate or compromise.

"But Max had a legal right..." I reply as the second to last wave of the set passes beneath us, steepening to burnished perfection. I'm barely able to restrain myself from a quick spin and launch. "I mean according to the law–"

"Law? What, you buy that 'Costa Rica as the Switzerland of the Americas' bullshit? This is Central fucking America, dude, and the end of the road at that. There's no law here. Max never understood that. It was his ignorance that killed him."

With this, he suddenly turns and with ponytail flying takes the final wave of the set, leaving me solo to wait out the ensuing lull. A rude move surely, and one perhaps calculated to make a point. He may like my nose-riding, but what he perceives as my simplistic position on the land conflict in Pavones has impressed him not a whit.

8

"Listen, Gerardo," I was saying as we slurped *arroz con leche* at his hutch in the bush, and on the rough-hewn west wall a Xerox-ed quote from José Marti fluttered in the welcome sea breeze. "I found a couple problems in the OIJ Police Report." My relationship with Mora had, in his perception, blossomed to the point where his problems were my problems. Things had even eased up with Mayela; she actually smiled at me when El Gitano and I had biked up earlier. And she'd given me a spoon with my coffee.

"What problems?"

"Well, Max's gun didn't have a clip in it. The clip was in his pocket." This wasn't just a run-of-the-mill type problem, it was a lollapalooza. It meant that Max had not fired a shot.

But Mora shrugged it off, slurped his *arroz*. "We found the other clip."

The *other* clip? And what did he mean by "we"?

Here's the story: the day after the shooting, some of Mora's crew were chopping the high grass at the crime scene and guess what? They found another clip. Brought it to Mora. Mora brought it to the OIJ.

Bingo, no problem.

I mean what could I say? (As I would find out, the pistol, a Lorcin .380, had been sold to Max with one clip. No one who knew Max had ever seen a second.)

Here were the same people who had attacked Max Dalton three days before his death, threatening his life, Mayela putting a knife to his throat... the same people who, armed with machetes and at least one handgun, had surrounded him on his own property before shots were fired... here these same people happened to be rooting around the crime scene and found...

But wasn't the crime scene secured?

I guess not.

"The other thing I was wondering about," I said, still nonplussed by the second clip revelation, "was why only one spent cartridge was found, a .32 from Aguilar's gun. None from Max's .380. There should have been four on the ground." (Both guns were automatics, which eject their spent shells).

This gave Mora contemplative pause. Mayela glanced at me over the frames of the reading glasses I'd given her; she put down her autobiography of Isabel Allende. Mora finally nodded, agreeing that this maybe was a problem. He then picked up his cell phone (his primitive hutch is also equipped with a beeper) and called the OIJ official in charge of the investigation – one Luis Avila – and told him that they needed to go back and find Max's spent cartridges.

After some chummy small talk Mora hung up, said they'd get on it, locate that evidence. Like they had with the second clip. (Metal detection equipment had already failed to turn up any shells from Max's weapon.) Also: It was a Sunday that day in the bush; Mora called the head of the investigation at home.

And there was more to come regarding OIJ's bizarre handling of the case: According to a very nervous government official I interviewed who had been at the scene of the shooting when the OIJ arrived (at about 9:30 PM, some five hours after the fact), an investigator had picked up one of the guns, fired it into air, then put it back down. In the dark, my informant couldn't be sure whether it had been Max's or Aguilar's. When I asked Mora about the shot-firing incident, he blithely confirmed it, adding that it had been Aguilar's weapon which had been discharged.

Further, in the OIJ Report, the serial number on Aguilar's gun does not match the number listed in its supposed point of origin, meaning that the source of the weapon was never traced.

Also in the OIJ Report: Max's legal advisor, Roberto Umaña, was spuriously misquoted in an apparent attempt to portray Max Dalton as being unstable and bloodthirsty when he returned to Pavones that last day. Based on my interviews with Umaña and others, such was not the case at all.

When I asked Gerardo Mora why he was initially arrested for manslaughter (he was quickly released), he told me because "some people were talking shit to the OIJ"; yet these people's testimonies were not included in the OIJ Report. Who were these people and what did they say? (*The Tico Times*, Costa Rica's English language newspaper, quoted a fearful, anonymous source as saying that non-squatter witnesses were "bullied into silence.")

9

My takeoff is late, one stroke and I'm in, then after a quick top turn to take the high line, I step directly to the nose. The first section is steep and feathering into the distance but I hang in there and make it onto the flat, then instead of backpedaling for a cutback, I stall from up front, edging my back foot toward the outside rail to point the board on a line less parallel to the wave face. I lean back in a semi-arch and think light and airy to avoid a pearl. When the wave walls again I return my back foot to the inside rail to get back onto the faster parallel track. I negotiate two more sections like this then the inside walls up and charges, not a thick top to bottom boomer but very fast and very long. I'm maybe half way through when I see I'm not going to make it. I backpedal and go to the bottom, finding I've gained enough speed on the descent to bottom turn around the end of the little bowl section. I climb back to the top and immediately go up front again for another extended green water nose glide. By the time I kick out I'm halfway to the squatter fish camp where the bay starts its sweep towards Langostino. Starting the long paddle back out, I find I'm aflutter and giddy from the ride, the perfection of the wave, the mindless joy of so much nose time.

I stroke by the two squatter kids, who grin, one calling out something I don't catch as my *norte* companion rips the inside on his short board. His wave sections unmakeably (one too many cutbacks) and he kicks out just outside of me.

We paddle back out side by side, babbling surf jive as if we were two normal guys sharing classic, empty warm water point surf in paradise.

February 25, San José, Costa Rica. Costa Rica's relations with the U.S. hit an historic low, as a diplomatic storm is unleashed by a comment made to the press by U.S. Ambassador Thomas Dodd, threatening economic sanctions against Costa

Rica by the U.S. if the shooting of Max Dalton is not properly investigated.
Reaction to the Ambassador's words comes swiftly at the Costa Rican Legislative Assembly when one member ends an anti-American tirade with the words "Take that, little gringos!"

10

By late February, my Mora dossier had thickened considerably as squatters who didn't like the man in the Langostino bush and his terror tactics came forward and told me...

About the clandestine inner circle meetings in the weeks prior to the shootout, organized by Mora, and from which ordinary squatters were banned.

About how Mora, Mora's son Esteban, Aguilar and Mora's brother-in-law Carlos Araya had been practicing their marksmanship with three newly-procured sidearms – two automatics and a revolver – on a secret firing range in the bush near Langostino, starting about a month before the shootout with Max Dalton.

About Mora's intimate connections to the political and economic power structure in San José. (Mora's cell phone records indicate that he averages one hundred San José calls per month.)

And about Mora's malfeasance with squatter funds, some of which were used to purchase unsquatted land in nearby Comte. Mora put the land in his father's name, since by law squatters cannot own property while they are actively squatting. (I confirmed the land purchase via a *norte* to whom Mora had tried to sell the 10-acre parcel.)

Another thing that had bothered me about the shootout was how it had turned out so perfectly for the squatter movement. One dead *gringo*, one dead squatter. The spilling of blood on both sides would be a convenient justification for a quick, clean resolution of the incident, since the apparent shooters were both dead.

According to rumor, Mora and Aguilar (the squatter killed in the shootout) had recently had a major falling out over Aguilar's desire to sell the rights to his squatted plot to a *gringo*, a serious no-no in the squatter code of conduct (although Mora was attempting to do this).

Mora's anger and a possible violent reaction to this sort of behavior had precedents, the best known being his late-night burning of the house of a 72-year old fellow squatter named Rufino Lopez, who had similar plans; the house had his grandchildren inside when it was torched. (They managed to escape.) Mora and his crew tied Lopez to a fencepost and beat him to near death.

Further, Aguilar was apparently missing a face card or two, a medio tonto (literally, "half an idiot"), according to neighbors who knew him well.

A logical choice as sacrificial lamb?

11

In early March my relationship with Gerardo Mora tightened further when I gave him a letter written by Danny Fowlie in prison in California and addressed to the Municipality of Golfito. The letter claimed that he, Danny, had given no one legal authority to sell his lands and that therefore all the ownership transfers since his incarceration were invalid. In theory this was a blockbuster since it supported squatter claims that Danny's holdings had no rightful owners and were therefore up for grabs. Mora could hardly contain his glee as he read and reread the letter.

But I failed to mention to Mora about other documents I had procured, one in which Fowlie clearly and legally did give complete power, to his then buddy Alan Nelson, the man who had subsequently made land-transfer deals, including – indirectly, through Owen Handy – the lease agreement with Max Dalton. The land transfers were legal.

"My plan for Pavones, my macro plan," Mora told me soon after I'd given him the letter, "is to preserve the beachland from Zancudo to Punta Banco and establish eco-tourist resorts on the land behind it, going all the way back to the Indian reservation."

This encompassed some 15 miles of coast, virtually all of Pavones and extended far back into the rainforest. Grandee Danny's ambitions were a vision of modesty compared to this. Mora coveted it all, the shebang plus.

"What about the squatters who say they want to farm the land?"

"They can sell food to the tourists, or guide them on hikes."

This surely gave a new twist to the "no land without campesinos" rallying slogan of the supposedly agrarian-bent masses. In fact, in both spirit and letter, the squatter laws were crafted to provide land to be farmed, not developed for tourism.

"Pilon would be a vital element, because of the geographical set up, right?" I asked. The hill road from Golfito descends and curves toward the beach at Pilon, making it a logical location for a resort complex. Max's property included the lion's share of prime Pilon waterfront. I knew, and Mora knew, that, as with the nearby settlement adjacent to the cantina, surfers would spearhead the influx of fun-in-the-sun-loving *nortes*.

Indeed, in his confidence in gaining control over Max's ranchland, which overlooks the classic point wave of my equinoctial surf session, Gerardo Mora, this simple campesino, had his name on an already-established "Eco-Pavones" website: "Come to Pavones," reads the pitch, and "Surf the waves on your surfboard. We have the third longest waves in the world..."*

Yes, it was the wave here that killed Max.

12

By mid-March the pieces of the Max Dalton/Alvaro Aguilar puzzle were starting to come together. Boiling down my foot-high mound of documents, newspaper clippings going back to the Fowlie era, and notebooks filled with interview transcripts and observations, the chronology of events that terminated in the deaths of Max Dalton and Alvaro Aguilar went as follows:

One month before the shooting, word leaks to the *norte* landowners that a squatter hit list has been issued and that Max Dalton's name is on that list. At about the same time, Mora, his son Esteban, his brother-in-law Carlos Araya and Alvaro Aguilar commence target practice in the bush at Langostino.

According to my informant, Juanito, the squatters are "waiting for a document" before proceeding with the hit.

On November 1st, two weeks before the shooting, Golfito Municipality Executive Jimmy Cubillo issues a document allowing Mora and his men to invade a small oceanfront piece of Max's land, supposedly to construct an icehouse. (The last clause of the letter is significant, stating that it does not limit future land seizures.)

At the same time, word leaks that Max will be the target of the hit.

Throughout the last month of Max's and Aguilar's lives, clandestine meetings are held, from which rank-and-file squatters are banned.

On November 10th, Mora and his men invade the disputed parcel, cutting Max's fence; they start work on the proposed icehouse. Over the next two days they invade Max's ranchland proper, building two thatched ranchos, ranchos described to me by Mayela Mora as of the type that would comprise the proposed Eco-Pavones tourist development. (Indeed, they were identical to the clutch of Eco-Pavones ranchos Mora had built just few hundred yards from his hutch in Langostino.)

Also on November 10th, about a dozen of Mora's men rough up Max, puncturing a tire on his Land Rover, telling him he's a dead man. Mayela puts a knife to Max's throat to underscore the threat.

Max goes to Golfito that same day to file a *denuncia* (the equivalent of pressing charges) against Mora et al for invading his land and attacking his person. Max has secured *desolojos* (legal evictions) several times over the five years he's owned his ranch and, though discouraged and angry, has

---

* Mora's website has since been removed from the World Wide Web.

little doubt he'll secure another, especially given the transparent illegality of the Cubillo document.

Mora also knows this: he told me so.

Through Max's legal advisors, Sarita Castillo and Roberto Umaña, and with assistance from the U.S. Embassy, Max is promised help on the following Monday by the Public Security Ministry. Castillo and Umaña, fearing that his life is in danger, urge Max to stay in Golfito until such help arrives. Max demurs, worrying about his cattle, which need his care. On November 13th, just after noon, he leaves for Pavones.

At approximately 4:30 PM, while trying to round up squatter cattle that had been driven onto his pasture land to provoke a confrontation, Max is gunned down, along with Alvaro Aguilar.

13

Aside from the aforementioned motive that Max's land was vital to Mora's proposed tourist development, there was a larger, more complex reason for the killing, one that explains why a general *norte* hit list existed before Max himself was singled out.

When I asked Gerardo Mora what he thought the result would be of the death of this landowning *norte* expat (presumably any *norte* would do), he told me this: "The United States government will pressure Costa Rica to solve the land conflict problem in Pavones and Costa Rica will do so by expropriating the land and paying off the gringos to leave." The expropriated land would then be given to the Costa Rican people; in other words, to the squatters. As leader of their local movement, the land would go to Gerardo Mora for his Eco-Pavones "macro plan."

Further, on October 9, 1997, one month before he was slain, Max Dalton went to the courthouse in Golfito to testify in a criminal trial wherein Gerardo Mora and a half dozen other squatters who would be present at Max's and Aguilar's killings were to be tried on usurpation (land theft) and assault charges, stemming from an incident in 1993. The trial was postponed when the San José prosecutor failed to appear. (This in itself is an eyebrow-raiser and perhaps a further indication of Mora's far-reaching influence.) But nevertheless, Max was on the verge of putting Mora and his crew in the slammer.

Again, it was right around this time that the hit list was issued and the target practice commenced.

14

The wind has remained down and with a mid-tide on the flood the surf has been getting nothing but better; bigger and better. Although I'm enjoying one of those sessions upon which future land-bound dreams are based, my new compadre has been distracting me from rapturous reflections with his continuing pugnacity regarding certain elements of the landowning *norte* contingent. No wonder I've never seen him in the cantina, I'm thinking, or even in the company of other *nortes*.

"What's your point?" I query, interrupting a tirade about the Logan/Clayton imbroglio, how both continue to do business – in the form of a sort of dueling *mordidas* (bribes) – with Jimmy Cubillo, the spectacularly corrupt municipality official at least partially responsible for the killing of Max Dalton.

"My point, shit-for-brains, is that those cantina phonies pretend to be all bent and outraged over what happened to Max, but name one that ever visited him at his ranch?" (When I met Max at his ranch a couple months before his death he effusively welcomed me, asserting that no one visited him any more – "They're all afraid.") "And take Logan," he goes on, "the way he's sucking up to your buddy Gerardo Mora, looking for help in running Clayton off the Sawmill property."

The enemy-of-my-enemy-is-my-friend kind of thing.

In fact, Logan had been one of my sources of documents helpful to Mora, once he'd had his change of heart about speaking to me. (And what a fountainhead of revisionist local history and specious revilement of his fellow *nortes* he was!)[*] Logan had made me promise to "tell Gerardo" of the documents' source; an obvious overture of friendship. A secret alliance between Logan and Mora surely had profound implications regarding the balance of power in this intrigue-ridden little down south Eden.

"But you know what?" I snap, having had it with my companion's supercilious antagonism. "None of the nortes around here tortured then murdered a 78-year-old man in order to steal his land." Now it's me with the wild eye. "Know what I mean, asshole?"

He's paddling towards me now and I'm briefly thinking I better prepare myself for a duke out, which I'll likely lose. But he pulls up and sits his board close.

"Listen, man," he says in a muted, tired tone, as if the air had been

---

[*] Like so many people who are lying and/or have something to hide, Logan also talked too much, spilling too many details in the process. Among the details was his relationship to Danny Fowlie, and that he still owed Danny $50,000 from a land purchase in 1991 (which was tantamount to an admission to ripping Danny off). Logan's revelations along these lines were, from his point of view, so dumb that at the end of the interview (which he allowed me to tape) he asked me to "forget I said that stuff about Danny." He then offered to sell me land at half the market price if he would "come off a certain way" in the magazine article. Soon thereafter El Gitano informed me that Logan wanted me dead.

sucked out of him. "Max and I had our differences. We'd argue, get drunk and yell at each other. But Max was my friend. Much as I disapproved of some of his attitudes and methods, his right-wing politics, I liked the old bastard. Max was the ballsiest man I ever met."

There is a silence and we look to the outside, where cats' paws are stirring the oily slick sea. "Wind's coming up," I say, and my voice, too, is hushed.

"A lot of my friends are squatters," he says thinly and I suddenly have an inkling of the degree to which his anger and frustration are based on conflicting loyalties.

"Same here," I say. "Most of them are basically decent people."

"But I'm no friend of Gerardo Mora."

"So what do you figure happened that day?"

"I've heard stories," my companion says after a pause.

"So tell me."

"You know how many shots were fired?"

"Three."

"Right. Three. Not five. That's key."

15

Indeed, with only three shots fired, and with those shots accounted for by the wounds in Max and Aguilar, how did Mora get the tip of his finger blown off?

One morning I was practicing with the 9mm Erik lent me, using a two-handed combat stance to pop rounds into an old surfboard propped up in the bush above my house. Having emptied a clip, I noticed my left thumb was bleeding. I'd been gripping the gun a little too high with that hand and the ejection slide had scraped it.

It hit me there and then: Mora had shot himself in the finger while he fired. In the heat of the moment of the confrontation with Max, and with a short-barreled weapon (a snub nose .38, say), it would have been easy to accidentally extend his non-trigger hand too far and blow off the end of his forefinger, especially considering Mora's long, lean fingers.

But wait. Mora's wound was on his right forefinger.

Mora is left handed.

And the shells. Why was only one shell, a .32 from Aguilar's weapon, found at the crime scene? (No bullets were recovered, supposedly.) Simple. Mora used a revolver, presumably the one he'd been practicing with for the month prior to the shooting.

Neither Max (again, whose gun was found clip-less) nor Aguilar ever fired a shot.

But what about the .32 shell they found? Doesn't that mean Aguilar fired?

No. Remember that the OIJ fired a round from Aguilar's gun that night. That's where the shell came from. If Aguilar had shot Max, they would have found two shells. (Why would the OIJ fire a round from Aguilar's gun? Two possibilities: To leave a spent cartridge at the scene, or to foul the weapon's barrel if the gun had been recently cleaned and not fired since; a clean barrel would have proved Aguilar had not shot Max. They may have also tried to fire Max's gun but could not since it was clip-less.)

And a tidbit from the autopsy: Max was shot from his right side, where, by the squatters' own accounts, Gerardo Mora was standing.

And then there's Juanito. At our last meeting I flat asked him who had killed whom, although I already knew the answer.

"Gerardo Mora killed them both," he said, then wished me goodbye, good luck and be careful. There was nothing more to say.

16

Sometime around the middle of March – my source could not pinpoint the exact date – the OIJ unsealed the clothes Max Dalton wore the day he was killed and shot them full of holes, supposedly in an attempt to determine what caliber bullet killed Max. They of course learned nothing from this, since fabric is flexible and raggedly perforated by bullets. What they did do, however, was prevent a gunpowder residue analysis from being performed – it had unaccountably been postponed for months – since the clothes were now contaminated. A negative test result would have indicated that Max had not fired his gun that day, which in turn would mean that Aguilar was shot by one of his own people.

The evidence that the OIJ was involved in the conspiracy to murder Max, if not in beforehand collusion then certainly in the ensuing cover-up, is overwhelming.

Other evidence indicates complicity by government authorities higher than the OIJ, both in the local municipality of Golfito and in San José. Indeed, given the severe on-going diplomatic repercussions which have resulted from the incident, it was inevitable that the San José administration would function as a behind-the-scenes force in the investigation, and hence in the cover-up.

17

And then there was Fajardo Fajardo (you're supposed to say it twice).

Throughout my investigation the name Fajardo kept surfacing in odd places, although no one seemed to know where he lived or how he could be contacted. A freelance spook variously described as a broker of guns, secret documents, government connections and clandestine information, as well as an all-around facilitator of the illicit, the OIJ Report revealed that Fajardo had sold Max the Lorcin .380 said to have been the weapon Max used to kill Alvaro Aquilar. And though claiming to be "like a son" to Max, Fajardo was seen in Golfito a few days after Max's death in deep conference with Gerardo Mora, and that same day tried to pilfer Max's six year's worth of legal documentation – much of which pointed an inculpating finger at Mora and his organization – from his ranch in Pilon.

At various times claiming to be in the employ of the Dalton family, the OIJ, and the U.S. Embassy, Fajardo, I had been warned, not only played both sides of the Pavones land conflict fence, but had no conception of what a fence was at all.

Although I had several possible scenarios regarding Fajardo's involvement in the killings, one of my interests lay in his potentially villainous connection to the weapons reputed to have been used, and perhaps to others as yet unrevealed.* To wit: the serial number on the bill of sale Fajardo gave Max for the Lorcin .380 does not match the number on the gun found at the crime scene (by one digit), indicating that Fajardo was seeking to legally disassociate himself from the weapon by making a "mistake" on the bill of sale.

In the case of Aguilar's Lorcin .32 – supposedly the gun that killed Max – the serial number on that weapon does not match the number listed on the government permit form by the owner of the piece, as given in the OIJ Report: a company named Securidad y Inteligencia Elite, SA (Elite Security and Intelligence, Inc). As mentioned previously, this implies that the real source of Aguilar's weapon was never traced by the OIJ; the surface appearance of the inconsistency being that Securidad y Inteligencia Elite's involvement is a red herring, irrelevant to the crime.

But further perusal of Seguidad y Intelligencia Elite's paperwork reveals that the company had two sidearms registered to it (and only two), the Lorcin .32 and a Lorcin .380. Again, the latter is the make and model of the weapon Fajardo sold to Max and which was subsequently found at the crime scene. (The serial number of the company's .380 is different by several digits from Max's.)

Is it possible that out of all the makes, models and calibers of side arms out there, this spooky-sounding company just happened to have registered to it the two makes, models and calibers supposedly used by Max and

---

* It's likely that, at the very least, Fajardo acted as an informant for the squatters, especially toward the end, when he was staying particularly close to Max. For example, Fajardo visited Max at his hotel in Golfito the night before Max was killed. Max, who trusted Fajardo, no doubt told him that help was on the way from the Public Security Ministry the following Monday. (They had promised to evict the squatters from Max's parcel.) Fajardo may very well have called Mora and informed him of this: Still another motive for the killing having taken place that day.

Aguilar that afternoon in Pilon – and no others?*

Given Fajardo's involvement in the weapons trade and his having sold Max the .380, if I could somehow tie Fajardo to Seguridad y Inteligencia Elite, the existence of a far-reaching conspiracy to eliminate Max would be all but confirmed. (In my repeated calls to the San José-based security company no one answered; my eventual visit to the address revealed a locked-up-tight office with no signs or indications that it had been recently active – indicating that it could have been a front used for the creation of a dead end in a paper trail of the weapons used.)

A swarthy down south version of Peter Lorre at his squirmy, toad-like best, Fajardo, the afternoon El Gitano and I met with him in a dim, raunchy Ciudad Neilly cafe, raised the art of verbal dodgery to a level best described as hilarious. But his prevaricational aplomb broke down visibly when I sprung on him the security and intelligence company's name, asking if he'd ever done business with them.

El Gitano and I exchanged looks as Fajardo did a classic double-take, then paused, his mind obviously racing. (Like many of the land conflict players I interviewed over the months of my investigation, Fajardo had underestimated the depth of the knowledge I already possessed, and was ill-prepared for incisive questions.) But Fajardo recovered quickly, issuing an exaggeratedly negative shrug.†

Although Fajardo's initially nonplussed reaction was not outright evidence, it was an important moment for me on the level of instinct; I'd begun to see conspirators everywhere and needed to assuage a nagging case of self-doubt.

"Listen, my good friend," Fajardo whispered in heavily-accented English, impatiently waving off my follow-up query as to why he was lying to me about virtually everything. I leaned across the rickety table between us while the creaking ceiling fan feebly stirred the fetid air and the tape recorder concealed in my pocket whirred. "If the truth about the death

---

* Given that the OIJ Report contained no less than four discrepancies in the serial numbers of the weapons in question, there is no way of knowing exactly what sort of chicanery was going on without examining the weapons themselves for their actual numbers. But one possibility, given this chicanery, is that Max was unarmed when he went out to deal with the trespassing cattle. Mora et al, knowing of this possibility in advance, had a twin of Max's Lorcin with them, to plant on his body after the killing. They also had a twin of Aguilar's weapon – since Aguilar of course did not know his role as sacrificial lamb, all bets had to be covered. This would explain the improbability of Seguidad y Intelligencia Elite possessing twins of both guns used that day, and no others.

† Let's assume that Seguridad y Inteligencia Elite's possession of the twins of the weapons used that day (and no others) is not a coincidence (my strong inclination). And let's further assume that Fajardo's double take reaction to my naming the spooky company indicates he is connected with it on some level he wishes to keep secret. Put the two assumptions together and Fajardo's intimate involvement in the conspiracy to kill Max becomes a virtual certainty, at least regarding the weapons used.

of Max is to be known to the world," he went on, "you know what would happen?"

I admitted that I didn't know.

"This government here in Costa Rica..." Fajardo waxed emotional now, vehemently stabbing the tabletop with a stubby forefinger for emphasis. "This government would *fall!*"

Silence as the forefinger rose slowly from the table, circled the space between us then gently came to rest against Fajardo's temple. Back to a whisper: "I know what happened to Max."

"So tell me."

A mock-helpless shrug as Fajardo finally got around to the real reason for agreeing to meet with me. "For that, my very good friend, I will need to be paid."

I smiled, having seen this coming. "How much?"

"One million dollars."

Although Fajardo's comical price tag for information implicating the government in Max's killing makes it suspect (as does his rep for treachery), wherever my inquiry led, his name kept surfacing in ways that gave me pause. One example: when I asked my weapons-savvy, metaphysically-bent surfbuddy Alex how he'd breezed through Costa Rican customs with a surfboard packed with cash and guns, he claimed he'd been under the paid protection of a government agent who had provided him with a uniformed escort through customs and immigration. Always on the lookout for new contacts, I'd then inquired as to the identity of his man. "A weird little guy named Fajardo Fajardo," Alex replied. "You're supposed to say it twice." *

March 17, 1997, Washington, DC. Senator Dirk Kempthorne of Idaho (Max Dalton's home state) co-sponsors a congressional resolution formally censuring Costa Rica for its mishandling of the Max Dalton murder investigation. Also signing were Senators Helms, Faircloth, Feinstein, Boxer, Gramm, Hutchison, DeWine, Smith, Chafee, Leahy, Coverdell, and Warner.

---

* More indirect but strong evidence of beforehand collusion in the murders on the part of the San Jose government lies in the unlikelihood that no bullets would be recovered from either of the bodies or the crime scene itself. Consider: we know beyond reasonable doubt that neither Max nor Aguilar were killed with the weapons said (in the OIJ Report) to be used. Had even one bullet (and there were three) been recovered, the "official story" would have been discredited by a ballistics analysis, rendering the otherwise intricate planning moot. Mora undoubtedly knew this but went ahead with the killings anyway. He therefore must have known ahead of time that had bullets been recovered, the evidence would be suppressed. Further, this collusion by the OIJ was unlikely to be solely at the local level, since autopsies would be performed in San José under the auspices of OIJ higher-ups. (After extensive and frustrating calls I was finally able to get someone involved in the autopsy on the phone. When I told him I was investigating the killings he at first got very nervous then hung-up on me. I never found out who he was, whether he was a medical examiner or administrator or what.) If medical personnel were in fact involved in the subterfuge, logic dictates that the cover-up extended beyond the OIJ. The only place to go from there is the San José administration itself.

18

I have come to surf the point break in front of Max's ranch this morning of the equinox because it is in the heart of Gerardo Mora's domain. I want him and his men to see me surfing here, for confusion's sake, to psychologically dilute the latest rumor about me, and potentially the most dangerous: That this aging, shaggy surf bum with the battered old pickup truck is a spy for the U.S. Embassy (in effect, the State Department).

I recently paid the embassy another visit (my first having been back in January) and filled them in on the progress of my investigation, under the condition that nothing I told them could be used in any way or passed along to anyone outside the room until I gave the okay, or in the event of my disappearance or demise.

Considering that the spy rumor surfaced within 48 hours of that meeting, plus the sudden materialization in Washington of information only I possessed, I have to assume that this promise was broken and/or there had been a major breach of security. (The timing strongly suggests that my intelligence was the impetus behind the senate resolution of censure, which was submitted to Bill Clinton less than a week after my embassy visit.)* Ambassador Thomas Dodd's statement to the national press that his people know more about what's going on in Pavones than the Costa Ricans (run as a front page headline in *La Nacion*, the country's most-read newspaper) when in fact the embassy people were totally clueless until my visit, is further evidence that I was blatantly betrayed by my own government: Anyone reading the story in which the quote appeared and wondering whence sprang the embassy's inside knowledge had only one suspect, yours truly, the lone *gringo* investigating the Dalton killing down in Pavones. And the refusal of the embassy's chief spook (his euphemistic title being "Head of Regional Security") to take or return my calls from Pavones when he knew I was at risk (and had assured me of assistance if needed) is still further evidence of the State Department's disregard for my well-being.

I am very definitely on my own here.

19

It's late morning now and the surf, though still sizable, is rapidly deteriorating from a rising south wind and too-full tide. Glassy, zippering wave sections I'd smoothly glided through a half hour ago – with the sibilance like a lover's sigh of my planing board reflective of a hydrodynamic equilibrium between lift and forward momentum – are crumbling

---

* The resolution is archived on the adjunct webite.

unevenly and the cross chop is creating a speed bump effect, exacerbated by the tendency of my rails and nose to catch smaller irregularities on the wave face: an overall detriment to the acceleration and sensation of control I crave.

The delicate combination of surface conditions, state of the tide and swell direction that had produced the morning's perfection has suddenly broken down. Although a non-surfer watching from shore would notice little change in the view before him, for a wave rider, for me, it's like a sudden and unwarranted slap in the face from the sighing lover.

So I prone out my last wave and come ashore, leaving my *norte* companion and the two squatter kids in the lineup, the *norte* way outside, probably waiting for a wave of sufficient size to offset the diminished surf quality, to come in on. In spite of some soul-baring on both our parts toward the end of our colloquy, I have not said goodbye to him nor have we made plans to meet again, and that's all right; the nature of acquaintanceships made while surfing are of a peculiar sort. Not necessarily casual or superficial, although they can be that; just... peculiar. I've often forged what I considered friendships over the course of several surf sessions then failed to recognize the other surfer upon running into him on land; or realized that we after all have absolutely nothing to say to each other when not in the water. In the case of my new surfbuddy of this day, I can easily picture him ignoring me should we meet again on shore, as he has been doing over the past months.

As I walk the beach towards the fish camp where I've parked my truck, a lone horseman trots by south bound, a ragged campesino. He's holding something large and rectangular as he rides, awkwardly with both hands, his reins looped over the saddle horn. I recognize the object as a solar panel of the type popular with *nortes* before the coming of electricity to Pavones in 1995. He regards me, grinning big, as he goes by, then rounds the next headland and the vast, sweeping curve of this majestic beach is empty again.

I place my surfboard in my truck bed – I've unloaded my camper, which sits propped up in my yard – and look around. I'm parked under a mango tree a stone's toss from the shack of a fisherman named Leonidas Zuniga, who was one of the squatters directly involved in the confrontation which ended the lives of Max Dalton and Alvaro Aguilar. Leonidas' little house and complex of lean-to sheds, worktables and beached *pangas* (dories) is close to water's edge, under the shade of a stand of hardwoods and nut palms.

I am also no more than a few yards from the fence that marks the seaward boundary of Max's property. Just inside the fence are the remains of Leonidas' former home, in which he and his wife and children lived before Max aquired the land from one of Danny Fowlie's corporations. Not much is left, just part of the foundation and a charred stump that was the support of one corner of the simple structure. As my new surf chum said, Max had taken a chainsaw to Leonidas' family's home, burned the rubble then destroyed the crops Leonidas had for years planted in the pastureland Max then used for his cattle; this was after Max had secured his first squatter *desolojo*, or legal eviction, in 1993, a year or so after he moved in. Leonidas, whom I'd interviewed in January, described how Max had also wantonly destroyed his wife's flower garden and the banana trees surrounding the house. By all accounts, and this is from both the local squatters and the *nortes* who knew him, Max had unnecessarily created added enmity from the start by not allowing Leonidas to dismantle and remove his house and reap what he could of his crops.

My own impression of Max, when I met him a couple months before he was killed, was of a proud and tenacious man, an obdurate man, yet a man not without humor. In spite of the fact that by that time his squatter problem had escalated to the point where confrontations were nearly continuous – he was virtually under siege by his neighbors – he evinced a cheerful, occasionally blackly comic stoicism and a dry wit. And indeed, I would have to agree with my *norte* surf chum: Given his sticking it out against overwhelmingly hostile forces in this remote place, this septuagenarian was in fact the ballsiest man I've ever met.

20

There is no one around and apart from the deep, rolling hiss of the surf and the chirping of birds it is very quiet. Standing by my truck, still dripping wet from my surf session, I look past a tall hardwood a hundred or so yards inland to the spot where Max and Alvaro Aguilar died. Past that, one to the south, one to the north, are the two thatched ranchos Gerardo Mora and his men were building on Max's pasture land before the killing, the beginning of Mora's planned tourist development. Past the northern rancho, barely visible behind a dense copse of high scrub, is Max's house.

I recently visited that house in order to interview Max's fiercely loyal, longtime ranch hand, a young Costa Rican named Macho, who had been with Max that fatal afternoon back in November. Macho had stayed inside the house when Max went into the pasture to deal with the trespassing squatter cattle. Minutes later, when gunfire erupted, he ran to Max's aid but was turned back by the threats of the squatters standing over his mortally wounded body. Fearing for his own life, Macho went on the run, immediately leaving Pavones for an inland hideout. I had caught wind of his secret plan to return – to briefly visit his father, who was now care-taking Max's house – and through an intermediary arranged to meet with him. Since Macho was the only non-squatter present that day, I considered his account vital.

Macho's was the strangest and most disheartening interview of my investigation. Macho lied to me about everything, even peripheral details. Some of his lies were so outrageous that had I not met him when I visited Max, I would have suspected that he was an imposter, a player in some nefarious plot to confuse my inquiry. But no, it was Macho all right, denying that Max had squatter problems in the days previous to the shoot out, denying that Max even owned a firearm, denying that Max had been at the courthouse in Golfito to file a *denuncia* two days before he died, and on and on. But there appeared to be no pattern to his lies in terms of either confirming or refuting any particular version of the shoot out; he was all over the place. There seemed to be no agenda behind the deceit.

But later, playing back the tape of our bizarre conversation, a pattern did emerge. Everything Macho said tended to portray Max a certain way: easygoing, tolerant, unconcerned with the squatter problem, and above all of nonviolent temperament; traits at odds with much of what I had learned about him. Then I remembered the long, hushed cell phone conversation Macho had had with one of Max's sons, Rick – a banker in California – just before my interview. I had been in fairly close touch with Rick for some time; he knew I was the only investigative presence in Pavones looking into his father's death, and he knew I would write about my findings. Although Rick and his twin brother Bob had been very active in pushing for diplomatic action against Costa Rica – they had hired a lobbyist to petition Congress and created a Max Dalton web site – and had professed a deep desire to see justice done, it occurred to me that a true and complete picture would reveal aspects of their father that were less than flattering. Had Rick told Macho how to respond to my queries, to shade his account in the aforementioned ways? And had Macho, this simple campesino (his name notwithstanding, a mild and diffident young fellow), gone to naively absurd lengths in an effort to please his benefactor (Rick was financing Macho's undercover seclusion), the son of the man he so revered? But whatever the motive, Macho's pattern of lies in portraying Max in a favorable light made absolutely useless whatever truths he really harbored about the murders.

It was dispiriting to be subjected to deceit from the faction of the conflict that in theory should have been most desirous of a full and veracious disclosure. How, at bottom, were these lies any different from Gerardo Mora's?

21

It's odd, how very quiet it is. Max's pasture land, some 80 acres spread out soporifically before me, is still as a painting: a tableau of troppo splendor, a pastoral New England with palm trees (sans squatters; they lurk, armed and squinty-eyed just out of frame). To the east, past the winding dirt track that Danny built and the sprinkling of primitive dwellings that line it, the bushy terrain rises gradually from the coastal plain to a snarly brawl of steep-sloped jungle, then precipitously rises further, the pale green hills merging into deep emerald mountains, which themselves culminate in the cloud forests of the interior. From where I stand it's a spectacle rivaled only by the panorama to the west, towards the sea.

I turn and look. Beyond the surf wrapping in from the south and freight-training across the arcing blue of the bay, some ten miles distant and clearly visible in the tropical dazzle looms the pristine ecological miracle of the Osa Peninsula, a true, unfettered wilderness. Its vast and towering presence so near creates a cozy, lake-like feel to the fecund, unsullied waters of the Sweet Gulf. Yet just a few miles to the south, the gulf's yawning mouth affords oceanic groundswells unimpeded access to the lush, point-rich coastline stretching north and south as far as the eye can see. But how perfect is this arrangement of land and sea, both aesthetically and as a sculptor of that voyaging force of nature expiring on the reef in front of me! The visceral awareness of this perfection underlies and reinforces my bond with this place like a secret shared between us.

Listen: The drift and implications of this chronicle – this goddamn murder investigation – have been to an extent misleading. The majority of my *norte* surfmates live here in at least surface amity with even the most militant squatters, by virtue of their having bought and settled upon unconflicted, preca-free land: land not previously owned by that legendary folk hero, that mythic waterman who would be king named Danny Fowlie. They are distant, if interested, bystanders in the frenetic struggle in which I have so deeply immersed myself.

My little rental house, my nestled niche by a banana grove on the bank of El Rio Claro, itself sits upon a secure parcel, unthreatened and serene, and a short downstream drift from one of the best surfing waves on the planet. And by dint of the effort expended and risks taken during my journey south, and after so much time locally spent, and given whatever personal qualities I offer to those preceding me, I have earned my place in the community here.

Yes, I do love this place.

Yet... and yet, what do I imagine will be the ultimate upshot to my involvement in these darker matters? It doesn't take much foresight to see the personal repercussions, once the secrets I harbor have been made public. Will not my next move in this chess game I'm playing with Mora (and with myself?) be a hasty withdrawal, another inevitable bolt? Is this supposed search for the truth after all no more than another symptom of my inability to commit, be it to a career, a woman, or even a place to live?

It's noontime and the sun is at its zenith. It bears due south now, and for the brief moment before continuing on in its astral journey it equally divides east and west. On this day of the equinox, this cosmic instant of balance and symmetry, I know that my time is running out in the paradise I've come so far to find.

22

The initial indication that something's amiss is Mayela Mora's agitated comportment, plus her sidelong glares as she stokes up her wood stove while El Gitano and I wait for her husband's tardy arrival: a reversal of the cordiality she's shown me over the past three months. I am in fact suddenly struck by my stupidity in being here at all, given the rampant rumor that I've been spying for the U.S. State Department, along with the repeated warnings my Pavones-savvy compadres Erik and Joachim have issued about my trips to the Langostino bush; and indeed, given the warnings of my local informants, who are directly privy to the whisperings of the squatter grapevine.

A half hour after El Gitano and I sit down, Mora arrives on horseback along with Mayela's brother, Carlos Araya, who himself has a violent history and had been a part of the conspiracy to murder Max. Mora dismounts and joins us at the table while Carlos sits his horse and Mayela stands close by, watching with narrow eyes. The Mora's hutch is wall-less and I can plainly hear Carlos's horse breathing just a few feet behind me, and the creaking of leather as Carlos shifts in his saddle.

Gerardo Mora's most striking physical characteristic is his eyes. Dark and intense, they've always met mine directly and steadily – one of the things I said to him at our first meeting months before was that I thought he had the eyes of a man strongly dedicated to his beliefs, which was absolutely true. (What I failed to mention was that I also thought he had the eyes of a killer.)

But today is different. Mora has a decidedly haunted look as he sits down, and his eyes will not stay still, will not settle. His level of agitation is palpable in the tautness of his body language, the unnatural carriage of his limbs. I feel my neck hairs prickle as I'm nearly overwhelmed by the sense that something bad is going to happen, right here, right now.

El Gitano is sitting beside me at the table; his stiff posture and bated breath reflect a nascent fear of Mora as well. Although I have not made him privy to my intelligence-sharing with the embassy, El Gitano knows of the rumor. The personal implications of his participation in my investigation must have finally hit home.

Whatever Mora is actually thinking, I assume it's related to the embassy-spy rumor, so my instinct is to try to diffuse that. Although he has not yet uttered a word, I immediately tell Mora that I've visited the American Embassy. Since presumably he already knows this, the admission does me no potential harm. Feigning anger, I launch into a tirade about how Ian Brownlee, the U.S. consul, would not even look at the document I'd brought: The expired land/lease agreement which proved that Max didn't own his Pilon ranchland. (Brownlee in fact already knew about the document.)

Mora is looking at me now, albeit suspiciously. I go on, lamenting the fact that the *norte* press has been relying solely on the embassy for the circumstances behind the shoot out. I assure him that my story will set the record straight.

Although my spiel is largely old news, Mora loosens up a bit and his steady gaze returns. Then, much to my relief, Carlos canters off; his lurking presence behind my back has made me edgy.

My impression, or perhaps my hope, is that I have persuaded Mora that the source of the spy rumor had simply misinterpreted the motive behind my embassy visit. (The *La Nacion* headline proclaiming, in effect, that "The Surf Bum in Pavones is a Spy!" is another matter...) Still, I get El Gitano and myself out of there as soon as it seems prudent to do so without creating further suspicion.

For his part, El Gitano has also been shaken up by the intense vibes at the Mora's. As we bike down the jungle path towards Pilon, he turns to me and says in his low, raspy, thickly accented baritone, "I have this feeling I'm going to get killed, man."

23

In retrospect, El Gitano's voicing of a personal fear of Gerardo Mora should have alerted me to his coming betrayal. As always with me, however, once a potential problem seemed over and done with I found myself shrugging off the overall experience, not foreseeing any repercussions down the line.

But repercussions loomed.

The next day Carlos Araya accosted me at the cantina and after some blathering, awkward small talk tried to be casual in querying where I lived. Thick, wild-man beard gone to seed, a congenital match of his sister Mayela's hostile, narrow squint, a rep as Mora's unquestioning sycophant and muscle, and with the implications of my harrowing Mora sit-down still a factor, I found myself on a sort of yellow alert, verging on red. This especially considering that the settlement adjacent to the cantina was not the Langostino boys' turf; it was the *norte* stronghold and since the slaying of Max Dalton very definitely hostile territory. Pilon and Langostino *precas* rarely ventured there.

As if to answer Araya's query about where I lived I pointed vaguely southward, toward the river, then suddenly excused myself, saying I'd be right back. I hoofed it quickly to the bar, where I pretended I had something vital to say to Joachim, who'd been casually observing the interchange, dripping wet in his surf trunks. "What's he doing here?" Joachim asked through his teeth, smiling as if nothing were amiss.

"Wants to know where I live."

Joachim, still smiling and feigning small talk, rolled his eyes.

Carlos was rubber-necking Joachim and me from across the room. Joachim and his partner Erik were former (and, to an extent, current) enemies of Mora and his cohorts, not only because the two had heavily armed themselves and fought back in the mid-1990s, provoking violent confrontations with the squatters on their own turf, but for how – once they'd reached a position of strength – they had negotiated with individual squatters, circumventing Mora's organization and hence subverting his power.

Billy Clayton, no doubt wondering what his arch enemy Gerardo Mora's brother-in-law was doing in his cantina, was eyeing me questioningly from behind the bar.

I terminated my faux confabulation with Joachim and returned to bid Carlos a quick *hasta luego*, before he could repeat his question about where I lived. Then, using a circuitous route, I biked to my secluded little house on the bank of El Rio Claro. I wasn't followed.

This all worried me a bit, although not unduly so – I already had an extensive shopping list of reasons why I might be in trouble – but the next afternoon the situation turned downright unnerving. I was enjoying a post-surf session drowse in my hammock when I looked up and here came Mora himself in a car, a nice late model sedan, being led by El Gitano on his bike. Led right to my house.

Rattled as I was, I maintained composure and invited the boys in for coffee, with Mora making small talk, much as Carlos had, and looking much more composed than at our meeting a couple days before. Mora was going to San José the following day, he said. "That's nice", I said. "What's up in San José?"

"I have a meeting with Rodriquez," Mora responded casually. "Before his trip to the United States." Miguel Rodriguez was the president elect of Costa Rica, due to take office in early May. He was going to the States to meet with Bill Clinton. One of the topics to be discussed in San José was the Max Dalton case; Mora was to brief Rodriguez on the situation. This of course was a bombshell of the first order – picture Dillinger having a sit-down with Roosevelt to discuss the state of the dollar – but at the time it was registering low on my psychological Richter scale. I was mainly wondering why Mora had come to my house and what had possessed El Gitano to bring him.

An indication was not long in coming. Out of the blue, El Gitano, who had plainly been drinking, said to Mora that he didn't think that Mora had shot Max Dalton and Alvaro Aguilar. Mora looked at me with a knowing smile, waiting for my reaction. I hemmed and hawed, mumbling something about unfounded rumors.

In truth, I was stunned. El Gitano had obviously spilled his guts to Mora about my having amassed evidence that Mora had planned the murders and himself been the shooter. He had no doubt done this to save his own ass, conveniently leaving out the vital role he himself had played in the gathering of that evidence.

Coffee finished, Mora got up to leave. Approaching his car, he tapped the hood and boasted that the government had given it to him. Then, as he fired it up, he looked at me with that same knowing smile and said, "You are my friend, right?" He said it in English, which was odd, and disconcerting. He'd not spoken a word of English to me before.

Mora tooled on by my banana trees then on down the rutted track towards Langostino, with El Gitano calling out that he'd see him later. Standing in my yard, with the muted resonance of surf breaking at the river mouth and the twitters, yodels and yahoos of the forest birds the only sounds, I looked at El Gitano, swaying slightly in moderate inebriation. He glanced at me then looked away. "I quit," he said, with an undertone of belligerence I'd not heard before, and a stiffening of posture.

"What?" I'd been paying him $20 a day for going on three months, more money than he'd ever seen in his campesino life.

"Gerardo got me a better job."

"Doing what?"

A shit-faced, woozy grin. "Working for the DEA." With that he mounted his bike and wobbled off.

El Gitano a DEA asset via Gerardo Mora? It was almost too ridiculous not to be true. DEA had been active in Pavones going back to the Fowlie era; and those guys would have no compunctions about working with someone like Mora, his terrorist activities notwithstanding. In fact, considering Mora's far-reaching connections and his obsessive desire to discredit Pavones's landowning nortes – some of whom (me included) had dubious histories to begin with – such a relationship made some sort of twisted sense. But true or not, the DEA job assertion indicated how tight El Gitano at least thought he now was with Gerardo Mora.

I was getting woozy myself. A possible Mora/DEA alliance... that call he'd made to the OIJ chief directing how the Dalton investigation should be run... his intimate ties to the local municipality... the Union Europa link... a new car from the government... the Eco-Pavones multi-million dollar macro plan... a meeting with president elect Rodriguez...

But again, it all paled in the face of one inescapable fact: El Gitano had painted a bull's eye on my back.

March 18, 1998, San José, Costa Rica. Under increasing pressure from the United States, the Costa Rican government issues a preliminary report on the Max Dalton case. It is a rehash of the squatter version that the incident was an unfortunate mistake, and that Dalton and campesino Alvaro Aguilar had killed each other in a duel-type shoot out. The deaths of Max Dalton and Alvaro Aguilar, the report says, are under continuing investigation.

24

May 5th, 1998. I'm at Puerto Limon, Costa Rica, watching my truck/ camper being loaded onto the Crowley Line ship *Senator*, for the sea voyage north to Miami. I'll be taking a bus to San José tomorrow, then flying back stateside the day after.

Even with three warnings that my life was in danger, including word of El Gitano's plan to plant a bomb in my truck (possibly on the orders of Gerardo Mora), I stayed in Pavones another five weeks after Mora came to my house, partially to mop up my investigation and partially because I was not yet ready to abandon the place I had come to see as home, or forgo the joys of the exquisite waves that break upon its shore.

When I did leave, it was not so much out of fear. Although I'd armed myself and took other defensive precautions (plus a preemptive leak to Mora that I'd already sent my information stateside), I had perhaps fallen into a Max Dalton-like stoicism. In truth, I left because I'd learned too much, not only about what happened to Max but about the opportunism and deceit of many of the *nortes* in Pavones, who themselves have covetous designs upon the land. I'd seen the dark side of the paradise I'd come so far to find, and in the end that vision depressed me profoundly.

THE AFTERMATH*

After leaving Pavones in late April, 1998, but while still in Costa Rica, I faxed my story[†] to my contact at *Men's Journal*, the features editor whom – a couple months later while I was back at Montauk – I would threaten to get the expense money I was owed. His initial reaction was better than I dared hope. He read the piece quickly, within a couple of days, and called with this rave: "We have an incredible story here, Allan, a potential award winner." He went on to assert that since the story was news and therefore of limited shelf-life, it should be gotten into print as soon as possible.

This was especially encouraging since aside from the time, effort, personal expenditures, and risk-taking I'd invested (the investigation had in effect also made me homeless), I felt that if run quickly, there was a chance the piece might actually result in the bringing to justice of Gerardo Mora; or, at the very least, publicly discredit him to the point where he'd lose his political and economic backing. Although initially my motive for looking into Max's death was of a professional nature, over the months it evolved into a personal crusade. By the end, I was obsessed with uncovering the truth and making it public.

So imagine my reaction when, after having been stalled for two months – during which time the publishing date for my piece was moved from August to "maybe November" – the editor curtly informed me that the story would not run at all, because, *"Men's Journal* does not solve murders." (During the course of my four-month investigation, this fellow had told me by phone that I was doing "exactly the right thing" in solving the Dalton murder myself.)

So now I was summarily cut adrift with a news story that was already old; for this reason, and perhaps others, I was not able to place it elsewhere.

---

* Although written largely in 1998, new thoughts were added to the epilog for my purposes in this narrative.

† I sent a 6,000 word version of what you've read here. (The article-length piece got lost over the years, the victim of one of my many crashed laptops.)

Upon my return to the States I contacted Idaho Senator Dirk Kempthorne's office in Washington. The aide I spoke to verified that the timing and the means by which the Senator had received the original inculpating information indeed indicated that it had been my intelligence – given to the San José embassy on the condition that it would *not* be passed on – that had been the impetus behind the resolution censuring the San José administration for its mishandling of the Dalton matter back in March.

I informed the aide that the final results of my investigation were that I now had definitive evidence of a conspiracy to murder Max, and of the Costa Rican government's complicity in the cover-up, if not the murder itself. Although the making public of the facts of the killings was the best way of seeing justice done, lacking that possibility I figured passing my story to Kempthorne was my best recourse. The resolution of censure had not had any real effect and my hope was that the full story (plus the foot-high pile of documents, interview transcripts and tape recordings that backed it up) would result in a renewal of the debate and further political and economic pressures being brought to bear on Costa Rica to properly resolve the Dalton affair.

The aide's reaction to my call – after "talking to some people" at Kempthorne's office – was more overt than simple disinterest. Not only did he rebuff my offer to testify before the Senate Foreign Relations Committee, but he did not even want to see my story. In fact, he was quite adamant about my not sending it. The Senator just flat did not want to hear it.

I was not surprised. Based on the State Department's attitude toward me and my investigation (as evidenced by the embassy in San José), I had already figured out what was going on: The initial hue and cry over the Dalton slaying was superficial at best. Costa Rica being the United State's closest, most stable ally in the chaos of Central America, the last thing Washington wanted was a political crisis that could result from too careful an examination of the matter, or of its implications regarding the safety of United States citizens residing in Pavones, and in Costa Rica at large. America's promise to protect her own had once again taken a back seat to political expediency.

In the end, my crusade to see justice done turned out to be a fool's mission. But back then (and now as I write years later) it was all okay. I regretted nothing. You have to give it a shot.

A piece of philosophy according to me: A truth is not dependent on popular perception. The masses, what it knows or does not know, what it believes or does not believe, is not a factor. In logician's terminology: To exist, a truth has one *sufficient condition*, which is that a single living person has knowledge of that truth, along with the willingness to reveal it. (Gerardo Mora et al's knowledge counts not a whit here, since the willingness to reveal is absent.)

In a world run amok with lies and deceptions on all levels, I truly could not get through the day without this deep-seated belief.

END NOTE

When I returned to Pavones in 2001, Gerardo Mora was very friendly to me. Since no story about my investigation had ever run, bygones were bygones – the old sports analogy "no harm, no foul" comes to mind. Plus, Mora had heard about the success of my memoir, *In Search of Captain Zero* (he even knew about the movie deal) and, he said, had seen my website. We both could make a lot of money, he suggested, via my helping him sell to rich *gringos* the large tracts of land he and his son Esteban now controlled.

In the four years since he murdered Max Dalton and his own cousin Alvaro Aguilar, this former hardcore communist had become a real estate salesman.

When asked how he came to control so much land – hundreds of acres – Mora avoided the question, but told me the titles were free and clear. (A lie, of course.) He also told me he had squatters on a couple of parcels but would soon have them evicted. Gerardo Mora said this without irony or self-reflection, which is to be expected from a sociopath, since sociopaths are capable of neither.

Part Four
On the Run

CHAPTER ONE

*The truth which makes men free is for the most part the truth
which men prefer not to hear.*

Herbert Agate

Second week in February, 2004. Slept but little last night. In fact, didn't conk out until around 3 AM, after I took a couple sleeping pills, strong suckers; one is plenty for most people. And like the codeine, you can get them over the counter in Costa Rica. Still, they almost didn't do the job.

Presumably you've read about my 1998 Max Dalton investigation. Okay, so have I. Which is a peripheral reason I couldn't sleep last night (the main one having to do with Lisa). Somewhere around Christmas – possibly during the writing of the chapter in Part Two mentioning that Lisa was baking tortillas at the Moras – I thought of including the investigation in this narrative. Thing was, at that time and up until my reading a few days ago, I hadn't considered the implications of making the matter public. I hadn't looked at the piece in several years and only had a vague recollection of it.

I dredged up the old file, which is labeled "Under Eden 1" – *Under Eden* being the working title of the book I was figuring to write after the *Men's Journal* fiasco; the story of Max, Gerardo Mora, Danny Fowlie, assorted side issues and characters (like Logan the Nutcase), the squatter wars; the surfy, wild west history of this paradise at the end of the road called Pavones, Big Turkeys.

So I paste the thing in sort of gleefully – gleefully because we're looking at a lot of words that I won't have to write; Part Three is already done, except for futzing and the rewriting of the epilog as a segue back to the present. So I'm gleeful. Then I read the thing and I'm not so gleeful.

Talk about denial.

Where do I think I'm going to be at – I mean every sense of "being at" – in the event that this book sees print and copies make their way down here, which would somehow be immediately, likely when the book is just in ARC, or even in manuscript?

Whaddam I, nuts?

The list of people who would be out for serious revenge on my sorry ass would be... if the phrase "all but endless" made sense – which it doesn't – I'd use it. Logan, assuming one of us hasn't already killed the other by then, is just one name on the list. In fact, he wouldn't even be at the top. I'd give him number two.

The top spot of course would go to Gerardo Mora. This based on the fact that he's already gotten away with two murders, not just conspired. His motive for killing me is self-evident, no? Okay.* Then we have Logan; give him number two. Ditto the motive. How about the OIJ (the Judicial Police), which at the very least was deeply involved in the cover up of the Dalton murder, possibly with forehand knowledge of the crime? Revenge aside, they might be inclined to off me in order to nip in the bud any further finger-pointing. Or how about higher-ups in the San José government who no doubt had approved the cover-up?

Virtually anyone mentioned in the Dalton investigation would make the list. Fajardo – whom I accuse of complicity in the crime – with his spook-connections, you name 'em. So many people having a motive would make it virtually risk-free for whomever actually does the deed – down here at Big Turkeys where the police give you the address of someone you're pissed off at and suggest you murder him.

But how about protection from my government? The U.S. State Department? As I point out in my Dalton investigation, the boys in Washington care not a whit for protecting U.S. citizens abroad, not when doing so conflicts with relations with a friendly, stable Central American country.

A lonely feeling.

But there's worse, way worse, news, in terms of lonely feelings. Last week, Lisa and I went up to San José, looking to protect ourselves from Logan. We met with our lawyer, Francisco, who could help by putting on the record what may happen – a bogus drug bust, say, like Logan's move against Mountain Mike. The second-to-last day of the four-day trip, Lisa had been out for the morning ordering construction materials (another reason for the trip). I was in the shower, having just gotten back to the hotel, the Balmoral, from a meeting with a newspaper reporter – using him to put stuff on the record. Just before my shower I noticed that Lisa's purse, big and green and funky, was on the chair. So Lisa had got back before I did and then she went back out for something. Fine. I came out of the shower just as she was opening the door – carrying no purse, of course, since it was on the chair.

Hi, babe. What's up?

---

* A while back Mora's son Esteban – who I occasionally run into surfing – out of the blue asked me to whom I have left my land in my will. What the fuck was with that?

Lisa said she was just getting back from shopping and did not succeed in ordering the stuff we needed.

Just now at this minute getting back?

Yes, she replied, seeming a bit rattled.

I was beset by a very bad feeling, based on the fact that Lisa was apparently lying about when she first got back. She could not have traveled across town in search of construction materials without her purse. All she had on her person was the room key (one of those electronic cards); she was wearing a dress with no pockets. The bad feeling I got was so bad that I couldn't deal with it right then. I went back into the bathroom to splash water on my face and look at myself in the mirror and think about this and I was all shaky. I was not ready for the implications of Lisa lying about where she had been; I was worried enough about bogus drug busts and maybe hit men.

Now, among other things, I was thinking about Lisa's "we" slip while describing her solo night in San José back in October after not keeping her story straight about why she didn't have the cell phone on her. Among other things like the night she spent alone in San José when she flew down to live with me and I couldn't get her on the phone at her hotel until the next morning, Lisa claiming that maybe her room phone didn't work that night (then started up working in the morning); and I recalled how she'd breezily described a guy she'd approached at a bookstore at the Atlanta airport between flights to ask about San José restaurants, a surfer who was on her flight. I thought about these incidents, among others, then gathered myself and came back out and told Lisa that her purse was on the chair when she came in.

She said no it wasn't; she had it with her.

I had to sit down. I really was not ready for this. Lisa's purse was on the chair when she came in – all she had on her when the door opened was her room key.

What does this mean? It means she was seeing her fuckbuddy that day. Why else lie about when she first came back? She came back then went out to see him, nearby in a café or, more likely, in another room in the hotel or in a nearby hotel, which is why she didn't think to bring her purse.[*]

Why else would she lie?

The implications of this make all this other stuff about me being murdered or set up look like... small stuff, to quote the asshole who wrote that dumb-ass book.

So, again, you want to talk about a lonely feeling?

---

[*] A couple of days after this incident, Lisa said, without thinking, "Even if I did go out without my purse it doesn't mean that much." To which I pointed out that it means a helluva lot: "It means you were lying about where you were, Lisa." To which she left the room without responding.

I've got to know the truth here – or prove the truth, in a way Lisa cannot deny. I've got to catch her unequivocally. My plan is to send her up to San José on some pretext or other and get her to take the bus, to save money or whatever. She'll go and I'll fly up and be waiting to catch her with her fuckbuddy.

Lisa herself solved the pretext problem, God help me. Here's what happened: When Lisa and I were up in San José as described, the day after the purse incident Lisa finally did order construction materials, which arrived at our property two days later via truck. The delivery didn't include a few things in the order. In all, some three hundred dollars worth of stuff; so the company owed us that much in money or exchanges. No biggie since we had to go up to San José again anyway within a couple weeks; we had unfinished business with the lawyers, plus I needed to go to my dentist up there soon.

Lisa talked by phone to the guy she placed the order with. She was on the office porch where the cell phone reception is best. I was downstairs but I could hear the conversation, although Lisa was not aware of it. It was very short; Lisa said there were problems with the delivery and that she would come up to fix them. When she got off the phone Lisa told me that the guy said he needed "original copies" of the invoices to fix the problem. Well, I was there when she paid for the order; the guy already had "original copies" – an oxymoron to begin with. And there was no time or place in the phone conversation for the guy to say that anyway. The whole conversation consisted of Lisa saying she would come to San José to fix the problem.

Lisa also said that since I was feeling down and agoraphobic these days, she'd go to San José by herself and take care of it all, even said she'd go by bus to save money. Her voice got breezy as she said this stuff.

The next day, when Lisa was walking the dogs, I called the same guy in the San José building-supply store and asked him if it was necessary to go up there to fix the problem with the order. He said no, of course not; it could be done by phone or fax.

So Lisa was definitely lying about what the guy said, making sure it sounded like she had to go back to San José, by herself to save money and to let me relax. This on top of what happened in the hotel, when she lied about where she was.

Sure, babe, go on up to San José.

So she'll get on the bus then I'll fly up the same day and check into the hotel and be waiting for her, in a nearby room. Follow her. Catch her with whoever is waiting up there to see her.

While waiting for my plan to crystallize, here's some other stuff, some loose ends, mostly about fear, and about where I am now, now meaning as you read this, not as I'm writing it – assuming I'm not dead:

I spoke to Lisa about what would be the consequences of this book being published with the Dalton section. I gave her Part Three, which she immediately read, me lying there beside her on our bed. When she finished she looked at me and said that the piece was good, which was a relief – Lisa reads a lot and is tough on writers. And she agreed that should it be published we'd have to get out of here, give up our home. Then she said that in spite of how much she loves our home – and she really does – she'll support me in my decision. Allan, she said, you're a writer, it's what you are. She'll change her life, again, and be there for me, support me in whatever is necessary. Because she loves me. Then she got out the massage oil and told me to roll over so she could do my back, feet and head, squeeze out the angst pus.

But it now seems that Lisa has a fuckbuddy up in San José, a Snowman (or Cityman) incarnation here in the tropical heat; it seems that she was carrying on with him while we were dealing with threats from Logan the Nutcase. It seems that Lisa has a fuckbuddy after the other lies and cheating and promises that the lying and cheating are over, and after Lisa read Part One of this, wherein I say that my worst nightmare is being in love with someone who is *dishonest*, and that Lisa is at heart a good and honest person.

That's *real* fear.

CHAPTER TWO

We make up horrors to help us cope with the real ones.
Stephen King

February 24, 2004. I'm on the run, I'm in hiding. I'm on the Caribbean island of The Horror fame; the island I did not name for fear of attracting more surfers, and at which my screensaver surf-photo was taken, and which appeared in *Surfer*. The computer with that screensaver, a desktop machine, is in San José, Costa Rica, stashed in my lawyer's office. In a sense it's in hiding too. There is too much stuff in its Word files that I don't want to lose or have leaked to the wrong people by leaving it vulnerable to a home invasion, fire or other catastrophe. I'm writing this on Lisa's laptop. Lisa is not here with me.

Everything has changed, including my plan to catch Lisa with her San José fuckbuddy by following her when she goes up there alone. Even this island has changed, at least from my point of view. An example is how this day has gone so far.

Remember back in Part One the idyllic image I drew of this little island jewel set in the blue Caribbean? Mentioned how my neighbor was playing soca music, which I like, the day I was writing, a Sunday, and how the fishermen were haul-seining in the bay below and how everywhere you look there is a postcard?

This morning at around 5 AM my neighbor started blasting on his stereo a tune I assume was titled "Stand up for Jesus" – a continual rap rhythm chant of nothing more than "Stand up for Jesus." This noise was on some sort of loop; it went on and on until after 7 AM. The speakers were those six foot-high jobs and just a few yards away from my door at full concert volume. Just at the point of losing my mind (and accepting Mohammed or Jim Jones as my prophet), I looked out my window and instead of a postcard of the men haul-seining in the bay below, I was looking at a riot down on the beach. A score of drunk locals throwing punches and even swinging cutlasses at each other. I don't know how the riot ended or if it ended; the mob fought its way out of sight around the point towards the surf break. It was a nice visual accompaniment to "Stand Up for Jesus."

A few minutes after the riot moved on, my DJ neighbor switched to full-blown island rap, a godawful perversion of the soca I like so much. I asked him to turn down the music. This was perfunctory; I knew he would not do as asked, and I knew the reason he would give, which was this: "Hey mon, it carnival time."

I had the misfortune to arrive here in the midst of Carnival. Carnival is supposed to be some sort of religious event, but it's actually no more than an excuse for the human beings who live on this island to behave even stupider than usual; hence the blaring music and the drunken violence on the beach.

Speaking of stupidity and violence. Yesterday, my first full day here, I was at the surf break and this local I've known for years walked up to me smiling and asking how I've been. Rather than answering his query I whacked him so hard it stung my hand.

See, last time I was here I did him a favor and by way of returning it he stole some money from me. Thing is, I'm edgy and cranky and really was not in the mood to see some guy who stole my money standing in front of me smiling and asking how I've been. Still, whacking him was stupid behavior on my part. I could have ended up in jail or he might have gone and gotten a cutlass and lacerated me; one or the other might still happen.

I don't like violence. In fact, whacking this guy resulted in a stomach ache that lasted for several hours. The last time my stomach was in this type of uproar was when I'd gone looking for the North American named Rich with the intention of blowing a few holes in his Jeep while he watched.

I'd let Rich stay in my house when I went to Montauk back in May – this was the trip wherein I found out about the New Year's Eve Guy and started worrying that he was The Cityman. When Lisa and I got back from that fiasco I found that Rich had swiped $300 from the house, money meant to pay our workers. I didn't go looking to whack Rich because Rich is bigger and stronger and younger than I am. He no doubt would have beaten me up. With people of this description, you have to make the point, and decisively so, that you're crazier than they are. This worked with Rich. He caught wind that I was looking for him with a shotgun, waved the white flag and summarily gave me back my money, saying it was all a misunderstanding. For the half day I was looking for Rich, though, my stomach was also in an uproar. As I say, I don't like violence.

Two days after my arrival here, Lisa called to say our cell phone wasn't working. Said she didn't know why; it just quit. Which means I can't call her;

she has to call me from the one public phone in the pueblo. This of course reminds me of the cell phone lies from the past, all of which resulted in the same situation – I can't call her. It also reminds me of a blurted query she posed last month, out of the blue: Did I think she'd brought her "nonexistent San José boyfriend" to Pavones? It also reminds me of my suspicions last fall that she has a local fuckbuddy, aside from the San José one.

The reason I'm here on this Caribbean island alone and in hiding is a result of events from eleven days ago. Just before dawn that day I was in my office working and was interrupted by the dogs going nuts at the gate. I went out there to find my mercenary buddy Ron looking upset, which isn't good; Ron doesn't upset easily. Plus, given the early hour, I knew something was afoot.

"Looks like our friend Logan put out a contract on you", were Ron's first words to me that morning, even before I calmed the dogs down or opened the gate.

I guide Ron in and over coffee he tells me the story. The previous day he was at the Panamanian border canceling my order for illegal guns to augment my arsenal (I decided that if I shot someone it would best be with a legal weapon) when he ran into a mercenary buddy from San José – there's a clique of foreign mercs that uses the city as home base. Ron had already spun some wild yarns about this crew so I knew about them. Four or five days previously, Ron tells me, his buddy saw Logan in San José looking for the nastiest of these guys, a bad-ass merc who mainly does "wet work," meaning hired killings.

"There's only one person he's crazed enough about to go to this guy," Ron tells me. "You." I know this is the case. Word in the pueblo is that Logan is seething over my sorry ass, going around telling people words to the effect that I'm history. He's told his men not to speak to Lisa's and my men, Flaco and his three brothers, Roman, William and Wilmar, plus their father Roman, Sr., all of whom, I believe, are loyal to me. Two of my expat-in-residence buddies, with tongues only slightly in cheek, told me that Logan's vendetta against me is a relief for them, and that Logan's brain is so busy squirming in his skull over me that he'll probably forget about his threats against *them*.

And of course I know for a fact that Logan is capable of using a hired killer to solve perceived problems – he'd offered Ron money to off Billy Clayton, according to Clay and confirmed by Ron himself. And let's not forget Gerardo Mora's assertion that Logan is "the most dangerous man" at Pavones.

I had some decisions to make that morning ten days ago. First, even given all the reasons to believe Ron, including his reaction to the unmotivated kindness I'd showed him, could his intelligence be trusted? Was he telling the truth?

Why would Ron lie about this Logan/hit man deal? Some possibilities occurred to me, but in a situation like this you have to assume the worst case scenario, meaning Logan had in fact paid someone to kill me. So I told Lisa, who had just gotten up – immediately sensing that all was not well – to pack light for fast travel and get in the car. We were getting out of there. Now.

CHAPTER THREE

You will think me lamentably crude: my experience of life has been drawn from life itself.

Sir Max Beerbohm

Ron offered to come with us as a bodyguard and suggested Panama as a place to hole up and regroup, but I opted for San José, notwithstanding that the presumed killers were based there. My plan was to use various means of letting Logan know that I was aware of the contract, and that other people knew, with the hope that he'd back off and cancel it. To this end I told our men – the Rodriguez brothers and their dad – that Logan had hired someone to kill me so they'd spread the word in the pueblo while we were gone. They'd also leak that I've left the country to arrange retaliatory measures. I'd already set up this notion via a chance meeting with Logan some three weeks previously in the nearby town of Ciudad Neilly, after I spotted him in a restaurant. He saw me as well and tried to avoid me but I ran him down and told him that I'd contacted people from my past and that anything that happened to me would happen to him. Logan had read *In Search of Captain Zero* and knew I was referring to the Colombians with whom I was tight when I was in the pot trade. Logan's response was mumbled bluster; he meanwhile jumped into his car to get me out of his face. But Christ I wanted to pop the fucker then and there.

At that time my implied threat to put a reciprocal hit on Logan was a bluff, but now real measures would have to be taken, or at least it had to appear so – again, if I'm to have Logan killed, even in a postmortem way, you think I'm going to outright say it here, in this nonfiction narrative?

We rolled into San José late afternoon, found a suitable hotel, a fleabag joint off the beaten track, Lisa and I in one room, Ron in an adjoining one. Assuming the worst case of the worst case – meaning that a professional killer was actively searching me out, was highly-motivated and had serious resources – I'd go to great lengths to keep our whereabouts unknown. We'd move every couple days, pick a hotel at random, definitely not one we'd used before, check in under false names, and pay cash for everything; no credit card trail.

My plan on how to make public Logan's hit on me was threefold. I'd use my lawyer to inform the Costa Rican authorities; I'd go to *The Tico Times*, which I'd already contacted on the previous San José trip (I'd given them a copy of the letter to the U.S. Consul); and I'd visit the Vice Consul, Nathan Flook – a great name, phonetically and alliteratively, for a State Department flunky, no?

First, I wrote another letter, this one to V.C. Flook directly, detailing the new information that Logan had put out a contract on my life – it was no longer just a possibility. I found Flook in the bowels of the building behind a bulletproof window tending to U.S. citizens with passport problems. Flook pretty much looked like what he was, a nondescript government bureaucrat. I introduced myself as a writer who had sent a letter to the Consul about being threatened by a nutcase at the end of the road down south at Pavones. I told him I now know that there is a contract on my life. I held up my new letter then went to slip it under the slot at the bottom of the bulletproof window. Flook's reaction was to take a wary step back and tell me to take the letter out of the envelope. Flook was apparently concerned that there was a bomb or possibly a weapon of mass destruction in the thin little envelope – hey, who knew where Saddam stashed his nukes?

Not a good start to our relationship, vibe-wise. Flook put the letter aside, told me he'll try to get around to it, then suggested I go the OIJ, the judicial police. I told him that wouldn't work since the OIJ is on Logan's dole. He looked behind me to see who was next on line.

Aside from conferring with our lawyer, Francisco, plus a high-powered colleague of his, I also visited *The Tico Times*. The timing was good; they were working on a story about Logan's conflict with the commercial fishermen at Pavones and had already interviewed a bunch of folks, Ticos and *nortes* alike, who told them that Logan is a loose cannon, if not an outright lunatic. And my credibility factor was high: the paper had done a profile on my life and times a couple of months before; my expat semi-celebrity status (Sean Penn and John Cusack wanting to play me and so forth) elevated me from some weirdo wandering in from the Central American landscape rambling on about hit men. Plus I had a gift for the *Times* journalists: documents linking Logan to Danny Fowlie, The Waterman Who Would Be King, in federal prison stateside. Logan had gone on and on to the paper about his law and order crusade down at the end of the road, to the point where the reporter already smelled a hypocritical rat. Logan had, on the record, vehemently denied doing business with Fowlie or even having met him, when the truth was that he, Logan, had twice visited Danny while Danny was in jail in Mexico in 1988, trying to cut a land deal.* I knew about the Mexico visits, not only from documents I possessed but because Logan had owned up to them in 1998 during my Dalton investigation; I had this on tape. Again, my knowledge of this and other aspects of Logan's sleazy deals is a big aspect of his desire to remove me from the realm of the living – now and back in '98 when he issued that first death threat. That and the fact that I surf rings around the asshole.

On the morning of day three I visited my flunky friend Flook again at the embassy – he had not returned my calls wanting to know if he'd read my letter. He looked up from behind his bulletproof window, not appearing to recognize me. I reminded him by saying that I was the guy from two days ago with hit men on his ass hired by a fellow U.S. citizen, and had he read my letter?

Haven't had time, Flook said, although he had come across and "looked over" my first letter, the one to the Consul. Flook suggested I go to the OIJ with the problem.

Look, I said – not even bothering to repeat that Logan has the OIJ in his pocket – all I'm asking is that you get word to Logan that the embassy has heard that he's threatening a fellow U.S. citizen and is there any truth to that?

"The U.S. State Department doesn't interfere in the internal affairs of other countries," said the federal flunky named Flook from behind the bulletproof glass. If not for the gravity of my circumstances this beaut would have precipitated an outright howl from yours truly, along with the observation that bombing other countries into oblivion and breaking every international treaty or convention ever written or thought of in the process could maybe be construed as interfering in their internal affairs.† But I didn't howl or make this observation. What I did do, though, was get a bit cranky; I couldn't help myself, and besides, the polite approach was getting me nowhere so what did I have to lose?

The intelligence I'd provided the embassy during my Dalton investigation was mentioned in my first letter, which Flook had "looked over," as was the gratitude of the Consul of that time, Ian Brownlee, plus that of the Head of Regional Security, the spook who left me hanging out to dry towards the end of my investigation after promising me protection if needed. So I reminded Flook that they'd sure as hell gotten involved back then, and they'd sure as hell taken an interest in me when *they* needed help.

---

* Fowlie will later claim he refused to do business with Logan because of the latter's history as a cocaine trafficker – which Logan freely admitted to – Fowlie saying he did not want that sort of association, given his own legal problems.

† I might have mentioned the State Department's threat to cut off aid if Costa Rica didn't sign an agreement exempting U.S. personnel from war crimes prosecution, which sounds like meddling, not to mention an admission to perpetrating war crimes.

Flook shuffled papers, said he'd try to find time to read my new letter. This was on February 17, going on two weeks ago. Not a word from Flook or anyone at the embassy since then.

CHAPTER FOUR

Why, sometimes I've believed in as many as six impossible things before breakfast.

Lewis Carroll

During this time in San José, I was concerned about my vulnerability; I had to assume that a killer knew that I was in the area. He certainly had photos of me, via my web site or print publications such as virtually any of the surf magazines or *The Tico Times*. He may have spread them around, to hotel contacts and restaurants often frequented by the expat community, which is a small one. As I say, I had to assume the worst case of the worst case. So I was very careful, didn't even give away to taxi drivers the name of my hotel; I'd have them drop me a block or so away.

In spite of my precautions, some unsettling stuff happened during the week Lisa and Ron and I were in San José prior to my coming to this Caribbean island. Upon reflection, though, this stuff may have had to do with Lisa's treachery, not any hired killer.

On the first day in the fleabag hotel I made a mistake. Lisa and I needed a starter motor for our car; we had the number of a German expat who ran a parts business in San José. I called the fellow and introduced myself, mentioning my Pavones surfbuddy, Kim, who had given me his number. The German said he could get the part, then offered to deliver it at my hotel and asked where I was staying. I told him – breaking my number one security rule.

About an hour later the mistake hit me; what also hit me was that, as mentioned, the San José expat community is a small one. If a killer was looking for me, it was possible that the German was part of his circle of cohorts. Also, have you ever heard of an auto mechanic who offers to deliver a car part?

We had to get out of that first hotel. I cut Ron loose, told him to go back to Pavones, and Lisa and I moved, not even telling Ron where we were going.

But during our stay at the fleabag hotel something else odd happened, although, as with the mechanic, I didn't immediately realize anything was amiss. Lisa had been bothered by a persistent cough; she just could not shake it. We'd settled in and Lisa had gone down to the lobby for something or other. When she came back she said she'd met an American guy staying at the hotel with his Tica wife and two kids; the wife was a doctor with an office in San José. The guy's name was David, Lisa said, a commodities broker from Miami, who was living in Costa Rica. Lisa theorized that he was one of those sorts that had "two families" – one in Costa Rica, one in the U.S., or maybe in the UK, where, she said, he did a lot of business. The doctor/wife would see Lisa about the cough that day, at the hotel, when she returned from her office. Today was some sort of special occasion in their marriage. Okay. Whatever.

That afternoon there's a knock at the door. Lisa gets up to answer; I barely catch a glimpse of this guy, a *gringo*, lean, with dark hair and a moustache, as Lisa steps outside to talk to him. I hear the guy say, "Do you have a blood type?" Lisa answers quickly, "AB." They step out of earshot to continue the conversation. Lisa comes back and says she has to meet the guy's doctor/ wife in an hour, at their room.

Okay. I'm somewhat distracted by this hit man business so I don't think much of this, although the guy's query about Lisa's blood type should have registered as odd. Why would a doctor – let alone the doctor's spouse – want to know that before seeing you?

So Lisa leaves the room at 6 PM, presumably to get examined in the hotel by the wife. I'm with Ron, discussing my general situation; I'm not thinking anything is weird, not yet. Lisa is gone about twenty minutes. Comes back and says the wife/doctor says she has an allergy.

The day after this I realized my mistake with the mechanic and we moved to another hotel, after which I had Lisa go to the mechanic's shop and pick up the car part. I shadowed her at a distance to see if anyone was following her to maybe lead him to me. This is how careful I was, how seriously I took the threat.

No one was following Lisa.

The next day I went down to the desk of our new hotel and asked if anyone was inquiring about me; asking if I was at the hotel and so forth. The desk clerk said no but that a man not staying in the hotel had hung out in the lobby for over an hour the night before, saying he was waiting for someone who was a guest. The guest never showed up, the desk clerk said, and the man left. I asked for a description.

A *gringo*, dark hair, and *flaco*, lean, with a moustache.

This didn't ring any bells regarding Lisa, not at first; I was mainly wondering if the guy was a potential threat to my life, but the next day I put the description together with the guy in the first hotel, and with my plan to catch Lisa with her fuckbuddy by following her to San José; the plan that was aborted when Ron told me about Logan's visit to the bad-ass mercenary. I had almost – not quite, but almost – put the Lisa/San José fuckbuddy problem out of my head. And the idea of Lisa continuing on with her fuckbuddy while I was actively on the run from possible hit men was... it was just too horrific a thought. But here are some of the things that now occurred to me about the San José fuckbuddy and the guy who came to our room at the first hotel:

Given that his "wife/doctor" had an office in San José (Lisa said), the couple obviously lived in the city or near it. Why then stay at this fleabag hotel, and with their kids?

Lisa got no prescription or even a recommendation of what drug to buy, nor did the wife give her a business card or office number – odd, if the couple was trying to drum up business, as Lisa theorized. According to Lisa, the blood type issue did not come up again; the wife/doctor didn't mention it. Which, again, begs the question of why a doctor's spouse, in setting up an appointment, would ask that; or even why a doctor would need to know it at all.* If the doctor had some weird theory of medicine then why didn't it come up in the examination? But what's my point here? Simply that nonsense in someone's already nonsensical story further raises the level of suspicion.

If the guy was Lisa's San José fuckbuddy he would have been a bit nervous coming to my room, no? This could account for a claptrap "medical" blurt – he would have instinctively wanted to immediately sound like a doctor's spouse. He fucked up, of course, not only with the subject of the blurt, but the way he phrased it: "Do you have a blood type?" I have news: Everyone has a blood type.

Also, Lisa sure knew a lot about the guy – aside from the doctor/wife-and-two-kids stuff – based on a brief meeting in the hotel hallway, the subject of which was supposedly her cough. What he did for a living, where he was from, that he lived in Costa Rica, that he did business in the UK, that his wife had an office in San José, that maybe he had two families, and that today was a special occasion. As I already knew, Lisa rambles on with details when she's lying. And her voice got breezy as she was telling me this stuff.

There was no charge for the medical consultation – still more odd shit – so no receipt. In other words, there was no way of checking if the story was true, or if the wife/doctor actually exists. I never saw her or the kids in the tiny hotel. And again, if the wife/doctor diagnosed her as having an allergy, why didn't she prescribe medication, or recommend what tests to undergo to find out what allergy she has?

There was also this: Lisa was obviously carrying on with her San José

---

* I would later contact a doctor/surfbuddy of mine and ask what possible reason a doctor would have for knowing someone's blood type before an examination. His reply was, "None at all."

fuckbuddy the day she came back to our room at the Balmoral without her purse, claiming to have been out shopping all morning and was just now getting back. We were concerned about Logan then too, if not as concerned as now. So, horrific as the thought was that she would still be carrying on, it was – let's face it – to be expected.

When I told Lisa I was skeptical about this guy and his supposed Tica wife/doctor, Lisa made another mistake via too many details/not thinking before speaking. She said that the next morning the whole family was downstairs having breakfast when we were doing the same, and didn't I remember?

Not only did I not remember, but I absolutely knew that there was no family having breakfast. Because of my situation I was extremely aware of who was in and around the hotel. I recalled precisely who was in the dining area (very small, like 5 tables): a Tico reading the paper over coffee and an older *gringo* having breakfast alone. No one else. No question of that.

Also, given that the wife/doctor had supposedly examined Lisa the previous day, some sort of "Hello, how are you feeling?" or *some* kind of exchange would surely have occurred, which I surely would have remembered. (Or Lisa would have pointed out the "doctor" who examined her, sitting a few feet away.) Not that this matters, since in any case I knew there was no one else there for breakfast, aside from the two guys.

But who knows, right? Maybe I'm disturbed and paranoid as Lisa theorized in response to my suspicions; maybe I'm blanking out the family for whatever reason, so I can be more miserable. I mean, right?

I went back to the hotel and persuaded the desk clerk to show me the check-in sheet. Lisa had pointed out the room the family was staying in; room 207. As I say, a couple doors down the hall from us. The hotel had maybe ten rooms.

According to the registry, room 207 on the date in question was occupied by a *gringo* named David all right. He signed in as "David Peter." "David Peter" is not a real, full name, not without an "s" at the end of "Peter." It is, most likely, someone's real first and middle name. In fact, when we checked in, for security reasons I had Lisa register for us, telling her not to use her real name. And there it was, in the register for our room: "Lisa Jean," Lisa's first and middle names. That's the way I used to check into places back in my pot-smuggling days and wanted no records of my movements; use my real first and middle names. This way, if you're asked for I.D., you don't look like a fool or worse; you can say that's the way you refer to yourself, a shortened version. Okay, we had a reason for checking in under a false, or partial, name. Why would this guy do that? One possibility that occurred to me was that he was there to fuck someone's girlfriend while the other guy was also at the hotel. The other guy being me. He would want no record of who he was, in case the situation went sour.

Number of occupants for room 207 that night: *One.* No family of four. "David Peter" stayed one night, the night we were there, then checked out. I asked the desk clerk if there could have been a mistake with the number of occupants. No way, she said. If the register says one occupant then it was one occupant, since they charge per person. When I told this stuff to Lisa she said the guy must've sneaked the wife in to save money. A commodities broker and a doctor sneak into a fleabag hotel ($15 a night) to save, literally, a buck? (On a *special occasion?*) I don't think so. Plus, what about the two kids? He sneak them in too? Plus, according to Lisa, they have breakfast – the four of them – right in front of the desk clerk? (The hotel is not only tiny, but you have to get buzzed in through the front door.)

In further trying to persuade me that nothing was amiss, Lisa came up with more details and, again, she made a mistake. She said she saw the wife's dress hanging in room 207; she saw this from outside, said she never went in the room. I looked at the room when I went back. The only view from outside the room through the door were of the beds and two windows. No place to hang a dress; the closet was on the near wall, out of sight completely.

If Lisa was lying about the family of four staying at the hotel – having breakfast and dresses hanging in the room and about the doctor/wife and so forth – and she surely was lying, then what does that mean?

The guy who came to our room was her San José fuckbuddy.

I build a case here, don't I, with my facts and deductions and rhetorical questions? As with Gerardo Mora as the killer of Max and Alvaro Aguilar, I feign objectivity and build the case, reveal to you the mounting evidence of ultimate treachery.

But here's the other side, what makes this case different, and please keep it in mind as we go: Lisa could not *be* like that. No, it's not possible.

You must understand that. No matter what else I say, whatever else happens, whatever crapola I come up with, you must understand that.

CHAPTER FIVE

Fasten your sea belts, it's going to be a bumpy night.
Joséph L. Mankiewicz, screenwriter

March 1, 2004. I'm leaving this Caribbean island tonight, going back to Costa Rica. All goes well with the flight, I'll be in a San José hotel room, the Holiday Inn downtown, before midnight. Lisa will meet me at the HI tomorrow morning, March 2nd, having flown up there from Pavones. My next plan to catch her with her San José fuckbuddy will come to fruition then or the next day, depending on how things go.

There's a coincidence here. Tomorrow, March 2nd, will be one year to the day since I found out Lisa had been screwing her ex-boyfriend and lying about it. I was in a San José hotel room when this happened; then I flew here and The Horror took place, plus the around-the-island romantic interlude during which I tried unsuccessfully to upset Lisa by pointing out that the hotel we were having breakfast in was where I had the best sexual week of my life, fictitiously speaking. All that possibly amusing (or self-indulgent) crapola. I can't stay at the San José hotel (the Balmoral) where I got this bad news, which would have been nice for symmetry and nostalgia. If there is a killer hunting me, he may be watching the hotels I've used in the past.

Last night was Oscar night on TV here on this fucked up little island. The Hollywood community, of which I used to be a member, was out in full peacock regalia to celebrate itself and its accomplishments over the past year. I nodded off about an hour in, then woke up around midnight. Took another sleeping pill. While waiting for it to kick in, the Best Actor award came up. Sean Penn won, for *Mystic River*. He looked fit, lucid and mellow, not like a stoned-out actor who doesn't read anything, to quote Steven, my treacherous, big-mouth Hollywood attorney. While Penn was giving his acceptance speech, I pictured him up on the silver screen playing me; I couldn't help myself. I also couldn't help picturing him down the Hollywood road apiece accepting another Oscar, won for his brilliance in playing me.

Something else happened while I was drowsing in front of the TV, eyes half-shut. During one of those tracking shots of the audience clapping and grinning and pretending they're happy that someone else won an Oscar, I caught a glimpse of someone I know. A woman I'd had sex with back when I was writing for *Miami Vice* and who had subsequently won an Oscar. (In a non-acting category, so don't get too curious.)

Seeing this woman reminded me of the time Lisa and I were watching satellite TV back home at Big Turkeys and an Al Pacino movie called *Simone* was on, and during the credits Lisa let out a squeal of delight and clapped her hands.

What, Lisa?

That was my friend (in the credits), the guy from *Magnolia*, Lisa said.

The Snowman. Great, Lisa, I was thinking, but I didn't say anything. I just sighed and got more depressed. Christ. Her *friend*. Lisa got all bubbly from seeing on the tube the name of the Hollywood guy she'd had the best week of her life with, sexually (since the sex was uncommitted).*

Last night, upon being reminded of a Hollywood woman I'd had sex with, I didn't let out a squeal of delight or clap my hands or get all bubbly. I just lay there like a slug, hoping I'd get to sleep soon. But I didn't. The recollection of Lisa's excitement at The Snowman's name on the tube somehow led me to worrying about Lisa's claim that the cell phone at Pavones wasn't working, and what that possibly implied about what she was up to. And then *that* worry – plus all the Oscar hoopla on the tube – reminded me that Lisa had recently claimed that she'd have to be "an Academy Award-winning actress" to fake so well her love for me. It was the second time she'd pointed this out, using those exact words.

So when I finally fell asleep it was with visions of carnival riots and guys I whacked and hit men chasing my sorry ass and catching Lisa with a fuckbuddy and Sean Penn playing me (and then winning an Oscar for playing me) and a Hollywood woman I'd had sex with (and who'd won an Oscar) and Snowmen in movie credits and Lisa up on the podium at the Dorothy Chandler Pavilion accepting an Oscar for faking so well her love for me dancing in my head.

---

* If for some bizarre reason you want to know The Snowman's actual name, you could now look it up via one of those filmography books or websites, by cross referencing the *Magnolia* credits with *Simone*. See who's listed in both.

CHAPTER SIX

It's not so much that you're still telling lies that bothers me.
What bothers me is that I no longer believe your lies.
Fredreik Nietchtze

March 4, 2004. I'm back at Pavones, in my office overlooking the Sweet Gulf. I flew into San José two days ago and Lisa met me at the Holiday Inn, Lisa having flown up from here. My plan to catch her with her San José fuckbuddy didn't at first go as planned so I had to improvise, change my plan yet again. Originally, I was to fly in before Lisa, meanwhile telling her that I'd arrive after her, allowing her to spend a night in San José by herself. I'd shadow her from her arrival, figuring she'd use the time alone in the city to have a fuckfest with the fuckbuddy, even if they'd already had a fuckfest at my house while I was on the run. Maybe he'd even pick her up at the airport.

Problem with my plan was that due to last-minute flight changes, Lisa knew she'd be arriving at San José after me and there was nothing I could do about it. Fresh off the plane, I checked into the Holiday Inn and thought about what to do when Lisa got in the next morning. Meanwhile, I contacted my spooky contact from the Max Dalton murder investigation, Fajardo. I was still thinking about "David Peter," the guy who came to the San José hotel room a couple weeks previously, just before I went on the run. Lisa's probable San José fuckbuddy. If David Peter had in fact checked into the hotel using his first and middle name, and if in fact he lived in Costa Rica, I figured Fajardo could help me find him, given his connections with the Costa Rican government, which keeps close track of foreign residents.

Although I well knew that Fajardo could not be trusted in any sense of the word – he had been at least peripherally involved in killing Max – and although the whole thing was a long shot, I figured I had nothing to lose. I'd provide him with the partial name "David Peter" and have him see what he could dig up. Farjardo was overjoyed to hear from me, like we were long lost war buddies reunited. He was, I knew, thinking about how much money he could extort from me. The negotiations were as expected, given Farjardo's price tag of a million dollars for providing me with the truth about Max's death, and about why that truth would cause the San José Government "to fall." After multiple phone calls and the concomitant haggling, a deal was struck. He'd get back to me.

My improvised plan to catch Lisa involved renting two adjoining rooms at the HI. I had a dentist appointment for the day after Lisa's arrival, during which Lisa would have several hours to herself. I'd blow off the dentist and instead wait in the adjoining room to see what she did. I could even listen to any phone calls through the connecting door. I also bought a tape recorder, which I'd leave on in the room whenever she was there alone.

First thing, the hotel people fucked up. When Lisa checked in, they sent her to the adjoining room, which was in my name but vacant; I was waiting for her next door. When Lisa realized I had rented two rooms she misinterpreted my motive, thinking I was sending her back to the States from San José and didn't even want to be in the same room with her. We'd had some blowups on the phone, including one over her changing her Yahoo password without telling me; we each had the other's passwords, for both business reasons and as a matter of trust.

Anyway, she lost it, had a full-blown breakdown.

Looking back, her hysteria and grief – the desperation with which she clung to me sobbing – over our perceived breakup was the cause of my plan's partial collapse; I don't handle that kind of thing well. My resolve was shaken. I calmed Lisa down and assured her that I wasn't sending her back to the States. I admitted why I'd rented the room, reiterated my suspicions about "David Peter," plus the time she claimed to have been buying building materials without her purse, plus the "we" slip in describing her night alone in San José; her inability to refrain from flirting with other men, and on and on.

She cried and cried and we made love and not only did my resolve get shaken, but I myself cried, after which I melted. I caved big time.

I caved because I knew Lisa could not *be* like that.

I didn't mention the tape recorder, however.

Lisa and I were hungry after the sex so I went to the supermarket to get cheese and wine. I surreptitiously turned on the tape recorder, which was still in my luggage on the bed, and went out. I came back from shopping and didn't deal with the tape, which was still running.

A few minutes later Lisa found the recorder in my bag. We had an emotional scene about trust and so forth and, in spite of everything, I was wracked by guilt. Lisa said let's listen to the half hour tape. I said no, I don't want to do it. I wanted to trust her, and show her that. It was crazy, of course. However, later, when Lisa went out, I listened to the first couple of minutes. Just Lisa turning pages in a magazine, a few coughs. I turned the machine off, leaving the tape where it was, about two minutes in; an eight of an inch on the take up spool. I put the recorder back in my bag and didn't touch it again.

The next day I went to the dentist; Lisa stayed in the room. Before leaving I considered taking the recorder to listen to the tape in the taxi. God help me, I didn't do it. Before leaving I did register exactly where the recorder was in my bag. Call it a half-assed premonition.

Three hours later I returned and noticed the recorder was in a completely different place in my bag; Lisa must have handled it. Lisa brought up the tape; she was jovial and breezy, that tone she uses when she's lying. She can't wait to see what I write about the tape, she said, referring to this narrative. (By now – and this is hard to imagine but true – Lisa had begun to encourage me to continue on with writing this book.) She said this three times in a few hours. Then she said this: "It's not like there are eighteen minutes missing," referring to Nixon's altered Watergate tape – a classic Lisa-blurt, as it would turn out.

We flew back here to Pavones and yesterday I was reading here in my office and decided to listen to the tape, just put it on in the background. The take-up spool was where I left it, it appeared, about two minutes in. I rewound and started it over. Six or so minutes in, I was brought up short, like an electric shock. There's a click and the sound of Lisa by herself in the room (the magazine page turning, her coughs, all the ambient sounds) ends and suddenly it's the next day, when I was gone at the dentist. How do I know this? The day I went to the dentist it was very windy. We were on the 12th floor and the wind was whistling against the window; it had come up overnight. We had remarked about how loud it was. This sound is very clear on the tape. Just that whistling wind after the click and nothing else, apart from a light bump one time, as if the recorder was picked up or moved. As a test, this morning I recorded over another tape and the click sound was identical to the one on HI tape – it was the sound of recording over the existing tape.

About 12 minutes later on the tape (after the sound of the wind) there are a few seconds of garbled sounds then another click (the tape being shut off, as I found from re-doing it on the other tape), then the original tape recording kicks back – the sound of Lisa and me talking when I got back from shopping before she found the recorder; no wind whistling. It was apparent that whoever recorded over the first recording had screwed up, waited too long to stop the rerecording.*

I confronted Lisa with this and she denied having recorded over the tape. We listened to it. She did not, could not, deny that the tape had been

---

* The tape I used was new, right out of the box, the recorder brand new. Also, I subsequently used the equipment for interviews. In eight hours of use there were no technical problems – not that technical problems were a possibility here, what with the clearly recorded sound of the wind.

recorded over. I said she obviously did it while I was at the dentist. How else could it have happened?

Here's Lisa's explanation: When she packed that afternoon, the tape must've gotten bumped in the luggage and the buttons got pushed. The sound of the wind, she theorized, was maybe recorded in the elevator on the way down to the lobby – wind blowing up the elevator shaft.

This is not even in any realm of possibility, for the following reasons: When I listened to the tape, I noticed that it was indeed where I had left it, about two minutes in. So here's how the machine had to have been "bumped in the luggage," how the buttons were accidentally pushed: First the Play or Fast Forward button, to advance the tape forward a bit, then the Stop button, then Record and Play simultaneously, then 12 or so minutes later the Stop button, then the Rewind button, then at two minutes into the tape the Stop button again, in order to leave the tape where I'd left it.

Plus, how to explain the sound of the wind and, other than that, silence, if the machine was being tossed around in the luggage? Also, if the recorder was packed in the luggage the wind sound would not have been audible. The theory that the sound of the wind was recorded in the elevator doesn't even deserve to be dealt with.

Impossible. Literally impossible. When I pointed this out, Lisa suggested the maid might have done it – meaning pushed all the buttons – saying she'd seen them watching TV in rooms.

This morning, after a tense and nearly sleepless night, I was here in my office listening to the tape again, desperately trying to come up with an explanation that doesn't imply continuing treachery on Lisa's part. Lisa came in, saw what I was doing and snapped, "Even if I did record over the tape, it doesn't mean much..." Here she shut up. When I asked her to repeat that, she left the room in a huff, saying the tape was my problem.

Lisa recorded over that tape, most likely because she had called her San José fuckbuddy when I was out, possibly to arrange a meeting the next day when I'd be at the dentist.

Why else would she record over the tape and then lie about having done so?

CHAPTER SEVEN

It is easy – terribly easy – to shake a man's faith in himself. To take advantage of that to break a man's spirit is the devil's work.
George Bernard Shaw

What was I thinking during this time? I mean about Lisa, not about the possible hit man hunting my sorry ass, or the *Captain Zero* or *Cosmic Banditos* movie deals, or the telling of the various back-stories, like that of my demented *Zero* book editor,* or my need to know everything about the Max Dalton and Alvaro Aguilar killings; plus a Meanwhile or two, the writing of this narrative being one example. And there was Mom, who was on my mind a lot during this time.

What I was thinking about Lisa was that Lisa could not *be* like that.

One recurring system of thought was that maybe Lisa and I were the victims of ridiculous fate – some pack of malevolent gods was toying with us, trying to ruin our happiness. In other words, maybe there were innocent explanations for the various incidents and Lisa-behaviors. This system of thought predominated early on, even right through The Incredible Bouncing Cell Phone And It's Various Destinations Incident (plus Lisa's "we" slip in describing her lonely night in San José), and which system of thought was buttressed by Lisa's otherwise near perfection as a mate and partner in life (I fear I've not made this clear): her kind and tender qualities, competence with practical matters, protectiveness (my Maginot Line) and so forth. In thinking about her blatant flirtations with other men... I didn't think about them, or tried not to. Ditto the lies she'd told early on regarding her dalliances (which was the word I tended to use, rather than, say, fuckfests) with her ex-boyfriend and the one night-plus-the-morning stand (if it was such) with The New Year's Eve Guy.

Oh, we'd argue and I'd occasionally grill her, as would be expected, but in the initial months since Lisa had moved down to paradise to live with me, our love and passion for each other mostly prevailed, and which

---

* After writing several more chapters about my demented editor and my then-literary agent, I excised them as being *small stuff* and Big Mo killers. You'll hear no more of them here; a sure indication of the deterioration of my sorry-ass life and times.

included daily sex of astounding duration and lust, plus plenty of take-fives. So, yes, we'd argue, but there was mainly bliss, if an uneasy bliss on my part, during this time.

But the effect of these mounting incidents was that my system of thought segued from the Malevolent Gods Toying With Us Theory to the Lisa Is Crying Out for Help Theory. In this one, Lisa's blatantly incriminating behaviors amounted to a need to be caught and then helped with her psychological problems.

My plan of action, my strategy, based upon the Lisa Is Crying Out for Help Theory was to persevere and finally catch Lisa in an act of infidelity/treachery in an in-your-face way that could no longer be denied. She'd then see how she was ruining our lives. And for what? Some occasional uncommitted dick (as a break from her full-blown Sex God)? My subsequent forgiveness of her transgressions would be profound proof of my love and commitment. Lisa's inevitable epiphany after being unequivocally caught would change her fundamentally and forever.

Meanwhile, in the face of it all, the Malevolent Gods Toying With Us Theory would occasionally resurface; but further incidents and Lisa-behaviors would soon invalidate forever any version of this one.

A couple of weeks after the Holiday Inn Taping Incident Lisa and I returned from a trip to the Panamanian border to order more construction materials. It had been a long day of driving on bad roads, and frustrations with blasé Central American incompetence. In unloading the car, which was in the carport immediately outside the front door, Lisa entered with my little shoulder bag and said, "I can't find the cell phone." She put my bag down, plus whatever else she was carrying.

I told her not to worry about the phone; I'd just seen it somewhere in the car and knew it wasn't lost. A few minutes later I was upstairs in my office, having brought my bag with me. Although I had no reason to do so, I opened the bag. The cell phone was in there. In retrospect, Lisa's assertion about not being able to find it was probably nagging at me: there had been several cell phone "disappearances" since the Incredible Bouncing Cell-Phone and it's Various Destinations Incident a few months previously. The phone had always turned up.

The phone was the sort that shuts with little hinges when you hang up and there was a receipt from the last hardware store we'd been to folded in there. I'd put the receipt in the phone myself, so as not to lose it.

I brought the phone downstairs, held it up, and told Lisa that I'd found it my bag.

Right, she said. Then it's not lost.

I asked Lisa why she'd put the phone in my bag.

Lisa denied having done that.

I said I hadn't touched my bag, which had been on the back seat, since the border.

Oh, right, Lisa said. She said she remembered seeing the phone bounce around in the console on the bad roads on the way back and thought to put it away.

Now she was affirming that she put the phone in my bag.

I asked Lisa where we were when she put the phone in my bag.

Back at the border, Lisa said.

I showed her the receipt from the store, which we'd been to *after* the border. So the phone was in the console on the trip back from that last stop, not in my bag. I also remembered that this was the case. Lisa, I said, since you were driving and my bag was in the back seat, how could you have put the phone in the bag between our last stop and home?

Lisa asked what my point was.

My point was that Lisa had put the phone in my bag *while unloading the car.*

Okay, Lisa said. So what?

By way of answering I wanted to know how someone could pick up a cell phone, stash it somewhere, and then *a few seconds later* say she couldn't find it?

Again, Lisa asked what my point was.

My point was that she was trying to demonstrate how cell phones get misplaced for innocent reasons. Keeping my tone light, I reminded her of her history with cell phones, starting with the lie about having left the charger in the city when she was really in bed with her ex-boyfriend. And remember the brand new charger that right out of the box didn't work (which was her stated reason for the phone being off) but the next day started working fine? I mentioned all the times when she'd turned off her phone after promising not to do that. And that for weeks of turning off the phone (after these promises), she kept doing so because she was back screwing her ex-boyfriend.

Lisa, I said, recapping, you were trying to prove that shit naturally happens with cell phones; they get lost or whatever with no sinister implications. I didn't mention what I was thinking, which was that to try to prove this via a sleight-of-hand deception *was* pretty sinister.

"I'm not that smart," was Lisa's blurt to this. Not that she wouldn't do something like that. She just wasn't smart enough to think of it.

"Smart got nothin' to do with it," I said, paraphrasing a favorite movie line.[*] I said this because Lisa's move was not smart at all. She should not

---

[*] The line was Clint Eastwood's (written by David Webb Peoples) from *Unforgiven*. Clint was about to blow away the evil Gene Hackman, who opines that since he was building a house, he didn't "deserve" his coming death. Clint replies, "'Deserves' got nothin' to do with it."

have said anything about the phone, let alone that she couldn't find it. She should have just waited for me to notice that it was missing, which probably would have been the next day, when all this stuff wasn't fresh. Then her ploy might have worked; or at least she wouldn't have got busted. Still another example of not thinking before speaking.

Lisa didn't deny the inevitable conclusion that she had put the phone in my bag while she was unloading the car – and that she then immediately claimed she couldn't find it. In the end, by way of final explanation/ qualification she said, "It had been a long day."

If you're in any way thinking Yeah, okay, maybe she was really just tired, an excuse to that effect, I ask you to do this: Put this book down, get up from wherever you are right now, walk a dozen feet, then see if you can bring yourself to say, "I can't find that great (or annoying) book I was just reading." Key to this impossibility is the "I can't find" clause, which presupposes you've been looking for the book, which of course you have not been.

Although I let the matter drop, I was thinking about it, and it bothered me. I was also remembering the last cell-phone "disappearance," which had happened immediately upon our return from the Holiday Inn Taping Incident. When we got home and were unloading the car, Lisa said those same words, "I can't find the cell phone." And, indeed, we turned our luggage and the car inside out looking for it. It was gone. Lisa "found" it the next day, claiming it was under the front seat. I'd already searched the car; it had not been under the front seat.

It was now obvious that Lisa was making a continuing, concerted effort to change my way of perceiving her phone deceits.

And it wasn't over yet. The very next day following the border trip we took the dogs for a walk on the beach down in front of the house. Upon returning and reaching our gate, Lisa held up her blouse, indicated its front pocket and said she'd dropped the keys to the gate and house somewhere on the beach.

Shit, Lisa! The spare keys were in the house… we'd have to break in… and our tools were in the house too… fuck!

Lisa said not to worry. She'd find the keys. She trotted back down our little dirt road toward the beach.

I was meanwhile thinking how unlikely it would be to find the keys on that beach; it's all rocks and one place looks the same as another, plus we'd traversed a good half mile during our dog walk…

But here came Lisa trotting back, smiling, holding up the keys. She was back so fast I could hardly picture her reaching the beach, never mind having the time to search…

"See, nothing sinister," she said as she unlocked the gate.

What? I didn't get it.

"I didn't call my boyfriend in San José."

What the fuck? Where did *that* come from?

Until that moment I wasn't thinking anything sinister was up with the keys. I was just relieved Lisa had somehow (instantaneously) found them. But this comment about not calling her boyfriend in San José – the phone was in the house – was the tip-off. Lisa was trying to connect in my mind the keys getting innocently lost with cell phones doing likewise. Or, for that matter, as on the previous day, cell phones innocently winding up in my bag.

See, nothing sinister, Allan.

Okay, I get it. Chronic dishonesty on someone's part wasn't our problem. With all these cell phones and keys falling and bouncing all over the place, the problem with our relationship was… gravity.

Gravity just would not stop fucking with us.

This stuff percolated in my head during the days following Lisa's sleights of hand until I finally couldn't keep my trap shut any longer. We were on the terrace sipping Chilean red wine and listening to the howler monkeys bellow in the bush out back and I turned to her and said she had to quit with the gaslighting behavior. My tone was conversational, as if I'd just pointed out a toucan sitting over there in the banyan tree.

What did I mean? Lisa wanted to know.

Cell phones, keys, trying to prove that they get lost or… whatever… innocently. Just please quit that stuff. It's upsetting me, I said. It didn't seem like that outrageous a request.

Although I'd seen versions of What Happened Next, I was not prepared for the intensity this time. Lisa was on her feet and in my face in half a heartbeat, screaming. In recollection as I write, and as reflected in my journal entry of that day, the only coherent words I retained from her tirade are "self-righteous" – which I believe referred to me and had negative subtext – and "changed my life." I also believe the figure of a quarter million dollars surfaced in this context, a reference to how much money Lisa would have made yearly if she hadn't given up her old life to come live with me, a claim I'd heard before, although not at this bullhorn volume. If it did work its way in, I was too busy beating a hasty retreat toward the bedroom to point out that Lisa had been unemployed at Montauk for the last three years, with no prospects other than local waitressing.

Lisa calmed down a few minutes later; head hanging and deep sighing, she was the very image of abject contrition. I don't know what happened, she said. Why do I always go crazy like that?

Because it works, was what I was thinking, but out of fear of her going crazy again I kept my trap shut.

The gaslighting accusation hung in the air as the tears welled up and phase two of Lisa's *modus operandi* for dealing with me was unleashed: uncontrollable sobbing and apologies and protestations of innocence and love and devotion and so on and on. And she clung to me and spilled tears onto my chest in her sorrow and grief and love.

My hope was that Lisa's attempts at altering my perception of the world to conform to her personal agenda – the very definition of gaslighting – would cease after my clear warning that I was on to her. And so it went, if briefly. Lisa returned to her role of perfect mate. And as had been our pattern, her blow-up and subsequent apologies led to lusty make-up sex and a post-clearing-of-the-air period of calm. But of course the air had not been cleared; it had been dirtied. And my inner turmoil, my bad thoughts, were difficult to hide; Lisa would catch me looking at her in a certain way and for a brief moment we would both know...

We would both know...

I did not know what Lisa knew...

What soon followed was a heightened frequency and duration of massages to squeeze out the angst pus, more and even jazzier home made pizzas, more "us against the world" assurances. Lisa's little love notes and sexy post-its became full-blown love letters, written as if we were involuntarily and gloomily separated by some vast distance (which metaphorically we of course were); multiple-page opuses oozing with desire and devotion. She would leave them around, often next to my computer so I'd come upon them in the wee hours upon rising for work – along with an occasional handwritten "private journal" entry accidentally left around the house; more florid prose extolling, among my other qualities, my astounding sexual prowess and how I'd "ruined [her] for other men." The phrase "my nonexistent San José boyfriend" would get worked in here and there, sometimes via ad hoc segues, which usually included reference to my irrational fears and unfounded insecurities. These private journal entries were especially significant since they were meant for her perusal only. They therefore represented a higher order of truth, could be taken as the gospel, even, in spite of their having been so carelessly left about, boldly labeled "Private" and easily subject to my well-known prying.

In other words, the gaslighting continued, if in a more subtle, theoretically tolerable form.

Then one predawn morning a couple weeks after Lisa's outraged eruption at my request that she desist from gaslighting me, I wobbled my way up to my office with coffee, cigarettes and codeine to carry on with the writing of this narrative to find something other than a love letter on my desk next to my computer. It was an Internet page Lisa had printed out, a treatise from a P.h. D in psychology named John Todd.

The Othello Syndrome

The delusion of infidelity of a spouse or sexual partner. It affects males and to a lesser extent females. Symptoms are recurrent accusations of infidelity, searches for evidence, repeated interrogations of the partner, tests of fidelity, sometimes stalking. Can appear by itself or in conjunction with paranoid schizophrenia, alcohol addiction or cocaine addiction. As in the play by William Shakespeare, the Othello Syndrome can be highly dangerous and result in the disruption of a relationship, homicide and suicide.

Sounds like me all right. Doc Todd all but mentions aging surfer/ memoir writers who live at end-of-the-road paradises as being particularly susceptible. On the other hand, there's that word right up front in the good doctor's classic illustration of circular reasoning/specious causation. "The *delusion* of infidelity." Seems important, that word. And the word begs a few questions, the most interesting being: Is it possible to suffer from The Othello Syndrome when, simultaneously, your girlfriend *is* fucking around on you? Is there a catch-22 or a double whammy here?

I may be paranoid but that doesn't mean everyone's not out to get me.[*]

---

[*] What's with the clause "As in the play by William Shakespeare" coming after the three supposedly related problems of paranoid schizophrenia, alcohol and cocaine addiction? Othello wasn't beset with any of this shit. In fact, he wasn't even delusional: he was being manipulated, yes, gaslit, by an evil underling. So what's with this syndrome being named after him in the first place? Should I be looking for some cackling Iago hiding in my bodega, trying to turn me against Lisa's sweet Desdemona?

CHAPTER EIGHT

All sin tends to be addictive, and the terminal point of addiction is what's called damnation.

W.H. Auden

I have a confession to make, in the form of an admission to a bit of nonfiction deceit I perpetrated back in Part One.

I'll quote from Part One, in reference to Lisa's former occupation before moving down to paradise to live with my sorry ass: "Lisa was, or is, a high-powered businessperson. In fact, she was, or is, so high-powered that I don't really understand what it is, or was, that she did, or does."

I was being disingenuous here. Hold on. I was lying like a slug. I knew full well what Lisa did, or does. I didn't want to disclose what Lisa did/does because of my agenda at the time of that writing, which was to portray Lisa in a positive way; I'd already decided that she was, to quote more crapola from Part One, "at heart a good and honest person."

That's my confession to a bit of nonfiction deceit.

What was with the deceit? What did/does Lisa do for a living and what does it have to do with my agenda back in Part One?

Lisa was in public relations, crisis management division.

Okay, so what's the problem?

With the possible exception of certain sorts of lawyering, public relations, and especially the crisis management end of it, is the most basically – meaning fundamental goals and methods – dishonest formal enterprise the mind of man has yet to conceive. Makes advertising look like death-bed-to-a-priest-confessional time.

I was so ashamed of what the woman I fell in love with did/does for a living that I lied like a slug, hid from you the truth.

Remember Bhopal? The toxic waste cloud released by Union Carbide that killed over 20,000 people in India back in 1984? What do you figure was the first thing the CEO Warren Anderson did when he learned of the catastrophic misery and death his company had perpetrated? See to it that medical and evacuation people were rushed in?

No. Anderson called Union Carbide's public relations chief, a guy named

Bob Berzok, to get on the crisis management, the spin control. "Spin" (or "spin control") is, of course, a euphemism for *lying like a slug*. And there's even a euphemism for the euphemism, a description/label/concept I really like – in the morbid sense – for its Orwellian ring. *Perception management*.

I'll just list, with no editorializing, some of the perception management projects Lisa's former PR company, Abernathy/MacGregor/Scanlon was involved in. Remember Suharto, the shitball motherfucker dictator (so much for no editorializing) of Indonesia back in the 1990s? In case you don't know: Suharto was responsible for the worst continuing genocide of that decade, in East Timor.* Lisa's company handled Suharto's perception management problems relating to his genocidal behavior. Tried to make him look like a nice guy, "our kind of guy."

Remember my old chum Michael Mann's tour de force, *The Insider*? Russell Crowe as Jeffrey Wigand, the tobacco industry's courageous whistle blower? Remember the smear campaign against Wigand in the flick? One of the senior partners of Lisa's company headed up that godawful piece of perception management.

Lisa claims that she wasn't involved in the above projects; let's assume that's true. Here are two projects she personally oversaw, according to Lisa herself: The meat industry was having image problems regarding slaughterhouses being inhumane, filthy and just all-around nasty. Plus with statistics and studies showing that eating meat is bad for you, meat consumption was falling (and, consequently, people were living longer, healthier lives). So Lisa went down to Texas (I think it was) to confer with the meat industry folks on how to perception-manage people into eating meat again. She also visited a slaughterhouse and found that they are in fact inhumane, filthy and just all around nasty. So there was that perception management problem as well.

I don't remember what Lisa told me about how this perception management campaign went, but *I* eat a lot of meat, along with my other bad habits.

Lisa also headed up the perception management of a toxic waste incident in Puerto Rico, went down there to fix the problem — not the problem itself, but the perception of the problem. It wasn't anything like Bhopal, though, she assured me.

Perception is truth is the underlying principle of the love of my life's profession.

---

* Both Bush I and Clinton supported Suharto in his genocide in the 1990s — sent him the military hardware to perpetrate that genocide — knowing full well what Suharto was doing. Clinton, in fact, called Suharto "our kind of guy" for his cooperation with big business (mostly oil) and repression of dissent. This support of genocide from the U.S. government goes back to the Ford and Carter administrations in the 1970s.

If at this moment you're not thinking that I'm perpetrating just a bit of perception management myself (notwithstanding that everything above is true, according to Lisa) then... no, you're not a fool; *not necessarily*. But I'll tell you what: You haven't been paying attention.

Which reminds me. *Dishonesty*. It appears that dishonesty is what this book is about. It's segued to that while I wasn't looking, so to speak. Obsession and pain, which I previously thought was what this book is about, or was about, has become a Meanwhile.

Perception management is a term I had better define. Since there is zero chance that it's in *Webster's New Universal Unabridged Dictionary*, I'll have to do it myself.*

Perception management is "The organized attempt to alter the understanding of the world of a person, group of people, or the population at large, in order to conform to a personal or group agenda– wherein truth is not a factor."

If this sounds familiar, it should. This definition is very close to the one I gave for *gaslighting*, in reference to Lisa's sleight-of-hand maneuvers with cell phones, plus her use of love letters, phony private journal entries, Othello Syndromes, and so forth, to alter my understanding of the world so as to conform to *her* agenda (that I'm delusional and she's innocent of rampant infidelities).

A result of the similarity between perception management and gaslighting is that Lisa was, in effect, professionally trained in the craft of gaslighting.

Gaslighting is Lisa's business and she has been very successful at it.

---

* I know *perception management* is not in *Webster's New Universal Unabridged Dictionary* because I tried looking up *spin*, which is the more commonly used synonym. Wasn't there (of course), not in the *lying like a slug* sense. Listen: After not finding *spin* in my fucking hundred-pound dictionary, I did something I should have done a long time ago. I flipped to the front to find out the year of publication of my edition. 1972. Christ. The shitball motherfuckers who put together *Webster's New Universal Unabridged Dictionary*, 1972 edition, have an excuse this time, since *spin* (in the *lying like a slug* sense) is a new word. Which in turn is an indication of how dishonesty has lately become a given in these sorry ass post-fucking modern times — or *post-post-fucking-*modern sorry ass times.**

　** Hey: What's with the word *New* in the title *Webster's New Universal Unabridged Dictionary*, (1972 edition)? Weren't the idiots at Webster's thinking ahead *at all* (back in 1972)? If they were to insist on leaving *New* in the title, they should have printed it in ink that fades over the years, no? A lot of words in that title, too, *needless* words, to once again refer to that great little book, *The Elements of Style. Avoid needless words.* I admit that dictionaries, *by definition*, so to speak, are not overly concerned with *style* but you'd think *some* thought would go into the title. What they should have done – what they *would have* done in a better world than this one – is lose the *New*, and lose the *Universal* and *Unabridged* too, since you get these points by looking at the thing, and trying to lift it. Just call it *Webster's Fucking Dictionary* and get on with it.

CHAPTER NINE

If there is a 50-50 chance that something will go wrong, then nine times out of ten it will.

Paul Harvey

Around this time the *Cosmic Banditos* screenwriting deal suddenly appeared to be going through. Why this should be after a year of procrastination on the part of John Cusack's company, New Crime, was a mystery; I'd pretty much given up on the deal. But suddenly, during the hit man and all the rest of the fiascos, I had a contract; Steven called and told me to sign it. Then I did something I'd never done before in the dozens of deals of my Hollywood life. I read the contract. Another premonition, maybe.

In spite of never having read a Hollywood contract – which is what I pay Steven to do – I do know a bit about the intricacies of deal-making. And guess what? I find a handful of fuck-ups, all in the other side's favor, including one that will immediately cost me $6,000. I have Lisa read the contract. Yes, she says, there are several fuck-ups, including one at six grand. I think of something. I look at the envelope the contract arrived in, via International DHL. The return address is from the other side, New Crime's legal firm.

What does that mean?

My attorney hadn't read the final version of the contract he's telling me to sign.

But get a load of this: Guess who the other lawyer is, the one who sent me the contract? Amy Nickin! After The Shooting Gallery went belly up she got a job with the firm that reps New Crime.

I know: It's relentless, plus ridiculous, this shit. But there you have it.

Anyway, it appears that Amy is at it again. (If so, the folks at New Crime have nothing to do with it, I'm sure. As with the original subterfuge, they and Cusack himself were out of the loop.)

I'm immediately on the phone to Steven, and with an attitude. Yeah, right, I see what you mean, Steven is repeating as I go over the contract, pointing out the fuck-ups, including the $6,000 doozey. Then I bring up his letting the other side — the Amy-frickin-Nickin side — send me the contract to sign, rather than sending it himself after reading it. You know who Amy Nickin is, I say. Then I quote him, pointing out how he called Amy "the most duplicitous lawyer" he ever dealt with. *That* Amy Nickin.*

To this Steven gets rowdy with me, which I expected. People tend to get rowdy when you absolutely, no question, bust them on a fuck-up or deceit. God knows I'm used to that sort of thing: it's how the love of my life gets through the day.

As Steven's rowdiness gathers steam, I'm remembering how he told everyone about the book I was writing, the book you are now reading, and the subsequent call from the *Zero* producer threatening a lawsuit. But instead of bringing up that piece of treachery directly, I interrupt with a related issue, asking if I can quote him in my book – in this book, of course – that "Sean Penn is just a stoned-out actor who doesn't read anything." Which was the excuse he used to not help get my "brilliant" draft to Penn.

This shuts Steven up for a moment, as I knew it would. Then, the Hollywood wheels in his mind having rotated, he says, "You can't publish that!"

"What's the problem?" I inquire (I'm tempted to add "ironically" as a modifier here, in spite of Stephen King's warning that the road to hell is paved with adverbs). "I mean since my book is not publishable." Which was the excuse he used in refusing to help me find an agent (for this book).

I use the ensuing silence as an excuse to hang up.

Steven calls back later that day and apologizes for his rowdiness, saying he's having a rough day up there in Hollywood.

That one precipitates a howl from yours truly.

---

* By the way, *duplicitous lawyer* may look redundant, but it's not. It's actually an *exponential whammy*, which is way more significant than a simple whammy or even a double whammy. An exponential whammy is when you take two concepts that look redundant and multiply them by each other; since they have the same numerical value (which is why they look redundant), this is identical to squaring one or the other (as in *duplicitous to the second power*). The number you get is a big one. In this case, you have to add the implied *Hollywood* to *duplicitous lawyer*. This further exponentializes the result (as in *duplicitous to the third power*), and hence you get into conceptual figures the human mind cannot comprehend.

CHAPTER TEN

Why shouldn't truth be stranger than fiction? Fiction, after all, has to make sense.

Mark Twain

Some Meanwhiles.

Our caretaker Roman's brother, Flaco – whose life I saved after he got bit by the deadly terciopelo viper* – along with the third brother, William, found a bale of cocaine washed up on the beach down in front – Pavones is a drug smuggling way point between Colombia and the U.S. of A. and shit sometimes ends up on the beach. Flaco and William tested the shit, word is, then decided that working for *gringos* (like me) was no longer fun. They took to smoking the shit and selling the shit and then when the shit they found on the beach ran out, took to sneak-thievery and outright burglary to keep having fun rather than working for *gringos*. They got ejected from their father's house for this behavior and so now have moved into the cottage I built for Roman, their brother, my caretaker.

So now I have crack-head thieves living on my property.

Soon after this bulletin from paradise some waves arrive from the Southern Ocean and one morning Lisa and I are surfing in front of the cantina. Surfing is my only escape, or source of relief – abatement, alleviation, amelioration, anodyne, to list just the "a"s from my thesaurus – from the fiascos and catastrophic shit. Aside from the physical beauty of the environment, there's the endeavor itself, the mindless, out-of-time rush of it... plus, nothing can... can sneak up on you out there. I'm talking more about assorted varieties of bad news and mindless drivel rather than hit men and the like, although there's that advantage too.

So I'm surfing and experiencing a bit of relief from all this and I look

---

* If you'll remember, I saved his life by getting him to the clinic in Comte in a record 18 minutes – normally a drive of 45 minutes over the worst roads you ever saw. This resulted in my local nickname going from "La Escopeta," or The Shotgun – a result of the time I went looking for Rich toting a shotgun with which to blow holes in his jeep – to "El Viento," The Wind, for how fast I got Flaco to Comte. Cool nicknames, no? Unfortunately, though, my nickname would eventually become "El Chivo," literally, "The Goat," but which means "One Who Wears Horns," i.e., a cuckold, which is not so cool.

shoreward to see Ron waving for me to come in.

This can't be good news, I'm thinking.

Ron sits me down on the seawall and lowers the boom of his latest gloomy tidings, in the form of a double whammy. First, my neighbor Carlos Lobo – a good hearted wild man I know well from my Max Dalton investigation – is now allied with Logan the Nutcase (who was Carlos's former enemy), and hence I should at all costs avoid him. The same goes for Marc Sherman, another Fowlie guy from back in the day. Sherman is my neighbor on the other side.

In other words, aside from a major Big Turkeys balance of power shift, I'm surrounded.

The really bad news, Ron goes on, leaning in, lowering his voice, is that Logan sent a Tico underling up to San José a few days ago and put a down payment on the hit, with the bad-ass merc that Ron doesn't know well.

I haven't said anything yet and continue to keep my trap shut. I want to see if this is going where I think it's going. It is. Ron lowers his voice further and suggests we do a preemptive hit on Logan, rather than merely set up a reciprocal one – I already told Ron that I arranged for this when I was out of the country, via my old Colombian cohorts. (Whether or not this is true I'm still not going to divulge.)

I shrug, and my overall noncommittal body language spurs Ron on.

Ron tells me that the job could be done for 20 grand, using himself as triggerman and his San José merc buddies to secure the weapon and for logistics, then to extract him from Pavones and from the country. The bad-ass merc who got the down payment to kill me will be pleased to keep the money and not have to do anything once Logan is terminated, Ron says. So he's no problem. Ron knows how to talk the merc talk all right.

Twenty grand. I happen to know that this sort of job here at the end of the road can be bought for under $1,000, via certain Panamanians at the border, at Paso Canoas. So I'm thinking Ron would probably use one of those guys and pocket the spare $19,000 and change. (Costa Rican assassins are notoriously unreliable and are to be avoided, notwithstanding the complexities and success of Gerardo Mora's assassination of Max Dalton. Goofy stories come to mind, like the Tico hit man who shot himself in the foot while waiting in ambush.)

It's around here in the conversation that I think to look out at the surf lineup to see if Lisa is carrying on with any guys. Her two-day flirtation with the surfer she invited to our house, which is going on a year ago now, is the original source of this constant concern (and reinforced by the various other in-my-face incidents), which concern is a distraction from the peace and beauty of the endeavor of wave riding. No, she's not carrying on with any guys out there right now. Okay. Good. One less thing. For the moment.

I tell Ron that I'm going up to San José next week anyway to see my dentist, and while there we'll talk further. I give Ron a few bucks for bus fare and food.

Keep your head down, buddy, Ron says.

Actually, I don't keep my head down, not at all. In fact, my attitude about being assassinated continues as it has been, alternating between not thinking about it and not giving a shit if I *am* assassinated.

A fine distinction, maybe, but there you have it.

CHAPTER ELEVEN

Do you believe in fairies? Say quick that you believe! If you believe, clap your hands!

Sir J. M. Barrie

My meeting with Ron in San José the following week sets a new record, reaches a new high, a hitherto un-scaled peak voltage on the doozey meter (another spectrum kind of thing). In fact, the doozey needle flies off the doozey scale.

I arranged for us to meet at a gambling casino bar/restaurant. Casinos are good places to meet if you're worried about hit men, rip offs, or other sorts of fiascos and catastrophic shit, due to in-place security.* A half hour late, Ron barrels in all sweating and discombobulated.

What's up? I query, sensing that something good is coming.

Here's what's up, according to Ron: He flew up from Big Turkeys yesterday rather than taking the bus because he's so worried about me and combed the merc bars looking for his merc buddy, the heavy-weight merc, in order to find out the status of the hit on me by the bad-ass merc – the merc he (Ron) doesn't know well. Ron can't find the heavy-weight merc and, coming out of a merc bar last night, gets attacked from behind, is knocked unconscious and wakes up in a cellar somewhere bound and gagged with duct tape and being hovered over by some heavily armed Ticos who don't say anything. Then the bad-ass merc comes in and un-gags him, wanting to know who Ron is, since he (Ron) has been asking so many questions about him (the bad-ass merc) in all the merc bars. Ron tells the bad-ass merc that he (Ron) is only trying to help a friend (me) who has a problem down at Pavones with a guy (Logan) and that he (the bad-ass merc) should know that his (Ron's) friend (me) is willing to do whatever it takes to call off a hit, should it be true that the guy (Logan) had hired him (the bad-ass merc) to kill his (Ron's) friend (me). Ron tells the bad-ass merc to call the

---

* It's for this reason that back in my pot smuggling days I often stayed at the U.N. Plaza hotel in New York City, where, because of all the diplomats, house security is massive; the added advantage being that the various sorts of cops that might give you problems are also kept at bay.

heavy-weight merc, with whom he (the bad-ass merc) is tight, to verify all this and to verify that Ron himself is a trustworthy merc, a veteran of all kinds of merc shit, a foxhole merc-buddy of the first order. The bad-ass merc leaves the room to call the heavy-weight merc, comes back and says that the heavy-weight merc did verify all of the above and that he (the heavy-weight merc) called in a favor with him (the bad-ass merc), asking him (the bad-ass merc) to call off the hit on me. Which the bad-ass merc did (call off the hit on me), at least according to him (the bad-ass merc). So then the bad-ass merc lets Ron go. Ron then talks to the heavy-weight merc, which was today, just a little while ago, and the heavy-weight merc verified that the hit is now called off, but that Ron now owes him (the heavy-weight merc) a favor.

Ron tells me that the situation is as if he (Ron) "dumped a dead nigger" on the heavy-weight merc's doorstep and now he (the heavy-weight merc) has to clean up the mess, like in the movie *Pulp Fiction*, when Harvey Keitel shows up after John Travolta accidentally shoots the black guy in the car.

I don't quite get the movie allusion, but I do get the drift.

Let me ask you something before I continue on with this: Which do you think is a bigger crock of shit, the above story of Ron's or Lisa's explanation of... say, how the tape got recorded over at the Holiday Inn? (Or, alternatively, Bush's reasons for why he bombs and invades other countries.) You can flip back to page 242 if you want to reread that one. Whaddya think?

Me, I'm not sure. It's a toss up.

Hold on. The answer is that Lisa's is a bigger crock of shit since at least Ron's crock of shit is *physically* possible. (I'm not sure of where to put Bush's reasons for bombing and invading other countries on the crock of shit spectrum. It's certainly somewhere way over toward the right end, in the area where X-rays would be if it were the electromagnetic spectrum rather than the crock of shit spectrum.)

But the point of all this – and I assume, I hope and pray, you're ahead of me here – is that Ron has been gaslighting me from the get-go. He made up everything, speaking of nonfiction.*

He did this, of course, for money, at first just the few bucks I gave him for expenses; then he tried the hit-on-Logan ploy, which would have been much bigger bucks, had I gone for it.

What do you think is going on *now*? With Ron's crock of shit story? The current one? (Yes, a pop quiz to see if you're paying attention.)

A hint. Key in Ron's crock of shit story is the end part, about dumping a dead nigger on the heavy-weight merc's doorstep.

What's going on, of course, is that Ron is setting me up for a shakedown. Ron is going to wait a little while and then approach me saying that he's having a problem with the heavy-weight merc, based on the "dead nigger" favor, a problem that can only be solved financially. Although there is no heavy-weight merc (or bad-ass merc or *any* mercs) involved in all this, at least not for the moment, Ron, if necessary, will come up with one, a cohort in the shakedown.

Now what am I thinking, sitting there with Ron at the casino bar/ restaurant in San José?

I have to nip this in the bud, is what I'm thinking.

But I have to be careful. I can't just explain to Ron that his story is a crock of shit and that he can forget about a shakedown. Why not? Because Ron would do what Lisa does, what Steven, my Hollywood attorney, just did, what everyone does when caught in something. He'd get incensed, get rowdy.† I don't need any more rowdiness in my life right now – as I say, I'm agoraphobic and depressed.

Sitting there with Ron at the casino bar/restaurant in San José, I come up with a plan, which you'll hear about, if you hang in.

One last thing regarding this hit man/Ron business: What was my original mistake? What was my fuck-up?

---

* Although I had no real need to verify that Ron's story was a crock of shit, I did – I'm the type who gives people all kinds of benefits of the doubts with their crock of shit stories. I called a contact I have with the puddle-jumper airline (Sansa) and found that Ron had not flown up from Pavones the day before. So he must've taken the bus. Since the bus takes 8 hours to make the trip, a simple perusal of the bus schedule proved that Ron wasn't even in San José the night before, let alone getting kidnapped there. Also, there wasn't a mark on him after being knocked unconscious outside the merc bar. That he didn't have the courtesy to punch himself in the face (so as not to further insult my intelligence) pisses me off. I often wish Lisa would do this as well, meaning have the courtesy not to further insult my intelligence in the crocks of shit she comes up with. Maybe punch herself in the face, metaphorically speaking.**

    ** A little (more) comic relief: One time Ron asked me for a few bucks to buy ammunition for his .38. Turned out his ".38" was a bang stick; a sort of spear gun for killing big fish. That's all the weaponry he had. So we were ready in case of a fire fight with a big tuna or marlin.

† I don't think Ron would use Lisa's alternate technique, uncontrollable sobbing and apologies and protestations of innocence, followed by a massage for me. His being a hardboiled merc, it wouldn't look right. (Steven *might* try the uncontrollable sobbing and apologies and protestations of innocence plus massage technique, but only under extreme circumstances.)

Think maybe it was my assumption that Ron's story of a Logan hit man was true?

No, that wasn't my *original* fuck-up. Besides, I pretty much had to assume the worst on that one, since, in general, assuming the worst seems to work out for the best.

A hint. My original fuck-up was from a couple years ago.

Right: Helping Ron with the 20 bucks when he was destitute and walking down the dirt road at Big Turkeys with his sad little cloth bag. That piece of unmotivated kindness is what got me into this current fiasco.

I doubt a day has gone by since she died that I haven't thought about Mom. But it was around this time that I started *talking* to Mom. Out loud, not just in my head. So far, the conversations have been one-sided, but what they usually involve is some sort of question, like, "What should I do, Mom?" Or sometimes I'll just say something that comes to mind, like, "Mom, I seem to be having some bad luck with people."

CHAPTER TWELVE

People do not wish to appear foolish; to avoid the appearance of foolishness, they were willing to actually to remain fools.
Alice Walker

Aside from the *Cosmic Banditos* movie contract fiasco, as described, it was right around this time that the *In Search of Captain Zero* catastrophe reached a possible turning point. The current option period was up. (To be exact, on February 18, 2004.) To recap the deal:

The studio (via Sean Penn, the other producer and the director) had not *bought* the rights to my book; they'd optioned the rights, a year at a time, at $5,000 per. So it was put-up-or-shut-up time on that date each year. I know: chump change, considering they'd already spent a couple hundred grand for my adaptation – the whole "it's-brilliant-then-it's-not-the-script-we-expected" fiasco – plus a producer's fee went to the above trio. Not chump change, in total.

Thing was, though, everything had gone so poorly that my feeling was they might let the option expire, stop throwing money into the fire. I certainly would have, had I been in their position. But hold on. A version of my catch-22 kicks in here, no? Something like *Anyone dumb enough to think there's a movie in my book in the first place is dumb enough to keep throwing money into the fire.*

And now there was another catch-22; or rather, the first catch-22 becomes a *compound catch-22*, which is sort of like an exponential whammy. Something like *Anyone dumb enough to think there's a movie in my book in the first place and then, in the second place, dumb enough to ignore a really good screenplay that somehow gets written, is certainly dumb enough to keep throwing money into the fire.*

So it was absolutely guaranteed that they'd keep throwing money into the fire.

I'm just realizing this now, as I write about it. At the time I thought maybe they wouldn't keep throwing money into the fire. And that would have been fine with me, since I'd get back the movie rights to my book. There was a problem here, though. Steven fucked up and failed to negotiate a buy-back clause in the contract, which meant that I'd get the book rights back but the studio and producers would still own the screenplay I wrote based on the book. The bottom line of this piece of Hollywood ridiculousness was that nobody could make a movie out of my book (at least not from the screenplay I wrote). Yes, still another catch-22, of the simple, classic variety.

But hold on. What's the problem here, really? If someone else, another studio, say, wanted to shoot my screenplay, couldn't they just buy it from the current studio/producers, those morons?

No.

Why not?

The studio/producers wouldn't sell it to them. They'd just sit on my screenplay and swallow the money lost.

Why would they do this?

Because if someone else made a movie from my screenplay and it was a hit, the studio/producers would look.... how?

Right: Foolish

So forget that.*

If no one could make a movie out of my book and, indeed, if I got the rights back it would cost me in option money not earned, then why did I want the rights back? I'm not sure, but here's an analogy that comes to mind: Imagine you're in love and your mate starts fucking someone else, some scumbag. You leave your mate, it's over. Then you find out that your mate and the scumbag are not fucking anymore. You're happy about it, even though it's still over between you and your mate.

Why are you happy about it?

Same thing here, somehow.

I wonder where that came from.

There was an amusing aspect to the option situation, though. Steven called and said the studio suggested that I extend the option *for free* – presumably because they figured that either, One, I liked them all so much, or, Two, money was not a concern of mine.

Insofar as it's possible for one to laugh in a Hollywood movie studio's face through an intermediary – in this case, one's attorney – from a cell phone at the end of the road at the bottom of Central America, that's what I did.

So they sent me the $5,000.

While the studio was busy making nonsensical proposals to my attorney and then sending me money, I was busy too. I mean aside from dealing with

---

* This particular studio *did* do this once, i.e.; sell back to the writers a screenplay they owned but didn't like. I've mentioned this one before, in another context. *There's Something About Mary.* Right: You wanna talk about looking foolish?

Lisa and her distressing antics, plus the hit man/Ron fiasco, plus crack-head thieves moving onto my property, plus my attorney telling me to sign a contract authored by Amy-frickin-Nickin without reading it, and so forth. I was busy trying to get my draft, the "brilliant" one – written before the one wherein I went into the tank – to Sean Penn. Aside from putting the draft on my website and asking anyone who knew Sean to please give it to him, I'd sent the draft to his Hollywood manager with a note asking him to read it and, if he liked it, send it along to Penn.* I knew this wouldn't work but I gave it a shot anyway. I knew it wouldn't work because Penn's manager was also the director's manager,† and the director, along with the other producer and along with the studio did not want Penn to read my draft. I also knew the manager wouldn't do anything as intelligent as reading the draft and giving it to Penn because (if you'll remember) the manager was one of the idiots who thought there was a movie in my book in the first place. Right: *That* catch-22 again (or a slight variation of it).

Regarding *that* catch-22: That catch-22 did not apply to Sean Penn because he still hadn't read my book (and hence had no reason to know there is no movie in it). I know this because I'd asked the other producer if Sean had got around to reading it. She told me no, but that Sean's wife, actress Robin Wright Penn, told her a copy of my book was sitting on their living room table.

"But you know Sean," the producer said. Meaning that a copy of my book's current location on Sean's living room table wasn't a whole lot of progress towards him reading it.

"No, I don't know Sean," I said. Not only did I not know Sean, but I hadn't seen him or spoken to him in quite a while -- since the breakfast meeting at the Four Seasons, actually, when the producer repeated how he gets involved early in the script stage and how I will enjoy working with him. So, no. I didn't know Sean, but I *was* getting the drift.

In case you haven't figured it out: I wanted to get my draft to Sean Penn because I figured he'd like it and straighten all the morons out – my draft would go back to being brilliant (plus I'd be a genius again). Which was why everyone was petrified of Penn reading it, since they'd *look foolish* if he did like it.

---

* It's still on my website (the aweisbecker.com one), so you can read it there too – see if I have my head up my ass like everyone else.**

    ** As Steven made sure to point out, putting my draft on my site was illegal since I don't own the draft, the studio/producers do. They could sue, Steven said. To which I say: Good luck to the fuckers! I imagine some Hollywood asshole in a suit with a briefcase showing up at Big Turkeys to serve me papers and getting accidentally shot by a hit man looking for my sorry ass or mugged by the crack heads on my property or bit by the deadly terciopelo viper.

† Still more Hollywood incest, and still another example of how I was surrounded.

Can you wrap your mind around all this stuff?

My other move was to dig up Penn's assistant's name and address and send the draft to her. Sent it off to Hollywood (the state of mind Hollywood, since her address is in San Francisco) from Big Turkeys then waited to see What Would Happen Next while all this other shit was going on.

As I say, it was a busy time.

CHAPTER THIRTEEN

My principal feeling about Hollywood is suicide. If I could get out of bed and into the shower, I was all right. Since I never paid the bills, I'd reach for the phone and order the most elaborate breakfast I could think of, and then I'd try to make it to the shower before I hanged myself.

John Cheever

While you and I – each in our different ways – wait to see What Happens Next with getting my *In Search of Captain Zero* screenplay draft to Sean Penn, I'll fill you in on more backstory on this fiasco. Bring you up to date, meaning the general time frame of the late winter and spring of 2004. Yes, a busy time for my sorry ass.

Remember my strategy meeting with the producer and the director at my Venice Beach hotel room? We were supposed to go over my draft but no one except me had a copy? The director was insistent that I remove passages from my screenplay that "couldn't make it to the screen" and then when I showed him a passage from a great screenplay that couldn't make it to the screen ("The Red Sox haven't broken any hearts yet") he scoffed and I wanted to strangle him? And then when I tried to improve a dumb scene he'd thought of (sea urchin spine removal via piss) he got contemptuous again, saying, "An actor would never let *someone else* piss on his foot!"?

Although during the subsequent meeting with the studio I mostly went surfing (in my head), one of the upshots was that the director would write an outline for the screenplay. I was supposed to use it in rewriting my draft, the once-brilliant one.

It was in late November, almost three months after the hotel room fiasco and the meeting following it when the director turned in his "outline." I received it by email at the end of the road. I read it, gave it to Lisa without comment, not even mentioning who wrote it.

Having read it, Lisa had a question: "What is this, a tenth-grade book report?"

That was Lisa's reaction to the director's outline. My reaction, which I shared with the producer, caused... the expression *the shit hit the fan* comes to mind.

For your edification and amusement I'm going to reproduce some of the director's outline plus my reaction to it. However, out of concern for your sensibilities, I'm limiting myself to about four pages. (The nightmare in its entirety is archived on the adjunct website.) The only set up you really need is the premise I salvaged from my book – virtually the only aspect of the book I left untouched. Again, the premise is this: *A middle-aged surfer gives up his straight life to search for an old friend and ex-partner in crime from their younger days, who is missing in Central America.*

Since there is no movie in my book, since I reinvented the story for the screen, I changed the main character's name from my own (Allan) to Alex. (I did this for the sake of... veracity.) The friend Alex is in search of is Chris (nicknamed Captain Zero). I've altered the memo in keeping with not using names, including that of the studio – I assure you that fear of a lawsuit is not the issue. It just works better this way.[*]

We pick up the outline as Alex leaves on his journey south to find his old pal. My comments, which upset everyone, are in **bold**. Notice how I get crankier as the fucking thing rolls along. (Also notice how the director tense-switches in mid-sentence in his initial voice over. Although he's lifting this stuff from the book, trust me that I didn't tense-switch in mid-sentence; I also didn't [and wouldn't] put a comma after "loneliness;" he's misquoting.)

> CUT TO:
> Alex drives out of town. His VOICE OVER; "I was not prepared for the loneliness, and sense of failure of leaving. I've broken so many promises I'd made to visit friends and ones dear to me. How do you say good-bye when in your heart you believe the parting is final?"

What's the point of this voice over? Voice over is intrusive if there's no good reason for it and I see no reason for it here. Alex's loneliness should be a subtext vibe that is done visually, not sledgehammered with voice over. If there is to be a v.o. here, it should be (at least in subtext) about Chris: Chris is what is on Alex's mind, not the other people in his life.

The problem of rambling off subject is endemic to this outline, as we'll see.

---

[*] By not using names the morons involved become more abstract and symbolic, *archetypical* even. Whoa: *Heavier.* Also, by not naming individuals it seems less like I'm picking on them. I as a person seem less cruel and vicious. I can therefore get away with more cruelty and viciousness.

CUT TO:
NEXT MORNING.
Alex is back on the road now entering Baja. Towards evening he pulls into his first Baja encampment. Campfires lined like little suns with planetoidal figures surrounding them. Alex's VOICE OVER: he talks about arriving at a place that is neither here nor there, east or west, north or south.

More voice over that I see no point to. Show, don't tell. And aside from the fact that the above v.o. book quote is wildly inaccurate, what is so out of whack about the place that such hyperbole is warranted? And if it is that weird, what are we saving for later, when, presumably (at the end of the road where Chris is), things are really fucked up? We are blowing our out-of-whack wad right up front, leaving nothing to escalate to. Also, there is a big difference between internal prose in a book and the way people actually speak. When spoken as actual dialog (or v.o.), this (inaccurate) line from the book is overblown and pretentious.

He's met someone here. They talk. This conversation allows us to find out what Alex is doing here.

Okay. I'll ask. What *is* Alex doing here? Not only *what* but *why*. (Although we don't necessary impart the why here to the audience, we as storytellers sure as hell better know the answer. Otherwise, there is no way to write the scene, since we don't know what Alex is really thinking, deep down. In a good story the protagonist may not know what he is thinking deep down, but the writer had better know.)

We also find out information from this person about the general lifestyle of Baja; the dangers, who the people are down there, what not to do, what to look out for etc.

I presume [the director] means that the guy does all this in dialog. This stuff should be imparted without expository dialog – through events, letting the audience *figure out for themselves* that it's dangerous down there. Besides, heroes are not told this sort of stuff. They already know. Especially Alex, who has been through more shit than this guy ever dreamt of. A scene like this makes Alex look like a tourist.

This may or may not be the place to insert the guys telling Alex;

"the only people who come down here are the wanted and the unwanted."

No, this is not the right place for that line. Another example of shooting our wad early, leaving little room for escalation. But anyway, to fixate on a line of dialog like this one is reflective of the overall problem with this outline. An outline of this length should concentrate on what *happens*, not little snippets of dialog. Here, pretty much nothing actually happens.

Alex is told how futile his search is? It's clear by everyone's reactions that searching for someone down here is not only futile but dangerous because most people come here so as not to be found. He's told to be careful whom he approaches.

Why is it futile? As I say in the book, the world of the traveling surfer is a small one. And it's not necessarily dangerous, nor do most people come to Baja so as not to be found. We're like a couple of hours south of San Diego. Still again, this sort of thing makes sense at the end of the road at the bottom of Central America, where Chris is, not here. This stuff is hyperbole and not true. (Real Baja travelers will be tossing stuff at the screen.) Plus, again, we have our guy being *told* stuff while he sits there like a tourist.

CUT TO:
Alex drives into a Mexican fishing village. He does more in- depth searching for Chris. Shows his picture. Alex is warned of danger to the south - three surfers were killed recently, he's told that his life may not be held in high esteem - don't travel alone.

Again: Show don't tell. And still again, our guy sits there and is told stuff. Not only told stuff, but told stuff we just heard in previous scenes, i.e., that's it's dangerous down there.

Also has the shark conversation at this point with the Mexicans who refuse to speak the word Shark. Guy in the conversation has one arm.

What does this have to do with anything? It does not advance the story, nor does it start up or pay off a subplot. AGAIN Alex sits there and listens to someone else: and STILL AGAIN, the exposition is about how dangerous it is

(sharks in the water).

Mercifully, I've cut out a big chunk here, most of the fucking thing. Please trust me that you've not been deprived of any brilliant stuff. (I in fact refrained from reproducing here the dumbest ass stuff, tempting as it was.) Towards the end now, as Alex finds his old friend and nothing whatsoever happens or is set up to happen:

CUT TO:
Denise, second phone call??? (May or may not be needed) Alex backtracks. Says he was wrong in previous call. She tells him she's found someone else.

Backtracks? Why? What has changed that would cause him to backtrack? Nothing, that's what. Our main guy cannot seem to come to any decisions about anything and then stick to them.

He's now void **(I presume [the director] means "devoid")** of all earthly connections aside from surfing.

Call me an insensitive brute (which has been done), but the many times women have dumped me, I never once felt devoid of all earthly connections. (The one time this did happen was in 1968 and a little purple pill was involved.)

By the way: how do you *show* this devoid-of-all-earthly-connections concept? How do you put it up on the screen – maybe the same way you do so with "The Red Sox haven't broken any hearts yet"?

CUT TO:
TALAMANCA ARRIVAL...

Alex, driving, approaches a group sitting in the shade of a large tree just outside of town, selling artistic trinkets.

After all the weird and dangerous and heart of darkness stuff from up in Baja – how it's where the Wanted and the Unwanted go and how people disappear there and how apocalyptic Bandido Alley was and on and on... after all that, Alex gets to the End of the Road, the End of the Line, the Bottom of It All and what does he find? Mellowed out hippies

selling artistic trinkets. What's wrong with this picture?

He shows them Christopher's picture. They say yes, he lives here and point down the road. Alex drives. A few miles down he sees a black woman.

Who's the black woman, Colonel Kurtz's cleaning lady? Damn it: What's the vibe of the end of the Road? Should be *Heart of Darkness* like we all agreed, like is (sic) in my first draft (flaws and all). Sure ain't in this outline.

Further along in this fucking thing (if you've seen enough, go ahead and skip ahead. Believe me, I won't be offended):

CUT TO:
Alex and Chris, at Chris' insistence, end up doing a long night of cocaine together. But something good, if only temporarily happens, they end up becoming close "just like in the old days." Lots of laughing. This is the first time they bond like the old times in the flash backs.

What flashbacks? The last one was so long ago that I don't remember it.

They discuss the days past, trying to one-up each other, big laughs and bigger stories.

Movie scenes are either Up moments or Down moments. From [the director]'s description, while these guys are smoking crack or snorting their brains out, the audience is supposed to be thinking, "Wow, isn't this great!"

Wait. I can't go on; I don't have the heart. [The director]'s outline ends with a drug deal gone sour that comes out of nowhere; no set up. It's so irrelevant that I'm not including it in this memo: you can't introduce the climax heavies in the third act, plus it's a cliché, plus it doesn't keep to the spirit of the book, plus there is no surfing involved.

What I've been doing here, picking apart each scene, is misleading. My quibbling over this stuff is sort of like that great moment in *Titanic* wherein the ship's architect adjusts a clock in the dining room as the ship is going down. (That was a wonderful touch, wasn't it? Said so much about that guy, in

about two seconds of screen time. *Without a word spoken.*)

Okay. Let me just say it. This outline is of no use whatsoever to anyone writing this screenplay, since there is no story here. And the problem is not in the details, in the execution, it's in the premises, or, rather, the utter lack of them.

You may be wondering why you optioned this book, given that there appears to be no screen story in the book story.*

Okay. There's more to this memo, but enough is enough! (Again, if you're interested in the storytelling process – how it should not be done – or in-over-the-top stupidity, you'll eventually be able to read the whole thing. But not now.)

First: What do you think of Lisa's assessment? Does the outline (minus my well-wrought comments) read like a 10th grade book report? I think she was kind. I'm thinking more like 8th grade, but I of course have an agenda (similar to the one I had in my comments on *Surviving Your First Year of Marriage*). Even so, I'd grade it a D, for its poor spelling, grammar, punctuation, comprehension and retention; the butchered quotes, a wrong name for a supporting character, a misunderstanding of what the book *is about*, and so forth. If this were a book report of whatever grade level, I might even accuse the kid of not fulfilling the assignment to read the book in the first place. (How the fuck did it take him three months to write this thing? Without my comments it was 10 pages. That's *nine days* for each page! And he claimed that this project was his number one priority!)

More sarcasm and all around vitriol, no? Getting tiresome, no?

Enough!

Let's get back on the subject of *me*, rather than the director, since me is what this book is *about*, aside from *dishonesty*. I mean fuck *him*. Okay. Why my anger, my outrage, as reflected in the memo? On one level, the most superficial, Lisa's not-thinking-before-speaking blurt about why she flirts openly with other men applies here as well: "Hey, maybe I just couldn't help myself!"

But the guy, the director, is just dumb, you might say. Give him a break!

The stupidity and incompetence of the director's outline – his dumbness – is not at the root of my outrage. Dumbness I can live with (I have more than a dose of it myself, via the Lisa issue). There's even a sort of sweetness to dumbness – the amusing flick *Dumb and Dumber* (from the same folks

---

* Yes, this sentence is my catch-22 disguised as a rhetorical question.

who gave us *There's Something About Mary*) comes to mind, among others. No. What pisses me off is unprofessionalism, discourtesy and ignorance. Like the unprofessionalism, discourtesy and ignorance of the director letting me work for a year and a half – with me sending him the pages as I went – knowing he had no interest in my draft, and then not even referring to my year and a half's work in his dumb-ass outline.

You wanna talk about a shitball motherfucker on top of being dumb?

On top of *that*, every movie writing contract has a get-back clause. After the writer hands in his draft the studio/producers have a period of time to digest it, then they supply "notes" upon which the writer's revisions are based; in this case they had two weeks, contractually. I handed in my draft in July. I finally got the "notes" – in the form of this completely dumb-ass outline – in December. *Six months*, half of which time was wasted crafting the dumb-ass outline. (During which I could not, ethically or contractually, take on another project.) It took them that long to get it together to insult me.

But it gets worse, or better, depending on whether you're talking about my life or this narrative. A shit storm ensued because I'd publicly insulted the director. Hold on. I *publicly* insulted him? Let me ask you something: Did you hear about it?

In fact, about three people on the planet read my analysis of his outline. Hold on. Okay. Four, if you include the studio executive's yes-man, who, in my view, should only count as half a person. So let's say three-and-a-half people read it. But somehow I'd *publicly* insulted the director. (I'd only sent the memo to the producer, who forwarded it to the director and a hacked-up version to the studio executive – so no matter what, I had not insulted the director publicly.)

An added problem, though, was I'd also insulted the studio – the executive (and by mindless extension, his yes-man, the half-person). How did I do that? See, the executive had written *his* own memo – extolling the outline's brilliance, how it was "soulful" and "had all the elements." (I'd love to be able to subject you to the memo, but I can't find the fucking thing.) So by pointing out that the outline is not only not soulful and not element-loaded but is completely dumb-ass, I also implied that the executive is a complete dumb-ass. A lowly *writer* had done this.

So there was a shit storm.*

Let me ask you something else before I continue on with this: Do you agree that the director's outline is completely dumb-ass? Christ, I hope so.

---

* Wasn't there also a shit storm in the fable "The Emperor's New Clothes"? What happened to the kid in that one, by the way, the one who started the shit storm by pointing at the emperor's naked ass? I'm not sure, but I think I saw him the other day stumbling around in a daze here at Big Turkeys.

It's a horrible thought that there's even one person out there that isn't with me on this one. Even if you've read my *Zero* screenplay and didn't like it you should now be completely on my side in the matter of this current fiasco. If not, there's very little hope for you and me.

But, believe it or not, it gets *still* worse. My movie agent – whom I would soon fire and whose reaction to that is the title of this book – joined in the shit storm against me, agreeing that I'd committed an egregious act with my memo.

I asked her if – never mind my egregious act for now – she thought I was right, and that the director's outline is completely dumb-ass.

It doesn't matter, was her reply.

It doesn't matter? You mean that my *hurting this moron's feelings* is more important than a multi-million dollar project? And how about the six months I've been waiting for "notes" so I can get on with the next draft? And how about that they expect me to *start over from scratch* after a year-and-a-half's work, using a completely dumb-ass outline to write from? And, further, I asked her if she could see why I got a little testy.

It doesn't matter. I shouldn't have publicly insulted the director.

But I didn't publicly insult him! I only sent the memo to the producer!

It doesn't matter.

Hey, wait a minute. Aren't you my agent? You know, my *advocate*?

Before she could say It doesn't matter or something about *public* insults or That's different or anything else, I said, How about they (one of them, any of them, all of them) reply to my memo? Show me how I'm wrong about that outline being completely dumb-ass.

They can't do that.

Why not?

Because I had publicly insulted the director. We were back to that one. (Was there some looping going on here?)

Okay, I said, and I shut my trap for now.

I had a plan.

I rewrote my memo, removing the sarcasm (talk about a writer sweating over something!), then sent it to everyone. I included a note apologizing for the tone of the previous memo, saying I'd been having a tough day in paradise, comedic words to that effect. I said that since they want me to start over using the outline to write the new draft, I needed them to reply to "my concerns" over the outline. *Concerns.* You wanna talk about a euphemism?

The silence was deafening.

The Christmas holidays came and went.

More silence. Now it was eight months since I turned in my draft and was waiting for "notes," so I could get on with my sorry-ass life and times.

My agent would not lift a finger in my behalf.

Steven, my Hollywood attorney, would not lift a finger, claiming... guess what? Conflict of interest! You know, since he represented the director and the producer as well as... as my sorry ass. Well... duhhhhh.... (Where was the conflict of interest when he was collecting commissions from everyone?)

The silence wore on.

While the silence is wearing on, let me ask you something else: Why do you think my agent and Steven, my Hollywood attorney, were arrayed against me in this matter? I mean their job is to be my *advocates*, and assuming that you agree that the outline is completely dumb-ass...

Why *wouldn't* they be on my side in this?

You know what comes to mind here? The three billion years of the evolution of life on earth. How nature or God or what-have-you went to a whole lot of time and trouble to provide humans with a brain capable of dealing with the issue of whether or not that outline is completely dumb-ass.

But you know what?

It doesn't matter.

See, the reason my agent and Steven were arrayed against me was this: The director was this wunderkind who'd arrived on the Hollywood scene out of the blue,[*] winner of the Sundance Film Festival *Palm du Horsemerde Medal* (I may be thinking another film festival, the one in France) as Best Director.

But hold on. The director "directed" a documentary that was almost all archival footage, so he didn't really direct...

It doesn't matter.

... all he directed were the interviews, the talking heads...

It doesn't matter.

But looking at that memo, it's obvious that you, Allan, are the one with the story sense, the talent, even, out of the two of you...

It doesn't matter.

But why? *Why doesn't it matter?*

It doesn't matter![†]

Okay. Enough.

What was the final upshot after all the *It doesn't matters* and *That's*

---

[*]   The Peter Sellers character, Chauncy Gardener, in *Being There* comes to mind.

[†]   In his memoir, *Adventures in the Screen Trade*, William Goldman theorizes that in Hollywood, "Nobody knows anything." Let me add this to that, and feel free to quote me: "It doesn't matter." Further, if neither "Nobody knows anything" or "It doesn't matter" fit whatever Hollywood shit you're trying to explain, try this one: "That's different." There you have it. The Complete Theory of Hollywood. In three acts.

differents, and public insults and silences wearing on? They cut me loose, sayo-fuckin-A-nara, Jack. In doing so they paid me for a bunch of work that, now, I'd never have to do.

Whoopee! Surf's up!

But why would they do this? Pay me off? Maybe because I'd publicly insulted someone, everyone (even though I *hadn't* publicly insulted someone, everyone)? You know, because they were *mad* at me?

If you're mad at someone you don't give him a bunch of money and tell him to have fun, go surfing. Do you? Me, I'm mad at someone I'd make him work for the bucks even if I know I'll never use the work.

So why didn't they make me work for the money? Here's why: To do so they would have had to reply to my memo on the completely dumb-ass outline. And they would not do that, under any circumstances.

Why not?

Is there any way they could reply to that memo without looking foolish?

Okay, but…

Remember what I said was the only real job of Hollywood people?

To avoid looking foolish. That's it. That's their job. Not making good movies or any movies, or using investor's money wisely or making a profit. None of that stuff. To avoid looking foolish. This avoidance of looking foolish includes – especially so – *looking foolish to themselves.*

That's what they meant when they said I'd insulted someone, everyone, *publicly.* I'd made them look foolish to themselves.

Listen: The avoidance of looking foolish in Hollywood (especially to themselves) is *a tough job.*

My mere presence on the project was a constant reminder of how foolish they are – or even my presence on this planet, which is why I'm adding them to the list of people who might be out to murder my sorry ass – and how poorly they were doing their real, their only, job.

I was fucking with their denial.*

Right: We're back to the D-word.

But…

No buts. No ifs, ands, just denials.

That's why they cut me loose.

I rest my case.

On second thought, I don't rest my case. There's more to come, then I'll rest my case. And guess who makes a cameo appearance to jazz things up

---

* You might remember my tale of the studio head who loved me and my work until I fucked with *his* denial by indirectly pointing out how foolish *he* was – that business about how the CIA answers their phone. He cut me loose too. Hey, I have a wide and deep reservoir of tales like these.

while I'm resting my case?
Brad Pitt!
The sexiest man alive!
I bet you can't wait!
Hooray for nonfiction! (*Whatever* it is!)
I love looping! (Ditto!)
Holy shit!

CHAPTER FOURTEEN

If you can't annoy somebody, there's little point in writing.
Kingsley Amis

A while back I promised I'd provide the specifics of how I was presented with the title of this book. I figure since I've made such a big deal of it, I better do it right. So aside from this preamble, this chapter consists of the email I sent my movie agent firing her, and her reply.

Some of you will be interested, some won't. That's just the way it is with readers. If you're one of the latter, just skip to the next chapter. You won't miss much and I won't be offended.

What I like about this chapter – plus others wherein I reproduce real stuff – is that it tends to reinforce this narrative as being of the nonfiction genre. The downside to this, of course, is that we don't know what nonfiction is, except that it's a load of horseshit. Yes, there's still another catch-22 around here somewhere.

As before (and for the reason already given), I've altered what follows to keep names out of it. Plus I've edited it slightly, in deference to Reader Big Mo, should there be any left.

February 4, 2003 - CONFIDENTIAL

Via E-Mail and Overnight Delivery

To: [My agent at the mega-talent agency
    where she is one of the pimps]
Cc: [The producer]

Re: Termination of Representation

I called the Writer's Guild contracts department, and after some background preamble about the deal told them the following:

That I wrote a 1st draft of my *In Search of Captain Zero* adaptation that the producer signed off on while I was writing it and again afterwards. That it was based on changes from the book that everyone – she, [the director] and [the studio], via our meetings – agreed on.

I said that the producer then gave it to [the studio], who then (after six months! Talk about a breach of contract!) gave me as "notes" an outline that makes no reference to, nor bears any real resemblance to (premises, structure, scenes, etc), my 1st draft. And that the premises agreed upon were gone. (If you ever bother to read [the director]'s unprofessional outline, you will find no resemblance to my draft. He couldn't even get the female lead's name right. What does that tell you?)

Anything inaccurate so far? Or don't you remember?

I asked if I was legally obligated to use this outline for my next draft.

They said no I wasn't obligated to do that, to write from an outline as described. That another treatment would have to be negotiated for, at the very least.

They said it doesn't matter whether [the producer] is my legal employer or [the studio], since even if it was [the studio], [the producer] – in signing off on my work as I did it – was the studio's representative.

They said that they would have to see my contract to formally pursue the matter, and maybe the draft and [the director]'s outline as well. I told them I'd get back to them.

By the way: Regarding the eight months I've been waiting for an okay to write the revisions, they said this: Depending on my contract, I probably should have been paid everything, or at least another installment, by now since it was the studio/producer side that caused the delay.

As my agent/advocate, did you know that?

Alexa Kent in the WGA's contracts department then asked what my agent has been doing about the problem. I told her the truth, that you said you would not call [the studio] on my behalf and that I should let the producer do it, who, I added, you also represent.

She was shocked to say the least.

She said that my "blowup" at the director is irrelevant, public or otherwise. (I didn't even bother to mention that if it was "public", it was [the producer] that made it so by forwarding it to other people.)

The head of the agency department next got on the phone. I asked if I could prevent you from taking any more of my money, given that you have refused to represent me in all of the above to [the studio].

Lou, the head guy, asked if I have a written contract with you. I said not lately. He said just contact [the studio] and have them send the money directly to me.

I said I'd get back to them as to whether I want to pursue these matters.

Maybe I have your attention, I dunno.

If so, let me add that you have some nerve on you, telling me how much money you got me. You make what? $20,000 for a few phone calls. I been doing nothing but this thing for a year and eight months, with you doing absolutely nothing when I needed help on issues I'm clearly in the right about.

You have refused to withdraw as my agent with class and grace.

You're fired, for reasons made clear in this memo.

Do not take any more of my money.

Refer any business matters to Steven.

If you say bad things about me I'll sue you and [your mega-talent agency] too.

How's that for whining? [Which she'd recently accused me of.]

Allan Weisbecker

P.S. You know what? I'm wrong. I did get some agenting from you, back in September, when I was in L.A., asking for help THEN with this mess. You remember what your advice was? Go into the meeting with [the studio] and tell them I'm working closely with [the director]. Remember that? Told me to go in and lie. Remember what I told you? "That lie will come back to haunt me." Lying may be standard procedure for you, but it isn't for me. Toughest thing I ever did was sitting there at that meeting not saying anything. (Actually, it wasn't that tough: I went surfing.) I wonder what the Guild would say about that piece of advice. I forgot to mention it.

Okay. A couple days later I got a response, via email. The body of the message was this and only this:

Can't you get along with anyone?

So there you have it.

CHAPTER FIFTEEN

Anything scares me, anything scares anyone but really after all considering how dangerous everything is nothing is really very frightening.

Gertrude Stein

A few days after the meeting with Ron in the San José casino bar/restaurant wherein he told the crock-of-shit story that caused the doozey needle to fly off the doozey scale, I executed my plan to nip in the bud the coming shakedown. Upon exiting the water after a morning surf session I found the shitball motherfucker sitting on the cantina seawall drinking beer with whatever was left of the expense money I'd given him. I put my board down and commenced pacing like I was really agitated or pissed off. Ron started to say something but I interrupted. I was going to do the talking, the bullshitting, the gaslighting, for once.

Your fucking San José merc buddies are full of shit, my friend, I said.

Ron started to say something but I interrupted again. I did some checking, I said. Logan wasn't in San José when your buddies said he was. He was right here. He didn't hire any hit man either.

Ron started to say something about Logan and a hit man… No, he didn't hire anybody, I said. I said I knew that for a fact, although I said I couldn't tell him *how* I knew. I said this because, unlike Lisa, I know enough to adhere to Rule Number One When You're Lying: keep details to a minimum.

Ron, my friend, I said, you've been played for a sucker. The whole hit man thing and the kidnapping was a set up so you'd owe them a favor. What's going to happen is that very soon the fuckers are going to try to get money from you.

See, this way I was able to point out that Ron's whole doozey meter-busting story was a crock of shit without calling *him* a liar. Here I believe Lisa's influence kicked in, her ability to work up rage or hysterical crying on command; her Academy Award-winning actress act. I got genuinely outraged, saying, When the mercs show up looking for money, tell them to come fucking see me. Tell them where I live and tell them to come on up. And tell the fuckers to come armed. I have my S & W thirty-eight under the seat – here I gestured at my truck – and I have rifles and shotguns all over the house. I'm fucking armed and I'm fucking *pissed off.*

I didn't have to interrupt Ron anymore. He just sat there dumbfounded. My tirade had come out of nowhere.

Ron, I said, you were behind me and now I'm behind you. And another thing, I went on – my outrage moved still further to the right on the outrage spectrum – no one is getting a fucking penny of my money, not even you. I paced, letting this one sink in. But listen, I said. I'll put my life on the line for you, like you did for me.

Here I ad-libbed, straying from the script I'd prepared. Ron, I said, I haven't been going to the dentist up in San José. I've been going to the hospital. I'm really sick. I bummed a cigarette from his pack and held it up. Looks like these fuckers have finally killed me. I lit it, saying, Fuck it, I'd rather go out in a blaze than in a hospital bed with tubes in me and shit.

Now Ron was really at a loss, with me having thrown him for this added loop.

In fact, I said, referring to my going-out-in-a-blaze comment, and here I paused and paced some more and then got calm and cold on him. More crapola: I'm going back up to San José in a few days for more treatments, I said. Give me some names and addresses. I wanna have a talk with these merc assholes.

With the terminally-ill doozey of a detail I'd broken Rule Number One When You're Lying but I figured it was okay in this case. Not only did it reinforce my lack of fear of violence, but it turned the whole bullshit fiasco in a new direction, which must have confused Ron even further.

Jesus, man, I'm sorry, was all Ron could come up with, referring to my terminal illness.

Give me some names and addresses, I pressed.

Ron said he didn't have any addresses and only first names.

Okay, give me first names and the names of the bars they hang at.

Just forget it, man.

You see those guys, I reiterated, really rolling now, and they try anything with you, you tell them to come up to my house. "No plata," I said, "just plomo." I was referring here to an old down south saying, *"plata o plomo,"* money or lead. If you can't pay someone off, you kill him. What I'd meant, in case Ron still didn't completely get the drift, was that I would not be shaken down. I'd go out in a blaze.

The conversation went on for a bit, got into philosophical crapola about death and so forth, but it's here, on the "No plata, just plomo" line, where I'd write Cut To if this were a movie script.

CHAPTER SIXTEEN

All moanday, tearsday, wailsday, thumpsday, frightday, shatterday.
James Joyce

My ad-libbed terminally ill detail was a nice touch. It didn't come completely out of the blue of my imagination, though. Thing was, I really wasn't feeling well, hadn't been for a while. I'd been getting the night sweats, fever, and chills. The chills, especially, were nasty suckers. Shivering right down to the bone kind of chills, which in the heat of the tropics is a really bad sign. I'd lost weight, too, noticeably, which was convenient for my credibility with Ron (and maybe good for my nose-riding), but I *was* sick.

Problem for now, though, was the added detail about my having to go to San José for "more treatments." It meant I pretty much had to go somewhere for a couple of days, leave Pavones, to keep my story straight with Ron.

I talked it over with Lisa, told her how I'd out-bullshitted Ron, that shitball motherfucker, and we decided I'd go for a solo drive up the coast, meanwhile telling everyone I was in San José at the dentist. I'd told Ron that the dentist was my cover story; that I didn't want anyone at Pavones to know I was terminally ill.

So I drove up the coast. I worried, leaving Lisa alone at the house. I worried about two things. One, just because Ron's hit man story was bullshit, it didn't mean that Logan *hadn't* hired a hit man to kill me. He was definitely capable of it. The old one about the paranoid guy who *is* being followed comes to mind (as does The Othello Syndrome, if you want to get goofy about it). The other thing I worried about (speaking of The O Syndrome) was that Lisa maybe had another fuckbuddy, maybe someone at Pavones, or in a nearby town like Golfito. I was not only remembering all her bullshit excuses to make solo Golfito runs (plus her "I gave it a shot" blurt when busted on one), plus oodles of other stuff, but something else had come up, still *another* of her not-thinking-before-speaking blurts. Two, actually. A couple of months previously she'd asked me, completely out of the blue, if I thought she had two boyfriends. Although this had occurred to me, it was a back burner possibility, one that I hadn't really pondered, one I certainly had never voiced or done anything about. Her San José "boyfriend,"

284

fuckbuddy, whatever, was a given and my main, my constant, concern.

Now, as I was about to leave, Lisa asked me, and, again, this came out of the blue (I hadn't mentioned "boyfriends" for a while), if I thought she had a local boyfriend, someone in Pavones. It was a variation on the two boyfriends theme except now she was zeroing in, telling me that the second one was right there under my nose.

So, aside from everything else, I had that thought to think about as I drove up the coast in order to keep my story straight with Ron about being terminally ill, leaving the love of my life alone at the home I built in paradise.

CHAPTER SEVENTEEN

The real comic novel has to do with man's recognition of his unimportance in the universe.

Anthony Burgess

Here's an example of a *bad sign*. It's a bad sign if you're in an ex-banana port Third World hospital and a doctor whose smock is a mustardy baby doo doo hue from bloody phlegm and human crud swarming with microbes as yet unknown to the A.M.A. comes running in your direction, hurdling over sore-ridden campesinos hacking and spitting, some of whom are actively dying, and which doctor (not "witch" doctor) is death-gripping your chest x-ray and wild-eyeballing your upright condition and you yourself like you're Christ arisen.

I exaggerate only slightly.

Holy shit, you should check out that x-ray. I just did, a moment ago, dug it up to look at the date on it, verify on what day this took place, since my journal from that day, April 6, 2004, is schizoid. One of my lungs, the right or the left, depending on which way the x-ray is facing and which way you're looking at it (or a confusing combination thereof), is a dense gray cumulo fucking nimbus.

This guy, this doctor, wasn't one of those who, over time, would ask if I've been under *undue stress*. This is not a question his typical indigenous-peasant patient could relate to (although they have *stress* aplenty, none of it is *undue*). What the doc did say, though, was that I was on death's doorstep with pneumonia and I had to check in to the hospital *inmediatamente*.

Lisa and I looked around at the moaning peasants, the cruddy, mustardy bedding, the barefoot *indios* bringing in pillows for their dying loved ones because the hospital didn't have any, and at the placard saying that visiting hours were from noon to noon fifteen (I'm not kidding).

Nah. Sayo-fucking-A-nara, Jack. I thanked the doctor, who had shown me kindness and concern – especially in his hurdling of actively dying people to get to me – then I signed a form saying neither my heirs nor the U.S. military would get pissed off if I keeled over on my way out of there, and we were out of there.

It took until the next day to make the trip north but I checked in to Cima Hospital in San José, a private clinic for foreigners and rich Ticos. I spent 11 days in a big private room that reminded me of the Holiday Inn where I taped Lisa calling her fuckbuddy. When I say I spent 11 days in the hospital, I really mean we, Lisa and I. To my huge relief, the admitting person said it would be fine if Lisa stayed in the room with me; there was big foldout couch, along with cable TV, high-speed internet and room service with great food. I eyed Lisa to see if she was pleased or bummed by the bulletin that she could sleep over, but couldn't tell. As soon as I knew I'd be laid up I imagined how my recovery would go, if it would go at all, knowing Lisa was at some hotel fuckfesting with her fuckbuddy, her *San José* fuckbuddy, since there maybe were two of the shitball motherfuckers.

Christ, think about it. Lisa leaves to go to her hotel and the nurse comes in to take my vital signs and based on those signs she presses her emergency button and the doctors rush in and can't figure why my vital signs are doing what they're doing and all they can think of is to ask if I'm under *undue stress.*

Just thinking about that scenario, an 11-day nightmare of that magnitude, makes the three hours I would spend in the dentist chair going through the worst pain in my life while Lisa was off fuckfesting with her San José fuckbuddy look like a clichéd day at the beach. I use the awkward "would spend" (I forget what you call it, future or conditional plu-something maybe) because that doozey of an incident hadn't happened yet. It will, though. So be patient, no pun intended.[*]

A couple or so things of note happened during my hospital stay. I called Sean Penn's assistant, to whom I'd sent my *Zero* screenplay draft, the one I wanted Sean to read. It'd been a month or so since she got it and I figured it was time to get in touch. I was expecting some Hollywood crapola but by now my condition had improved (I was no longer on death's doorstep) so I figured I (plus my vital signs) could deal with it. (I'd had a quart of the funkiest pink liquid scum you ever saw drained from my lung.)

Penn's assistant reminded me of Lisa in how she would come up with irrelevant details to make a point that in any case had nothing to do with anything; how she could talk around stuff. There was also a breezy quality to her voice, which Lisa uses when she's lying. I'm not saying that Penn's assistant was lying about anything, *not necessarily,* but when you can't follow what someone is going on about, there's something going on. Yes, I've done the research on this.

The point of sending my draft to Penn's assistant, and I made this clear

---

[*] I'm writing this from pretty far in the future from April, 2004. I know a lot of stuff you don't, of course, but not everything. Mainly meaning that I still don't know how all this shit is going to end. Which is a huge source of stress, although I'm not sure if the stress is *undue* or *due.*

in my cover letter (which explained about the *Zero* deal, even though she no doubt knew of it), was to eventually get Penn to read the draft. My suggestion in the letter was that Penn's assistant read it first and, if she liked it, pass it along to Penn with a recommendation. I did this because of the way it works in Hollywood with reading stuff: No Hollywood person reads stuff unless it's handed to him with a recommendation by another Hollywood person. There's a catch-22 here, of course, having to do with following the chain of Hollywood people handing stuff to read to other Hollywood people until you run out of Hollywood people and then there's no way to get the chain started in the first place, if you get my drift.

Right from the get-go in this call I amended my request, suggesting to Penn's assistant that she just read the first 30 pages of my draft, which was up until the first turning point, not counting the one that kick starts the yarn in the beginning. It was a pretty strong turning point, the one on page 30, I felt, and would hook a reader into wanting to find out What Happens Next. So I suggested this and then Penn's assistant, in her reply, lost me. She went on and on with me hardly saying a word, then towards the end said something that implied that she might not have time in the near future to read the first 30 pages of my draft.

I looked at my watch. You know, I said, it might have been more efficient if you'd just said okay to my suggestion to read the first 30 pages of my draft, which suggestion I made 20 minutes ago, since you'd be finished reading by now, or close to it, then you wouldn't have had to explain all that.

What followed was one of those Hollywood silences so familiar to me. One of those silences that means someone is looking foolish, *publicly so* – meaning to herself – and is aghast and nonplussed and unable to undo either the foolishness per se or the public-ness thereof. A rush of insight of the unpleasant variety.

That pretty much ends this installment of this fiasco. There's plenty more to come, though.

I got a couple of calls from the States while I was in the hospital. One from a friend up at Montauk and one from the shitball motherfucker Hollywood writer who's envious of my modest Hollywood and literary successes. This is the guy I describe back in Part One as "trying to sound all rosy and happy for me but I could imagine his green-with-envy complexion and forced grin – picture a seasick jackass chewing on a swarm of yellow jackets." This was when he heard of my *Cosmic Banditos* deal with John Cusack, having already heard of the *Zero* deal with Sean Penn. Now, his having somehow heard of my hospital stay, I'll amend that description just a bit. Here, in his phony concern for my health we delete the *green-with-envy* and *seasick* stuff, and his grin was no longer forced; he was, rather, unsuccessfully trying to suppress his grin (as he inquired with great concern about my health). But you can still picture his grin as being like a jackass chewing on a swarm of yellow jackets.

I'd love to be able to say I came up with the *jackass chewing on a swarm of yellow jackets* allusion myself but the truth is that I heard it somewhere years ago, don't remember where, and have been saving it to use somewhere. It's one of those rural down home-isms that knocks my socks off. By the way, as I write these words here at the end of the road it's raining really hard. It's raining *like a tall cow pissing on a flat rock.**

As I hung up with the shitball motherfucker Hollywood writer I wondered how he had heard I was in the hospital. Only a few people in Montauk knew and there was no connection between my Montauk friends and Hollywood. Christ. Maybe the guy was involved in the whole Ron/Logan/San José merc/hit man conspiracy. *Maybe he's at the bottom of it.* Or maybe… *maybe he's Lisa's San José fuckbuddy.*

Just kidding.

Here's another one: *The paranoid man is simply the man with all the facts.*

Before leaving the hospital I called Steven. I was feeling a lot better and was in the mood to fire him, for the big-mouth treachery and incompetence you already know about. But before I could fire him Steven came up with a bulletin that distracted me: the *Zero* studio and the producer(s) (plural if you consider Sean Penn a producer in more than title only) were hunting for a new writer to do the adaptation. This was good news, in the narrative sense. See, I knew I (or, rather, we, you, kind reader, and I) was (were) in for more hilarious Hollywood shit, based on another writer adapting my book under the tutelage of the dumb asses who had come up with and/or approved of that outline. But for now, the point being: The idiots were throwing still more money into the fire.

Not only that, Steven went on, but the studio et al were looking for a partner in the *Zero* movie deal in order to defray the expense of the other writer and of the production itself. In other words, they were looking for other idiots to *help* throw money into the fire. Steven said that they had approached Quiksilver, the mega-buckola surf wear company. Okay. I knew that a couple of the head guys at the company were big fans of the book; I had even met one of them.

So this was all interesting. In fact, it was so interesting that when I hung up I realized I forgot to fire Steven, which was why I'd called him in the first place.

---

* Point being that when you hear gems like these, remember them, or, better, write them down. They come in handy. I mean if you're going to write a book (but not *someday*).

CHAPTER EIGHTEEN

As Gregor Samsa awoke one morning from uneasy dreams he found himself transformed into a gigantic insect.

Franz Kafka

Finally, in the waning days of May (2004) I got hold of Sean Penn's direct email address – I was getting nowhere with my pleas for his assistant to read my screenplay (or just the first 30 pages) and forward it to Penn if she liked it. Here's what I wrote.*

To Sean Penn
via email

Dear Sean,

We've met (at the Four Seasons), and spoken on the phone. I'm the author of the book *In Search of Captain Zero*, and the screenplay adaptation of the book, although you may not be aware that such a screenplay exists.

I've always admired your work; the projects you do, not only as an actor but as a director. I believed [the producer] when she told me you "get involved early in the script stage." I let her (and, technically, you) option my book. I sweated over four drafts. Almost three years' work, two and a half years more time than I've ever put into a screenplay. (I've written or rewritten about 20; I have screen credits on features and numerous TV shows.) My book was a tough, tough adaptation. I had to reinvent my book's internally driven, anecdotal, nonfiction story for the screen. (The key was finding the ending my book did not provide; the noir, *Heart of Darkness*, mythical finish I had promised everyone – you may recall this promise, made at our Four Seasons Hotel breakfast meeting.)

---

* In the following email exchange I edited out details either you already know about or were boring. For veracity's sake the full versions are archived on my website.

During the writing and rewriting I kept asking [the producer] when you were going to get involved (especially after she went from my screenplay being "brilliant" to "it's not the screenplay we expected"). Suddenly it was, "Oh, Sean doesn't read." (I didn't believe this.)

The *In Search of Captain Zero* screenplay I wrote is the best work I've ever done. I wish you'd read it. Your assistant has a copy. I have fine-tuned it further, but that version will do for now. (In fact, I'm not even asking you to read the whole draft. If act one – up to page 30 – doesn't knock you out, toss the thing. I know how busy you are but I'm really only asking for a half hour of your time.)

Yours truly,
Allan Weisbecker

I'll combine Penn's response to my email with my response to his response. Again, I've cut it down a bit, with the full version archived on my website. My responses to his letter are in **bold**. One other thing: In the email subject box Mr. Penn wrote: "Genius screenplays and other entitlements." His use of the word "entitlement" aggravated me, as you'll see.

CLYDE IS HUNGRY FILMS

June 9, 2004

Hello Allan Weisbecker,

Yes, liked the book and wanted to be involved.

You had not read my book at the time of the deal you made to produce it. My point here is this: If you're going to give Sage and Morally Superior Life Lesson advice, you might consider not leading off with an outright prevarication.

Regarding your use of the word "entitlement" in the subject box to your email (referring to me, I assume) and to your disingenuous claim (below) that "Hollywood" is merely a place on a map: The H-word as I use it and as everyone in the movie business understands it (or should) refers to a state of mind that allows someone in your position to get 25k (from the studio) and not have to do anything except show up two hours late for a breakfast meeting (at the Four

Seasons) and not apologize (since you don't believe other folks' time is of any importance), except to say that you had "a pharmaceutical night" (people not subject to entitlement do not advertise their drug abuse problems) and light up a cigarette in a busy restaurant – not only a rude, but illegal move (I smoke, btw). Entitlement. You actually used this word in reference to me. Wow.

...and by the time the screenplay came to my attention, so had it come to my attention that you had published the screenplay on the internet. Whether or not that was your right to do, I don't know, but I'm not interested in projects that have been pre-read by the public at large. For me, it's akin to doing a revival, the magic lost.

Maybe 200 people have read my screenplay. You call this the public at large? This makes it a... revival? Wow. Here's some news. Screenplays get read. Hey: books get read. Did you know that *Mystic River* was a book before it was a movie? The story got read by the public at large. A revival? Please.

In a rambling paragraph Penn says that the last time he checked, "Hollywood is just a city on a map."

But I would always warn a writer not to put his fingernails into hyperbolic comments made. Considering oneself a genius can be a lonely affair and create disproportionate hostilities, ie. don't let initial comments infuse the old ego. Motion picture scripts always need the personalization of the director.

I do not consider myself a genius any more than I consider you one. Mozart was a genius; the rest of us, as you say, are just getting by. I mentioned [the producer's] comments as an example of my frustration level at her flip-flop (in my screenplay going from "brilliant" to "not the screenplay we expected"). In rereading my letter, this seems completely obvious. Perhaps [the producer] was right in her oft repeated comment, "Sean doesn't read."

It is, after all, a collaborative medium into which you've stepped foot.

Of all your doozies, this one is my outright favorite. Yes, it's a collaborative medium and guess what? Along with [the director] and [the producer], you are my other collaborator.

In your Sage and Morally Superior Life Lesson Advice did it even occur to you that you are my collaborator? What level of denial are you living under, Mr, Penn? My courteous, respectful, borderline fawning letter to you was nothing more than a plea for help from my contractual, paid collaborator. (One who supposedly "gets involved early in the script stage.")

I think you're a very good writer

Again, I doubt that you've read anything of mine before now. [Note: He still hadn't read my book, let alone my screenplay.]

I'm sure you worked very hard on the screenplay and I know what that's like but there are people living in Hollywood who are working very hard on screenplays too. And I have found that many of them are just as genuine as those at the end of the road, at the bottom of Central America, and those in Boston, Baghdad, and beyond.

Your denial is showing again: The other genuine people working very hard on screenplays throughout the world do not have Sean Penn as a paid, contractual collaborator.

The "Hollywood" attack works for me about as well as the "Nigger" attack on blacks or the "Evil" attack on Muslims. None do much to move life forward and I believe that it is beneath a talented writer. But if you want to continue writing things like that I would suggest you move to the corner of Sunset and Doheny where you will find lucrative work at People Magazine or The Star or The Enquirer.

How about this for a thought: Instead of spending whatever time you did with your Sage and Morally Superior Life Lesson advice, why didn't you spend that time reading the first 30 pages of the screenplay on which you are a contractual, paid collaborator (and which is all I asked of you)? It might've actually taken less time. [Note: Again, I cut out quite a lot of Mr. Penn's letter: It truly would have taken less time to read 30 pages of my draft.]

Of all the ironies inherent in your message, this one is perhaps the biggie. (I made the same comment to your assistant, by the way, who did most of the talking during our lengthy calls.)

If you live in paradise, as you said in your letter, enjoy it. It's special. You're special. We're all special. Isn't that special. But of the many writers who are gifted, I afford my time to those of good will and unpublished screenplays.

As anyone reading my letter would see, I wrote you with respect and goodwill. And what do I get back?

I hope that you will re-group and spend more time with your talent and your paradise and less with bitterness and barrages. We're all just gettin' by.

Bitterness and barrages? Again, what letter were you reading? Did you read it or get coverage?

Sean Penn

Okay. A few days after sending the above I got this email from my collaborator:

Allan,

I got about as far as the money issue...FYI I was never paid one red cent... Genius? Or sad little man dwelling in his own obnoxious self-importance? I got a feeling I know which option you see. In either case, I'm sure you're doing yourself and the world a lot of good down there in Central America and therefore, despite my own selfish interest, I encourage you to stay there until something that resembles death...

Disgusted,
Sean Penn

If Penn in fact never got any money, I'd say he has some firing to do – his manager and accountant at the very least, since – according to the producer, who should know – his contract *did* include a 25k up front fee, the same as hers.

I'll not go into the fractured syntax and bad sentences and other nonsense in his replies (I had pushed some buttons, though, hadn't I?), except to repeat that it sure would have been easier if in his capacity as producer on this project he'd just taken a quick look at the first 30 pages of my screenplay.

But the point being: Can't I Get Along With Anyone?

CHAPTER NINETEEN

Think, in your head, now, think of the most... private... secret...
intimate thing you have ever done secure in the knowledge of its
privacy... Are you thinking of it?... Well, I saw you do it!
                                                            Tom Stoppard

Summer of 2004.

Since the fiascos of that winter, Lisa and I had had our ups and downs,
mostly downs, but somehow we were still together, technically. I did not
love her anymore, not in the normal, healthy sense. But I did *need* her. With
Lisa, as with the codeine, the cigarettes, the rum, the coffee, and even with
the writing of this dispiriting narrative, I was in the grip of a full-blown
addiction.

I see that now. But at that time I was too occupied with denial to see it,
or anything else, clearly. I was so busy with denial that I was *in denial about
being in denial*. To put it another way: I knew I was in denial – and watch
how I out-self-reflected myself on this – but I figured since I knew it, and
pondered it so much, so freely and generously admitted it to myself, I was
above it. A double whammy kind of denial, with a bit of a catch-22 as a
Meanwhile, no?

No one knows shit about why he does anything.

But still: I'm pretty sure I was hanging in with Lisa, needing her, not
because I needed Lisa *herself*, but because I needed *to be in love*. Make no
mistake: *Being loved* – or the illusion thereof, which is actually the same
thing for the illusionated – was wondrous and beautiful, and Lisa, God
knows, was a proficient illusionator (not counting the cheating and lying
and gaslighting). But *being in love* was sublime.

One time a while back (just prior to Lisa's "in another realm" and
"beyond the pale" two-day flirtation with the surfer at the cantina) Lisa
and I were sitting on our bed after a lengthy take five and, panting in spent
lust and lingering passion, I was suddenly overcome emotionally, saying
I was truly happy for the first time in my life and that was because I was
in love.

Lisa's response was interesting. For a flicker her eyes went sad and she subtly, reflexively, shook her head. My impression then, and which impression rattled me, was that she was saying "Don't be." Happy that is.

Armed as I am now with more knowledge, knowledge a part of me intuited even then, I see that this spark of mercy or pity or humanity was surely an anomaly – my heartfelt profession should have vindicated Lisa's relentless efforts to woo me, reassure me, and, indeed, outright gaslight me, given her agenda. But, rather than exultation, she let fly a beat of melancholia, and a glimmered warning.

Out of character, no? But for a desperate character so needing to *be in love*, hope is where you find it. The recollection of Lisa's sadness and her warning had been a justification for clinging, if by a torn hangnail, to the Lisa Is Crying Out For Help Theory.

But beyond that, beyond whatever human need I harbored, I was dimly aware of something else, something deep and dark and related to the dreads I sought to shake.

During that summer (2004) Lisa pumped the Perfect Woman well nearly dry, with her love notes and sexy post-its and angst pus-removal massages and jazzy home-made pizzas and earnest assurances that I'd ruined her for other men and it was us against the world. How could I doubt her? She exclaimed yet again in heartfelt rhetorical inquery, since she'd "have to be an Academy Award-winning actress" to fake her devotion to me. Meryl Streep had nothing on the love of my life.

In July, Lisa went off to New York to visit her family. There were no cell phone shenanigans this time – she didn't activate her New York cell for the brief trip. But there were shenanigans. I'll not jeopardize Reader Big Mo here with an inventory of indications that more infidelity was afoot, as it clearly was. To make matters worse, in the couple days before her return Lisa pelted me with devotional emails and sexy phone messages; even a breathless paean wherein she was thinking about me as she satisfied herself. Clear and present gaslighting, so to speak, possibly to put me at ease regarding her stateside doings, and also regarding her forthcoming solo night in San José before taking the puddle jumper to our paradise at the end of the road.

There's only one way to put it as I waited in San José for Lisa's return, having told her that I was at home at Big Turkeys (to reassure her she'd have a night alone in San José): I was *crazed* to catch her with her fuckbuddy, the San José one. And my journal notes reflect my frothy obsession. Try to follow my convoluted thinking in the following, which is from my journal of the day before her arrival, as I lurked in San José, planning various ambushes.

I let her stay in room for a while, maybe an hour or more. give her time – maybe guy will come right away or she will go to his room (so I don't answer her call and then call back in 20 minutes and tell her where I am, to see if she is in room. if she is not in room and didn't leave hotel, she is in other room). then call and say I wanted to meet her at airport but cab got a flat and missed her. didn't want her to think I was trying to catch her so I am 5 minutes away, she may then call him to alert, from room, will be on the tape recorder. if she is not in room when I call, should I wait or leave a message right away that I'm in sj and coming then go to her room?

What did I say were the two concepts comedy/humor/whatever are based on? Right: Obsession and pain. So if you laughed at my notes, it's okay, I'm not offended. In fact, if you howled, busted a gut, you're my kind of guy or gal. (*Doctor Strangelove*, the funniest movie of all time, was about the end of life on earth.)

The tape recorder mentioned was to be planted in Lisa's hotel room before she arrived, mainly to pick up any phone conversations. But such was not necessary, as it turned out. Preliminary Plan A — my observant presence at the airport when Lisa arrived, to see if her San José fuckbuddy would meet her -- proved to be all that was necessary. All that was necessary for the *worst moment of my life* to transpire. Yes, what was coming was the worst moment of my life, not even excepting Mom's death, God help me.

I bought a big bouquet of flowers, with which I'd be waiting. (If you're laughing at *that* image, again, great.) Some irony: after all my Machiavellian scheming and after all the Alternate Plans that ran the length of the alphabet, I finally decided it was all too convoluted and stupid and that if Lisa came out of customs and was not met by her fuckbuddy, the San José one, I'd appear smiling with the flowers and make like my presence at the airport was a surprise gift. We'd reenact our first kiss: "The kiss that changed my life," is how Lisa referred to that moment in front of the passenger arrival door upon her first visit; this was some year and a half previously. We'd then hop a taxi and grope each other as we did then, and upon arrival at the Balmoral we'd tear off our clothes and consummate our lust with nervous passion, hardly uttering a word, and soon be going at it again in the shower.[*]

---

[*] To be more accurate, *I* was nervous in my passion, quite so. Lisa was not; she was merely hot to get naked and on with it. This difference did not bother me at the time – I was concerned with performance – but later, when Lisa claimed she had not been with any men except her ex-boyfriend and her ex-husband for over 12 years, I wondered at her casual sexual aplomb with a new lover.

Hold on. *What was I thinking here?* That if the shitball motherfucker San José fuckbuddy didn't meet her plane, all was fine and dandy? There was no trouble in River City? Was the D-word roaring out my name from the peanut gallery or was I just plain stupid or nuts or afflicted with some serious battle fatigue?

If Lisa did meet up with her fuckbuddy, the San José one, and after I'd flattened the shitball motherfucker's nose against his face (for the insult of his coming to my room during the Fleabag Hotel incident), I'd press the flowers into Lisa's shaking hand and look into her fearful and guilt-reddened eyes and say, "Lisa, we're going home now. I'm going to help you with your problem. You're going to get well. You're going to become a real human being." (I'd practiced my appeal in front of the mirror and still remember it verbatim.) Yes, the flowers were a nice touch, no matter which of the two wildly disparate scenarios transpired.

Unfortunately, there was a third possible scenario — the one that would provide me with the worst moment of my life.

Need I point out that I planned my airport vigil with due diligence? Or that I checked with the airline multiple times to see that Lisa's flight was on time? And finding that it was on time need I point out that I left the hotel an hour earlier than necessary in case of traffic or an accident or a 10.0 earthquake that might destroy the road and I'd have to somehow make it on foot through the rubble to meet the flight?

Vantage point was vital. Across from the passenger arrival door at Juan Santamaria International is a two-tiered parking garage with an overlook of the terminal. Perfect. Twenty yards across the access road at about a 45-degree downward angle lay the taxi stand and just beyond it the little booth where you buy your taxi voucher. To get to your cab you pass through a narrow gate, right there in my unobstructed view. Lisa, who would be lugging two huge suitcases packed with power tools and which weighed nearly two hundred pounds total, would need at least five minutes to buy the voucher, get help with her freight, secure a driver then load up the taxi and pull away.

If she took a taxi.

The high position was also ideal in that I had to avoid Lisa spotting me before I ascertained that no fuckbuddy was there to meet her: As any deer hunter in a tree stand will tell you, animals rarely look upwards for possible peril from predators or other dangers. It was a foolproof vantage point, I figured.

Need I point out that I kept mind-wandering or even eye-blinking to a minimum from the moment the first passenger from Lisa's flight exited customs, bought his voucher and bolted in his taxi? Or that an hour afterward when I still had not seen the love of my sorry-ass life appear I commenced to worry? She had not called our cell, which she surely would have done had she missed the plane, and there was no crowd for her to get lost from sight in; the passengers exited in ones and twos every half minute or so.

What was going on? Had one of her huge suitcases not made the Atlanta connection and was she dealing with that fiasco? Was customs harassing her about the power tools?

Time passed. The dribble of passengers trickled to nothing. I descended to ground level and asked the taxi dispatcher if all the passengers from the Atlanta flight had come out. "Si, señor," he said. "Todos salierion." They've all gone.

I looked at the passenger arrival door, which because of my high angle and the building's overhang, I could not quite see from my vantage point.

A bad gastro feeling now, not my writer's queasy gut but more of the sort you may be familiar with: When you've made a dumb, completely avoidable mistake with catastrophic implications and would give anything to undo it. That sort.

I had to sit down, right there on the curb. My knees were, quite literally, weak.

Once you exited the passenger arrival door from customs it was only a few yards to your left to the taxi area, but if someone was picking you up you turned to the right and followed a path to the parking garage. Having always taken a taxi from the airport, I hadn't realized this. Neither did I realize that I could not see the path to the garage from my vantage point.

Lisa's San José fuckbuddy had met Lisa's flight all right, and I had blown it. While I fixated on the taxi area the two of them had walked by me, *right* by me, just below and to my left, holding hands or groping each other impatiently, perhaps, and I hadn't seen them because of my faulty goddamn angle of view.

Do you understand why I say this was the worst moment of my life?

After so many months of awareness of Lisa's infidelity, her outright treachery, and after all the incidents, way too numerous to recap, and after literally dreaming of the moment when *the lies would have to stop*, and after laying awake for the last couple nights concocting Plans B through Z… after all of it I fuck up everything with such a stupid Preliminary Plan A error?

What a clown I am!

And do you see why the San José Airport Incident would seem to indicate that, aside from nothing in my life working out for the best, *nothing in my narratives works out for the best either*? No, you don't see that? Consider this question, then, although I've asked (and answered) it before: What is the essence of storytelling? Right: Conflict. *Escalating conflict*. Problem is, conflict cannot keep escalating forever. So in order to end the escalating conflict, you need what? A *confrontation* followed by a *resolution*.

The San José Airport Incident should have provided my confrontation and resolution. But instead of a confrontation and resolution, what happens here? I'm sitting on the curb with my thumb, plus my head, up my ass.

But wait! Is there hope yet? Maybe... just maybe Lisa was one of the last passengers out and she and her San José fuckbuddy are still en route to the hotel, the good old Balmoral, and since they have to stop at the Tracopa bus terminal first to send off the huge suitcases, maybe I can get to the hotel first...

I grabbed a taxi driver almost literally by the throat, forced a 10k *colones* note into his hand and told him to get me the fuck to the Balmoral right *now*.

I don't remember much about the 15 minute hell-bent cab ride to the city (normally 25 minutes), except my body being tensely arched and twisted, head between my knees in the shotgun seat, grimacing and muttering and moaning and cursing and asking Mom how I could have fucked up so badly.

An added problem, a related fiasco: Having scrapped all my Alternate Plans as too convoluted, I'd not tried to hide the fact that I'd checked into the hotel – this would have been very difficult anyway, since the Balmoral staff knew Lisa and me well and always greeted us by name. When Lisa arrived they'd say, "Allan está aquí," Allan is here, or some such giveaway. And that would be that. Lisa would tell her fuckbuddy – waiting outside or an expected phone call away – to keep the hell out of there.

So my only hope was to get there before Lisa did.

I barreled into the hotel, still clutching that stupid bouquet – what a clown! – to find my front desk buddy smiling and saying, "Lisa está!"

Did you tell her I was here?! I wanted to know.

"Sí, claro!" Yes, sure!

The worst moment of my life, not even excepting Mom's death, God help me, was now a continuing condition, and would be so for a long time. Even now, it lingers. *Especially* now, as I write about it.

As I rode the elevator to Lisa's floor all I could think about was the misery I was now experiencing, and how to get rid of it. There was only one possibility, a faint, faint hope that this was just a nightmare and not reality. My hope was that Lisa would say that she hadn't taken a taxi from the airport; maybe she'd met someone on the flight who had a car in the garage and who offered a ride. Something like that. As long as she didn't claim to have taken a taxi to the hotel...

Lisa was in the shower as I entered, trying my damnedest not to look too wild-eyed. She heard me and exclaimed over the running water how happy she was when they told her I was at the hotel.

Right.

She came out with a towel around her and I smiled – a jackass chewing on a swarm of yellow jackets again comes to mind – wanting to know how was her taxi ride from the airport.

Fine, she said. The usual.

The nightmare was confirmed as reality.

Must've been tough handling those big heavy suitcases by yourself.

Yes, she said, jovial and breezy as ever. Took me like ten minutes, what with getting the taxi driver and buying the voucher and the loading...

I was at the airport, I interrupted. You didn't take a taxi.

There was fear in Lisa's eyes as she insisted she did take a taxi.

I have to ask you something before I continue on with this. Do you believe me one hundred percent without doubt that Lisa did not take a taxi from the San José airport? In other words, do you believe my eyewitness account? And you do realize, do you not, that if you believe my eyewitness account and if Lisa was lying and did not take a taxi, it means she was picked up by her fuckbuddy, the San José one? You do realize that, right?

But if there's doubt, even the tiniest bit about either of these issues, fine; I'll here dispel it. Or, rather, Lisa will, with her not thinking before speaking. I didn't even have to prompt her further. She got all bright-eyed and even breezier (still another adverb on the road to hell) in her detail-rich story about coming out of the passenger's exit, first lugging one huge suitcase out of customs then the other, and then buying the voucher and then getting the taxi driver to help and how long that took and, anyway, how could I miss her in her bright yellow dress, which she then pointed to there on the bed?

Indeed, there was no way I could have missed her in that bright yellow dress. Or if she'd been wearing camouflage either. Hey, I couldn't have missed her if she'd taken some bad-CIA movie invisible woman spy elixir and all that was visible coming out of the passengers' exit door at the airport were the huge silver suitcases, moving on their own into a taxi. Or how about this image: I couldn't have missed her if she'd taken some bad-CIA movie invisible woman spy elixir that didn't completely work and all that was visible coming out of the passengers' exit door at the airport was her pussy – the cause of all this – moving on its own into a taxi with the two huge silver suitcases.

Those flowers are for you, I said, adding a bit of self-effacing irony to the fiasco, meanwhile indicating the stupid bouquet on the bed next to Lisa's bright yellow dress, the one I couldn't miss her in.

Lisa kissed my cheek in thanks for the flowers, as if I were the attentive male end of a normal, happy couple. Then, maybe as a reward for my being so thoughtful and romantic, she sat down on the bed, opened her notebook to the back page and commenced to diagram the taxi area at Juan Santamaria International. With circles and arrows and stick figures and her arrival time up top and doodles in the margin, Lisa proceeded to repeat her story of how she caught a taxi.

Christ. Didn't she know how much worse she was making all this with the detailed and, anyway, irrelevant garbage? Did she think if she just kept talking and diagramming and breezing it up I'd forget she was fucking *lying* and all this would go away?

I was staring at the taxi area from twenty yards away, Lisa. You did not take a taxi back from the airport with two huge suitcases and in your bright yellow dress.

Look! The taxi driver's phone number! Lisa went on to say she'd talked to the taxi driver on the way from Tracopa about coffee plantations in Heredia and took his number. She sometimes did take *taxista's* phone numbers if she liked them. Yep, there was a phone number and a name, above her goddamn diagram of the area I'd been staring at for over two hours almost without blinking.

Call him, she said. He'll verify that he took me from Tracopa to the Balmoral.

Wait a minute. What about the taxi that picked you up at the airport?

I let him go at Tracopa, Lisa said. She said she changed taxis.

Lisa saying she'd changed taxis at Tracopa was proof that she was lying about taking a taxi from the airport – if you doubt my eyewitness account – although there is yet more proof looming. Bear with me on this.

Lisa, I said, why would you switch taxis at Tracopa?

To save money.

What? Lisa, all you do is at the airport you tell the driver that you're going to the Balmoral but need to stop at Tracopa first to drop off the bags. Since the fare to the city is fixed, if you switch taxis it costs you *more*.

Lisa said she didn't want to argue with a taxi driver.

In fact, Lisa loves to argue with taxi drivers. But no matter, because no Costa Rican taxi driver would jeopardize an airport fare by arguing about an extra stop. Never, since there are a hundred more drivers waiting behind him. And Lisa well knows this — in the total of four other times Lisa has flown in to San José and had to go to Tracopa before the hotel, she has never once switched taxis at Tracopa. One time, even *after* this incident, and with me with her, she said this to the driver: "Two stops. Tracopa then the hotel." Bad perception management, Lisa.

Plus. if you'll remember, Lisa had her passport stolen at Tracopa, a traumatic event that makes her taxi-switching claim even more absurd, if that's possible. She would never have allowed herself to be between drivers, with no one to watch her stuff.

So there is no way Lisa switched taxis at Tracopa. Not in this world, or even in a different (or slightly better) one. Lisa's fuckbuddy, the San José one, had brought her from the airport to Tracopa, whence she took a taxi to the hotel; this so the hotel staff wouldn't see her with the shitball motherfucker, since they know us so well.

Need still more proof that the love of my sorry ass life was lying yet again about her inability to help herself when she's hell-bent for uncommitted dick?

By now it was late afternoon. I had to lie down. Two reasons. To let the stress properly do its work, and to avoid Lisa switching modes from bright-eyed and breezy to screaming with veins popping about having changed her life to come live with me at the end of the road, her favorite harangue, which I sensed coming if I pressed her on her lies. Lisa lay down with me and tenderly rubbed my back; it wasn't an angst pus-removal massage, but close. In spite of everything I halfway dozed, or passed out, whatever. I don't remember if I dreamed, but assume not. I hope not.

We had dinner in the room. I ate little and said little. Lisa was... still breezy. But afterward, something occurred to me. A rush of insight. A big one.

I asked Lisa to see her notebook. I told her I wanted to call the taxi driver who brought her from Tracopa, as she had suggested. See, I didn't doubt that Lisa had taken a taxi from Tracopa to the hotel, for the reason stated – she would never have let her fuckbuddy drop her at the Balmoral. My rush of insight – and I mentally kicked myself for not realizing this before – was that the taxi driver would remember how Lisa got to Tracopa from the airport; say, with a gringo, probably in a private car, and which gringo, by the way, was maybe named "David" (and had the middle name "Peter"). The two of them – the taxi driver and Lisa's San José fuckbuddy, be he a David or no – had undoubtedly pitched in together moving the big heavy suitcases. *I had her after all*, I figured.

Lisa fished her notebook out of her big green purse – *that* purse – and handed it to me without comment. I opened to the back page. It was blank. I thumbed through the book, thinking I was mistaken about the diagram and phone number being in the back. No diagram, no phone number. Nowhere in the notebook.

Lisa, you drew the diagram on the back page under the phone number, right?

The smile under Lisa's nod was... what... quizzical? Or a bit triumphant, in spite of herself?

Lisa's rush of insight about the Tracopa taxi driver having seen her with her San José fuckbuddy had preceded mine. It had probably come as soon as she spoke without thinking, saying I should call the taxi driver, at which time I was distracted just by the absurdity of the idea that she had switched taxis. So while I was dozing after the back rub or while I was in the bathroom, or whenever, she tore out the page and disposed of it; crumpled it up and threw it out the window or flushed it.

After examining each page – overkill since you couldn't miss that whacky diagram -- I handed the notebook to Lisa and asked her to please find the page with the diagram and phone number.

Mystification. I don't understand, she said. It was right here in the back.

It disappeared? Disappeared from the notebook in the last couple hours?

It's just not here.

Can't explain it?

No, I can't.

Okay, Lisa.

So if you doubt my eyewitness account: There you have it.

Later that night, in the dark of our room, I fucked the living hell out of Lisa. As I banged and heaved and grunted my stomach was in an uproar and in my mind I was saying to the love of my life that if dick was what she wanted dick was what she'd get, even if it wasn't uncommitted dick but only my sorry-ass Sex God dick. This was the first time my fervor and stamina were motivated by rage — and maybe something deeper and darker than that — not passion or even just animal lust.

I'm quite sure Lisa didn't notice the difference.

CHAPTER TWENTY

*It is closing time in the gardens of the West and from now on an
artist will be judged only on the resonance of his solitude or the
quality of his despair.*

Cyril Connollly

Remember Fang, my adopted dog, whose name was taken from the title
character in Jack London's *White Fang*, my favorite childhood book? I
mentioned her briefly in the context of making a phone call to the *In Search
of Captain Zero* movie producer, when the producer flip-flopped (the first
time) from my adaptation being brilliant (and so forth) to being "not what
we expected." I was on the beach with my cell and Fang was a little puppy
wandering around underfoot as I listened to the latest Hollywood horseshit
and my writer's queasy gut flared.

That was March of 2003, just before my trip to the Caribbean isle where
The Horror would soon take place. Now it was August of 2004, a week
after the San José Airport Incident, the worst moment of my life, and Fang
was a full-grown dog. By God she was a handsome animal, close to 60
pounds and trim and all rippled muscles and adorned with a gorgeous
short-haired tawny coat. Although Honey, the dog I'd brought from the
States in 2001, held a special dog-position in my heart, Fang had emerged
as my other favorite of our pack, which numbered four, soon to be five,
when the now-grown puppy (Fang's cousin) we'd given our caretaker's
brother, William, came back to us near death from malnutrition. William
now being a useless crack-head thief after finding the bale of cocaine on the
beach, he was too fucked up to care for the dog, whose name is Kaiser.

But in her maturity Fang had developed behavior problems. Although
as gentle and loving as a dog could be with Lisa and me, she was too
protective, very aggressive with visitors (especially Costa Ricans) and now
with the other members of our pack. A pit bull mix, she had for some weeks
been asserting her dominance with other dogs. It got to where walks on the
beach were difficult; Fang would immediately attack any neighborhood
mutts we came across. Then she started up with our own dogs, first
Aleeza, my German expat buddy Joachim's (of Joachim and Erik fame,

the ass-kickers from my Max Dalton investigation) Australian Sheppard mix, which I'd adopted when Joachim abandoned Pavones. (He had family matters to attend to in Germany, but he told me he also left because he "couldn't stand the place anymore.") Poor Aleeza would run off and hide in the jungle after Fang's assaults, sometimes staying gone for days. Thing was, Fang was not satisfied when Aleeza would roll over in submission. She'd go for Aleeza's neck, try to kill her, only letting up when screamed at, beaten and bodily pulled off her quivering, squealing victim.

But what a joy that dog was too. The smartest of them all, Fang had a mischievous side and was a constant source of amusement. For example, having so many dogs to contend with, Lisa and I decided that only Honey would be allowed in the house. Having been raised as a stateside suburbia house dog (I adopted her when I was caring for Mom in North Carolina), it would be traumatic and unfair to discipline Honey about coming inside. Besides, Honey and I had so much history; she was the princess.

Fang didn't like being banned from the house. She didn't actually say anything but it was obvious she was aggravated. So what she'd do was very gradually *encroach*. See, we usually left the door to the patio open, and there was literally a line there, a small step down separating inside from outside. At first Fang would lie down with just her nose crossing the line, a very uncomfortable position with her neck crooked to raise up her nose, with the rest of her a few inches below the doorsill and the line it represented.

So you notice that Fang's nose is over the line and you don't say anything. You turn your back for a moment and then her whole head is somehow over the line. Maybe you give her a disapproving look but you still don't say anything. Just a dog *head* inside the house isn't too bad an infraction, right? Then you turn your back again and her shoulders are now inside, the rest of her hanging very uncomfortably off the step. Here's where you throw her out.

Then the whole process repeats itself. Nose, head, shoulders. Out. Again. Nose, head, shoulders. Out. But as time wears on and you get tired she'll manage to wriggle half her body across the line before she gets the boot.

Fang was *relentless*. And you'd never actually catch her in the act of encroachment. She'd look to be innocently asleep when she was, I'm quite sure, watching through slitted eyes for you to turn your back so she could wriggle unseen a few more inches over the line. This started to bug me. But no matter how many times I'd pretend to be busy, whirl around thinking Gotcha, I never caught her. I'd even leave the room, make noise somewhere else in the house, creep back and peek around the corner. Never caught her.

Well, Fang outlasted us. One day we just gave up, called for all the dogs to come on in. Boy, there was joy in Dogville that day. Four, five, six dogs, I don't remember if Kaiser or one of the other puppies was there, how many dogs showed up for the party. But while the other dogs were jumping around in celebration, Fang was cool about it. She just lay there in the middle of the room, *her* room, eyes amused and triumphant, her attention alternating between Lisa and me.

I had to laugh. Fang laughed along with me, the way certain dogs do.

When a dog outlasts you, in essence is smarter than you, and when you laugh at that dog's cleverness and stamina and then the dog laughs along with you at her own goofy victory, you are in the presence of a special canine soul, in my view.

Let me just add this and I'll get to the point: Fang would have laid down her life for Lisa or me, without hesitation. No question of that.

But on July 31st, 2004, Fang tried to kill Honey. If Lisa and I hadn't been right there, Honey would have got her throat torn out and bled to death. The racket was so prolonged and horrendous that our neighbor Carlos Lobo heard it way down on the beach. Honey is a small dog, chubby, as sweet as they come, possessed of no aggressiveness or guile. She was snoozing in the carport when Fang set upon her. As it was she suffered a gash on her neck.

I tied Fang up on a tether and went inside to think. I thought and I thought but I knew what had to be done.

Fang had to be put down.

I thought about alternatives. That night I tried to sleep on it but couldn't. Lisa thought maybe we could give her to someone, but I nixed that. Who would take her, if we were honest about her problem, which we would have to be? No *gringos* we knew would. Costa Ricans will tie dogs up on short rope, toss them scraps, no affection let alone love. No life for a dog like Fang. (Fang was also a chicken-killer, which is death sentence amongst the locals at Pavones.)

But how to do it? I thought of the vet in Ciudad Neilly, a couple hours away. Doc Andres was a kind and competent fellow but there was no way I was taking Fang to be put down there. As a puppy when she'd gone for her shots she'd freaked out, as most dogs do in veterinarian's offices. She'd certainly remember and get upset. I wanted her last moments to be tranquil and happy.

It would have to be done here at home, where Fang was happy.

But who should do it?

I thought of our caretaker, Roman, with whom we were having problems, his fucked-up crack-head brothers staying at Roman's cottage on our property. But the real problem with Roman was that he was Costa Rican. A Tico campesino will kill an animal – doesn't matter if it's a cow or a horse or a pet dog – and it's no big deal, no emotion, no regret. (This is merely an observation.) That wasn't right, not with this dog. Whoever did it had to have compassion and love for the dog.

I had to do it myself, of course. I'd been thinking and thinking all around that.

So the next morning I untied Fang and played with her for a while in the yard...

... okay... shit... this isn't easy... the writing...

... I played with Fang for a while in the yard, then I shouldered my shotgun and led her out the gate and to our lot across the little dirt road to the spot where I'd already had Roman dig a hole, a deep one. I sat down.

Fang looked at me and then she sat down too, close by and with her back to me.

The jungle birds were chirping and the howler monkeys were quiet.

I should tell you something. I looked in my journal notes for details on this matter but there wasn't much. Only this entry, which was on the next cyber page after my ramblings about the San José Airport Incident, which had occurred on July 23: "August 2, 2004. Killed Fang yesterday." That's it.

So this is all from memory. I'm quite sure I have it right though.

I sat there for a while with Fang sitting close by with her back to me. She was just quietly looking around. I put the shotgun barrel to the back of Fang's head and pulled the trigger. I was surprised that the shotgun went off. I thought maybe it would misfire or something.

Fang was now lying on the ground in front of me but I thought she was still moving so I panicked and emptied the rest of the magazine into her. Three more shots. I don't remember rolling Fang into the hole but I must have done so because when Lisa came running up a bit later Fang was down there. The expression on Lisa's face was one of surprise, as if she hadn't thought I'd do it, kill Fang, even though I told her that's what I was going to do when I shouldered the shotgun and led Fang off.

Then Lisa was hugging me and crying and talking but it took a moment to hear what she was saying. Lisa was saying that Fang was a good dog but who also had a bad side and so I had done the right thing.

Now my eyes focused and I was able to see Lisa clearly as she repeated that Fang had a bad side and had to be put down. Lisa said this without irony or self-reflection, which is to be expected from a sociopath, since sociopaths are capable of neither.

Hearing Lisa repeat that I had done the right thing in putting Fang down, I found myself imagining Lisa sitting in front of me where Fang had sat. I imagined putting the shotgun barrel to the back of Lisa's head and pulling the trigger. Rolling Lisa into the hole with Fang and piling dirt on their bodies. Going back to my house and having a rum and O.J., or maybe a glass of Chilean red wine.

PART FIVE
The Real Thing

CHAPTER ONE

Sure is a mess, ain't it, Sheriff?
If it ain't, it'll do until a mess shows up.

Cormac McCarthy

October 29, 2005. On the run. In hiding. Usual place, the Caribbean island of The Horror fame. I'm on the run and in hiding because my life may be in danger back in Costa Rica.

I know: That sounds familiar.

I arrived yesterday and plan on keeping my whereabouts secret while I finish this narrative. Only a couple of trusted surf buddies know I'm here – no choice since they're here too – plus one other person, whom I'll get to, plus explain why I'm back here in hiding again. Try to hang in, please.

After the Airport Incident – the worst moment of my life – and then having killed with a shotgun my beloved dog Fang in the late summer of 2004, I wasn't in what you might call tip-top shape, and Lisa wasn't helping matters (aside from her angst-pus removal massages and jazzy home made pizzas and sexy post-its and love notes and letters and assurances that I'd ruined her for other men and it's us against the world): She just *would not stop* with her gaslighting. In fact, as I soon found out, she'd been upping the gaslighting stakes without my knowing it. The first revelation: For at least the past eight months, since the events starting in February, she'd been going to my friends in Pavones with bulletins about my obsessive jealousy and irrational suspicions; telling my friends that, in effect, I'm nuts. This came to my attention while I was visiting a long-time Pavones expat couple, Candyce and Phil.

Having learned that I'm nuts, I ask Candyce and Phil what sort of background and details Lisa gave them about my being nuts – my obsessive jealousy and irrational suspicions.

Lisa said she'd burned bridges when she came here to live with you, Candyce says.

That's it? She'd *burned bridges*? Nothing about her having cheated and lied for the first few months of our relationship and then got caught at it? I mean just for starters.

No, nothing like that, Candyce says. She says you've been tape recording her and accusing her of cheating on you, among other things.

No details about the tape recordings and accusations? Like why I might do these things?

No.

Did she say anything about the tape recording?

Only that it got screwed up.

It got *screwed up*? That's all?

And you're... obsessed with it.

Obsessed with it?

Allan, she's very upset. She loves you so much.

She's come to us like twenty times since last winter, Phil says.

Twenty times?

Something like that. At least.

She cries and asks us what she should do. This is Candyce again.

Cries? I'm too dumbfounded to do anything but repeat the bulletins Candyce and Phil are bombarding me with.

Hysterically, sometimes. She's very upset.

When I asked Lisa why she'd been gaslighting my friends, aside from me, with lies by omission and outright lies, telling my friends I'm nuts, she screamed with veins popping that she needed support since she'd given up her life to come live with me and look what I was doing to her and to us, then later she cried and apologized for screaming with veins popping.

In fear of actually *going* nuts – in fear of making Lisa's gaslighting a self-fulfilling[*] prophecy – I knew I had to get out of there, get away from Lisa, get away from my home. I needed to regroup, find a place where I could lie down and not be interrupted while the stress properly did its work.

Here's where I did something dumb.

Hold on. If that last clause didn't precipitate a howl and then a moment later your blurting the following, words to this effect: *You mean as opposed to all the smart things you've been doing*? then truly, there's little hope for you and me. I mean I howled, just now, having realized what I'd written – written without irony or self-reflection.

I've used these words before – *without irony* or *self-reflection* – twice, in

---

[*] A beaut of a self-word, no? Unfortunately, having to travel light I left WFD behind when I bolted back to this island. I'm going to miss not being able to find important words from this narrative in it, especially *self* words.

describing characters in this narrative, claiming that they said certain things in this manner. Lisa is one. Remember the other? Right: Gerardo Mora, the man who murdered Max Dalton and his own cousin, Alvaro Aguilar. I also theorized that sociopaths are capable of neither irony nor self-reflection. *Sociopath.* There's a word I had better define. But not now. The dumb thing I did – the *latest* dumb thing – is more important.

Instead of going somewhere where nothing fucked-up could happen – a monastery in Tibet, say, where the monks are not allowed to speak to anyone, let alone gaslight them – I thought I'd take a little trip into my past, go visit my old friend from my (first) memoir, Captain Zero himself, who lived over on the Caribbean side of Costa Rica.

Since I have to assume you haven't read *In Search of Captain Zero,* I'll disclose some stuff. You might recall these words from Part One, referring to what happened when I found my old friend, whom I'd gone in search of in that narrative:

"I went through a bunch of shit, then, at the end, pretty much just went through more shit."

Point being: Instead of going somewhere where nothing fucked-up could happen, I was going somewhere where something fucked-up was virtually *guaranteed* to happen.

You wanna talk about dumb! What was I thinking?

I tell Lisa I'm taking a little trip into my past and hop a bus. I know while I'm gone Lisa is going to do all sorts of fucked-up things at the end of the road but I put that out of my mind (so to speak), or at least try.

So I arrive at the little town where my old friend lives, which, by the way, is also at the end of the road at the bottom of Central America, except on the other coast, the Caribbean coast, and *within minutes* something fucked-up happens. And the fucked-up thing that happens doesn't have anything to do with my old friend; *that* fucked-up thing would have to wait until the next day. *This* fucked-up thing comes completely out of the blue. I say *out of the blue* even though I should have seen it coming. God knows I should have.

I get off the bus, walk into a hotel and there's this guy standing near the front desk wearing a knit ski cap in the tropical heat. He looks familiar but for a moment I'm blanking. The guy looks at me and lets out a breath and has to sit down. Then he says one word:

"*You.*"

Christ. The way he says that one word, *you,* is as if the main reason why the world is so fucked-up is standing right there in front of him, in the personage of *you,* meaning *me.*

Now I remember the guy and I smile at him, meanwhile wondering what the problem is, why he said *You* the way he did, and why he had to sit down before he could say it. *You.*

Don. Good to see you, I say.

Don won't even look at me. He's staring at the floor, shaking his head.

Your book, he says.

What?

It screwed me up. My life.

In a sense, the main reason why the world is so fucked-up is in fact at that moment standing in front of Don, in the personage of *me.*

I'm talking about the D-word.

Here's the deal: I wrote about Don in *In Search of Captain Zero.* He appears in two chapters, one about a surfboard he was making for me, and then again in one wherein I ask him why he's living so far south, at the end of the road at the bottom of Central America...

> "This is one of the last places they'll get to," Don said.
>
> "Who?" I inquired.
>
> "The vanguard of Satan's warriors," he said, in the same laid-back, reasoned tone he'd used to discuss surfboard design.
>
> I stared at Don, giving him time to grin and say, "Gotcha!" but his gaze remained level and serious. He picked up his bottle of Pilsen and ran a finger along the edge of the label. "See that bar code?"
>
> I said that I did.
>
> "There's no Mark of the Beast on that bar code yet."
>
> "I'm not following you," I said, but I was starting to get the general idea.
>
> "Six-six-six. The Mark of the Beast," Don explained, ever patient and easygoing. "It's not there. They haven't infiltrated this far south yet."
>
> "What do you mean?" I asked and immediately regretted it. I didn't want to be subjected to any more evidence that this guy I'd known for more than two months and liked very much was in fact out of his mind.
>
> "Up in the states they're already implanting the chips."
>
> Computer chip implants in the brains of the unsuspecting multitudes, perpetrated by the satanic conspiracy of multinational...
>
> Nah. Sayo-fuckin-A-nara, Jack. I was out of there.

Everyone read your book, Don says. Read that stuff about me.

He's still sitting there shaking his head, still hasn't looked at me. He isn't angry. He's *sad.*

I don't know what to say so I just stand there.

I wasn't well back then, Don says after a bit. His voice is... still sad.

Don gets up and takes off his ski cap. There's a scar on the top of his head, running from one side to the other.

I had a brain tumor, Don says, and then he's gone, out the door.

I got a room and went up to it and sat on the bed and quietly wept.

Before you even think of letting me off any hooks: Although I was sorry for what I had done to Don, I was mostly feeling sorry for *myself*.*

There's humor here, though. For the past couple of months, while I was going through the worst moment of my life and then killing my beloved dog Fang and then at that moment when I was sitting on a hotel room bed at another end of the road weeping for what I had done to Don and because I was feeling sorry for myself, I was supposed to be writing the screen adaptation of my novel, *Cosmic Banditos*, for John Cusack's company.

A goofball comedy about The Meaning of Life.

You gotta laugh at stuff like that, no?

More humor: Remember when I was in the hospital I told you that if you were patient (no pun intended) you'd hear about how Lisa *would be* off fuckfesting with her San José Fuckbuddy while I was in the dentist's chair going through the worst pain of my life?† By now that had happened, so I can tell you about it. The short version: A couple of months after my hospital stay I hired a guy with a camera to follow Lisa while I was at the dentist and he showed up that day with a newly broken leg, a cast on it from his toes to his crotch. He couldn't have followed a slug on a garden fence, let alone Lisa hell-bent for uncommitted dick.

Again, you gotta laugh at stuff like that, no?

I stayed in my room that night, didn't go out. After my weeping interlude I went briefly down to the desk to call Lisa, try to gauge what she might be up to while I was gone. I'd planted a voice-activated tape recorder in our bedroom before I left but harbored faint hope it would pick up anything interesting, like her fuckfesting with someone in our bed. Too much

---

* Since you're reading this it means Don read it first in manuscript and gave me permission to use it. Had I not cleared with him my use in this book of the quote from *Zero* that screwed up his life I'd be a worse shitball motherfucker than anyone else. (My pilgrimage from this island to visit Don is described in the "Cut Chapters" section of the adjunct website).

† Remember the "Is it safe?" scene from *Marathon Man?* Imagine that except no one is asking you any questions.

ambient noise, what with the open-air windows and so forth. Dogs barking out front, even a bird tweeting on the patio would set it off. The one-hour tape was probably gone through already.

But one must live in *some* hope to get through the day.

I told Lisa what happened with Don and she said that was terrible and sympathized with my guilt and then she told me she loved me. Said she was writing me letters while I'm gone.

I asked her to please leave my friends, our friends, out of our problems and she said she would and that she was sorry for lying to them about me behind my back, although she didn't use the words "behind your back," let alone "lying." I had to fill in those blanks myself. She said it was wrong to do that and she was *really* sorry. I wondered how someone could do something for almost a year then suddenly realize it was *wrong*.

That at this stage I could wonder this sort of thing about Lisa is still another example of the level of denial I was living under.

CHAPTER TWO

I spent the afternoon musing on Life. If you think of it, what a queer thing Life is! So unusual, so unlike anything else, don't you know, if you see what I mean.

P.G. Wodehouse

Here's where I had better define *sociopath*.

Sociopathy is a word that psychologists, psychiatrists, psychotherapists, "social scientists," and other types of witch doctors who have their heads up their asses often use to explain bad behavior. In other words, they cite sociopathy as a *cause* of bad behavior.

A while back I claimed that the fellow who came up with The Othello Syndrome, a witch doctor with a Ph.D.* in something or other with the uninteresting name of John Todd, was a perpetrator of circular reasoning/ specious causation. Here's what I mean by that: Let's assume that Doctor Todd, in listening to Lisa in an Academy Award-winning-actress account of our life together (including hysterical crying with real tears), would nod sagely and diagnose me as *having* The Othello Syndrome. Then Doc Todd would sit back (meanwhile possibly lighting a pipe), smug in the delusion that he's explained why I sneak around planting tape recorders and lurk at airports and so forth.

Aside from Doc Todd having his head too far up his ass to realize that Lisa was lying about everything to begin with, he hasn't explained *anything*. His reasoning is circular and therefore specious: He explains my behavior using The Othello Syndrome, saying I have it, right? If you then asked him how he knows I have The Othello Syndrome, he'd say because of my behavior. That's circular reasoning and is absolutely useless.

A thought: Since aging surfer/memoir writers have as much right to come up with syndromes as anyone else, I think I will: The Head Up Your Ass Syndrome, or HUYA Syndrome. According to me, the HUYA Syndrome supersedes all other syndromes and hence prohibits anyone suffering from

---

* What does Ph.D. stand for anyway? Try this: You go to college first for a B.S., right? Okay, we know what B.S. stands for, as in Bull Shit. Then you get an M.S., which stands for More of the Same. So, obviously, Ph.D. stands for Piled Higher & Deeper.

it from coming up with his own syndrome. So if you happen to be at a psychotherapy symposium or some such – possibly one where people are supposed to *get in touch with themselves* – and someone is going on about a syndrome he came up with, your job is to yell "HUYA! HUYA! HUYA!" to shut him up. If this catches on it could do some good for this sorry-ass world.

Anyway, sociopathy is the same sort of circular reasoning/specious causation as The Othello Syndrome. It is not a cause of anything. It's a description of behavior, bad behavior. That's all it is. There are a few witch doctors who insist that they know this, but in the next breath *diagnose* someone as being a sociopath, then sit back (and light a pipe), smug in the delusion that they've explained the cause of the sociopath's bad behavior.

To put it another way: Sociopathy is not a *disorder,* caused by *a lack of a conscience* (which is the witch doctors' theory) but is another spectum kind of thing, and the spectrum is the *honesty-dishonesty spectrum.*

So let's define *sociopath* as someone who is way, way over on right-hand end of the honesty-dishonesty spectrum, where X-rays would be if it were the electromagnetic spectrum instead of the honesty-dishonesty spectrum.

Someone who is so far over on the right end of the honesty-dishonesty spectrum that he or she will do whatever is necessary to get what he or she wants.

That's enough, isn't it? No psychobabble necessary.

Listen, though. Key in the above is the *whatever is necessary* clause. And key in that clause is the word *whatever.* When we say *whatever,* we mean just that: *No limits* as to behavior, or lying about behavior.

This is what separates the sociopath from you (I hope) and me.

With Lisa, *what she wants* is to get uncommitted dick and not get caught at it.

No limits.

That's what we're dealing with.

There you have it.

CHAPTER THREE

That is one last thing to remember: writers are always selling someone out.

Joan Didion

So back to my fool's mission at the other end-of-the-road paradise at the bottom of Central America, this one on the Caribbean side. I woke up the morning after I arrived, and after I'd gone through the scene with Don. Instead of getting on the next bus out of there before anything else fucked-up could happen, I went out into the world to find my old friend, whose real name is different from the name I use in my (first) memoir, *In Search of Captain Zero.* I changed his name for the reasons I tried to give in my Author's Note, or Note on Veracity, which Note caused my demented editor to go ape-shit while simultaneously being pleased as punch – she would use the Note to scare the living shit out of me by suspending publication of my book. Remember that stuff?

If not: Part of the reason for the name change was that I'd put my old friend in some backstory tales which in reality he had been absent from. I felt it would somehow be less dishonest if I changed his name.

Right: The D-word in action yet again!

While wandering around looking for my old friend I ran into Don; it's a small town. I asked him if he'd have breakfast with me and to my surprise he agreed. So we went to a little *soda* and sat down.

It went well. In a sense, anyway. Don forgave me for what I did to him in *In Search of Captain Zero.* This is why I say that *it went well* and also why I say *in a sense, anyway.* The latter, my qualification, is due to this: Don is a really nice person. I don't mean in the *nice guys finish last* sense, although that old one may be true, depending on your definition of *finishing last.* I mean in the decent human being sense. Someone you instinctively know will not steal from you or gaslight you. Someone who is on the opposite end of the honesty-dishonesty spectrum from, say, Lisa or Gerardo Mora. Or Mora's son, Esteban. Or Bush or Cheney or Rumsfeld or Carl Rove or Condi Rice or Tony Blair or any of the other shitball motherfuckers who are actively responsible for the world being so fucked-up. See, Don being a decent human being and his forgiving me made me feel worse about everything, if that was possible. If you get my drift.

A striking characteristic of the honesty-dishonesty spectrum, by the way, is how crowded it is on the right-hand end, where all the shitball motherfuckers are bumping into each other, elbow to elbow. In contrast, on the left end you can stretch your legs, wave your arms, do jumping jacks, all unhindered by a mob scene. There's even enough room to play some tennis, if you can find anyone around to do so with.

Don and I bonded a bit that morning, possibly for this reason: Both of us had a problem that had endangered our physical health and caused irrational behavior. His problem was a brain tumor, mine a sociopathic female. The difference being that his problem had been removed, by a team of surgeons, and now he was okay, he was fine. I was not okay, not fine. No team of surgeons or any other team could remove my problem. It was completely up to me to remove it.

The fragility of body and soul, plus how closely the two are connected, comes to mind here, somehow. Plus, as usual, the D-word.

Speaking of the D-word – and now we're getting to the other fucked-up thing that happened – I soon found my old friend on the beach near the jungle shack he was squatting in, and some fucked-up things happened with him immediately, within minutes; but the main fucked-up thing happened a couple of hours later. We were having lunch at a *soda* and my old friend started reminiscing about old times, old times from my book, even though at one point he'd threatened to sue me for *stealing his life*, via my book.

You wanna talk about loads of horseshit?

But okay. He was reminiscing. Fine, so far. In theory. Problem was that of all the old times from my book he had to choose from to reminisce about, my old friend chose old times from which he had been absent. In case you're not getting my drift: The way it actually happened, my old friend wasn't there, in the old times he was reminiscing about. I'd *made up* his being there, when I wrote my nonfiction book. And my old friend kept grinning at me as he reminisced, then he would pause, hoping I'd pitch in, maybe add a detail or two to his reminiscing, for rhythm and pizzazz.

I'll put it another way, and I apologize in advance if it turns out he had a brain tumor: My old friend was out of his fucking mind. Nuts.

I didn't need this, not right then at that moment in my sorry ass life and times.

Sayo-fuckin-A-nara, Jack. I was out of there.

CHAPTER FOUR

No evil dooms us hopelessly except the evil we love, and desire to continue in, and make no effort to escape from.

George Eliot

When I got back to my home at Big Turkeys after my visit with Don and my old friend at the other end of the road I found out that Lisa had been fucking someone in our bed while I was away. No, not the voice-activated tape recorder I'd planted. That was a symphony of dogs barking and birds tweeting. What happened was that I came back a day earlier than I told Lisa I would.

Surprise, honey!

No, I didn't catch her in the act. That would be asking too much of life.

After Lisa kisses me and tells me how glad she is I'm home and how much she missed me I go into the bedroom to unpack, also figuring to retrieve the tape recorder, which is hanging on the back of the big tiki next to the bed. I immediately sense something's not right. The bed is a rumpled mess, which is unusual since Lisa makes the bed as soon as she gets up – a tiny aspect of how wonderful she is as a mate – but that's not what's wrong. I sit down on the bed. Look around. The candlesticks aren't where they were when I left; they're closer to the bed. One has been moved to the night table on my side, plus they've been burned way down.

But that's not really it either. I look at the stereo. I have a premonition. In two years of living with me I don't believe Lisa has even once played music in the bedroom unless she's in the mood for sex and wants to set up a seduction. I pick up the stereo remote from the bedside table on my side and click it. An old Beatles album comes on. That was not the CD that was in the machine when I left; in fact, we've never played that one before. But that Lisa has been playing the bedside stereo is not really what's wrong either, although things are starting to add up.

I put the clicker back on the bedside table, which is cluttered. Amidst the clutter is a bottle of sex oil. It isn't the sex oil Lisa uses when she massages me to squeeze out the angst pus. That sex oil is way over on her side of our huge bed, in her bedside table. This sex oil is the special, expensive kind that is flavored, so when you're licking someone you get a nice taste, piña colada in this case. Lisa and I have not used this sex oil, the tasty, expensive sex oil, in a long time. Months, maybe. It was not on the night table when I left.

The rumpled bed, the burnt candles moved closer to the bed, the music… but the sex oil is what does it. I'm pretty goddamn sure Lisa has been fucking someone in our bed.

Lisa comes in the bedroom and so I get up and leave, going to get something from the car, I tell her. I just really have to get away from her for a minute. I don't make it to the car. I get to the living room and have to sit down and think. Lisa almost immediately comes out of the bedroom and goes to the kitchen, does something there. I get up and go back to the bedroom. I do this not only to get away from Lisa, but now I'm figuring to lie down, for the usual reason.

Everything is as I left it in the bedroom except that the sex oil is no longer on the night table on my side, which is still cluttered. I open the drawer. The sex oil is back in there where we keep it. Lisa didn't want me to see the sex oil out on the night table, so she put it back in the drawer while I wasn't looking.

Now I *know* Lisa has been fucking someone in our bed.

I don't say anything about this that day, nor for a while after. I don't want to alert Lisa that I know she's been fucking someone in our bed. I need to know *who* she's been fucking in our bed. This need is based on my general need to *know everything.*

When I do say something I phrase it as a question. I ask Lisa why she put the sex oil back in the drawer while I wasn't looking. Lisa's answer is this, after she pauses to think about it: She used the sex oil to masturbate while I was gone and was self-conscious about it.

Some questions come to mind:

Why would Lisa cross over our huge bed – it's six and a half feet square – to get sex oil from my night table to masturbate with, when she has her own sex oil on her side? Plus, I cannot recall Lisa using sex oil on herself anyway.

Or how about this related one: Did she use the expensive, tasty, piña colada-flavored sex oil because she's figured out how to lick her own pussy while masturbating?

And *this* one: She was *self-conscious** about masturbating? With *me*?

Here's the image that comes to mind. Lisa sues me for libel based on this narrative. During the trial Lisa is on the stand and after an Academy Award-winning actress caliber monologue about how it was us against the

---

* Where's *WFD* when we *really* need it?

world until my mind became addled due to The Othello Syndrome, the subject of the sex oil on the night table comes up, her motive for hiding it so I wouldn't see it. "I was self-conscious about masturbating," Lisa says, and she chokes back an embarrassed sob and averts her eyes after a quick glance at the jury.

Now the cross-examination, and I force my lawyer back into his seat as he starts to rise. I'll handle this myself.

I remind Lisa how much she loves – used to love – to turn me on by masturbating in front of me and how she'd tell me how she masturbated while thinking of me when I was away and how she'd masturbate on the phone sometimes.

Lisa denies all this, insisting that she's self-conscious with me about masturbating. She blushes and chokes back an embarrassed sob. The blushing and sobbing is not lost on the jury, which feels for this embattled and humiliated woman.

"Okay," I say, and with a flourish strip the shroud from the easel that has been set up in front of the jury, revealing a poster-size photograph of Lisa splayed naked on our bed, half the fingers of her right hand disappeared in her pussy and her expression into the camera way over on the right-hand end of the leering spectrum.

Pandemonium. Flash bulbs from the paparazzi pop, reporters dash from the courtroom feverishly making notes. An elderly woman in the third row of the packed gallery faints. As the judge pounds his gavel and yells for order and threatens to clear the courtroom I commence to unveil dozens of photos – all well lit and composed, me being a professional shooter with national magazine covers to my credit – of Lisa masturbating and obviously enjoying being photographed while doing so. I save the best of the lot for last: Lisa diddling herself with what looks like a malevolent version of R2D2 – I'm talking *voltage* here, plus bells and whistles and disco lights blinking and Cyndi Lauper blaring in sensaround that girls just wanna have fun.

I exaggerate only slightly.

As the judge pounds his gavel and the woman in the third row is administered CPR, I point at the rear screen TV being wheeled in. "I'm not finished!" I bellow. Then, in my best sportscaster's voice, "Let's go to the video tape!"

My slightly sledge-hammered point being that Lisa was lying when she said she hid the sex oil because she's self-conscious with me about masturbating.

Armed as we are now with a lot of knowledge, and given the sex oil and the sex oil lie and indeed the whole post-fuckfest vibe upon my surprise return home, does anyone out there doubt that Lisa was fuckfesting with someone in our bed?

But with whom? Her San José fuckbuddy, down from the city for a fuckfest visit, or her local fuckbuddy, someone right there under my nose? Or both? Together (a Lisa-sandwich fuckfest) or separately? Or neither, maybe another guy she picked up surfing and invited up to our house, *my* house?

Although it will take a while, I will find out. You will too, if you hang in.

CHAPTER FIVE

...righteous indignation, blushing modesty, weepy sadness...
(c)rocodile tears at will are a sociopathic trademark.
Martha Stout, Ph.D.

The above quote is from *The Sociopath Next Door,* a book by the credited witch doctor, Martha Stout, who, as noted, has a Piled Higher & Deeper in some area or other of witch doctor stuff, witch doctory, whatever you call it. Hey, witch*craft*!

Hold on. How can I quote a witch doctor's writings to make a point when I go so far out of my way to accuse witch doctors of having their heads up their asses (let alone of practicing witchcraft)?

Through paying attention, it's possible to learn something from people who have their heads up their asses. In this case, by *paying attention* I mean ignoring the witch doctors' theories on... on just about anything. For example, Doc Stout, Piled Higher & Deeper, goes on and on about *a lack of a conscience* being the *cause* of sociopathic behavior: Since anyone who *lacks a conscience* is a sociopath and since a sociopath is by definition someone who *lacks a conscience,* the two concepts mean exactly the same thing. Which means that to try to say sociopathy is caused by a lack of a conscience is the very definition of circular reasoning/specious causation. Although Doctor Stout calls herself a scientist, there is no science here whatsoever. It's a dumb-ass theory, no matter how many witch doctors with Piled Higher & Deepers repeat it, which many do. In fact, it's not even a theory at all. (The bedrock of science is this: If you have a theory that something causes something else, there must be, at least in principle, a way of proving the theory is correct. But more importantly, the theory must be *disprovable.* Since the *lack of a conscience* theory is neither provable nor disprovable, it's not a theory at all. It's nothing, apart from some words strung together.)*

But why burn all these words on witch doctor discrediting, which, by

---

* When confronted by a nonscientific theory, renowned physicist Wolfgang Pauli would label it "not even wrong." I love that.

the way, is pretty much popping off fish in a barrel? Why not shut my trap, let the witch doctors I quote sound brilliant, and get on with the *story*? (Reader Big Mo.) Because it would be *dishonest*. I would rot in Writer Hell if I did that. I'd rot down there like Bob Woodward is surely going to rot, for one. In fact, if there's a real hell with flames and poisonous rivers and hordes of shitball motherfuckers writhing in agony – sounds like New Jersey, no? – I'd rot down there too. Fuck that.

Further, as you'll see if you hang in, this witch doctor stuff ties directly to what, in the end, this book is *really* about. What this book *is about* has again segued to something else while I wasn't looking. From obsession and pain to dishonesty and now to... what?

To *why the world is so fucked-up.*

But back to witch doctors, learning something from them. What I'm interested in is witch doctor *observations of dishonest people*. Martha Stout, Piled Higher & Deeper, has by her own account interviewed or otherwise observed hundreds of people who either are sociopaths or have somehow in their lives been subjected to sociopaths.*

So I pay attention and learn something, mostly about patterns of behavior, what sorts of behaviors go with other sorts. This can have predictive value (what to be ready for) and even some explanatory value (but not much). As I say, though, you have to pay attention, wade through some psychobabble.

For instance, after some psychobabble Doc Stout says the following, based on her observations of hundreds of sociopaths and the victims thereof.

A sociopath who is about to be cornered by another person will suddenly turn into a piteous weeping figure whom no one, in good conscience, could continue to pressure. Or the opposite: Sometimes a cornered sociopath will adopt a posture of righteous indignation and anger in an attempt to scare off her accuser...

Lisa's M.O., no? In common, everyday practice Lisa combines these two sorts of behaviors in a one-two sociopath punch, sometimes the weepy shit first, but usually the righteous indignation/anger first, then the weepy shit, plus heartfelt apologies.

Observations such as the above quote from *The Sociopath Next Door* – and this chapter's epigraph from it – can have another benefit: *to reassure me that I'm not nuts.* By way of explanation: Back at Big Turkeys, after finding out that Lisa had been lying to my friends about me behind my back for going on a year, I tried to explain the situation to these people – Candyce and

---

* Witch doctors are not dumb, let alone fools; *not necessarily.* The problem is solely the location of their craniums with respect to their posteriors, and the depth to which the former is inserted into the latter.

Phil, Kim and Sassy, plus Alex and Amy (who own the local surf shop), Amy especially having been a major Lisa-gaslighting target – give them the background and, especially, the details of my life with Lisa, her blurts and flirting behaviors and the various incidents, from the Incredible Bouncing Cell Phone And It's Various Destinations Incident (plus the "we" slip), the Purse Left Behind in the Hotel Room Incident, the Fleabag Hotel Incident and how there was no family of four having breakfast that morning; how Lisa recorded over the Holiday Inn tape then claimed the maid did it; how Lisa and her San José fuckbuddy slipped right by me when I staked out the airport clutching a dumb ass bouquet; how the sex oil on the night table was a dead giveaway; and how Lisa had been perpetrating sleight of hand maneuvers with cell phones and house keys, plus bombarding me with phony journal entries and Othello Syndrome printouts... and... and the result of my explanations was this: I sounded like *I am in fact nuts*.

What had my dear friend Lesley asked me?

Are you out of your fucking mind?

Doc Stout, God bless her, has a whole sub-chapter on gaslighting, which of course is Lisa's specialty, both professionally (perception management, or PM) and in her personal life, in getting what she wants, i.e., uncommitted dick and not getting caught at it. Rather than quote her, I'll sum up Doc Stout's observations on gaslighting:

The sociopath's surface charm (another sociopath hallmark, one which Lisa possesses big time) and reasonableness makes the sociopath's behavior incomprehensible to "normal" people. Since it doesn't seem believable that anyone could *be* that way, people around the sociopath, especially those not directly subjected to the behavior (Lisa's and my friends, say), will just refuse to see the truth. The point being that my attempts to expose Lisa for what she is only resulted in further doubts being cast on my sanity. And remember that Lisa had already been actively casting doubts on my sanity for going on a year.

Here's another quote from poor Doc Stout (whom I shamelessly use *and* abuse), this one regarding the perception of sociopathic behavior.

Speculate as we may, we cannot imagine *why*. Nothing sounds believable, so we think there must be a misunderstanding, or maybe we have greatly exaggerated something in our observations.

Although a woman being obsessed with uncommitted dick is far from unbelievable – just find a woman who perceives sex the way a man does – what is unbelievable is that anyone would simultaneously go to such outrageous lengths to prove to his/her supposed mate – and to the world – undying love; and then, when continually busted on cheating behavior

– rather than back off – *redouble* those efforts; redouble them to the point where the lying and the gaslighting and the concoction of explanations/ qualifications becomes a *full time job* and a *tough one*. Which begs a question: If uncommitted dick is so important to Lisa, why not just dump my sorry ass (Sex God or not) and get on with the uncommitted dick-getting, minus all the hassles of getting caught? Here's another observation from the good doctor.

> People who are sociopaths report that they crave extra stimulation almost continually. Some use the word *addicted*, as in *addicted* to thrills, *addicted* to risk. (Italics in the original.)

The risk-taking motive surely fits. Think of the risk, the thrill, when Lisa had her San José fuckbuddy come to our room at the fleabag hotel, and then pulled off a mini-fuckfest with him in 207, two rooms down from where I was hanging with Ron, arguing about hit men*; or the risk, the thrill, of how she *just would not stop* with her cheating, no matter that I knew she was doing it and was trying to catch her. Doc Stout again:

> Like drugs, the games have to be done over and over, larger and better...

By "games," Doc Stout is referring to the domination game, which she has observed is the be-all and end-all of sociopathic behavior. *Winning* the domination game, that is, which is played against other people. (In the case of Bush and his gang, against the world at large.) True, Doc Stout is making causational assumptions again, but how else to explain Lisa's relentlessness in pursuing not only uncommitted dick but her ceaseless (and transparent) attempts to gaslight me, which had evolved to a full time job?

Why else would she continue with this loony behavior?

Why not just dump my sorry ass?

Because she was playing the domination game against my sorry ass.

Not convinced? A couple of weeks after the fiasco with my old friend, in October 2004, when Lisa was in New York alone, she started going to Al-Anon, which is a support group for people who are subjected to the dispiriting antics of drug addicts and alcoholics.

Why Al-Anon? Since The Othello Syndrome/Morbid Jealousy angle had not flown very well on its own, Lisa decided to dabble in pathology theory, quickly becoming an expert on the clinical roots of my compulsive

---

* If you think they didn't have time since Lisa was gone for less than 20 minutes, recall that it was Lisa who came up with the "take-five" concept, which, by definition, means they had plenty of time for one.

suspicions and obsessive jealousy. I was now the victim of chronic drug and alcohol addiction, which are well-documented causes of paranoid behavior, according to Lisa's latest Internet printouts and tearful sorties to my friends at Big Turkeys. She had also expanded her target audience to include my friends at my former home of Montauk, via emails and phone calls. Lisa's perception management was now an *international* campaign. Jeffrey Wigand, the tobacco industry insider/whistle blower and victim of the smear campaign by Lisa's former business associate had nothing on me!

But that Lisa would go to Al-Anon and gaslight complete strangers, people who could not serve to buttress any of her lies to me or my friends, since we would never meet them, seems too nutty to be true, no?

What was it that Doc Stout observed?

Speculate as we may, we cannot imagine *why*.

CHAPTER SIX

Three quarks for Muster Mark!

James Joyce

During this time, the summer of 2004, I did a stateside run to do some business and also to almost lose my mind. The *almost losing my mind* part wasn't an actual planned purpose of the trip, I mean not per se; it just worked out well that way.

Aside from the near mind-loss aspect, which I perceived as a negative, and aside from whatever fucked-up shit Lisa was up to while I was away, my stateside time was fruitful, in theory. I met with the people at John Cusack's company, New Crime, in good old Hollywood (the state of mind Hollywood, since their offices are in Venice, California). We had a couple of meetings and blabbed about how I'd approach the adaptation of *Cosmic Banditos*. This is worth a few words.

One thing first: I liked the folks at New Crime. They were smart and nice.

Right: Someone I *can* get along with!

Right: Holy shit!

Right: We'll see how long *that* lasts.

There were problems in adapting *Cosmic Banditos* to the screen – not in the league of my other book, but problems nonetheless. Aside from the narrative voice (which is the main source of humor) not translating to the screen, there was the ending problem, in that the book ending wouldn't work for the movie, at least not directly translated.

So in thinking about this – and I have to give myself credit for thinking about it at all, given all the fiascos and catastrophic shit that were going on while I was thinking about it – I came up with a general approach.

Since the theme of the book is a quest for The Meaning of Life, which is ridiculous to begin with (doubly so if you count the context of my real, actual, sorry-ass life, but I didn't bring that up in our meetings), let's go for it, I said, push the ridiculous envelope, nudge the story even further toward the right-hand end of the ridiculous spectrum, via an over-the-top, Indiana Jones From Hell goofball attitude. Hey, The Meaning of Life makes

Lost Arks and Temples of Doom and Last Crusades as quest objectives look like... *small stuff*, no? The folks at New Crime liked the idea.

Okay. In order to accomplish this, we needed a "bigger" ending than the book provides. In the book, our lunatic bandito Meaning of Life Seekers corner a hapless physicist they've been stalking and, in the course of demanding to know The Meaning of Life, accidentally blow up his house. (The physicist's daughter, who, by the way, is a nymphomaniac, is a vital aspect of the ending.)

Not enough at stake here for an Indiana Jones-type ridiculous ending, so how about if we go the distance in upping the stakes, and have *the fate of the universe* at stake at the end of the screen story, via an accident precipitated by our bandito gang? But instead of accidentally blowing up the universe (rather than a mere house) — tough to imagine since there is nowhere for the universe to blow up *into*, if you get my drift — the universe would be in danger of *poofing out*.

The fate of the universe? It might poof out? A tall order, no?

I proposed we move the ending from a family barbecue to a particle accelerator. In case you don't know, particle accelerators are these wild-ass devices that goose subatomic particles to near light speed and smash them together in order to reproduce the conditions at the birth of the universe, the Big Bang. I'm talking *first causes* here. What happened *in the beginning*. God stuff.

Heavy, no?

Believe it or not, a few years ago, physicists, in designing a really big particle accelerator, worried that a particle-smashing experiment might accidentally... poof out the universe. Really. I'm not kidding. They analyzed this possibility in deciding if building the particle accelerator was a good idea. In the end the physicists decided to go ahead and build the accelerator because they calculated that the universe would probably not accidentally *poof out* in one of their experiments.

Probably not. I love that.

Details. Our crew of lunatics includes an unbalanced Indie Jones type (to be played by Cusack), a full-blown bandito named José (even if he's a woman): sombrero, crisscrossed bandoliers, the whole *we don't need no stinking badges!* bandito nine yards, maybe to be played by Benecio del Toro, plus a psychotic municipal bus driver the boys kidnap while they're laying waste to a San Francisco gay bar called The Crisco Disco West. Plus one other character, my favorite, a dog named High Pockets. In their quest for The Meaning of Life they all tend to drink a lot of tequila, except High Pockets, who has an obsession for Milk Bone Flavor Snacks For Large Dogs (he's a *large* dog). Everyone has his own whacko obsession.

Got that?

Another problem is that the book provides no specific heavy; the boys are being pursued by every law enforcement agency known to man but we never *meet* any of the pursuers. So for the screen story we needed to personify the forces of antagonism, the bad guys trying to thwart our boys on their monumental quest.

How ridiculous could we get here? Since the quest begins in then passes through Central America, how about if we play it out in the 1980s (instead of the 1970s, as in the book) during Reagan's antics with Iran-contra? This way, the heavies could be real people, historical characters, i.e., not only Reagan, but CIA director William Casey and that other sleazebag felon, Oliver North. Imagine this: The Casey character (who in real life got off the Iran-contra hook because he had a brain tumor and would soon croak) himself gets obsessed with The Meaning of Life (due to his brain tumor) and marshals the CIA and Ollie North to beat our guys to The Meaning of Life-punch, so to speak. A Meaning of Life conspiracy/scandal would be made public during the Iran-contra hearings by doctoring footage of the real testimony, a la *Forrest Gump*. (How the physicist's daughter, the nymphomaniac, would fit into all this was to be worked out.)

What you should be thinking right now (aside from all the brain tumor stuff lately, which is a coincidence), is Whaddam I, nuts? To put it another way: As I well knew, speaking of thin ice and fiascos and catastrophic shit, this was either going to be a whiz-bang helluva screenplay or a complete, utter crock of shit, possibly even *the worst screenplay in the history of the world*.

That I subjected myself to this pressure, this *undue stress*, rather than just adapt my book more or less as is, is partly what drove me to the brink of losing my mind.* But there are other payoffs to these details, including, believe it or not, my prediction that Bob Woodward is going to rot in Writer Hell.

The first payoff is that the folks at New Crime arranged for me to visit the particle accelerator at Stanford University to see what it's like and to talk to some physicists. So I zipped up to Stanford, and this was where I almost lost my mind, hovered on the brink thereof.

How to explain?

Without repeating my usual litany of fiascos and catastrophic shit, entertaining as that can be, let's just say that stuff continued to pile up.

Hold on. Stuff piling up. A few days before I left on this stateside trip, some more stuff piled up, in the form of another paradise-at-the-end-of-the-road bulletin. Remember Logan and Ron and the nonexistent merc hit

---

*   One reason why I like to reinvent my books for screen stories might be this: I've already told the book story, so why do it again? That would be boring. On the downside, however, we have the losing-my-mind repercussion.

man? That fiasco has been quiet for a while, no? Well, here it came again: Ron and Logan were conspiring on something and money had already changed hands, in the predictable direction, Logan to Ron.

One way to interpret this is that Ron, having burnt me out in the buckola-extorting department, approached Logan with the notion that *his* best move would be to assassinate *my* sorry ass before the reverse transpired, and that he, Ron, would do it for 20k, then no doubt hire a Panamanian for under a thou so he could keep the 19k and change. Since this approach didn't fly with me, why not try it with Logan? In fact, if you think about it, it would be surprising if that shitball motherfucker Ron *didn't* give it a shot. (He'd have to hurry up with this plan, otherwise I might die of my terminal illness first and ruin everything.)

So there was that, in the Stuff Piling Up Department, as I researched my goofball comedy about the universe poofing out – a pretty accurate interpretation of what would happen, from my point of view, if my sorry ass did get assassinated, come to think of it – plus The Meaning of Life.

The actual brink of losing my mind, i.e., a full-blown nervous breakdown, occurred around sundown on my second day at Stanford, as I was sitting on the bed in my hotel room thinking about everything, including something that happened earlier that day. Plus, the phone in my room was ringing. This didn't help matters.

Here's a theory I agree with: If a wildly-advanced alien civilization visited planet earth the result would not be wanton destruction like in Spielberg's godawful version of *War of the Worlds*. (Nice special effects, Steven, but where was the *story*? What was with that *dues ex machina* ending?) What would really happen would be quieter but just as deadly: world-wide angst, severe depression and then a collective human race full-blown nervous breakdown, due to human beings realizing how insignificant, how completely fucking *clueless*, we really are. Imagine, say, a slug on a garden fence suddenly realizing what he is, a slug on a garden fence. Talk about a bummer of a rush of insight.

All the stuff piling up had a lot to do with what was coming next, but after speaking at length to a theoretical physicist named Stephon Alexander, who was way, way over on the right-hand end of the brilliant-human spectrum, I felt like a slug on a garden fence. I felt insignificant and clueless. For some reason, that Stephon found me amusing and that we got along so well made me feel even more like an insignificant and clueless slug on a garden fence. Go figure. Maybe I was simply *in the mood* to feel like that.

By the way, when I asked Stephon why he became a theoretical physicist, his answer was this: "I was angry at God."

Speaking of God stuff.

The phone was still ringing as I sat there on the hotel room bed hovering on the brink of a full-blown nervous breakdown.

Here's my best shot at describing what I was beset with: *terminal loneliness*. Yes, that's it, terminal loneliness, which was overlaid upon something deeper and darker in my psyche – I'll refer to it as *dark shit* – of which I was only dimly aware, and which was somehow the converse, the opposite, of the loneliness.

To sum up, to belabor the obvious: I was a mess.

Probably the last thing you want to do when you're a mess hovering on the brink of a full-blown nervous breakdown due to being beset with terminal loneliness is answer the phone, especially if the main reason for your condition is apt to be on the other end. The last time I spoke to Lisa down at Pavones, which was the day before my brink hovering, she informed me that she met some guy, a surfer, showed him some land, and was going out that night to find him and drink some beer with him at the cantina. She said this as if she was telling me she was taking the dogs for a walk on the beach down in front. (Lisa would later apologize, promising she would never go out drinking with some guy when I'm not around.)

Still more stuff piling up. My terminal loneliness was slightly exacerbated by a book I was reading as part of my research. It was a book by Bob Woodward. A nonfiction book. Hovering on the brink, with Bob Woodward's nonfiction book on the night table, I answered the phone, knowing full well that had it been Lisa telling me how much she loves my sorry ass, I'd go over the brink then and there, completely swallowed by terminal loneliness, and that would be that; my mind would pretty much *poof out*. That's how serious my brink-hovering was.

It wasn't Lisa. It was the girl at the front desk who'd checked me in and she was telling me that if I needed anything, anything *at all*, I should call her or come down to the front desk. She was off work tomorrow and the next day, she said, and in case I needed anything then, she'd give me her home number.

She was propositioning me. Even in my condition I knew that. And boom! I was pulled back from the brink, and terminal loneliness regurgitated my sorry ass back up from being swallowed. I don't mean I was suddenly fine and dandy, but I knew I would weather the brink hovering. And I did weather it. (I checked out the next day and never saw the front desk girl again.)

I'm not going to analyze the whys and wherefores of this little piece of business saving my sorry ass from a full-blown nervous breakdown caused by terminal loneliness (plus who knows what the dark shit was) except to say that thank God it was only much later when I realized that the girl at the front desk might have had a sorry-ass sap much like myself at home, a sap who was also beset with terminal loneliness due to the love of his life's relentless pursuit of uncommitted dick – in this case, mine. That was a piece of self-reflection I did well without, at the time.

Odd, isn't it? That I'd be pulled back from the brink of losing my mind by a phone call from a girl on the make at the front desk while I was researching The Meaning of Life and talking to a physicist who was angry at God.

Odd, but that's what happened.

CHAPTER SEVEN

They say in my country that the Dark Lord can govern the storms in the Mountains of Shadow that stand upon the borders of Mordor. He has strange powers and many allies.

J.R.R. Tolkein

The nonfiction book by Bob Woodward I was reading and which slightly exacerbated my terminal loneliness and nudged me further towards the brink was called *Veil, The Secret Wars of the CIA*. I was seeking a better handle on the CIA's antics in Central America back in the 1980s, which is the time frame of my reinvented screen story about The Meaning of Life.

Not only did I not get a better handle on the CIA's antics in Central America back in the 1980s, or anything else, but my reading of *Veil* resulted in a rush of insight of the negative variety, a dispiriting one. Woodward's book is so packed with lies by omission and outright lies, plus blatant perception management, that it's safe to say that the book itself *is a lie*. See, I already knew a bit about the 1980s, having been around then (including *in* Central America) and having paid attention to what was going on while doing so. In fact, all one need to have done during the 1980s – aside from being around – would have been to be conscious, i.e., not comatose, to realize that Woodward's book, his nonfiction book, is a lie. One example: Endings. Important, right? Woodward sees fit to end *Veil, The Secret Wars of the CIA* with a lie on every level you can lie in a nonfiction book. He ends it with a chapter describing a personal visit with CIA director William Casey on his deathbed (from the brain tumor).

About two sentences into this, I *knew* Woodward had *made up* the scene. Remember that when it comes to *making up stuff*, I know whereof I speak – the old one, *you can't bullshit a bullshitter* comes to mind. (Others have opined the same regarding that scene, based on looking into dates and hospital records and the like.)

But I could have forgiven that lie, which was only about facts, i.e., Woodward's deathbed visit to Casey having never happened. I've lied about facts myself. Sometimes it's okay, sometimes not. What Woodward does, however, in the deathbed scene he made up, is to lie in subtext as well — in what is really going on — which kind of lying is a *sin*, for the commission of which writers will rot in Writer Hell.

Here's the scene: Casey, on his deathbed, admits to having known about the diversion of Iran arms sales funds to the contras. The subtext here is that Casey didn't have anything to do with the diversion. He *knew about it*.

Technically, Woodward wasn't *outright* lying. But what he left out of his fucking narrative is that Casey *knew about* the diversion because he had been instrumental in planning and executing it.

A whopper of a lie by omission, no?

Another thing Woodward left out of his fucking narrative about the CIA in the 1980s involves drug trafficking by the contras. Casey and his protégé, Oliver North, didn't just *know about* contra drug trafficking, they were likewise directly involved in the okaying of it, plus the cover-up. (In 1989, Oliver North was barred entry into Costa Rica for being a known drug trafficker.) In *Veil*, Woodward doesn't even *mention* the contras and drug trafficking, let alone that Casey and North knew about it, let alone that they were directly involved in the okaying and subsequent cover-up.* Since the contra war in Nicaragua was one of the secret wars of the CIA of the title of Woodward's book, one would think that the CIA's involvement in drug trafficking to finance that war would bear mention, no?

Since other journalists from that time knew about all this, how did Bob Woodward miss it? The answer is that he didn't miss it. He just left it out of his fucking narrative, for reasons related to Woodward having turned into a shitball motherfucker toady of the powers that be.

Of Bob Woodward's nonfiction books since *All the President's Men*, at the time of my brink-hovering I had only read *Veil, The Secret Wars of the CIA*. Out of (morbid) curiosity I went on to read two of his subsequent books. In *The Commanders*, purported to be the definitive history of the U.S. military's overthrow of Manuel Noriega, Woodward devotes *one sentence* to U.S. history with the Panamanian dictator. Here it is, the one sentence:

> Although he once had been one of the CIA's key Latin American assets, the administration now viewed (Noriega) as an outlaw and an enemy of U.S. interests.

In his definitive history, Bob Woodward justifies the invasion of another country by telling us... nothing whatsoever...

Do you think maybe Woodward left out some stuff about Noriega's

---

* There's a surf break in northern Costa Rica called Ollie's Point, so named because it's near a clandestine landing strip North's cohorts used to run cocaine into the United States. Point being: If the ragamuffin surfers who named the break knew about North's smuggling activities, why didn't this legendary *journalist*?

relationship to the CIA in his fucking narrative? I mean aside from not even *mentioning* the CIA's collusion with Noriega on drug trafficking (likewise to fund the contras) and aside from not even *mentioning* the list of treaties and international laws solemnly signed by the United States that were broken by the invasion. Nor does he *mention* that the unilateral aggression of invading another country without "imminent threat" (or any threat) is the same crime for which Nazis were executed at Nuremburg. Noriega being an "outlaw" (a drug trafficker) was fine and dandy as long as some of the drug money made its way to the illegal war the CIA was supporting, but when the dictator quit cooperating, colluding with the CIA in big-time criminal activities, he was now an "enemy of U.S. interests" and his country was fair game for invasion.

But my favorite lie by omission, one near and dear to my heart, comes in Woodward's *Plan of Attack* – his definitive history of our conflict with Saddam Hussein. Woodward does better, wordage-wise, in this one, devoting *one whole page* (out of 450) to U.S. history with "The Beast of Baghdad." A little problem, though: In his one page history Woodward skips from the 1970s to the 1990s, leaving out the 1980s. *Not a word about the decade of the 1980s.* Right: The decade during which the U.S. and The Beast of Baghdad were close allies and the U.S., under Reagan then Bush I, was actively and knowingly aiding and abetting The Beast of Baghdad in his crimes against humanity.

Thing is, Bob Woodward himself classifies his books, his nonfiction books, as being "somewhere between the news and the history books."

Let's take him on his word on that.

See if you concur: People who provide a democratic society (like what the United States is purported to be) with *news* (meaning journalists) should maybe *question* what the shitball motherfuckers in power tell them about their antics. Same goes for the writers of history books, which mold the minds of our children.

Bob Woodward does not question *anything* the shitball motherfuckers tell him. Woodward just parrots their lies and perception management as facts. Bob Woodward's books, his nonfiction books, which are something "between the news and the history books," *are lies.*

That I had this rush of insight about the journalist who in the 1970s questioned everything and in so doing uncovered the truth, then followed the truth wherever it led, even to the toppling of a president, and who was a hero of mine, and who was now the personification of why Orwell was an optimist and hence of *why the world is so fucked-up*, slightly exacerbated my terminal loneliness.*

---

* If the rewriting (or erasing) of history, which is what Woodward does in his books, sounds vaguely familiar, this was the protagonist Winston Smith's job at the Ministry of Truth in George Orwell's *1984*. Smith, along with the rest of the world of that story, was intimidated, threatened, bullied, into denial/lying via "jackboots on human faces." That the jackboots are unnecessary in the real world of today to get Woodward (and the rest of the mainstream media) to rewrite history is the basis of my observation that Orwell was an optimist.

CHAPTER EIGHT

The optimist proclaims that we live in the best of all possible
worlds; and the pessimist fears this is true.
James Branch Cabell

There was a Meanwhile that occurred on my stateside trip to research my
goofball comedy about The Meaning of Life and to almost lose my mind
that deserves special mention.

Remember Danny Fowlie? Danny, The Waterman Who Would Be King,
the big-time pot smuggler, Underground Empire insider and mythical
founder of Pavones back in the 1970s – boon companion to the likes of
Robert Vesco and machiavellian fiscal spook Norman LeBlanc? Danny,
whose flight to avoid arrest in the mid-1980s inadvertently precipitated the
squatter wars, and hence the eventual murder of Max Dalton?

After 18 years in federal prison at Terminal Island, California, Danny
had just been released on parole and was living near San Diego.

For various reasons, some straightforward and some (I suspect) complex,
I wanted to meet the man, sit down with him, talk some story, maybe find
out some things. The straightforward aspect of my motive was related to
my long-term aspiration to expand my Max Dalton investigation into a
book – or by this time maybe to include it in this book – and also to my
need to know the truth, *to know it all,* a need that's apparently a chronic
personality disorder I harbor.

This aspiration and my need to know the truth were also my underlying
motives for staying on surface-friendly terms with Gerardo Mora, his wife
Mayela, and their son Esteban, mother and son also being privy to not only
the details of the Dalton assassination – Esteban having actively participated
in it – but to the continuing land disputes at Pavones. The Moras, having
literally gotten away with murder, were an arrogant and big-mouthed lot
and – remembering how during my investigation Gerardo in particular
would blithely blurt self-incriminating particulars – the closer Gerardo
figured he and I were the better. I even theorized that someday, if I played
it right, the patriarch Mora might outright acknowledge his having been
the planner and the shooter, and maybe reveal his San José government

co-conspirators; another detail I'd missed back in '98.

Lisa knew of my motives in this and continued to be an asset in cementing my relationship with the Moras, through her visits to their *finca* (farm), just down the road from our house. Although, as I say, her friendship with this murderous family was a bit disconcerting, I knew there was no practical downside, let alone risk. In a subtle way, in fact, quite the contrary. Given my problem with Logan the Nutcase, a relationship with the Moras was an advantage: whether it was Logan or Gerardo Mora who was "the most dangerous man" at Pavones, Logan would be less inclined to move against me if he figured it would displease Mora, whom everyone, Logan included, feared. In the end, I did little to discourage Lisa's continuing relationship with the family.

So, aside from whatever end-of-the-road wickedness to which the Moras were privy, the one missing element in my need to know it all about local history was Danny Fowlie. I'd corresponded with him since his release, had sent him *In Search of Captain Zero*, which among other confessionals recounts my own experiences as an international pot mover back in the 1970s; I assumed that this would create an up-front birds-of-a-feather bond with Danny. Indeed, my title page inscription to him averred that it was only via blind luck/ridiculous fate that he'd done a long stretch of hard time, while I had not. Another version of the *there but for the grace of God go I* sentiment, which to this day I take quite seriously. (Holy shit, my life could have gone so differently!)

Danny loved my memoir (and said he laughed his ass off at *Cosmic Banditos*), and even approved of an article I'd written on the history of Pavones for a prestigious surf magazine, only correcting me on one faux pas regarding his life and times.* When we spoke by phone and I told him of my Hollywood trip, Danny insisted that I stop off in San Diego so we could get to know each other.

Danny met my flight. Although the Danny-photos I'd unearthed in my investigation from '98 were two decades old (Danny was now in his early 70s), emerging from customs into the crowded terminal, I zeroed in on Danny and he on me instantly. Our grins were mutual and real.

I worry, I sweat, over your understanding the significance of my meeting this man, and of our getting along so well. Although my account of the Max Dalton investigation reflects Danny's influence on the history and culture (and even on the actual topography) of the place I'd made my home, the truth is that there is nothing about Pavones that is not steeped in Danny's benign early influence. The stupendous subsequent flaws, the violence, the

---

* I'd asserted that the DEA had been chasing Danny for years before he went on the run to Mexico, where he was eventually captured and extradited. Danny vehemently denied this. It was *the FBI* that had been chasing him for years. I apologized and stood corrected.

greed, the corruption that followed Danny's summary exit were of the sort that might result when a kind and loving parent leaves a room full of toys to the devices of a group of toddlers in the worst of the terrible twos.

This I already well knew. And I also well knew that Danny's former associates had run amok with his land holdings while Danny was in the clink, perpetrating greed-motivated malfeasances through bribe-driven land transfers, some of which were nothing short of hilarious in their bald-faced cheek. The squatters, even Mora himself, notwithstanding his violent proclivities, had nothing on certain of the Big Turkeys gringo contingent in terms of avarice.

And I myself was not totally innocent. The land I'd bought and upon which I'd built my home, and indeed the land I'd invested in with Lisa as my invited partner, were part of a tract of former Dannyland. The potential error I'd made went back to my '98 investigation, when in looking into the well-rumored subterfuge by Danny's former associates I'd seen documents that appeared to give one of Danny's long-time cronies – a best buddy from childhood named Alan Nelson – the right to transfer land titles, including those of the lots I eventually bought. In our subsequent correspondences, Danny claimed that the documents were bogus. Although I was twice removed from the original deal, having bought from the second owner after the possibly illegal transaction, and not having seen evidence that Nelson's legal status was anything other than what he said it was, I assumed I was on solid ownership grounds. For me this was strictly a moral issue. I wanted to clear the air with Danny. I was worried about how this would go.

That of the dozens of landowners involved in questionable Dannyland deals that had gone down since Danny's incarceration I was the only one to show up and own up to an ethical – if not legal – indiscretion had an immediate effect on The Waterman Who Would Be King (we were hardly out of the airport parking lot when I did my owning up). By my departure for Hollywood and subsequently to the Stanford particle accelerator (and my brink hovering) Danny had given me a document absolving me from future litigation on his part – a gesture that moved me greatly. There was no *quid pro quo* here, except that in my writing about Pavones I would tell the truth. Danny's generosity was largely motivated simply by his liking me.[*]

During my four days as Danny Fowlie's house guest, Danny allowed me extensive formal interviews on his life and times and the history of

---

[*] Months later, when I caught wind of Danny's need to immediately get some money to his San José lawyer, I transferred $10,000 to that lawyer's account, as a way of showing I was not all talk. I offered another $15,000 if he needed it, but Danny demurred. The money was neither a gift nor a loan – I just made it clear that I would not accept repayment. This was a matter of respect for a man who deserved it.

Pavones, plus complete access to the records archived in his garage; a literal mountain of fascinating historical papers, including correspondences and legal documentation implicating current landowners, my neighbors, in outright land fraud. I was now the possessor of still more explosive dirt, especially regarding Logan the Nutcase, who, according to the documents I saw, colluded with Norman LeBlanc back in the early 1990s in misappropriating several hundred acres of prime Dannyland. I also copied and stashed a document that tended to confirm Danny's assertion of Logan's history as a cocaine trafficker.

Logan. Of all the treacheries Danny had been subjected to, Logan's were at the top of the shit list. My problem with the Nutcase, which I related to Danny, was no doubt a peripheral factor in our bonding. The enemy of my enemy is my friend kind of thing.

And I had some information for Danny. Through copious bribes and other subterfuges, Logan had finally succeeded in wresting control of the Sawmill parcel from Billy Clayton, who'd thrown in the towel and bolted back stateside. The Sawmill, the plum of Pavones, with its perfect wave in front of Danny's now-crumbling manse from back in the day, and with all its history and all the lingering "vibrational traces of bros past," including the true legends of the surfing subculture who had sojourned there, was now in the hands of a fool, a nutcase, albeit a dangerous one.

Danny and I discussed the future, worst case scenarios. We agreed that given the millions of dollars at stake, plus Logan's history, methods, and mental instability – his conspiring with Ron to off Billy Clayton comes to mind – one worst case was that Danny might be the target of a stateside hit. So there was that. And what with the recent conspiring between Logan and Ron, which most certainly had to do with my sorry ass...

To re-quote Cormac Mc: *Sure is a mess, ain't it, Sheriff?*

Before leaving, I made a promise to Danny Fowlie, one which I would keep. I would be his eyes and ears at Pavones, regarding Logan and others who had apparently misappropriated Danny's land, the Moras being high on this list, as well as a former Fowlie underling named Marc Sherman and Sherman's partner, an utter scumbag named Eric Kloos, plus a powerful and well-connected Tico who had taken control of, then sold, the cantina. I was taking a chance here, I knew, compounding my already threatened status. If Logan, or indeed Mora, or indeed any of them, learned of my alliance with The Waterman Who Would Be King, I would certainly be at greater risk. So another thing Danny and I held in common was that we were both threats to the vital interests of dishonest, extremely treacherous men. We would have to be very careful.

Aside from a couple of trusted surf buddies, Danny is the one person who knows I'm on this Caribbean island, hell-bent on finishing this narrative.

CHAPTER NINE

Day by day the little thump of insult. Day by day the tapping on the nerves, the delicate assault on the proud stuff of a man's identity.

Laura Hobson

Here's how it went upon my return home from my researching The Meaning of Life and the universe poofing out and my brink-hovering and visiting The Waterman Who Would Be King.

After a Hello-I-missed-you-soooo-much-darling hug and kiss I dumped my bag in the bedroom and went to take a shower, Lisa meanwhile unpacking for me. She neatly folded my shirts and put them in my clothes drawer. She always did stuff like that, took care of my needs, aside from her mission as my buffer, my Maginot Line, plus the massages to squeeze out the angst pus and the jazzy home made pizzas and love notes and assurances that I'd ruined her for other men and it's us against the world.

Thank you, dear.

The next day I wanted to go online, check email for bad news, maybe peek at my books' Amazon sales rankings in order to feel better about myself, or at least my writing. So I needed the cord that attaches the cell phone to the computer, which I'd brought with me on my trip.

Where was it? Looked in my bag from the trip, which was empty, Lisa having unpacked everything. No phone cord. Lisa helped. We looked high and low. No phone cord. I must've left it somewhere, maybe up at Stanford while I was hovering on the brink. Lisa was sympathetic, saying I hadn't been... myself for a while. Forgetful and... you know... not *myself*...

I found it! This was Lisa, in the bedroom, a few minutes later. Found the phone cord in my clothes drawer. Said she was hanging up my shirts and came across it.

Great! What a relief. Thanks, Lisa.

Then, immediately, some things occurred to me.

Lisa, you unpacked my bag, right? Unpacked everything.

You were tired from the trip so I thought I'd do that for you.

The phone cord was in the bag. Only place it could've been, right?

I suppose.

So *you* put the phone cord in the clothes drawer.

What's your point?

You had to have put the cord in the drawer while you were folding shirts.

What's your point, Allan?

The cord is way too bulky to accidentally fold in a shirt, so you put it in the clothes drawer on purpose, even though you know how important that cord is and that it belongs upstairs in the office.

Lisa does not respond to this.

By the way, why did you suddenly, in the midst of the phone-cord crisis, start hanging up shirts you'd neatly folded and put in my drawer yesterday?

You know what, Allan?

Yes, I do know what. You were doing it again. Trying to show me that shit just naturally happens with cell phones, or cell phone cords, whatever. Which somehow proves that there's nothing sinister going on when phones bounce around and get lost under pillows or beds or under car seats or the chargers get left in the city or don't work then work fine and the phones get turned off after three hundred promises that that won't happen again.

From now on...

But there's a difference this time, Lisa. The difference being that you made me think that *I'd* lost the cord, since I was the last one who had it.

From now on you can unpack your own bag.

This time, regarding my observation that she was gaslighting me again, Lisa didn't scream at me with veins popping then later apologize for screaming at me with veins popping. She just calmly said the above about me unpacking my own bag and then left the room, maybe to go to the kitchen to make a jazzy home made pizza. I forget. Point being: Lisa's whacky, transparent attempts at making me think I'm losing my mind and then her getting caught at it were pretty much a formality between us now, a sort of a quirk in our relationship we had come to accept and to live with.

And then there's the sex oil, the tasty, expensive sex oil quirk, how there would be less of it whenever I returned home, even though Lisa never again used that sex oil with me, nor when she'd masturbate or diddle herself with R2D2 as a seduction approach. It was never again left out on the night table then put back in the drawer when I wasn't looking, though.

That was a positive.

I write these italicized words from the future, after it all went down, after all the events and all my weaknesses played out, plus my one strength, and after the writing of all of it. I add these words just before this book goes to press and I'll be unable to say anything more to you; these are the last words I'll write.

Norman Mailer calls writing "the spooky art" and that is very apt, for many reasons, but for me it has to do with you, the personal you. You. You are a very spooky entity to me.

You are spooky because you mean everything to me, yet I know nothing about you except that you are right now reading these words.* Do you understand the bond I feel with you, the depth of it? I am giving you a lot but you are no less returning that. I speak of your time and of your attention, the two most valuable things you have to give. Thank you for that, for having come this far with me.

But instinct tells me that if it hasn't happened before it has certainly happened now, with these incidents of the sex oil and the phone cord. You consider me a fool.

You must understand something: I don't fear that you think me a fool, nor do I fear that you don't like me.

I only fear that you don't care. Don't care What Happens Next. Don't care what I've written on the pages you have not yet read.

To put it another way: I have chronic tinnitus, ringing in the ear. Sometimes the ringing is so loud – like a siren going by – that I can't believe everyone can't hear it. I fear that this book is like that.

That's my fear right now as I write these last words.

---

* What time of day is it now as you read? Are you on your couch, stretched out in the early morning, maybe on a Sunday, your mate cooking breakfast, Eggs Benedict, say; your favorite Sunday breakfast (mine too). Will you talk about me and my book as you eat together? Or will you be alone with your breakfast, reading this lonely book?

CHAPTER TEN

Life for each man is a solitary cell whose walls are mirrors.
Eugene O'Neill

Timing.

There have been some interesting examples of timing since I arrived on this island. One occurred last week, just after I finished sweating over the chapter about almost losing my mind at the Stanford particle accelerator while researching The Meaning of Life and the universe poofing out. You may recall from that chapter that the day I almost lost my mind I had spoken to a theoretical physicist, Stephon Alexander, who I claimed was so far over on the right-hand end of the brilliant human spectrum that he inadvertently made me feel like a slug on a garden fence, which in turn nudged me a little closer to losing my mind.

I hadn't communicated with Stephon for almost a year and a half. As I recall, a few days after my return to Pavones from that trip I sent him a short email thanking him for the interview – I left out the slug on a garden fence/losing my mind stuff, of course – and he sent me back a short You're welcome email. And that was that. Again, this was almost a year and a half ago.

So then last week I finished the chapter in which Stephon appears, and two days later I got an email from him. Yes, out of the blue.

This isn't really what I mean by timing, though. The timing: The day his email arrived happened to be one of my bad days. How to describe one of my bad days?

On one of my bad days it's like I *wake up* beset by my after-writing throes. I've got a profound sense of fatigue, of loss of essence, right from the get-go, without even getting any work done. If you theorized that on one of my bad days I feel like a slug on a garden fence you wouldn't be far off. You can work in some terminal loneliness if you want, also.

In his email Stephon hopes I remember him and says he enjoyed our talk at Stanford. A couple of sentences about how he's doing but basically he just wants to say Hi. I was so grateful for this email that I came within a hair's breadth of doing one of my weeping routines. The effect of the email was maybe like when the girl at the hotel front desk called to proposition me, which pulled me back from my brink-hovering. It was like that except much more so. I suddenly felt almost normal. I think this effect was due to a connection with another human being, however tenuous. In Stephon's case, not just that but with another human being whom I perceive as special. That a special human being would remember a brief encounter with me after so much time had passed and take a moment to communicate with no ulterior motive made me feel less hopeless about the world. Unmotivated kindness does this also, witnessing it.

I need to explain why I think Stephon Alexander is a special human being, and if you hang in you'll see how this connects to other things.

When we sat down for our interview at Stanford, the first thing I told Stephon was that I'm a dilettante. Stephon stopped me. "That word," he said. "What does it mean?"

"Dilettante?"

"Yes. What does it mean?"

I told him it means that I know just enough about theoretical physics to make a fool of myself in talking to an actual theoretical physicist.

"How do you spell it?"

I didn't really know. I told him there are some "l"s and "t"s but I didn't know how many of each, plus there is an "i" somewhere and at least one "e." Stephon was nodding, taking this in, filing it away somewhere.

Then I asked him why he became a theoretical physicist and he said because he was angry at God.

Hold on. Let me ask you something. Let's say that for some reason you're being interviewed because you have expertise at something. Someone, a Hollywood screenwriter, say, shows up and you do a formal interview. And let's say the interviewer starts out by saying something to the effect of how smart you are, but in doing so uses a word you're unfamiliar with. Here's the question: Would you stop him and ask what that word means?

Neither would I.

Why is that? Because our main concern would be how we're perceived. This would be the case in any situation with a stranger, but especially in an on-the-record interview, and even more especially if the premise of the interview is that we're smart.

Stephon did not care how he was perceived. Or, rather, he may have cared, but his need to know something, a truth about the world, minor though it was, was more important.

If people – you, say, plus me – worried less about how we're perceived, we'd worry less about self-image (still another self word), too. Which means we'd be less likely to believe untruths simply because they make us feel more comfortable about ourselves. Please trust me on something:

The belief in untruths is the primary reason why the world is so fucked-up. In fact, all the reasons why the world is so fucked-up depend on people believing untruths. I know that I'm right on this one thing.

Stephon Alexander *is not* one of the reasons why the world is so fucked-up, which is enough to make him special. In fact, that's my definition of special, as in special human being. Someone who is not part of the problem of the world being so fucked-up.

And listen. Stephon Alexander knows some secrets of the universe. Trust me on another thing: That Stephon asked me what "dilettante" means and how you spell it is as much a reason for his knowledge of some secrets of the universe as his astounding innate brain power, his intelligence.

This angry-at-God thing. Stephon grew up in a poor section of the Bronx, New York. As a child he was confused by all the misery around him. The confusion led to anger at God, since he had been told that God created Everything and Everything must include the misery all around him. So he wanted to understand how God could have done this. Stephon, having been blessed with astounding innate intelligence, even as a young person sensed that he would not come to understand about God through studying religion or philosophy or anthropology. He was tempted by art, he told me, particularly the art of jazz music. But he decided to dedicate his life to physics, the area of it that looks into first causes. What happened in the beginning.

If anyone ever comes close to a real understanding about God it will be a physicist, someone like Stephon Alexander. It will not be a Pope or an ayatollah or a rabbi or a Buddhist in a monastery or some shitball motherfucker blabbing away on Sunday morning TV. The reason for this is simple: Without knowing *how things work*—what causes what—there is no possibility of knowing anything else. It's all just words strung together and circular reasoning and specious causation and *made up* stuff and other crocks of shit. All of it.

Another thing. That Stephon was tempted to dedicate his life to art, to jazz music, is significant also. In fact, Stephon does dedicate himself to jazz music, to playing it on a saxophone, when he's not looking into first causes.

To sum up: In seeking to understand God, Stephon Alexander looks into first causes and plays jazz music on a saxophone.

I love that.

Although he grew up in the United States, Stephon was born in the Caribbean, on an island. I believe that this heritage is part of what makes Stephon special. The spirituality of his people. He told me a childhood story about his grandmother that gave me the shivers.

The island on which Stephon was born is this island, by the way. The little island from which I write.

CHAPTER ELEVEN

When you're writing, that's when you're lonely. I suppose that gets into the characters you're writing about.

Dick Francis

By late September of last year (2004), soon after the stateside trip I describe – a bit over a year ago from now as I write from exile – Lisa was gone from Big Turkeys, gone back stateside with no plans to return. It, our relationship, appeared to be over. *It* had just got to be *too much,* even for two people as disturbed as we were, each in our different ways. Need I elaborate here? I think not.

But at the same time, each in our different ways, we just *would not stop.* Lisa was relentless. I was still the love of her life, the one and only, the man who had ruined her for other men and so forth and so on, as reflected in daily emails and tearful, passion-rife phone calls and ground-mail letters and care packages to our P.O. box in Golfito.

And me? How to explain what I was thinking, if you can call it that, during this time? Try this for starters: Lisa's presence in my life had rattled me and depressed me to the point of near incapacity; I had become completely dependant upon her in my full time job of just getting through the day.

You wanna talk about a catch-22?

Yes, just getting through the day had become a full time job, and a *tough job.*

I'll tell you what: I will never again harbor that scintilla of contempt I used to upon hearing of some battered woman who didn't just up and leave her batterer. And you likewise might hold off judgment of my weakness until you've been through it. *It* meaning… I don't know… even *now* I don't know what *it* was. You'll know *it* should you go through *it,* God help you.

Aside from my weakness, here reared again my need to *know it all* about Lisa, which I can only compare to my need to know it all about what happened to Max Dalton: seven years after the old man's murder, how could it possibly matter who was Mora's San José government co-conspirator, or whether his son Esteban did this or that, or even if Mora directly fessed up (to what I already knew) due to our surface-friendly relationship?

Knowing it all about Lisa meant not just the facts of her relentless treacheries, but I needed to know the answer to the big question, the ultimate one, which was a version of my own constant challenge: *How does Lisa get through the day?*

But the complexities compound themselves still further.

How to explain?

Nonfiction.

Three problems with it… whatever it is, whatever I'm doing here. The first two are obvious.

Veracity. Am I purposely misleading you, i.e., lying like a slug, including by omission, in order to further some agenda other than telling the truth?

Memory. Assuming I'm not lying, do I have my facts right, the important ones, via notes or tapes or mental reconstructions, be they mine or someone else's?

Obvious stuff (if a bit oversimplified so I can get to my point).

What's not so obvious and what's vital to understand – not only here, in whatever it is I'm doing, but out there in life itself when someone is spinning you a yarn – is what I'll refer to as the *uncertainty principle*. I borrow this concept from subatomic particle physics, quantum physics, which is the branch of science that seeks to understand the underlying nature of reality. (Which on a certain level is what any sort of storytelling is about.) For our purposes, the uncertainty principle states this: *You cannot measure something without changing it.*

That this is true in nonfiction – that you cannot *tell* a story without *changing* it – is for me inarguable. The uncertainty principle is completely aside from, and unrelated to, veracity and memory. You ask someone what happened yesterday, they may lie and/or may not remember correctly in the tale they tell, but the uncertainty principle is there too, another obstacle in the path to the truth, or what *would have been* the truth had the tale not been told.

A writer cannot get around the uncertainty principle by being more careful, more honest, or even by being a better writer, any more than a physicist can hope that a more accurate measuring device will not change the phenomenon he seeks to understand. And likewise the reader cannot avoid the uncertainty principle simply by paying better attention or being more skeptical. We're both, you and I, stuck in this dispiriting conundrum.

Most often the uncertainty principle is a subtle, hidden factor and is never acknowledged, should the writer even be aware of it. But here it so clearly jumps out, almost literally off the page, that I give myself minimal credit for owning up. By way of explanation: Events starting from the time of Lisa's departure from Pavones in late September of 2004 were to a large extent *caused by* the writing of this narrative. To put it another way: Aside from my need to know it all, including *how Lisa gets through the day*, and aside from my weakness and my dark shit, whatever it was, *I needed an ending to this book.*

The Airport Incident, wherein through sheer stupidity I'd missed Lisa and her fuckbuddy, the San José one, strolling arm-in-arm to his car in the parking lot one floor below while I clutched that stupid bouquet, represented the ending I'd blown, the confrontation followed by the resolution I craved, both in my life and in the description of it, i.e., this nonfiction narrative. For agonizing, queasy-gutted months I was crazed to make up for that.

To finish up the Cormac Mc re-quote: *If it ain't, it'll do until a mess shows up.*

Me-as-a-writer couldn't let this narrative (the Lisa through-line, which has taken over) go out with a whimper, so to speak, as it surely would if I just got on with my life without Lisa, which was clearly what me-as-a-person should have done, and was yearning to do. The me-as-a-writer would have to hang in until a mess showed up, dragging me-as-a-person, that poor sap, along with him.

The uncertainty principle in brazen, shameless action.

Do you get my drift?

Good.

Pressing on.

CHAPTER TWELVE

You can tell a lot about a fellow's character by his way of eating jellybeans.

Ronald Reagan

Election night, 2004, I'm at home at the end of the road with my pups, trying to get through the day, the night, and I have a visitor to put in perspective the impending popular approval of George W. Bush, plus my impending trip north to join Lisa in New York to try to work things out.

Hold on. Work things out? *Work things out?*

Hang in.

Clay, the ex-pro surfer who informed me of the aborted Logan/Ron deal to whack Billy Clayton, roars up on his ATV, and he is *fucked up.* But holy shit is he fucked up. And Clay comes bearing the predictable gifts: joints, a six of Pilsen, and a packet of blow. Although by now I had cut my codeine intake down to four (Tylenon 3 equivalents) daily, on less dispiriting days and as a challenge abstaining altogether, seeing George W. Bush on the verge of popular approval gooses my craving to feel normal, or possibly to feel *just plain fucked-up* (a fine distinction lately), so I'm vulnerable to Clay's plying me with a blend of consciousness-expanding smoke, mind-dulling liquid, and happy powder. Expanded, dulled, and happy, all at once. Sounds right and reasonable, all things considered, no?

"Listen..." here comes Clay's first coherent pronouncement after his doggy-cuddling and doggy-baby talking, beer-bottle opening, and then staring at me for a long moment as if trying to remember who I am. "I did not fuck your girlfriend, bro."

I sense a long night looming, but maybe an interesting one.

I steady Clay's hand as he attempts to light a local-herb bomber, his eyes crossing as he gauges which of the many joint-images jiggling upon his retina he should fire up. Then, glowing reefer in one hand, Pilsen in the other, Clay weaves his way to the couch where he dumps a half gram or so of cocaine onto the glass coffee table top, saying again, "I did not fuck your girlfriend, bro."

As I contemplate various tacks I might take with Clay's denial-bulletin,

Clay draws out and hoovers up a thick white line, passes me the straw then says it yet again.

"I did not fuck your girlfriend, bro."

On the tube, on CNN, there are red states and blue states and the number of Americans who voted for George W. Bush in either a red state or a blue state appears on the screen. The number strikes me as high, since it's more than zero.

"Clay," I say, finally deciding on my response to his denial of fucking my girlfriend, "I never accused you of fucking of my girlfriend. Never said that to my girlfriend or to anyone."

Clay hands me the straw and, believe it or not, says, "I did not fuck your girlfriend, bro."

No point in keeping my head about me in this company, I'm thinking, as I huff my first line of cocaine since the previous millennium. In fact, I can't remember the last time I did the shit.

More or less out of the hazy blue: "She's no good, bro." I sense Clay is referring to my girlfriend here. To Lisa.

"Why do you say that?" I of course have my own theories on this subject, but I'm curious as to Clay's take on it, especially given his reiterations of not having fucked the woman he's claiming is no good.

Clay waves off my question as being either irrelevant or too obvious to deal with. He fumbles with the joint and the straw. He's still cross-eyed, literally. His right eye appears to be monitoring the election results on the other side of the room while his left eye fixes upon me; so I focus on his left.

"Rum?" This is Clay.

I pour him a tumbler to go with everything else. One for me too. We clink to the surf gods and drink. We huff and we puff and we swill, then, inspired, Clay apparently decides to more or less answer my question about why my girlfriend is no good, and I'll now dispense with quotation marks since the night soon gets too fuzzy to justify them.

Clay: Ever notice how everything is *hers*?

I have noticed. Lisa does refer to everything as *hers*. The land we bought together is "My land," our *cuiador* (caretaker) is "My cuiador," our building project is "My project." Our car, my car actually, is "My car." Nothing is "ours."

Even your house, bro. Your house.

Lisa, in inviting someone over to the house I built before she came to live with me (including surf bums from the break in front of the cantina), would phrase it this way: "Come up to my house if you want." This quirk/habit became so disconcerting I actively tried to break her of it, for weeks correcting her each time she'd say "my," but to no avail. She just couldn't help herself, apparently. I finally gave up.

Clay is shaking his head and repeating that Lisa is no good then opines that I'm better off without her, bro.

Clay knows that Lisa has flown the Big Turkeys coop. He does not know of my coming trip north to try to "work things out" and I refrain from enlightening him. I don't want to derail his train of thought, such as it is, with that bulletin.

At some point on the tube, and it could have been here, CNN shows a clip from one of the debates between George W. Bush and his opponent, John Kerry. Not in the clip, nor at any other time in the debates, does John Kerry expose certain big lies George W. Bush has told, although it would have been easy to do so. The reason John Kerry does not expose these certain big lies is that these big lies are perpetrated by both political parties, the current most blatant example being that the U.S. invasion of Iraq has anything whatever to do with *spreading democracy*.

What happened that night at karaoke? I ask Clay. I'm not actually changing the subject from Lisa being no good and my being better off without her, not much. I'm referring to the girls' night out from several months back, which night eventually resulted in Lisa telling Clay, plus Alex and Amy and others of my friends that I'd accused her of fucking Clay on the beach in front of the karaoke bar. I didn't find out about this lie for several weeks, during which time Clay avoided me.

Lisa came home drunk after her night out with the girls. It would only be a slight exaggeration to say *roaring* drunk. Her friend, *our* friend, Gayle, a married *gringa* expat, drove her home. All giggly and weaving around the living room and breezy as all get out, Lisa described how she'd had a few then gotten up and sung "Wild Thing" to Clay. She was a big hit at karaoke night, she said.*

The next morning I ran into Clay and good-naturedly asked him if he'd had fun last night, figuring we'd share a laugh about his status as a "wild thing," which he pretty much is. Here was his response and he got shifty in delivering it: "I left before Lisa got there."

It seemed a bit odd that even Clay, drunk as he no doubt had been, wouldn't the next day remember a babe singing "Wild Thing" to him in front of a packed house. And why would he deny having seen Lisa when I hadn't asked him anything about Lisa, or even mentioned her name? That was more than a bit odd, no? And if he left before she got there, how did he know she was there at all?

These are some questions I asked myself at the time. Also, when I say Clay got shifty as he issued his nonsensical blurt, I mean he got *shifty*. His

---

* If you find it strange that a ramshackle bar on the edge of the jungle at the end of the road at the bottom of Central America *has* a karaoke night, I can only say that yes, Big Turkeys is a bizarre place all right.

body stiffened, he couldn't look at me, he immediately did a segue-free change of subject – you name it in terms of shifty, he got it.

Later that day I queried Lisa on her theory of my exchange with Clay. Lisa pointed out that Clay is a drunk and don't ask her to explain his drunken nonsense. Not her problem, she said, and I didn't argue, didn't bring up her hangover or how drunk she herself had been the night before.

I then asked a simple question. Was she ever alone with Clay that night?

Absolutely not. Okay. That was that. And Lisa was right. Clay *is* a drunk.

A few days later I asked Clay how he could have forgotten about Lisa singing "Wild Thing" to him. Clay said he had blacked out the evening. Although this didn't explain his non sequitur about having left before Lisa got there – if he'd blacked out how did he know he'd left before she got there is a peripheral aspect of this nonsense, on top of the original aspect, which is that even had he not blacked out he couldn't have known Lisa got there after he left since he wasn't there to witness her getting there – I let the matter drop, filing it away in the Stuff Piling Up Department, somehow finding room for it in there.

Back on election night, Clay is saying that it all started at karaoke, shaking his head as he comes up with this one. I ask what he means as the monumental other bullshit drones on from the tube across the room.

This is what you think, bro, according to your girlfriend. That our affair started that karaoke night.

Christ. Now I'm accusing her of conducting an on-going affair with this clown.

I repeat that I never even considered that, or that he fucked my girlfriend even once.

I did not fuck your girlfriend, bro. I swear.

We were back to that one, along with the "I swear" tag. "I swear" is bad news in the sense that whenever someone says it, whatever came before it is likely to be a falsehood. I've done the research on this also.

Clay then starts in on an alibi about his movements that night, his first of several that are to come. Tells me who he did fuck that night. Someone other than my girlfriend, of course.

I guess you didn't black out.

Whaa?

You told me you blacked out that night and now you're remembering all these details, months later.

Here's Clay's slurred response, and I can only assume he's misread me, interpreting my observation as simply a compliment on his memory, and is now seeking to further impress me with its acuity: "Lisa told me that under no circumstances was I to tell you that we left together that night." I use quotes in this case because the words are exact, their significance having resulted in my making a supposed bathroom run and jotting them down immediately. I was on the *nonfiction case*, buzzed as I was.

Absolutely not. Again, this was Lisa's answer to my query as to whether she had been alone with Clay that night. Although I have not framed her words in quotes, I do believe they are exact.

So something is amiss here.

Furthermore, why would a bro – a surf bro or any bro – tell his bro that the bro's girlfriend is no good? This sort of thing has ended friendships (broships?), even when the bro didn't fuck the other bro's girlfriend. So if a bro tells his bro that the bro's girlfriend is no good and all he can come up with as a reason for saying this is the bro's girlfriend's misuse of pronouns ("my" as opposed to "our") there is something going on here.

The misuse of pronouns does not warrant a bombshell of this magnitude.

Does it?

So Clay is holding back the real reason for repeating over and over that my girlfriend is no good (and I'm better off without her). No doubt about that.

It's possible that Clay has other information regarding my girlfriend being no good, like she fucked someone other than Clay, but given all this other Clay shit, his bizarre guilty behavior, his denial litany, his whopper about leaving before my girlfriend arrived at the bar, his blurt about my girlfriend telling him that under no circumstances was he to reveal that the two of them left together that night, and so forth, the logical explanation is that he himself fucked my girlfriend, if not that night then maybe some other night.*

<u>Female baboons copulate with all the males of their troop except their sons.</u> The passage my girlfriend underlined from *Love Warps the Mind a Little* resonates on a couple of levels, not to dub Clay a baboon or anything.

A possibility: My girlfriend fucks Clay then spreads the news that I accused her of fucking Clay as a way to discredit me. She does the deed then uses the idea of the deed, since it's so horrendous and unbelievable, to further buttress her point that I've lost my mind, when the truth is I never accused her of doing what she actually did do.

Can you wrap your mind around that?

This would be pure and even inspired sociopathic shit, no? *No limits.*

A question: Do you remember what you were doing on election night,

---

* In April of 2007 I received an email from a reader of the U.K. edition of this book who said that in January of 2006 he'd seen Lisa and Clay going at it "hot and heavy" one night near the beach at Pavones. So at the very least, Clay did fuck Lisa "some other night." (The email is archived on the adjunct website.)

2004, how your night went?

This was how it went for me, as I tried to get through the day, the night, of the popular approval of George W. Bush.

CHAPTER THIRTEEN

He had felt like a man rushing to catch a train he was anxious to miss.

Helen Hudson

Two weeks after election night, in the creepy aftermath of George W. Bush's popular approval, I'm up in New York sitting in a witch doctor's office, Lisa in a chair to my left, the witch doctor himself, whom Lisa and I refer to as Doc Bruce, benignly facing us from his just slightly-elevated chair, Piled Higher and Deeper diplomas plastered on the wall behind him – but Christ is he a deeply-piled fellow! A full-blown shrink!

A good question, two or three actually: A witch doctor's office? With Lisa? Whaddam I, nuts?

I'd written a letter to Lisa's brother, Marc, detailing Lisa's sociopathic behavior, her various infidelities and deceptions and treacheries and blurts and bizarre gaslighting maneuvers, which were motivated by the domination game she was playing with my sorry ass: Imagine that all the dispiriting Lisa-behaviors I've so far chronicled are lifted and strung together in a 40-page, single-spaced, 16,000-word, Joe-Friday-nothing-but-the-facts-ma'am epic. The document was not a work of literary genius; I readily admit that. (On a certain level Dante-esque, it fell short of the Italian's flare for imagery.)

As I knew there would be, there was a shit storm, with Marc and with Lisa herself. But unlike most shit storms I've created simply by telling the truth, this shit storm had an upside once it ran its course, blew out to sea, so to speak. After tearful Lisa-entreaties of the usual sort, Lisa herself came up with this doozey of a concept: She would reply to my version of events point by point and then I would come up to New York, where we would consult with a shrink to see if we could "work things out." We would use our co-written document as a counseling device.

To repeat: Whaddam I, nuts? Yes, no question, but there was method in it. That Lisa would lie in her response to the letter was a given, but since aside from something being wrong with Lisa, there *is* something wrong with her, I also knew she would fuck up (from her point of view) and reveal many truths while in the process of lying. See, I needed proof for this narrative that everything happened as I describe. My hope was that Lisa – rather than completely rewriting history – would try to perception-manage events, leaving the facts more or less intact. That she would do this *in writing* was vital – she would not later be able to call me delusional or a liar regarding what had happened between us. Yes, as clear-cut an example of the uncertainty principle as you'll ever come across, as the events of the tale are directly affected by the telling.

Lisa's response to my letter would exceed all expectations. (Her PM lollapalooza is archived on the adjunct website, which I'll direct you to in due time.)

But the real upside, at least in my deranged mind, was that heads up their asses or no, witch doctors, with their extensive observations of sociopaths and nutcases of other ilks, will surely see the handwriting on *this* metaphorical wall.

I'd be vindicated by the very situation Lisa had set up!

Talk about hoisted by her own petard!

The ending I so craved was at hand!

But right: The Banana Peel Effect was about to kick in.

Back to Doc Bruce's office, Lisa and I facing him. Although the following is not Doc Bruce's opening line, it's nearly so: "I'm not interested in facts." (As usual, quotes mean exact words.)

Doc Bruce issues this beaut in response to my defining why Lisa and I are there, which is to have a third party mediate a disagreement between us, my side being that Lisa is a sociopath obsessed with copping uncommitted dick, then, having copped said dick, pathologically lying about it, and, further, engaging in a relentless attempt to make me and everyone Lisa and I know (plus sundry strangers) on two continents[*] believe that I've lost my mind, in order to cover up the truth of her obsession with copping uncommitted dick and then lying about it. I leave out the domination of my sorry ass as Lisa's underlying motive so as not to confuse Doc Bruce with causation theory, fearing he might be working on some sort of syndrome of his own. Christ, I could end up with one being named after me, which would be depressing.

Lisa's side of the disagreement being that I'm irrational and delusional due to chronic substance abuse and the inevitable upshot thereof, the dreaded Othello Syndrome (plus a dose of Morbid Jealousy). It's one or the other, I tell Doc Bruce, meaning Lisa is a sociopath or I'm delusional, and

---

[*]   Three continents, if you count when Lisa lied to her mom Fran when Fran was in Italy.

the facts needed to bear out my version are contained in the document he's read, meaning my Marc letter and Lisa's reply to it.

To repeat Doc Bruce's response to this: "I'm not interested in facts."

While I'm absorbing this, a statement the magnitude of which is up there with *you'll never change my mind about anything* in its dispiritedness, my eyes wander to Doc Bruce's wall-mounted *bona fides*, his glut of Piled Higher and Deepers, the sum total of which equal Doc Bruce defining himself as a scientist. Being an M.D., he's studied all the physical sciences, from chemistry to physics to biology and so forth, and, I assume, has at least *heard* of the scientific method, which involves the attempt to understand phenomena. Facts would seem relevant in this quest.

Yet Doc Bruce is not interested in facts.

I forcibly fold my hands in my lap; I'm shaking in anticipation of strangulation urges which have not yet actively surfaced. But okay. Without my asking, and possibly in response to my pained expression and white knuckles, Doc Bruce explains what he is interested in: "What I'm interested in is exploring the dynamics of your relationship with Lisa." To my surprise, Doc Bruce does not light a pipe, smugly or otherwise, as he says this. He just sits there looking wise and benign.

What I want to know is how Doc Bruce could possibly understand the dynamics of my relationship with Lisa without knowing if one of us is a sociopath, or the other delusional. This is the question I pose. Seems like a good one, no? While Doc Bruce talks a lot to this query but says nothing, I rummage in my bag for the Holiday Inn tape that got "screwed up."

Look, I say to Doc Bruce... I gather my logic... You read about the Holiday Inn Taping Incident in our relationship epic (with Lisa's reply, 73 pages, which is now piled on Doc Bruce's table under his wall-mounted Piled Higher and Deepers). Why don't we listen to the tape and see if either "it got bumped in the luggage" or "the maid did it" is plausible, in this world or even in a slightly stranger one, maybe a world where the laws of physics take days off down in Costa Rica to rest up.

I lead off with the Tape Incident because Lisa did not take issue with the facts as I put them forth in the Marc letter; the same facts I have put forth here. And since the tape is *physical* evidence, my being delusional is irrelevant to Lisa's status as a sociopath. (Which in turn is evidence that you *can* suffer from The Othello Syndrome while simultaneously your girlfriend *is* fucking around on you.) Further, since Lisa had – I'll use a lawyerly term here – stipulated to my version of events, and even put in writing the above ridiculous explanations for the gap on the tape, all one need to do is listen to the tape to know she herself had "screwed it up." Which would mean – extrapolating to the other incidents (the Fleabag Hotel Incident, to name just one) – that without doubt Lisa is guilty of...

well… everything. And therefore is a sociopath. This logic has the feel of inarguability, no?

No, no! Doc Bruce holds up his hands to halt my rummaging for the tape. Doc Bruce quite adamantly does not want to hear the tape.

Doc Bruce: The important aspect of the tape is why you went to that length. It seems excessive behavior.

What? Hasn't he read the goddamn fucking letter? I mean, *why* I went to that length is because…

Lisa loves this. She brings up my drug and alcohol addictions as the underlying reason for the taping. This throws the discussion onto a tangent from the real point, but the tangent's upshot is a bummer for Lisa. After querying me on my codeine and alcohol intake, Doc Bruce says that although it's a problem, it is not the cause of my delusions, if any. In fact, he says, codeine, being an opiate (if a very mild one), if anything would *lessen* that sort of delusional thinking.

A big-time setback for Lisa; she'll now have to come up with an alternate pathology for me being nuts. Weeks of research and Googling and multi-national gaslighting defenestrated. Sitting to my left, the love of my life visibly deflates. Has nothing to say.

In my bag I also have the cell phone cord Lisa stashed in my drawer upon my return from my brink hovering; among my evidentiary props I also have a t-shirt (a Stanford particle accelerator t-shirt, as a brink-hovering or Meaning of Life or What Happened in the Beginning reminder, perhaps). I want Lisa to demonstrate how the three-foot long phone cord could have gotten "accidentally" folded in a shirt, which was the only way it could have gotten "lost" in the clothes drawer innocently – as I already know, a physical impossibility. This is important as proof that Lisa was not only copping uncommitted dick and then lying about it – the implications of the tape would nail that one down – but trying to gaslight me into thinking I had lost my mind.

Only a sociopath, I say, would try to make the love of her life think he's lost his mind because he figured out she was fuckfesting with someone in San José while she thought the love of her life's life was in danger, among other times, one being when he is away researching The Meaning of Life (plus brink-hovering); fuckfesting in the love of her life's own bed in the house he built in paradise, and using the love of her life's expensive piña colada-flavored sex oil in doing so.

Doc Bruce will have none of it, no demonstrations as proof that Lisa has been gaslighting me, or, indeed, that she is a sociopath. That knowing this one way or the other is the purpose of our $300 sessions with the guy is irrelevant to him.

Facts, who needs em?

A scientist?

Remember my Head Up Your Ass Syndrome?

HUYA!

But it quickly gets worse with Doc Bruce, as Lisa further demonstrates why she was successful at her former line of work, public relations crisis management – institutional gaslighting. As it turns out, Doc Bruce, notwithstanding his Piled Higher & Deepers – or possibly because of them – is fish-in-a-barrel time for Lisa. Keeping in mind that *perception is truth* is the bedrock of Lisa's worldview, let's look at the first of the Ten Commandments brought down from Mount Orwell by the original PM messiah:

Perception Management Commandment 1: *Thou shalt always maintain plausible deniability.*

The problem is that plausible deniability is usually an obvious illusion, if one pays even a modicum of attention; the lies become self-contained (still another *self* word!). *Self-contained* lies meaning that it's not even necessary to outside fact check to notice them. Bush's lies about why he bombs and invades other countries are a good example here: you merely connect his speeches together, consider them one, and go back over them. In this case, even less than a modicum of attention-paying is necessary.

As an example of Lisa's perception management/gaslighting that is not contestable I bring up a whopper in Lisa's reply to the Marc letter – her new version of the New Year's Eve fuckfest.

> I found my night with Robert (the New Year's Eve Guy) to be unsatisfying and realized later on what a dumb thing I had done, while at the time I thought I was being so liberated.

Whoa! What happened to the sex being top-notch because it was "uncommitted" and the guy knew how to please a woman and Lisa had orgasms and they needed two condoms because they did it again in the morning and then she bragged to Vanessa about how great it was with the Brando look-alike? Now it was *unsatisfying*? Lisa was lying right in my face, knowing that *I know* she's lying, to give a positive impression to Doc Bruce, trying to say she's not really "that kind of girl."

As I try to point all this out Doc Bruce cuts me off with "He said, she said."

What?

"'He said, she said' is not useful."

Plausible deniability.

I believe I growled here, involuntary and low and way back in my throat, like Fang used to do when a Costa Rican approached within five feet of me or spoke to me in above a whisper.

I turn the growl into a throat clearing to conceal my feral reaction. Okay. All right. I move on. I have a trump and by God I'm going to play it and I assume Lisa is dreading this because she knows about it. I tell Doc Bruce that I've exchanged a flurry of emails with Lisa's ex-boyfriend after I sent him the Marc letter to offset Lisa's gaslighting of him about me, the back and forth Q & A that resulted clearly putting the lie to virtually everything Lisa wrote or said about her relationships to the two of us, going back to the very beginning. Everything is a lie: what she did, when she did it, how many times she did it, and how she felt about doing everything she did. As I bend to my bag to extract the relevant email printouts, Doc Bruce once again holds up his hand to stop me. Given that "He said, she said is not useful" will not really work here (since Lisa's ex and I are together on this – a sort of bonding-of-the-saps – it would be more like "He said, he agreed, she said"), he says, "He's probably lying." Doc Bruce adds that Lisa's ex wants Lisa back and therefore cannot be trusted in what he says. Here I have a rush of insight: Lisa prepared Doc Bruce in advance for my bringing her ex's correspondences into the fray. How else would he know, or think he knows, what Lisa's ex wants?*

Perception Management Commandment 2: *When plausible deniability is in jeopardy, thou shalt discredit the source of the truth, preemptively if possible.*

"How about if we just take a *glance* at his emails?" I say, and my voice is getting squeaky as I finally intuit the utter hopelessness of this shit. Look, I ramble on in desperation, when the poor bastard read my Marc letter he realized that Lisa had manipulated us both. I wave an email. He says it's okay to use his emails here and even says to call him from this session! He's waiting by the phone right now! (I might have added "like a lifeline on *Who Wants To Be A Millionaire*" but didn't think of it.)

Doc Bruce shakes his head, possibly at my lack of insight into human motivation.

Me: If he wants to get her back why would he expose her as a lying, treacherous sociopath? Mightn't that sort of *piss her off*?

Lisa lets fly a snort of derision at this but doesn't say anything.

---

*   That Lisa set up our appointments allowed her to work in various preemptive lies via her version of the background of our relationship, while subtly indicating how *sincere* she was in solving our (or, really, *my*) problems. Also, Lisa wrote the checks to pay for our sessions (I'd reimburse her later, she suggested); this was another subtle maneuver along these lines, I suspect.

Let's get back to exploring the dynamics of your relationship with Lisa, Doc Bruce says, ignoring the inevitability of my logic.

Now strangulation images actively surface.

I take a moment to review the positives and negatives of strangling Doc Bruce. I would certainly feel better, which is a positive. And isn't my feeling better what all this is about? So wouldn't strangling Doc Bruce be behavior that is *in the spirit* of the tenets of psychotherapy?

On the negative side, were I to strangle Doc Bruce it could buttress Lisa's theory that I'm nuts, no? I mean it wouldn't look good:

"Allan strangled the psychiatrist we went to see to try to work things out."

Given everything, this would be an oversimplification, I think, notwithstanding the essential truth of the statement, were I to in fact strangle Doc Bruce.

...please bear with me for a moment...

Imagine a doughy guy in his late forties, slightly florid complexion, russet suit jacket and loosened tie defining him as a serious academic, yet casual and approachable... Hold on. Just imagine a pompous witch doctor so we can get on with it, okay? Imagine the witch doctor appearing wise and benign in his slightly elevated chair facing the love of my life and me, saying he wants to explore the dynamics of...

...and boom! I'm on him, in a whiz-bang blur I have him bent over the table under his framed Piled Higher & Deepers and I'm banging his fucking head onto the Marc letter and meanwhile gripping the bitter end of his tie with my right hand and sliding the knot down tight onto his doughy neck with my left, Doc Bruce's florid complexion waxing still more so, which complexion is quickly sliding up to the right-hand end of the visible light spectrum, all the way from red and orange on up to violet, past which light is no longer perceptible to the human eye...

Please add a little tongue-protrusion and eye-bulging to the strangulation imagery.

My strangling Doc Bruce is an Up Moment, as opposed to a Down Moment, for this narrative – even though my strangling Doc Bruce didn't happen, even if it's *made up*. An Up Moment unless of course you're Doc Bruce himself reading. Or Lisa or for that matter Logan the Nutcase or any of the Mora family (reading a translation, except Esteban, who's pretty fluent in English) or my demented editor or either of my former agents or Sean Penn or anyone involved in the Zero movie deal or...

...and so forth.

For any of these people Up Moments and Down Moments in this narrative are reversed, I think.

There's either a catch-22 or a syndrome around here somewhere.

CHAPTER FOURTEEN

Life is an offensive directed at the repetitious mechanism of the Universe.

Alfred Lord Whitehead

I not only sent the Marc letter to Marc himself and to Lisa's ex-boyfriend, but gave it to Alex and Amy plus my surfbuddy Kim and his wife Sassy at Pavones; this to offset the gaslighting Lisa had perpetrated to convince my friends that I'm nuts, in the delusional sense. Here was the result: After reading the Lisa through-line of this narrative with all else edited out, *none of them believed that Lisa had been screwing other men or had done anything deceitful, like lying or gaslighting me or them.*

I put the above in italics to underscore this question: How could this be? Here's how, and it goes directly to why the world is so fucked-up, i.e., people believing untruths: *Notwithstanding evidence to the contrary, human beings will believe whatever makes them feel most comfortable about themselves.*

That these people had a sociopath living among them, and that they had been completely fooled by her, made them too uncomfortable to accept the obvious truth – good old Doc Stout in *The Sociopath Next Door* observes that this is a common phenomenon. It was less distressing to accept that I'm delusional than that their friend Lisa was faking her weeping-woman/ innocence routine, let alone has a hole where the soul would normally be. This in spite of my having introduced them to Lisa when I brought her to the life I built in paradise.

And now with Doc Bruce we have a supposed scientist and impartial observer who likewise can not, or will not, accept the truth.[*] You want to talk about a lonely feeling? Possibly the loneliest feeling in the world is

---

[*] Doc Bruce's reason for not recognizing Lisa as a sociopath was that in his experience sociopaths do not seek psychiatric help. That Lisa was not seeking psychiatric help but rather was engaging in gaslighting behavior aimed at Doc Bruce himself (as well as me) did not, would not, could not, occur to him, even in the face of incontrovertible evidence. Right: the D-word again. Speaking of which, get a load of this: After Amy read the Marc letter and voiced denial of Lisa's treachery, I asked her to explain the HI tape, how it got "screwed up." Amy's response was that maybe Lisa recorded over it because "she farted on the tape and was embarrassed." To repeat: Do you think I could make up this shit? But god*damn*, I wish I had the imagination.

knowing the truth and as a result being thought delusional. (On the level of hair-pulling frustration as opposed to gut-wrenching angst, the director's dumb-ass outline comes to mind here too -- everyone but me perceiving it as "soulful" and "possessing all the elements.") Which may be as much the root cause of my terminal loneliness (and perhaps my dark shit) as Lisa herself, her treachery.

But, predictably, it gets worse.

CHAPTER FIFTEEN

It was a cold bright day in April and the clocks were striking thirteen.

George Orwell

The two or so weeks I spent in New York in November of 2004 was the worst period of my life. But there was humor (of the usual sort) too. Aside from Doc Bruce – a full-blown witch doctor – Lisa arranged for us to see a couples' counselor, a fellow trained in mediating disputes between warring "life partners." Since our counselor, Rick, lacked a Piled Higher & Deeper (I believe he did have an M.S., a More of the Same), we referred to him as Rick, not Doc Rick. The humor reared at the end of our second session when Rick told us this, with a voice-tremor: "You two are both fucking nuts and I can't see you anymore." (Notice the quotes.)

Rick, a substance abuser "in recovery," was so rattled by Lisa and me, our lunatic act, that I suspect he feared for his sobriety if further subjected to our presence on his office couch. And remember that Rick was exposed to warring couples every day, multiple times per day. So we must have been – to once again quote Lisa (in describing her own flirting behavior) – "in another realm" from that which he was used to.

Lisa's and my reactions to being fired as patients were somewhat different. Me, knowing Rick had whacked the nail right on the head in his diagnosis of us both being fucking nuts, and seeing the panicky look on his sweat-beaded face, I convulsed in uncontrolled laughter. And by then I sure *needed* a laugh, no matter whence it sprang.[*]

Lisa, in contrast, and in the manner of a true sociopath, got outraged, demanding to know what the hell Rick meant by that and then exclaiming in righteous indignation that "There's nothing wrong with *me!*" This precipitated more volume and higher pitch in my hilarity, which in turn

---

[*] Remember Peter Sellers' Inspector Clouseau's boss in *The Pink Panther* series, whom Clouseau drove to lunacy? The sweating, the wild, roaming eyes, that great facial tic? (A tour de force humor-based-on-obsession performance by Herbert Lom.) That's the fictional character that comes to mind when I think of poor Rick and his reaction to Lisa and me trying to "work things out."

heightened Lisa's outrage. Lisa's outrage and my hilarity then fed off each other in a chain reaction phenomenon that so disconcerted Rick that he appeared to be searching for the nearest exit from his own therapy chamber.

But the humor did a fast fade a couple of days later when a dark moment, the first of three, loomed.

CHAPTER SIXTEEN

It is stupid of modern civilization to have given up believing in the devil, when he is the only explanation of it.
Monsignor Ronald Cox

My dark moment, the first of three.

A few days before I bolt the Apple, solo, no Lisa, take my flight back to Costa Rica and then the puddle jumper to Pavones, to my paradise at the end of the road at the bottom of Central America, Lisa and I are in our sublet apartment – which, believe it or not, belongs to a friend of the New Year's Eve Guy* – and I'm trying to take a break from whatever horrendous thoughts I'm having, unsuccessfully. In truth, and I realize this is going to sound ridiculous, I could use an angst pus-removal massage, but I don't have it in me to ask for one and Lisa isn't offering. Leaning on the credenza that separates the living area from the bedroom, I contemplate Lisa, sitting on the bed thumbing through a magazine. Although all the stuff piling up is now on the verge of critical mass, all I can think about is how Lisa lied about virtually everything to Doc Bruce and to poor Rick, with me right there, knowing I know she's lying. (Had I begun my formal research on sociopathy, I'd know that a blasé disregard for someone knowing a sociopath is lying is a sociopath hallmark.)

Hold on. One more incident; I think it's worth the words. As soon as I touched down at the Apple I bought a new cell phone (right, still more cell phone shit), an expensive Motorola, one that I'd be able to use down at Pavones, but mainly I needed one in New York. A week of hell with Lisa goes by, right? Lisa is having lunches with friends, whom, she says, lend her moral support in these troubled times. In other words, Lisa's list of gaslighting victims is ever growing.

This gives me the idea of seeing an old girlfriend of mine, with whom I have stayed friendly since we lived together back in the 1990s. Lisa knows this, and that my relationship with my ex is strictly platonic.

---

* This is just a small aspect of the preponderance of evidence that Lisa was fuckfesting with the New Year's Eve Guy in New York — the implication being that the New Year's Eve Guy was in fact The Cityman all along.

Notwithstanding this, and notwithstanding that Lisa is also lunching with her ex-husband,[*] I can tell Lisa is agitated by the idea of my seeing my ex in *my* need for moral support. She doesn't actually voice her agitation, but the grinding molars are a bit of a giveaway.

The day before I'm to go see my ex, Lisa comes into the bedroom of our sublet apartment where I'm lying down and hands me my new cell phone, saying I should call my ex to confirm our date. I think it odd that Lisa would make this suggestion; her concern is phony at best and anyway confirmation isn't necessary. So I put the phone down, let my head loll back to allow the stress to continue doing what it does best. Some time later I need to make a call, I forget to whom, and as I dial the number the phone lights up like a strip joint marquee -- the sucker is blinking and buzzing and vibrating like Lisa's R2D2 device, doing everything but let me make a call. Pissed, I take the phone back to the store, where the technical guy opens it and says it's fucked-up from water damage, which the warranty doesn't cover. I'm thinking the guy is trying to avoid replacing the phone, so I have him Fedex it to the factory. Sure enough, it comes back "Water damaged." A brand new cell phone works fine for a week, never goes near water, and now it's completely inoperable due to water damage.

Armed with all our knowledge, particularly regarding Lisa's cell phone pranks, what do you figure the chances are that Lisa did *not* sabotage the cell phone, dip it in a glass of water or whatever? (Not to belabor the point, but it's one of those phones that folds shut, so you could probably put it under a shower and water would not get into the electronics.)[†]

I have to give Lisa credit for the double-duty effect. The cell phone sabotage not only punished me for wanting to see my old girlfriend, but also accomplished the usual – showing me how shit just happens with cell phones.

Lisa's old Gravitational Theory as the cause of our problems had now segued to... I dunno... water damage... it took a lot of water to fuck up that phone... let's get hyperbolic and call it the Tsunami Theory, dub this incident the Tsunami Incident.

Okay. My dark moment, the first of three.

"You know, Lisa," I say as I lean on the credenza in our sublet Apple apartment while Lisa thumbs through a magazine on the bed, "with the shit you've been doing, you're dabbling in an area I can only describe as... *Evil*."

---

[*] That Lisa habitually cheated on her ex-husband was revealed in a classic Lisa-blurt. The story of this is archived on my website in the Cut Chapters section.

[†] If it seems nutso that Lisa would hand me the phone knowing it would immediately not work and knowing I'd probably find out it was water damaged and therefore know she'd sabotaged it, consider how she could not lose here. If I accused her of what she in fact did do, she could then tell everyone: "Now he thinks I sabotaged his phone!" as further evidence that I'm nuts.

Listen. I don't casually toss around words like *Evil*, especially when I capitalize and italicize them (which my voice-tone did also), so this is the voicing/writing of a new and significant concept on my part. I really, *truly*, do not fuck around with words like *Evil*, use them lightly.

What Happens Next is my dark moment.

Lisa looks up at me from the magazine then resumes thumbing through it.

That's it, my dark moment.

How to explain how Lisa looking up from a magazine then resuming thumbing through it could constitute a dark moment?

I've used a few movie allusions here, maybe too many, but in this case I really need to, because of how a visual image can sometimes impart a rush of insight more effectively than written words, no matter how well-wrought. The movie I refer to here is *The Exorcist*, and the image is when we first realize that the little girl, played by Linda Blair, is possessed by the devil: she's sitting on the bed and her head spins all the way around.

No, Lisa's head did not spin all the way around while she was sitting on the bed in our sublet Apple apartment, but when she looked up at my mention of the word *Evil*, it was like that for me, meaning my interpretation of the moment. To explain strictly in words: The manner of Lisa's looking up, the way her head moved, had a quality about it that made my neck hair prickle. It was like a marionette's movement, controlled by some unseen force or intelligence, and the look in her eyes as she briefly contemplated me leaning on the credenza contemplating her was disquieting in the same way. It was as if someone, or some*thing*, else was staring out at me from in there.

I do not deny that my precarious mental state at that time may have been a factor in my perception, but I don't think it was. Still, if you choose to discount my reconstructed portrayal as voodoo shit – in a sense I would respect you for this sort of skepticism – so be it. There is still significance in the moment I describe in that, be it real or "in my head," it was a factor in future events. In short: Due to this dark moment, the first of three, both me-as-a-person and me-as-a-writer knew that the worst, or the best (depending on which one of us you refer to) was yet to come, if I hung in.

To put it another way: I now knew without doubt that — as with me when I was a Hollywood screenwriter, and as with Coca-Cola – Lisa was *the real thing*.

372

PART SIX
Package Deals

CHAPTER ONE

Art, like morality, consists in drawing the line somewhere.

G.K. Chesterton

More timing.

As I write from exile on my little Caribbean island, it's January 15 (2006), which means that tomorrow is, or was, depending on your view of tense and of mortality, Mom's birthday.* But that's not the timing I refer to. I mention it because Mom is on my mind more than ever these days. For instance, last Sunday, a week ago today, I thought about Mom while the New York Giants played the Carolina Panthers in a playoff game. As I say, Mom was a big pro football fan, especially regarding the New York Giants. I am too, although I am hard pressed to explain this.

The game was not shown on TV on this island, but I kept track of it online. While doing so I imagined watching the game with Mom at her home in North Carolina. Mom would have been in a little conflict about the game since (having moved from New York) the Carolina Panthers was now her home team. She would have been rooting for the Giants, though, no question. In matters of loyalty, even to a football team whose players have no loyalty to anything except money, Mom was unshakable.

So I imagined Mom sitting on the edge of her couch watching the game, eyes bright, leaning forward, maybe using a bit of body English to effect the trajectory of an errant Giants' pass, then complaining about play selection, saying they should have given the ball to Tiki, like any dumb-ass guy football fan would do.

The Giants lost big, 23 – 0. Mom would have been disappointed that the Giants' season was over but would have said something to the effect that there's always next year. She would have said this even had my imagining been in the 2000 – 01 season, meaning that Mom would have known she would not be around for next year. She did not dwell on her coming death, not in front of me. Once I overheard her tell Ellen that she was afraid,

---

* I wrote this chapter during the writing of Part Five then stuck it in here. So it's out of whack chronologically. (Structure!)

though. This made me afraid for a while.

But the timing.* Three days ago I had CNN playing in the background as I worked on this book. I often do this, mostly out of morbid curiosity about what new lies are being told, not so much by the people who run this sorry ass world but by CNN itself. Still another fine distinction, a very fine one.

While I was working a promo came on telling me that a writer named James Frey was going to be on *Larry King Live* that night and that there was controversy that his book, his nonfiction book, his memoir, *A Million Little Pieces*, was not nonfiction but rather was fiction. *Made up.*

The timing I refer to is in this. See, three days ago I decided that this chapter, the one I'm writing now and you're reading later, would deal with the possibility that this book, this nonfiction book, this memoir, is fiction. *Made up.* Completely or a lot or a little. The idea that you may think this is a major issue for me.†

Larry King Live comes on at 10 PM here, which is late for me since I get up very early to write – around "first chicken," as the expression goes on this island; I'm usually long gone to nodland by 10 PM. But sensing relevant bullshit looming, I hung in for the show. In the morbid sense, it was worth it.

I read *A Million Little Pieces* about a year ago, at Pavones. In case you don't know: *A Million Little Pieces* purports to tell the true story of James Frey's life as a criminal, scumbag, and drug addict, then his rehabilitation and how he cleaned up and became a decent guy. Frey does a lot of owning up in the book. A lot of self-reflection.

Or so he says.

Wading through all the lies and perception management from Larry King Live – to which I'll return – and also based on a bit of research I did over the past three days, here's the story in brief.

James Frey wrote *A Million Little Pieces*, his first book, a few years ago. At that time Frey was calling his book a novel, fiction. He could not find a publisher; something like 17 houses turned him down. Then one house said they'd publish it but only if it were labeled nonfiction, a memoir.

---

* In case you're a big pro football fan like Mom was: As I write this footnote it's the next round of the playoffs and the Steelers and the Colts are going at it. It's 14 – 0, Steelers, but right now, just before halftime, the Colts are driving. Maybe you remember where you were and how you were feeling right now.**

    ** The Colts' drive was stopped at about the Steeler's 5 yard line. They settled for a field goal.***

        *** Later, at night now: The Steelers won the game after a wild-ass finish.

† As you'll see if you have the stamina to read it (on the adjunct website), Lisa's response to my letter to her brother Marc verifies my factual account of virtually everything you've so far read. (Plus she somehow simultaneously lied all over the place.) That Lisa proved that I'm not lying (or mistaken) about any of the incidents in our relationship is spectacular news for this narrative, especially given this James Frey shit storm.

Since I'll soon cop some moral outrage, I'd better do this first: play How Would That Go? I'd better Put Myself In James Frey's Place:

I write a book, a novel, fiction, a story I *make up*. I sweat over it for a long time. While writing it my forehead maybe even bleeds. No one will publish it. Then someone says they'll publish it if I agree to claim the book is a memoir. Nonfiction. I agree to do this even though I know the book is not nonfiction. In other words, I agree to lie like a slug. (By the way, I'd love to have been a fly on the wall at the meeting wherein that proposal was made. How it was phrased and so forth.)

Believe it or not, so far I'm on James Frey's side in this, more or less. I've in essence been there, more or less. In the writing of my (first) memoir, *In Search of Captain Zero*, there came a time when I made sort of a similar decision. In order for the story to hang together, to have sufficient Reader Big Mo, I'd need to do some lying; mainly putting a character in some backstory tales from which he was actually absent. I didn't *make up* the backstory tales, just his presence in them. You know this; I've owned up. In fact, I tried owning up at the time of the publishing via my Author's Note, which I tried to call A Note on Veracity. You even know that the real-life character I put in some backstory tales from which he was absent now seems to believe he was actually present in them.

But again, Frey agrees to claim his book is *non*fiction when it really is fiction.

As I say, I'm still more or less on James Frey's side here. I'm not in love with what he did but I'm hanging in with the poor sap because I understand the obsession and pain he no doubt experienced over his book. There is a real difference between what I did and what James Frey did, but still, with my book I was diddling around on the same spectrum, the lying-in-your-writing spectrum. (I have no patience with euphemisms like "taking liberties" or "artistic license".)

But then, as a result of the re-labeling, and of Frey's agreeing to lie like a slug, not only does the book get published but it's a howling success. Oprah hails it on her show from here to next week. Literally. First she hails it on her show one week and then the next week she hails it again, this time with James Frey on the show, who she hails as well. She hails him for changing his life so monumentally and for writing so honestly about it. Suddenly the poor sap is no longer a poor sap; he is a celebrity and his book is selling like hotcakes, mostly due to Oprah. (That one person's opinion can single-handedly have this effect on a book's fate is depressing, by the way, but that's another story.)

Here's where Putting Myself In James Frey's Place becomes a little dicey, in that I have to be careful. There are fine lines, fine distinctions, matters of degree and spectrum kind of things involved, plus the human frailties we all are heir to. I'm not talking about *A Million Little Pieces* itself; no fine lines there. James Frey's book *is a lie*. A complete crock of shit from one end to the other. He *made it up*.

In fact, before Frey's book was publicly exposed as a lie, I already knew; I knew it was a lie from reading it, and I remember the moment I knew it was a lie. Early on, Frey checks into a rehab clinic and is sent to have extensive dental surgery, root canals and so forth. Frey writes that since he was a drug addict in rehab the dentist couldn't use Novocain because Novocain is a drug. Frey describes the agony of this in excruciating detail.

Utter horseshit. Since Novocain is a *non-intoxicating drug*, there would have been no problem in using Novocain to dull the guy's gums.* By this time I was already suspicious of the book's veracity, but this scene did it. I knew that I was dealing with an author who not only was lying but doing so in an insulting way, since the Novocain lie is so transparent; as transparent as, say, Lisa's lie that her one-night stand on New Year's Eve was unsatisfying. There's a word that describes the attitude behind telling a transparent lie and figuring no one will notice, and the word is *contempt*; as in contempt not only for the truth but for the reader's intelligence. Although my intelligence was insulted I kept reading *A Million Little Pieces* anyway, out of curiosity to see how far Frey would go. I wanted to see if perfect characters would show up to create more emotion and buttress the crucial turning points that Frey *made up*, and which would result in a perfect ending that makes you go, "Wow, that's *heavy*." Sure enough, this came to pass.

No, the fine lines are not regarding the book itself, which, and I must repeat, is a complete crock of nonfiction shit, and an insulting one at that. The fine lines are in what Frey did next and continued to do: Frey ran amok with lying like a slug. He went on the talk show circuit and did a major book tour, going out of his way in assuring everyone that his book is true and that everything happened as he wrote it.

One more time: *Nothing happened as he wrote it*.

But if nothing happened as he wrote it, where are the fine lines? Here: What was Frey supposed to do? He got sucked into lying like a slug because he loved his book and had worked hard on it and believed in it as fiction and now, suddenly in the spotlight, what was he supposed to do? Own up? Admit he'd been lying like a slug?

What would *you* do?

There's still no moral outrage on my part, although I don't think I would have done what Frey did had I been in his situation. Lying in your writing is one thing, lying about whether you're lying in your writing is another. But

---

* Once again the scene from *Marathon Man* comes to mind, but in this case it would be the patient asking the question, to the dentist, the question being, "Whaddare ya, nuts?" Then: "Gimme some fucking Novocain, you shitball motherfucker!"

that's just my view. (You might recall I got pissed off at Frank McCourt for this – the quotation marks issue.)

So there are fine lines with this James Frey business (and in your life and my life) but eventually there also comes *a moment of truth*. A moment of truth does not involve fine lines. A moment of truth is clear-cut and it always involves… what?

A *crisis decision*.

For James Frey the moment of truth, the crisis decision, came when his book was exposed publicly as a lie, exposed in a way that is inarguable. Which brings me back to Frey's appearance on *Larry King Live*, and Frey's crisis decision, which was one of What To Do Next?

Frey had some choices; three, I think, although there may be variations. That there is choice is the linchpin of a crisis decision — no choice, no crisis decision.

One: Keep his trap shut. Disappear if necessary. Take a vacation to, say, a monastery in Tibet, where the monks not only have probably not read his book but are not allowed to speak, so even if they had read it they couldn't ask Frey anything to which he'd be tempted to lie like a slug.

Two: Own up publicly and completely and then weather the shit storm.

Three: Perception manage the situation, i.e., continue to lie like a slug right in the face of the truth. Should this be the option taken, Frey would slide over to the right-hand end of the lying-about-writing spectrum, and indeed the honesty-dishonestly spectrum. In the latter he'd slide into the area inhabited by Lisa, the Moras, plus Bush, Cheney, Rove, Rice et al – the Orwell-as-an-optimist area. Oh. Add Bob Woodward to that list.

Frey took option number three. That he was no doubt under considerable pressure to do so from his publisher, and probably from Oprah and her corporate PR people, plus others, is irrelevant. The moment of truth, the crisis decision, was James Frey's and James Frey's alone. This is another hallmark of a crisis decision – it cannot be blamed on others.

On *Larry King Live* Frey lied about everything and did so in a way that outraged me; he did it in pure Orwell-as-an-optimist, public relations crisis-management doublespeak. In other words, he lied but figured he maintained plausible deniability that he lied. I really hate this kind of lying. Reminds me too much of the love of my life, who used to make a ton of money telling people how to make use of plausible deniability, and who makes use of it herself in order to get through the day.

Perception Management Commandment 3: *When all else fails in maintaining plausible deniability, thou shalt find a catch phrase that sounds good and repeat it no matter what the question or issue you're faced with. Also known as a "talking point."*

"I stand behind the essential truth of my book." If the shitball motherfucker spouted that one once, he did so 20 times, often as an answer to a question like this one:

"Did you embellish any events from your life?"

"I stand behind the essential truth of my book."

Fine, James Frey, but I'm sure Herman Melville would say the same about his book about whaling and good and evil and man's place in the universe. Thing is, though, Herman Melville – aside from being above checking his book's Amazon.com sales ranking – was not claiming *Moby-Dick* as non-fucking-fiction.

Have you gotten the idea that I'm not on your side any longer, James Frey, you lying sack of shit?

Speaking of outrage, listen to this: The lying sack of shit had his mother on the show to help him lie. To help him lie about lying in his nonfiction book. And about lying about lying about lying.

His *mother*!

You wanna talk about moments of truth?

You wanna talk about contempt?

You wanna talk about a shitball motherfucker?

But in a sense, the larger sense, it gets worse. During the call-in period, the callers were screened (you bet they were) so none were outraged about Frey's lying -- they all said words to the effect that Frey's book was an inspiration and that they stood behind Frey.

Worse still, the guy who exposed Frey's book as a lie was interviewed and said that his outfit, thesmokinggun.com, had gotten a ton of emails about Frey and *half* of them not only stood behind Frey but were outraged that thesmokinggun.com exposed Frey's lies. Extrapolating: Since about four million people have read Frey's book, two million of them not only do not care that it's a pack of lies, but, further, are outraged that the lies were exposed.

Think about that for a minute.

Oprah calls in. Pretends her call wasn't arranged in advance; she actually says she had to keep calling because the line was busy.

More contempt.

And guess what Oprah says? Come on, take a wild stab.

Oprah says she stands behind the essential truth of James Frey's book.

By now Oprah well knows that James Frey not only lied to her about everything while she was reading his book (and weeping over it), but she also knows he went on her show and lied about everything again (plus lied about lying), to her and to millions of people. Hoodwinked her and everyone else and made himself rich and famous in doing so.

And she's standing behind him.

How could that be?

Because Oprah didn't want to… to what?

Look foolish. Right: We're back to that one.

Oprah, the most trusted woman on the planet, pretends her call wasn't prearranged and then tells the world that lying is okay. This so she wouldn't look foolish.

Relentless, this shit, these reasons why the world is so fucked-up, no?

My final word on James Frey: He's supposedly been clean and sober for thirteen years, right? People are worried that due to his current problems he may backslide, get into drugs and alcohol again, right? Which could ruin his life or maybe even kill him, right?

Give me his address and I'll send him a bottle of rum and a vial of painkillers. Get him started.

CHAPTER TWO

A bird flies, a snake crawls, a change of typewriter ribbons.
Charles Bukowski

At the end of Part Five I intimated that I'd hang in, meaning it wasn't yet over between Lisa and me, the excuse for this lunacy being my realization that Lisa is *the real thing*, plus the related issue of my need for an ending to this narrative, an example of the uncertainty principle – the tale being affected by the telling. Unfortunately, there was more to it in my motive – the dark shit I've referred to – and the expression *sick puppy* comes to mind. For now suffice to say that I did hang in and the hanging in almost cost me my life, twice, not counting my bout with pneumonia, which was likely caused by the chronic Lisa-induced stress I was under. So three times, really. My presence here on this island, the details of which I'll get to, is accounted for by the last of these life-threatening situations.

So the me-as-a-writer overruled me-as-a-person (who yearned for escape from Lisa), although the latter also knew that on a very real level all I had that was meaningful in my life was this narrative, the writing of it. Aside from surfing, that is, but even my passion for wave riding was debilitated, plus my timing out there tended to be off. One day I had to come in from dizziness and double vision, conditions that recurred another time driving home from the pueblo and which forced me to pull over; then, once the dizziness passed, to drive the rest of the way with one eye closed.

That playing this game with *Evil* would cost me further grief and plenty of it did not really occur to me. It should have. Although, since the New York trip's dark moment, a certain macabre clarity had been attained, I was still pretty much out of my mind. I wanted to see if in my life with Lisa the point would be reached that screenwriting guru Robert McKee calls The End of the Line, where turning points run out and meaningful options diminish to zero. To sum up: I was still a fool but of a different sort than before. I was a thoughtful, insightful, highly intellectual fool.

So by mutual agreement Lisa returned to Costa Rica, Lisa figuring we would try to work things out (whatever that meant to her), with me professing to go along with her when I was actually operating under the twisted closet motivations I've semi-described. She arrived on New Year's Eve, 2004, almost exactly a month after my dark moment, the first one. I met her flight at the San José airport. There was some symmetry here, New Year's Eve being a day so meaningful to our relationship, plus the airport meeting itself. Lisa's view of our reunion at the customs exit door was that it reminded her of her initial arrival in March, 2003, the "kiss that changed my life," that piece of utter horseshit. For me, the recollection was of the worst moment of my life, when I let her and her fuckbuddy, the San José one, slide right by me due to rattled stupidity of the not-paying-attention sort. In fact, more or less to torture myself, I got to the terminal early and positioned myself as I had that day, verifying what I already knew: There was no way I could have missed Lisa catching a taxi with her two huge silver suitcases and bright yellow dress, or even dressed in camouflage, and so forth. Having relived that – you'll either be pleased or disappointed (in the morbid senses) to know I shit-canned the clownish bouquet – and now seeing Lisa coming from my vantage point, I quick-stepped down the escalator and we had our passionate reunion, the difference now being we were *both* faking it.

So it's New Year's Eve. We make our resolutions over dinner.

One: We will not lie to each other in any way.

Two: We will not be disloyal to each other in any way.

Three: We will not talk to others about our relationship in any way.

Right: Take a moment to finish your belly-laughing

Me, I'm cold and humorless about it all as I write; probably a bad sign.

I don't know why I do this, maybe it's the champagne, maybe it's something else, but late that night I say to Lisa, "I know what you've done, Lisa, and I'll forgive you for it if you just stop doing it."

Lisa's reply: "*Fuck* your forgiveness!" Outraged, she then says this: "You have to *believe!*"

Perception is truth.

I say Never mind, I'm just a little drunk, something like that, then I fuck Lisa.

It doesn't take Lisa long to break the first resolution, no-lying, just a few hours. Next morning, New Year's Day, 2005, she tells me she needs to find an open pharmacy to buy birth control pills. There's a problem here. When Lisa went solo back to New York in the early fall, she told me right away by phone that she quit taking her birth control pills. This of course was a PM way of saying she wasn't fuckfesting, nor had she any interest in fuckfesting. Now, since I remember she bought several packets of b.c. pills before leaving in September (they're way cheaper down south), she should have plenty left. I of course know she hadn't quit taking them while alone in New York, since with Lisa fuckfesting is a constant and urgent phenomenon.

So I ask what happened to all the b.c. pills she had in New York.

A beat, then Lisa says this: "I accidentally put them in storage."

Accidentally. I love that. As I look at my watch to gauge the exact time elapsed since our resolution-making – eight hours and some-odd minutes – I suppress a perverse grin.

As a formality I try to picture Lisa *accidentally* taking her b.c. pills out of her makeup case and putting them in storage. Hold on. Since Lisa perceives sex the way a man does, let's reverse the situation. A couple is separated for many weeks and the male end claims fidelity during the separation, a total lack of interest in the opposite sex. Then, the couple having been reunited, the female end inquires what happened to the twelve-pack of condoms that were in the male end's toiletry kit back when they last parted. The male end says, "I accidentally took them out of my toiletry kit and put them in storage with my winter clothes and stereo equipment."

A howler, no?

I keep my trap shut in the face of this, partially because Lisa does have plausible deniability here, how *she* defines it (and, for example, how Bush and his gang define it), so to challenge her would not be "useful." Plus, I'm figuring if I let this slide Lisa will forget about it and there will be a payoff down the line.

So resolution number One is… right… defenestrated. (I'm starting to love this word.)

Resolution numbers Two and Three meet the same fate less than a week later at Pavones, in one fell swoop. The No disloyalty and No talking to others about our relationship resolutions include Lisa refraining from perpetrating her gaslighting litany about my substance abuse problems to anyone. Although it was a blatant lie to begin with, due to Doc Bruce's rejection of it as a cause of any delusions I might be subject to, Lisa in any case no longer has this one in her arsenal.

Since Lisa is in charge of the building of a spec house on one of our lots and since she has no experience in contracting, she's hired my surfbuddy Kim to help. Kim built his own house at Pavones and is fairly knowledgeable, although Lisa likes to point out (to me) how he fucks up in design and other matters. But anyway, Kim is at our house after a day's work and Lisa asks him if he'd like a beer.

Yeah, sure, he says.

Lisa opens the fridge and says, "There's only two left but Allan's not allowed to drink." She says this right in front of Kim, plus me.

Outraged, I don't say anything, not right then, but I grab one of the beers and tell Lisa we'll split it. I don't want a beer – it's only about 4 PM and I don't drink before sundown – but I need to make my point, mostly to Kim, who's standing there looking awkward at all this. Boy am I pissed, and it's obvious.

A while later Kim leaves and I demand to know why Lisa told Kim I'm not allowed to drink, breaking Resolutions Two and Three, the loyalty and talking about our relationship ones. In fact, since the assertion itself is a lie – I can drink whenever I want – she also broke resolution One again, No lying.

"I didn't say that."

"What?"

"I did not say that."

Perception Management Commandment 4: *When all else fails in maintaining plausible deniability, thou shalt just outright lie, no matter how transparent the lie. Anything is better than admitting the truth.*

There's a problem in Lisa's maintaining plausible deniability with this whopper, though, and his name is Kim. Kim was right there as a witness to this one. So two days later I hunted up Kim and said this: "Remember the day before yesterday when Lisa said I'm not allowed to drink?"

"I don't recall that."

He doesn't *recall* that?

I'll not string out this scene: Kim refused to admit what he heard, and he clearly *had* heard it – I could tell by his unease at the obvious conflict between Lisa and me over the beer, the way I immediately had one after Lisa claimed alcohol for me was off limits. He did not forget that in 48 hours. So not only was Lisa lying and gaslighting me but now my bro Kim was too. I say gaslighting here because the two were, in effect, trying to make me doubt my own perceptions. I then recalled that Kim and his new-agey wife, Sassy, had read my Marc letter and had denied belief in Lisa's treachery. I figured that since the beer incident Lisa had gotten to Kim first and persuaded him to lie for her; or he just instinctively did it to protect her, seeing as how I'm a nutcase paranoiac who is maybe capable of anything.

As with Clay, my affection for Kim as one of my Pavones bros is now on the wane, as is my patience with his and Sassy's "We all love you, Allan" crapola (the "in spite of your being nuts" being unspoken), plus their "Always create peace" voicemail outgoing message, plus their continued use of the words "energy," and "negative energy," the latter applying to my Marc letter, I assume, from their dumb-ass reaction to it.

Given his lying for her, I decide that I'll no longer stand up for Kim in the face of Lisa's denigrating him – Kim, according to Lisa, is "a wimp," "a cheapskate," plus his son "is a whacko," plus his dumb-ass oft repeated claim to being the "best longboard surfer" at Big Turkeys makes her laugh, and so forth. All true (I like his son, actually) but give it a break already, especially considering that Lisa refers to Sassy as her "best friend" at

Pavones. Now she has the jerk so gaslit and cowed that he's lying for her.

So no more standing up for Kim. Fuck him and his "negative energy" avoidance and creating fucking peace on his stupid voicemail.

I've always hated that dumb-ass new age crapola anyway.

CHAPTER THREE

The difficult character in comedy is that of the fool, and he must be no simpleton that plays the part.

Miguel de Cervantes

Barry. Barry is an ex-pro volleyball player who was building a house next to mine and with whom Lisa fuckfested in our bed when I was away in the summer of 2004, using our expensive piña colada-flavored sex oil, and my Beatles album to dampen Lisa's ah ah ah ah ah pre-orgasmic anthem. How I initially came to the tentative conclusion that Barry was the fuckfestor, and then subsequently knew without doubt it was he, is worth some words since fuckfesting in our bed – *my* bed – in the home *I* built in paradise is clearly an escalation in Lisa's progression of betrayal.

Barry was my prime suspect in the fuckfesting from the get-go for several reasons, not the least of which was a string of Lisa-not-thinking-before-speaking blurts. Her long-ago doozey about the female sportscaster not allowing love to stand in the way of fucking a lot of athletes also applied here, Barry being a big, strapping ex-pro athlete (no question that a Yes went off in the love of my life's head upon first meeting him). That he was right there next door, his uncommitted dick just a few yards away, was a factor also, temptation-wise. Nothing like a little proximity to get the fuckfesting rolling.

Lisa's first blurt was in response to my asking if Barry had been to our house while I was away during any of my absences – my brink hovering at the Stanford particle accelerator, my drive up the coast to keep my terminal illness story straight with Ron, or my dumb-ass visit to my past and my old chum Captain Zero. This query came soon after the Sex Oil Lie Incident. Lisa's response was this: "Barry's never been through the front gate."

I had to love that one for its surface truth/lie by omission aspect, which is a Lisa hallmark.* See, I'd already figured that Barry would not use the front

---

* In *Without Conscience*, a book about sociopaths by Robert D. Hare (Piled Higher), one chronically dishonest female interviewee brags that she often "salts the mine" with a "nugget of truth." "If they think some of what you say is true, they usually think it's all true," this sociopath theorizes (breezily, I'd bet). In other words, own up to something minor, leave out the horrendous rest-of-it: Lie like a slug, but by omission. This is an M.O. of perception management (institutional lying) as well, Lisa's highly-remunerative vocation.

gate in coming over to my house to flesh-pile with the love of my life, since someone, our caretaker especially, could easily spot a front-gate trespass and tell me later. So I Put Myself In Barry's Place and in my mind's eye saw him finding a breach in the fence line facing his property to make his entrance. So Lisa was probably telling the truth when she said Barry had "never been through the front gate." (Think about it: Why would someone answer in this way the simple query of whether she had a visitor? How about a simple "No"?)

Then another time Lisa fucked up, forgetting her implied claim that Barry had not visited her during any of my absences, and said he'd come over once "to borrow a broom." This, I knew, was another example of a lie by omission, of salting the mine with a (tiny) bit of truth, i.e., revealing that Barry had been in my house, but for an innocent reason. Lisa, breezy as all get-out, then improvised that she was upstairs at the time and didn't actually see Barry when he showed up looking for a broom.

Lisa's mistake with this blurt became evident when I asked how she knew Barry'd borrowed a broom if she didn't interact with him on the broom-borrowing sortie. This took Lisa aback for a moment, then she claimed Barry had borrowed it from Maria Louisa, our maid, who was in the kitchen. When I queried Maria Louisa on this she adamantly denied Barry's broom-borrowing; he'd never done that.

So Lisa was lying. Her salting the mine – and not adhering to Rule Number One When You're Lying, i.e.: keep details to a minimum – as usual, backfired. Then, not being able to leave well enough alone and quit while she was behind, when I wasn't around Lisa tried to get Maria Louisa to change her story about Barry and his broom need. Later, Maria Louisa related to me how Lisa, in her bizarre attempt to rewrite history, broke down crying about my "unwarranted suspicions" about Barry. Maria Louisa, who'd been with us for two years and is intensely protective of the house, stood fast: No broom borrowing had transpired with my neighbor. And even this simple campesina told me she saw the phoniness of Lisa's weeping act.

Through still another blurt I was able to reconstruct how Lisa initiated her fuckfesting with the guy – and you can bet she was the instigator. Although I never actively grilled her about Barry, my suspicions were becoming obvious, so Lisa, out of nowhere, came up with this one: "You should see Barry's wife. She's beautiful." This, I assumed, was supposed to indicate how unlikely it was that Barry would be interested in fucking Lisa, since his wife is so beautiful.

Perception Management Commandment 5: *When plausible deniability continues to be in jeopardy, thou shalt confuse the issue through misdirection.*

Problem was, aside from the obvious misdirection of the blurt, Barry's wife has never been to Pavones.

So my natural inquiry to this was, "How do you know she's beautiful?"

"There was a picture of her." Notice the passive phraseology.

Lisa was digging quite a hole for herself and although she knew it she just kept excavating. She had visited Barry at his new house "for some reason" while I was away and he showed her the photo. That Barry was having marital difficulties also came out here, as Lisa continued to wail away with the shovel, dirt flying. Now she and Barry were swapping problems-with-their-mates stories. Lisa truly cannot help fucking up once her mouth gets going.

Here's how it went and you can take it to the usual place and earn some interest: Lisa goes over to Barry's on some pretext and in the course of her pursuit of his uncommitted ex-athlete dick the subject of mates comes up, probably via Lisa, Barry relating his marital problems, showing Lisa the wife-photo in the process. They may or may not be sitting on his bed at this point – Barry has little furniture in his house-in-progress, so it's likely. Using the commiserating about mate problems as a segue, Lisa, inspired, works up some weeping, spilling her guts about my unwarranted suspicions about her infidelities, her "nonexistent" San José boyfriend, and so forth. She needs support, she says, the same gaslighting technique she uses with our friends. One thing leads to another with the weeping and then the support she needs from Barry becomes uncommitted dick, her goal after all.

That Lisa is now doing what she says I falsely accuse her of probably never occurs to Barry; he's not the brightest bulb in the marquee to begin with and, anyway, who cares? Lisa is a fine piece of ass, if you ignore her little problem of… of having a hole where her soul would normally be.

Their fuckfesting moves over to my house; this for convenience and so Lisa can answer any phone calls I might make from wherever I am – should she not be home I might get suspicious. Which brings up another Lisa-blurt that fits with my already-formed theory of how all this went.

After the sex oil fuckfest in our bedroom, and with my apparent suspicions, Lisa would be nervous about continuing to carry on there, due to the open-air windows. Her little ah ah ah ah ah ah pre-orgasmic anthem, which can get quite raucous, might be heard by our caretaker; indeed, if he got really nosy he could conceivably even peek through the hedge and see with his own eyes the candle-lit fuckfesting going on downstairs while I was elsewhere. So Lisa would move the fuckfesting upstairs to the bed in my office, which being glassed in for the air conditioner is basically sound-proof; plus being on the second floor no one could peek in. They'd do it up there for privacy. I have no doubt whatsoever that this was the case.

Lisa, during one of our phone calls: "I got stung by a scorpion in the downstairs bed so I've been sleeping upstairs."

She just can *not* help herself with her salting-the-mine blurts.

But hey, her fuckfesting with Barry is still plausibly deniable.

What is not plausibly deniable happens soon after Lisa's return on New Year's Eve (2004) and a couple of weeks after the incident with Kim. First, some chronology/disclosure: Due to his and my Pavones comings and goings I hadn't actually seen Barry since August, before their fuckfesting began; he had been gone on extended stateside business.

We now are in February of 2005, a month after Lisa's return and my concomitant hope that *some* sort of ending to all this will present itself. Lisa and I are in Golfito at the supermarket and I'm outside waiting for Lisa to finish up the shopping when Barry shows up – again, I hadn't seen him since August, before the fuckfesting. He sees me, I'm hard to miss leaning against our big green Explorer right out front, but he tries to keep going. This is my next door neighbor, a fan of my books, and although we're not buddies we're always friendly, always take time to catch up after one of his extended absences. In fact, it's a ritual that when he comes back to Pavones he visits my house, bringing a bottle of wine for the three of us and a Cuban cigar for me. Nice guy, friendly guy, if not real bright. I mean the *nice* modifier *in theory*.

Hey, Barry! I say, and now he can't ignore me. He turns in mock surprise. I never, ever have seen anyone as nervous and shifty-eyed as this guy when he reluctantly steps over and tries to act normal. He's making Clay, with his "I left the bar before Lisa got there" shiftiness look downright James Bondian in suavity. This is when, in a literal heartbeat, I go from heavy suspicion to no questions or doubts that he's the one Lisa had been fuckfesting with in our bed – both beds, upstairs *and* down – draining our expensive piña colada-flavored sex oil reserves in the process. As Barry rambles on with his stuttering nonsense, my stare hardens, although I'm at a loss as what to *do* about this, at least right now, given the fucking plausible deniability of the situation.

I interrupt: "Lisa's in the super. Go say 'hi.'" There's some subtext to the way I say this, plus my hard stare, but since Barry has not yet looked me in the eye, he's unaware of the latter.

"Oh, yeah! Right!" His voice actually cracks. Jesus Christ. I can't help but wonder how this ex-pro V-baller used to handle the pressure when down match point, side in.

Barry was headed for the market and can't very well not go in now; I shadow him through the supermarket's front window as he grabs a cart inside and starts wheeling it around, randomly it appears. Even through the dirty window and from 30 feet the guy looks panicky. A minute or so later I watch as he encounters Lisa near the vegetables. They speak no more than a couple of words and then Barry keeps right on going. The guy's been gone for like five months, our neighbor with whom Lisa has visited and swapped life stories, and he doesn't even stop for a reunion chat. The fucker is too rattled by his encounter with me, and by his fear that I'm doing what I am in fact doing, i.e., observing his act; me, the guy whose girlfriend he fucked.

I go in the super and come upon Barry squatting by stacks of tuna cans. He's just plucked three cans from the shelf. He looks up, sees me, and the three Tesoro del Mar (Treasure of the Sea) cans go *flying*. The sight of me standing over him caused him to lose physical control of tuna fish cans. This is an ex-pro *athlete*?

While Barry is blushing and mumbling and fumbling, trying to straighten out the tuna-can chain reaction he's precipitated, I glance down the food aisle. Lisa is at the far end, observing all this. She quickly looks away, wheels her cart out of sight. I can't help but wonder if Barry's comical incompetence will affect her fondness for fuckfesting with him. Probably not. Dick is dick and it doesn't much matter what kind of jerk it's attached to, as long as it's uncommitted.

Outside, a few minutes later, we run into Barry again. He's loading his car; seeing Lisa and me he gets jumpy; as he roars off he yells in a high-pitched voice, "I'll be over with wine and a cigar!" As I say, this has been the ritual with our neighbor when he returns to Big Turkeys.

This time, of course, is different. Barry does not come over with wine and a cigar.

In response to my prediction that Barry will not come over with wine and a cigar and having figured out why I'm saying this, Lisa comes up with the following beaut: "I ran into Barry and he said he hasn't come over because our nice wood depresses him."

She's referring to the *cachimbo* I used in the construction of my house. It's true, it's nice wood – and it's the same nice wood Barry has on order for his house. But our *nice* wood, even though he's using it too, now *depresses him*, so he doesn't come over, as is the custom. This according to Lisa. (At least she didn't claim *her* nice wood depresses him.)

The reason I couldn't make up any of this shit is this: I'm simultaneously not smart enough and not dumb-ass enough, if you get my drift.

A couple of incidents, although there are a half dozen of this ilk: Lisa and I are having a post-surf session lunch at the cantina and I spot Barry pull up. He comes into the cantina, hasn't seen Lisa and me yet and Lisa hasn't seen him. My staring at him causes Lisa to turn and look. At just that moment Barry turns his head and sees the two of us sitting there. His and

Lisa's heads simultaneously and reflexively *snap away* from each other, both pretending to be interested in something else. It's the guilt-ridden reflexivity of their head movements that knocks me out. There's no thinking involved.

"Jesus Christ, Lisa," I say. "I mean, fuck."

"What?" Lisa wants to know, feigning innocent confusion.

Plausible deniability.

Lisa and I are on the way back from Golfito. A half hour outside of town there's a river you cross via a little ferry, a flatbed outboard-powered barge that holds four cars. As we drive on, Barry's Trooper appears behind us on the dirt ramp and stops. I look. What's he gonna do, I'm wondering, not drive onto the ferry? There are no other cars waiting and I know the idea of being stuck on a ferry with just Lisa and me will shake him up big time. I mean he really doesn't want to drive on; he's *exuding* not wanting to drive on. But under the circumstances he pretty much has to, so he does.

"Hey, Barry," I say, as I approach him during our little sea voyage. "Long time no see." This is meant sarcastically, of course. It's really a lack of eye contact, not a lack of seeing, that I'm talking about. Barry has *seen* me plenty.

Believe it or not, with no motivation or segue, Barry immediately starts in about how he's not interested in getting involved with any women. Women are nothing but trouble, he opines, then, again with no segue, says something about some babe who's coming to visit him, a physical therapist or something (who never did show up).

Where's Lisa during this dumb-ass monologue?

She's ten yards distant over at the ferry rail pretending to be fascinated by the upriver view. Christ, what's her excuse for not coming over to say Hi to our neighbor, the one she visited while I was away to swap mate-woes stories with? Doesn't either of them have a clue how to feign naturalness?

Barry is drunk on his ass, by the way – it's about two in the afternoon – clutching a plastic cup brimming with what, from the color and familiar aroma, is rum and coke, mostly rum. Yes, I knock back a few after sundown, but this guy is a full-blown drunk.

Listening to Barry's slurred homily about not being interested in women these days (although there's one coming to visit him), I keep glancing at Lisa, who, finally realizing how weird and inappropriate it is that she's not acknowledging our neighbor, saunters over.

Silence. Neither says hi to the other, nor do they look at each other. The vibe is in another realm of *awkward*, at least for the two of them. In a perverse way, I'm sort of enjoying this. Barry, now even more rattled, in a desperate effort to break the silence extends his rum and coke toward Lisa, saying, "Some rum, Lisa?" His hand is visibly shaking as he makes this ridiculous and gauche offer in broad daylight on a ferry ride.

"No, thanks," Lisa says, and even she seems disgusted by this jerk's lack of grace under pressure.

"Jesus Christ, Lisa," I say as we drive off the ferry. "I mean, fuck."

"What?" Lisa wants to know.

Plausible deniability.

One morning I walk my fence line, looking for Barry's non-"through the front gate" way onto my property in order to cop some Lisa-pussy. The hibiscus hedges, palms, and various decorative shrubs I planted in 2001 when I bought my property are now a thick tangle, basically impenetrable from the outside, even aside from the semi-snake proof chicken wire fence that circles my land. So I walk my hundred or so yards facing Barry's lot (there's someone else's cottage between us, but the owner is never around), finding no break in the tangle until I'm down almost to the end where the land drops precipitously from my plateau to the coastal plain. Here it is, I'm thinking, as I examine a gap in the hedge; there are even some freshly broken limbs and twigs where Barry cleared the natural break further. But then there's the fence itself, waist high, topped with barbwire. Even with Barry's long legs it'd be a chore to get over; a minor slip and he'd be in danger of snagging his scrotum, which would be counterproductive given his mission. I look down and actually laugh. There's a pile of thick ceramic tiles stacked up against the fence, a half dozen of them, a platform from which he could easily step over the fence with no scrotum-snagging.

I can't believe it. The fucking guy, aside from his ridiculous behavior around me – his in effect yelling in my stupid, hangdog face that he's been fucking my girlfriend – has also constructed a convenience for doing so, and left it there. I mean the only route in, since *he's never been through the front gate*, is this break in the hedge line and there it is, right at my feet, the only stack of fence-leaping-facilitating tiles for probably a hundred miles.

Didn't the moron think I might *notice* his little stairway to heaven?[*]

Between Lisa's blurts, this guy's slapstick tuna can act, his stuttering and neck-bending avoidance of eye contact… and now this… I'm a cuckold and a fool but these two are the fucking clowns, no?[†]

But notwithstanding the humor and the clownishness, I am getting *pissed off*.

Something will have to be done.

---

[*] I was so astounded that I went and got my camera to document Barry's little stairway. The photo is on the adjunct website.

[†] Last month as I write my new caretaker Marcos called and informed me that Lisa has been surreptitiously spending nights at Barry's next door, trying to keep their fuckfesting a secret from the pueblo, as it of course wouldn't look good, given her many protestations of "absolutely no interest in the guy." (In her gaslighting of me she also branded Barry "just another dumb gringo" and "a drunk.")[**]

[**] Later, I got an email from a Pavones female, telling me that Lisa admitted to screwing Barry, her rationalization being that since I accused her of it, "the thought was not so bad."

CHAPTER FOUR

For the sin ye do two by two ye must pay for one by one.
Rudyard Kipling

I had two alternate plans to resolve the matter of Barry. The one that most appealed to me involved Lisa's refrain that my sorry ass had "ruined her for other men." I'd give new meaning to that one, was what I was thinking.

I take a solo trip to the border town of Paso Canoas to hunt up a certain Panamanian there, Hector, a guy I met through an associate of "The Facilitator." I know where to find Hector: at the whorehouse on the Panama side where I'd gotten semi-raped in 1998 during my Max Dalton investigation when the alpha whore didn't like my attitude. I'm hoping she'll still be there, for some peripheral symmetry, I suppose. She of course is not; it's been six years since she didn't like my attitude and a whore's life at a Central American border town is no day at the beach; six more years of going tits up and legs spread under the denizens of that particular *beau monde* and… maybe it's best that my image of her remains un-updated.

Hector isn't around either, hasn't been for a couple years. This is predictable as well; assassins with per-hit going rates of under a thou are not apt to have a lot of job security, or alive-on-planet-earth security, for that matter. But the whore I'm querying gets the drift that I'm up to no good and says she'll call a guy she knows who's the same cool kind of guy as Hector was. I should sit down and wait for him.

My intention is not to hire someone to murder Lisa, and for this I feel some measure of shame. I considered it, but due to my own selfishness nixed the concept. By way of explanation: that Lisa would precede me in exiting what has been so aptly and lyrically referred to as this *vale of tears* is not only a deeply unsatisfying notion but a genuine bummer. Given the age difference and my bad habits, I'm counting on her living far beyond my passing. Serves her fucking right, is the way I look at *that*. Also, that it will be only a virtual eye blink in creation's muddle before she's old and wizened and ugly and bereft of uncommitted dick or any dick likewise is a wonderful thought. I mean: *then what*? May she live to be 110!

But the shame in not hiring someone to murder Lisa? What's up with that? It would be nice if you're ahead of me here: Ridding planet Earth of Lisa would have been the right thing to do, in the moral sense. This is so obvious that to explain my reasoning would be foolish, a waste of words and God knows we have enough words here as it is. I'd either be preaching to the choir, or, if you're not already with me on this, trying to indicate which way is up in the void of deep space; no mean feat.

So, no. My foray into the border town underworld is not with murderous intent, but to gauge the feasibility of having Lisa's face rearranged -- as I say, to give a more honest and meaningful twist to my having "ruined her for other men." (I'd be out of the country when it went down.)

I know: I've lost some of you.

What can I say?

But as you should have already figured out, I didn't do it – otherwise I wouldn't be owning up in this nonfiction narrative. What happened was that I never met Hector's understudy. After about ten minutes of waiting, having a cup of coffee in the whorehouse, I pretty much fainted. Didn't actually fall over, but close. Hammered by dizziness and double vision plus a bad rush of agoraphobia,[*] I had to get out of there. Making the "momentito" sign to the whore I'd talked up, I stumbled out of the whorehouse into the harsh blast of midday and to a nearby fleabag hotel, got a room and lay down.

Christ but this shit, this dark shit, whatever it was, was really fucking me up.

An hour or so later I was able to drive and went back to Pavones and Lisa and my next door neighbor Barry and my friends who think I'm delusional, Alex and Amy and Kim and Sassy and Candyce and Phil and the rest, plus my caretaker (at the time), Roman, and his crack-head brothers, who, along with their father, were in the midst of trying to extort several thousand dollars from me. Having been told to get off the property, they were now squatting on my land and had been sabotaging my water system and threatening to muster a large scale squatter invasion. So now I'm usually armed, carry my S &W .38 when I leave the house.

This was pretty much the welcome home vibe after passing out while trying to hire a Panamanian hit man to rearrange the love of my life's face.

I settled on my alternate plan, which was more symmetrical than the hit man plan anyway, mainly because I myself would carry it out. (The uncertainty principle may have been at work in my need for a symmetrical

---

[*] Predictably, witch doctors can't seem to agree on what agoraphobia *is*. In my case it's an aversion to interacting with people on a more complex level than hi-how-are-ya. Negotiating with a Panamanian hit man for the rearrangement of the love of my life's face would seem to apply here.

resolution; it's hard to say.) Simple: I would walk over to my next door neighbor's house, empty my Browning 12 gauge into its façade, do likewise with my S & W .38, then walk back home, into the house, grab Lisa by her thick mane and drag her kicking and screaming to the front gate (which Barry has never *been through*), throw her pig ass out, lock the gate, dump her shit over the fence, then walk back to the house – *my* house, not her house or our house – and then, gazing out at the Sweet Gulf and surrounded by my pups, have me a rum and O.J. or a glass of Chilean Red.

Repercussions? Barry wouldn't do a fucking thing. No cops would be called, no retribution of any kind. His guilt-ridden inability to even look me in the eye pretty much assured me of that.

If the shotgun blasting of a house has a familiar ring: a while back I'd gone out hunting for my house sitter Rich, who'd tried to steal my money, with the intention of blowing a few holes in his Jeep while he watched. I'd taken this route because Rich was bigger and younger and stronger than I am, and I needed to demonstrate that I was crazier than he. Same with Barry, who had me by half a head and a good 40 pounds. A dimwit, but a big, well-muscled, ex-pro athlete dimwit. Getting beat up by Barry, given the sum total of the circumstances, was an absolutely unacceptable scenario. My use of firearms would cancel any such thoughts the shitball motherfucker might have. The drift of my antics might even run him out of town, out of guilt or cowardice or whatever.

So there was that.

Although my bros, indeed the whole pueblo, would now consider me flat insane, there were upsides. Logan, for one, would now be scared shitless of my lunatic ass. I'd have no more problems with him. Ditto Ron, whom I'd come to realize was not as hardboiled as his cultivated image.

Another upside was that my nickname with the local campesinos would revert to La Escopeta (The Shotgun) from El Chivo (One With Horns), which was a peripherally comforting thought. Plus, Roman and his crack-head brothers and greaseball squatter cohorts would likely think twice about their invasion plan. Still another offshoot, so to speak, was that I'd have even more of my pick of waves when a big south swell arrived. Who's going to play pecking order games in the lineup with a certifiable lunatic known as La Escopeta?

Lisa, I assumed, would bolt stateside, maybe back to her ex-boyfriend, who, as it turned out, she had continued to torture through all this with hints that they would someday once again be a couple. In her relentless domination game, Lisa excluded no one, gave up on no one, no quarter given. *No limits.*

So my plan sounded good, notwithstanding my agoraphobia and aversion to violence. Speaking of which, you'd think my stomach would be in an uproar here, no? Not so. A sort of calm settled in, contemplating my Wild West scenario.

A related issue: Have you of late noticed a lack of reference to my writer's queasy gut? What's up with that? Gone, cured, no more unpleasantness in my duodenal area! My theory is that my gut had been *pickled*. I think the centipedes had pretty much been *fossilized*. Or maybe they just lost heart due to my stamina, how I outlasted them. The Battle of Thermopylae comes to mind, metaphorically. When a few hundred Greeks held off an army of a million invaders. *Or so the story goes*, if you get my nonfiction drift.

I was still subject to my after-writing throes, though. But holy shit, *those* fuckers were worse than ever.

Back to my plan. I didn't want any witnesses to my O.K. Corral extravaganza in case Barry did decide to involve the authorities. Without witnesses and since Barry – predictably for a "dumb gringo" (Lisa's description) – speaks little Spanish, I might be able to bullshit my way out of it with the cops. Right: With the holes all over Barry's house and my literally-smoking guns, this would be a stretch. But down at Big Turkeys where the cops suggest you murder someone (and give you his address) to save them paperwork, and the best of them are still the same José Jimenez meets Inspector Clouseau comedy act as back in '97 when Max got whacked, my worries of serious legal problems were minimal.

Likewise, I wanted no witness to Lisa's by-the-hair expulsion from my life. Being the way she is, I knew without doubt she'd go screaming and bawling to the cops with tales of her violently psychotic mate. But again, with no witnesses, not a mark on her – except maybe a bare patch on her skull where the follicles gave way (possibly revealing a 666 tattoo on her scalp) – and the chauvinistic Latino culture, the cops and I would probably wind up at the cantina tipping Pilsens and swapping old ones of the "if they didn't have a pussy there'd be a bounty on 'em" variety.

So conditions had to be right. As part of Barry's avoidance of me, I assume, he'd made himself scarce, was over-nighting at a cabina near the Piña bar (of karaoke night fame); he was rarely in evidence during the continuing construction of his house.

So I waited for him to be at his house, Lisa to be home with me, and no one else around.

While we're waiting for conditions to be right, let's deal with the Meanwhiles, with which my sorry ass life and times during this period was jam-fucking-packed, and, thank the narrative gods for the needed rhythm, there's some humor coming, plus a victory for me, if you hang in.

CHAPTER FIVE

You call this a movie script? Give me a couple $5,000-a-week
writers and I'll write it myself.
Joseph Pasternak, movie producer

The day Lisa and I ran into Barry at the super in Golfito, I picked up an International DHL package at the puddle jumper office, which is just down the way from the super. The package contained the new *In Search of Captain Zero* screenplay, the result of the studio/producer having hired another screenwriter, the cost of whose labors was shared by Quiksilver, the mega-buckola surf-wear company that was now pitching in with the tossing of more money into the *Zero* movie-deal fire.

But a good question: Why would the studio/producers et al send *me* the new screenplay, given my persona non grata status (to say the least) with them (and Hollywood in general) and indeed with Sean Penn (the other contractual producer), whose brain was no doubt still squirming with fervent wishes for "something that resembles death" to befall my sorry ass? (But holy shit Sean would have been pleased to know how my real life was going!)

The answer to this good question resides in *timing*. As any standup comedian worth his salt will tell you, with jokes, with comedy/humor/ whatever, timing is everything: the efficacy of a punch line, i.e., whether you laugh or heckle the sap on stage, is determined by the timing with which it's delivered.

So in a sense, the *for me* sense, the punch line to the joke that was the *Zero* movie deal was at hand, and the timing was good for both my real life and our purposes here.* See, the end of the last contractual option period was fast approaching (February 18, 2005), which meant that come that date the studio/producers would not have the option of a re-option unless I

---

* I say *for me* because given that the deal started in July, 2001 and was still going nowhere at high velocity in February of 2005 (and continues its voyage to oblivion a year later as I write), its eventual fruition (a movie getting made) or abandonment (the cessation of money being thrown into the fire) seems unlikely to occur any time before the universe finally decides whether to keep expanding forever or start its contraction back to what physicists call the Big Crunch. Point being: It's unlikely I'll be around for either of these events.

chose to give it to them via an addendum to our contract. If I refused the addendum, in order to retain the rights to my book they'd have to buy it outright, the remainder of the purchase price (after the option money already paid) being 140 grand. Some fairly serious money, certainly from my point of view.

Before I press on with further ridiculousness: I hope you'll let me off the greedy shitball motherfucker hook when I say that I just wanted to get as much money as possible out of this fiasco, the whole 140 grand being my goal. Although I coveted the money itself, at this point I also needed some sort of a victory in my life. I hope you understand.

In describing my *Zero* deal legal position as February 2005 rolled around, the phrase *in the catbird seat* comes to mind, although I had to play this exactly right. Evidence of my catbird position is that in about mid January I started hearing from the producer, chit-chatty calls and emails, affable in the extreme, as if all had gone fine and dandy between us in this fiasco. In her transparent attempts at bullshitting me into giving them the option addendum she assured me that I would *love* the new screenplay, since it stuck so close to my book – she had evidently forgotten my various voicings of the catch-22 that there is no movie in my book.

But the point being that when, out of the usual sort of curiosity, I asked to read the new screenplay, the producer couldn't very well refuse me since she was desperate to butter me up into giving them the option addendum.

So the screenplay arrives on the day Lisa and I run into Barry at the super in Golfito and there is even more timing and symmetry in this, which should make you suspicious that I'm diddling with facts, i.e., *making up* some stuff: You'll just have to trust me on this matter since although I have a witness to the following scene in Lisa, it's becoming increasingly difficult to picture her backing me up in any assertions I might make in this narrative. The added timing and symmetry: While Lisa was at a muni office taking care of paperwork, with me waiting in the car, the producer called my cell for more bullshitting and to see if I got the new screenplay they'd DHL-ed. Lisa returned to the car sometime during the following:

Yep, I said to the producer, the screenplay is right here on my lap. I hadn't opened the package yet, figuring to stretch out on the living room couch at home, open it then, get the effect of its contents in one fell blast, so to speak – hence it would be better if I was lying down at the time. I mean I knew what would be in there, more or less. As the producer started in on how much the other writer loved and respected my book, plus me as a writer, I was inspired to open the package, figuring to take a glance at a random page as sort of a goofball accompaniment to the producer's ramblings. I didn't get any further than the title page. There were two mistakes on it; three, actually. Again: *On the title page.*

The writer, as part of his respect for me, had misspelled my last name in crediting me as the author of... "the novel" blah blah and so forth. *Novel?* My book of course is not a novel, which means fiction (right: m*ade up*); it's a memoir, nonfiction (right: *whatever that means*), a point that's pretty hard to miss if you're paying any attention whatsoever while reading it. So that's two mistakes. The third one is that in film credits the convention is you use the phrase "From the Book by"; you don't use "Novel" or "Memoir" or "Complete Crock of Shit" (I'm thinking of James Frey's book, should the movie deal I've heard about come to fruition) or whatever, in any case.

After my laughter subsided I pointed out all this to the producer (minus the James Frey aspect, since his book hadn't yet been exposed as a complete crock of shit), adding that three fuck-ups on the title page is not a good sign right out of the gate. I was able to laugh at the ridiculousness of this because I had not yet run into Barry at the super. That fucked-up turn of events would happen in a few minutes. So my mood had not yet gone to dark and borderline murderous.

As it turned out, it took a while to get through the new *Zero* screenplay, my being busy with border trips to arrange for the rearrangement of the love of my life's countenance and passing out while waiting for Hector's understudy; then the planning of my O.K. Corral extravaganza, plus the matter of the coming squatter invasion, plus being the eyes and ears of The Waterman Who Would Be King, plus keeping track of Logan and Ron's rumored deal-making, which maybe had to do with my assassination – by Hector's understudy for still more symmetry? Regarding this matter, I was still vacillating between not thinking about being assassinated and not caring if I was assassinated if I did happen to think about it; *that* fine distinction.

Right: Plus *getting through the day.*

Still another Meanwhile: My sex drive slid way over to the left-hand end of that spectrum after the Barry scene at the super. As sick a puppy as I was regarding sex with Lisa, I wasn't sick enough of a puppy to get past the ex-pro V-ball-player's dick images that would surface regarding what had transpired on my bed. The sporadic sex Lisa and I did have would usually be of this sort: It's the dark of night and we're in bed and I'm trying to mind my own business (meaning not conjuring specific ex-pro V-ball-player dick images), and suddenly Lisa is down there under the sheet rooting around and pretty soon locates my sorry-ass dick and with the expertise gleaned from her vast experience – and my dick having a mind of his goddamn own – she eventually gets the desired response and is grinding away on top, with me trying to get to the profound sense of fatigue and loss of essence as quickly as possible, which I do. Lisa immediately slides off saying, "Gotcha!" in obvious satisfaction, not of the sexual sort, but that she's been successful in causing me the loss of some of my essence.

I suspect that whatever fantasies I may have had during these trysts were of shootouts at O.K. Corral extravaganzas and, possibly, Doomsday Machines. Memory fails. (Yes, we'd come a ways since Lisa's "otherworldly" claim days, or, for that matter, me as a Sex God not wanting to think about mastodons after going boom. Or, for that matter, my assertion that with Lisa, *this is it*.)

During *all of the above* I exchanged calls on the coming Zero deadline with Steven, my treacherous, big-mouth attorney, whom I had still not fired. In fact, given *all of the above* (with some and-so-forths thrown in), I had nixed altogether the idea of firing him. Through the process of elimination I was starting to view Steven as my best buddy.

Steven's plan was to try to extort (not the word he used) another 10k or so out of the studio/producers for an option extension addendum. He doubted that they'd cough up the whole 140. This after the studio called and suggested, as they had exactly one year previously, that I extend the option for *free*. I'll not subject you to my reaction to this one. (A minor bright note/ bulletin from Steven: the executive who had written the memo extolling the director's outline as "soulful" and possessing "all the elements" had been canned. I had spoken to his replacement, however. Predictably, there was a shortage of wattage in getting *his* bulb to glow.)

Hold on. I forgot to mention my view of the new screenplay. How to best accomplish this in the fewest words? Try this: The title page was the screenplay's strongest element, for the humor in it, if unintentional. *The worst screenplay in the history of the world* assessment again comes to mind, meaning that the extant screen adaptations of my two books – not counting my own – were in a dead heat for the honor.*

In scheming how to best extort as much money as possible from this fiasco, I quizzed the producer regarding who, outside her little circle of idiots (not my exact words), had read the new screenplay. This was a vital question. No one, she said, to my relief. The new screenplay "needed a polish" before dissemination, she added, which the other writer was currently working on.

It needed a *polish*? To return to a *Titanic* allusion, this was like claiming that the ship, if raised, would only need some fresh paint before its next try at a trans-Atlantic crossing.

---

* Believe it or not, the new screenplay was written from the director's dumb-ass outline. When, on the phone, I voiced to the producer my *concerns* (that euphemism) about the screenplay, I referred directly to my response to the dumb-ass outline, which had caused the shit storm way back when and which had made them all look foolish *publicly*. Although I omitted the sarcasm, dulled the edge of my rapier wit, my critique was pretty much verbatim. This was somehow all new to her. At the end of the call she thanked me profusely for my insights, saying that I could "give a seminar on screenwriting." Truly, there is no way I could make up this shit.

The producer went on to inform me that after the polish they were going to send the new screenplay to a slew of Hollywood mega-folks, including Brad Pitt, with the notion of a Pitt/Penn match up. Hey, maybe there would be conflict between the two stars in deciding who plays my old buddy, Captain Zero (who, perhaps fittingly, had lost his mind) and who plays me (ditto, come to think of it).

Speaking of minds (and having lost them), mine wandered to a possible *Variety* headline:

Pitt Plus Penn Pugilize Pursuing Pal Pic Part!

Thing was, given her agenda (wheedling a cheap option addendum), the producer could not have done a dumber-ass thing than issue the Brad Pitt bulletin. In fact, the bulletin may have cost the whole gang of them $140,000. See, when I combined the Brad Pitt fantasy with the concept that no one outside her little circle of idiots had yet read the new screenplay, I realized that if I stuck fast and demanded the whole 140k, they'd give it to me. This is what I mean by the timing being perfect for my greed-driven purposes: As soon as Pitt's people or any people read the new screenplay and responded with something along the lines of "Whaddare ya, nuts?" a dose of reality might actually set in, making the coughing up of another 140k less likely.

By the way, assuming there's some bizarro alternative universe out there where this movie actually gets made, my preference in who will play me leans toward Pitt, since Penn, given his sentiments toward my sorry ass, would likely go into the tank. Meaning in his playing me.

But the final upshot: I told Steven to put on his lawyer game face, tell the fuckers that no addendum was in the offing and to put up or shut up, and by God they did. On February 19th, 2005, a check for $140,000 arrived at my accountant's office in North Carolina, to augment the $200,000 they'd already paid me for my once-brilliant adaptation, plus options.*

Aside from my dizzy spells and double vision and agoraphobia and the *all of the above* distractions in my life, and given that my mental state was a sandwich or two short of a picnic, that I was able to rally and outthink some of Hollywood's finest minds, including that of Steven, my treacherous, big mouth attorney, was pretty impressive, no?

But I wasn't yet finished with Hollywood in terms of greed-driven extortion; I was out of my mind and rolling now on a bunch of levels, aside

---

* The next day, February 20, 2005, I heard that Hunter S. Thompson blew his brains out at his home in Colorado. But Christ! Please! Can't I even have a small victory, i.e., extort six figures from Hollywood, without another whiz-bang zinger of a terminal loneliness trigger to offset it?

from the O.K. Corral extravaganza one. By way of explanation, a question: What about my deal to write the adaptation of my other book, *Cosmic Banditos*? It was now February, 2005, some six months after my meetings with John Cusack's people at New Crime Productions (plus my brink hovering at the Stanford particle accelerator). Shouldn't I have long ago finished the adaptation and shouldn't the movie itself currently be playing in a theater near you?

What's up with that deal?

If you'll remember, on my stateside trip six months previously I'd pitched my various bizarre thoughts on how to reinvent *Banditos* for the screen and had been given the okay by Cusack's people at New Crime. The plan was that I'd put that stuff in writing in the form of a preliminary outline. I somehow did so (no mean feat considering… *right, all of the above*) and emailed it to them in mid-September. Contractually and decorum-wise, they should have gotten back to me with notes within a couple of weeks, plus a go-ahead to start the screenplay itself. Guess what? Now, in February – again, six months, half a year later – *I had not yet heard from them*. Not a word.

If you're thinking I must have gotten cranky at this added example of Hollywood nonsense – think again. The *last thing* I needed during this period was a go-ahead to write a goofball comedy about The Meaning of Life. Without a recap of events since the previous summer/fall, which might raise the final page count here into four figures, let's just say that my mood was not exactly conducive to *comedic* thinking. Imagine going through election night with Clay then rising and shining all amped to write howler scene sequences and dialog about The Meaning of Life. Ditto with visions of strangling Doc Bruce and Lisa's Linda Blair act (while my sabotaged cell phone buzzed and blinked in my pocket) dancing in my head. Enough said, drift-wise.

So, that the folks at New Crime had somehow *just flat forgot* about their deal with my sorry ass – aside from being ridiculous – was a gift from the gods, narrative and otherwise. But now, in February of 2005, with my mood edging ever to the right-hand end of the demented spectrum, and with my *Zero* deal victory still fresh, I had Steven call New Crime to demand payment for the *Banditos* first draft screenplay that not only had I not written, but had been – and continued to be – *incapable* of writing.

A ballsy move, no? And New Crime coughed it up – another $50,000 or so going into my coffers – along with an apology for their tardiness. Even then, and certainly reviewing my behavior now as I write, my move, though legal, seems questionable. I mean, as I say, I *liked* the people at New Crime. (Plus, as you'll see, Cusack and New Crime subsequently did me a favor without which this book might not even exist.)

What can I say, except that I was not in the mood to cut *anyone* any slack.

Not only all this, fiscally, but I'd just sold two parcels of Pavones land Lisa and I had invested in, to the tune of another couple hundred grand. You'd think being financially flush would raise my spirits at least a smidgeon, no?

No. Or, rather, only indirectly. One day, as a way of *getting through the day*, I commenced work on a list of... no, not of women I've had sex with – that one was frozen-stuck at 119, the figure having gone up by one due to a change of heart about the alpha whore who semi-raped me, who was now included in the total* – but shitball motherfuckers who, with all my money, I could have professionally assassinated. My thought was that I'd hunt up Hector's understudy and make a lollapalooza of a package deal with him -- assuming he didn't assassinate me first via a deal with Logan/Ron.

Even limiting the list to people who'd annoyed me just since 2000, the turn of the millennium, I soon realized that Hector's understudy would probably have to do some farming out. Plus, with how long he'd be on my payroll, he'd probably hit me up for a dental plan.

To include my list here would be ridiculous, in terms of clarity and brevity (especially), as well as rhythm and pizzazz. I will say that I left out heads of state and corporate CEOs, figuring they would be above Hector's understudy's proficiency level – Bob Woodward was the closest to these types who made the final hit list. (Oprah would have been on it had I known at the time that she was going to stand behind the essential truth of James Frey's book.)† Still, the fucking thing was endless. Even after I crossed out all the Hollywood shitball motherfuckers (figuring that they were too dumb-ass to be held morally responsible for their behavior), it occurred to me that it would take a fortune more along the lines of Bill Gates's to get it all done, even considering Hector's understudy's already low per-hit going rate, without any package discount I might negotiate.

I exaggerate only slightly.

But I did blow off a little steam with my list, which was a positive.

So now February rolled into early March, and Barry continued to make himself scarce. (All this shit transpired in under two weeks: Busy, busy, no?) The one time he was home alone, a weekend with his workers off, Lisa was off somewhere, doing whatever fucked-up thing she was doing. And another time when it looked like conditions were perfect and, armed to the teeth, I stumbled in Barry's direction (I was having a dizzy, double-visioned day), a carload of his gringo friends arrived before I reached his

---

* My reasoning: Although money was involved in the semi-rape, I'd already paid her when the semi-rape was committed, so she must have semi-raped me for reasons other than money. See what I mean?

† That Oprah later tore Frey a new asshole only pissed me off further, since she was obviously reacting to the media's contempt that she hadn't done that in the first place.

property line.

But I persevered. I kept my Browning 12 and S & W .38 well-oiled and within easy reach, Lisa figuring this was related to the coming squatter invasion. I'd occasionally take the Browning 12 out and fire a round into the ground. It had misfired on me once, so I was worried. It's hard to think of a greater humiliation than a shotgun misfire while you're trying to blow a hole in the house of a shitball motherfucker who fucked the love of your life in your own bed. There's some depressing symbolism in that sort of turn of events, if you get my Freudian drift.

So as February became March my O.K. Corral extravaganza waited to happen. Waited until Something Happened Next, a lightning bolt that would change everything.

CHAPTER SIX

A problematical situation for which the only solution is denied
by a circumstance inherent in the problem.
Webster's Collegiate Dictionary

I still don't have a dictionary and have decided that on a matter of principle I'll make it to the end of this without one. I came across the above definition of catch-22 in Kurt Vonnegut's *Timequake* (in which *Webster's Collegiate Dictionary* is attributed), which is one of the few books I threw into my bag when I bolted from paradise back in October. Given my frequent use of the term, it's a nice coincidence that in *Timequake* catch-22 is formally defined, especially via a dictionary from Webster's, since I have a bone to pick with those bastards for the way they left out so many words vital to the understanding of this narrative in their mammoth *Webster's New Universal Unabridged Dictionary* (or *Webster's Fucking Dictionary*, WFD), my favorite example being *nonfiction*. (WFD lacking in *self-reflection* is up there too.) If you'll remember, I also took issue with Webster's for their use of needless and misleading words in the title *Webster's New Universal Unabridged Dictionary.*

A related question: What's with the word *Collegiate* in the above Webster's other-dictionary title? Knowing a bit about publishers, *those* shitball motherfuckers, I assume it's a point of sale device to get college students to buy the fucking thing, not only because there are a lot of college students out there (all but the dumbest asses of which are potential dictionary buyers), but also calculating that when the college students who buy *Webster's Collegiate Dictionary* graduate they'll figure they have to buy another dictionary now, since the *Collegiate* in the title no longer refers to their circumstance. Perhaps they'll graduate, so to speak, to *Webster's New Universal Unabridged Dictionary,* the implication of the title of which is that this one is the real thing, as opposed to the *Collegiate* one, which, they now must assume, was abridged, i.e., some words were left out, words they may need now that they're out in the real world.

I'm not kidding here. I'm dead serious. If you don't think the marketing pricks at Webster's were thinking along these general lines, you're not a fool, *not necessarily*, but you're edging along in that direction at a pretty good clip.

But the point being: We can't even dictionary-shop without getting gaslit.

A positive, though, is the above definition of catch-22, which is a beaut, I must admit. In fact, it's so good that I'm surprised Webster's didn't stick it somewhere on the cover, not only as a point-of-sale device to impress college students with the brilliance of their wordsmiths, but to inform them as to what they can expect from the college experience and then real life itself, if they don't hang themselves or take a flying leap from the psychology building's roof before cap and gown day.

A half-assed segue: Speaking of being gaslit by dictionary wordsmiths who tell us what catch-22 means and O.K. Corral extravaganzas and real life and falling in love with sociopaths and hanging yourself and taking flying suicidal leaps, the lightning bolt that changed everything was another chest x-ray, which informed me that I had lung cancer and would be dead within a few months.

You wanna talk about a banana peel?

CHAPTER SEVEN

*'Then you should say what you mean,' the March Hare went on.
'I do,' Alice hastily replied; 'at least – at least I mean what I say
– that's the same thing, you know.'*

Lewis Carroll

Writing from two months later (no, I'm not dead yet), and having decided to insert this chapter here (structure!), and having briefly broken my no-dictionary rule, I came across another mammoth motherfucker. The title: *Webster's Third New International Dictionary* (under that, the subtitle *Unabridged*). I'll not subject you to my analysis of this one, nor remark on its marketing theory's contempt for our intelligence, nor will I rhetorically inquire about the difference between *International* and *Universal* (I of course refer to my abandoned *WFD*), nor will I publicly wonder how either adjective applies to a book of *English language* usage, nor will I get outraged at the rampant disrespect for *words* evidenced by a dictionary publisher, nor will I get into more personal issues, like how important words are to my sorry ass.

But the real point is that I have big news. Predictably, it's of the *good/bad* variety. The good news is that I gave *nonfiction* a shot in *Webster's Third New International Dictionary, Unabridged* and guess what? It was fucking there! (Why is it not defined in a *Universal* dictionary but is in an *International* one, if both are unabridged?) The bad news is the definition, which is this: "Literary works other than novels or stories."

A question: What does this tell us?

The answer: Not a fucking thing – telling us what *nonfiction* isn't, is like defining *apple* by saying it's not a grape or a pomegranate. Not only that, but by including "stories" in the (very) short list of shit that *nonfiction* isn't, Webster's has its head even further up its ass (HUYA!), since it defines *story* thus: "A connected narrative of important events." Which means it's claiming that, say, history books – not to mention this current narrative – are not nonfiction, which they clearly are (putting aside your possible snide observation that the events of this narrative are of no importance).

Not a word about *making up stuff*, or not doing so, and of course no mention of *lying like a slug*, or not doing so.

If you think about it, the wordsmiths at Webster's are actually saying this: "*Nonfiction* is a load of horseshit."

The expression *I rest my case* again comes to mind.

One more question: Wouldn't it be nice if *someone* just *one time* came out and told the truth about *something*, instead of jerking us around?*

---

* Or, alternately, if they don't know the truth, say so. As in: "*Nonfiction*: We don't fucking know what it is."

CHAPTER EIGHT

Writing a book is a horrible, exhausting struggle, like a long bout of some painful illness.

George Orwell

First: The best of you out there, meaning as readers, are still laughing at the chest x-ray/cancer bulletin:

What's with this guy and his fucking life!?

I mean give me a break!

Still more looping: *You ain't seen nothin' yet*!

Some semi-nonfiction deceit semi-owning up: With my claim that my chest x-ray *informed me* that I had lung cancer and would be dead within a few months, I was doing some diddling, some parsing. Nothing on the order of "it depends on what the definition of 'is' is" from our 42nd president, or what *unsatisfying* means regarding one night stands from the love of my life, or the chickenshit non-definition of *nonfiction* from the wordsmiths at Webster's, or how the U.S. government defines the word *spread* when it says it only wants to *spread democracy*, but diddling and parsing nonetheless. See, after seeing the chest x-ray and after the doctor at Cima Hospital in San José hemmed and hawed and, avoiding eye contact with my sorry ass, rambled on about the *possibility* that I did *not* have lung cancer and the *possibility* that I would *not be* dead in a few months, I spent the next three weeks assuming I had lung cancer and would be dead within a few months. I mean with all the cigarettes and and-so-forths.

Turned out I had tuberculosis.

But see, in a very real sense, the x-ray *informed me* of what I claimed it did.

Still questionable, my diddling and parsing? Sorry.

No diddling, though, no parsing, when I said that the x-ray/lung cancer bulletin, false though it turned out to be, *changed everything*.

It changed everything for me and for my next door neighbor Barry and the façade of his house, which would now remain un-buckshot and .38 dumdum-peppered, although until now the shitball motherfucker didn't know that. It changed everything for Lisa, too, in that the hair-pulling expulsion from my sorry-ass life and times did not happen either. Instead, she got to do her Mother Teresa routine (proving once again that it's us against the world) and was also provided with a substitute for her discredited theory that substance abuse was the cause of my delusions that she was anything other than a perfect mate.

It was the tuberculosis! Now, along with my dizzy spells and double vision and agoraphobia and overall weakness and angst, the tuberculosis was precipitating chronic attacks of The Othello Syndrome! Plus Morbid Jealousy!

Whoopee for Lisa!

Tuberculosis used to be called consumption (and was invariably fatal). Consumption does what the word itself implies: it consumes you, saps you physically and psychologically and in my case maybe spiritually, since my spirit was already so severely sapped.

With my history of getting sick, my Cima doctor insisted on an AIDS test, figuring that was a possible cause of my immune system breakdown. An interesting concept, no? I'd had a negative AIDS test a few months before Lisa moved in with me and I hadn't fucked anyone else (or even considered it, until recently) since being with her, well over two years. So I said this to Lisa while we were waiting for the results: "Be interesting if I have AIDS, huh?" There was innuendo here.

Lisa: "It's not possible that I have AIDS." Straight face; no irony, no self-reflection.

The test was negative. Sort of a bummer, since had I had AIDS, Lisa would have also, since she would have given it to me.

This was too much to ask of life.

Another scene I'm fond of: We're in New York, at Sloan-Kettering, where I found out I had tuberculosis, not cancer. One of my doctors looked at my medical history, including the negative AIDS test. Asked me if I've been under undue stress, a question I'd heard enough times that the understatement in it had run dry.

When I related this to Lisa, including my answer that Yes, I've been under undue stress, Lisa said, "What do you mean, stress because of the problems with your screenplays?" Straight face; no irony, no self-reflection.

Witchdoctors claim that sociopaths do not have a "mental disease," disease as in "dis-ease," since they feel just fine about themselves and their behavior and inner life. I understand what they're getting at here (although they're on thin ice in their cavalier use of words), but I still take issue with it, at least in Lisa's case. For example, when Lisa said, "What do you mean, stress because of the problems with your screenplays?" I'm pretty sure she was not *consciously* gaslighting me. She may not have even been knowingly telling an untruth when she said it was impossible that she has AIDS.

411

I believe Lisa just rewrites history to suit a view of herself as a normal, good and honest person. What I'm getting at is a revision of my observation that sociopaths do not necessarily have a *mental disorder*. When someone can rewrite history *and believe the rewrite*, doesn't it mean something is very wrong? Does it really matter if this person feels fine about herself (is not in dis-ease) or does it even matter that she is successful in dealing with complex day-to-day problems, which Lisa is? And anyway, with her blurts and bizarre and transparent attempts to gaslight me and on and on, is this even a person who deals with life in a manner that is *sane*, notwithstanding her success in gaslighting other people?*

Lisa and I spent a couple of fun-filled weeks in New York, during which time I got another bulletin from paradise. One of my neighbors, whom I had helped sell some land and done other favors for, had heard about my health-related absence and took advantage of it. He was bulldozing an illegal road through my property to raise the value of the land I'd helped him sell.

Hooray for paradise!

But right: *Small stuff* in the overall picture.

Although the cancellation of the cancer/imminent-death bulletin was a relief – I *think* it was a relief – there was a long road to recovery ahead for my dis-ease-ridden, sorry ass.

I mean that on several levels, of course.

---

* Further evidence that a Lisa-screw needs clockwise rotation: On December 4th (2004), within hours of my leaving New York after my first dark moment (the Linda Blair act), Lisa started posting Amazon book reviews; the books were all of the self-help genre, dealing with delusional mates and psycho-jealousy (one is titled – what else? -- *The Othello Response*). In her critiques Lisa claims to be a victim of a delusional mate afflicted with The O Syndrome and recommends Al-Anon to her sisters in misery. This behavior one-upped the lunacy of her Al-Anon visits, since she was now not only gaslighting complete strangers (who could not buttress her lies), but strangers she would never even meet (Amazon readers). One way to interpret this behavior is that Lisa is indeed living in a world wherein she believes her own lies. (One of the other book titles contains the word *self-deception*. You gotta love that.) In this world there are two Lisas, one who fucks as many men as possible then lies and gaslights, and the other Lisa, who is the innocent victim of her delusional mate and is unaware of her soul-less counterpart. This would explain my dark moment: The first Lisa was thumbing through the magazine, but at my mention of *Evil*, the second Lisa briefly surfaced to shoot me a look, then retreated, and the first Lisa went back to magazine-thumbing. Something like that. I theorize (plus wax witchdoctory myself, for which I apologize), but this would also explain Lisa'a innumerable revealing blurts – the two Lisa's were continually fighting it out for control of her mouth. (The URLs to Lisa's Amazon reviews are on the adjunct website.)

CHAPTER NINE

"You know what you can do with free will?" said Prince.
"No," said Trout.
"You can stuff it up your ass," said Prince.

Kurt Vonnegut

As I write it's February 28, 2006. Carnival time on this little island, as it was two years ago when I had my rough night watching Sean Penn win an Oscar and I saw a woman in the audience who'd won an Oscar and with whom I'd had sex and then I imagined Lisa accepting an Oscar for faking so well her love for me. There's a double overhead north swell wrapping around the point just down the coast from where I write, perfect waves, what I live for, and I'm too dizzy and weak and shaky for a go-out.

One of my dogs back in Costa Rica, Tigre (a good boy), died, and I'm having a tough time with it. Marcos, my caretaker, told me this by phone. That Tigre may have been poisoned is not helping in my dealing with his death.

No, this time don't laugh, please, at the relentlessness.

So this morning instead of surfing I stayed here at home... not *home*, since I don't have one, but here where I'm living right now, the same house I was living in two years ago on Oscar night – the same TV set I watched on the table by my laptop – curled up like a poisoned slug on my bed and reading more from *Timequake*. I like to read, reread, K.V. when I'm stressed and depressed; it makes me feel more normal. In a sense reading K.V. is similar to unmotivated kindness, witnessing it, which I've said kills some of the hopelessness.

Here's some stuff from *Timequake* I underlined when I first read it and I hope you'll find it of more significance than female baboons copulating with all the males in their troop.

The premise of *Timequake One* was that a timequake, a sudden glitch in the space-time continuum, made everybody and everything do exactly what they'd done during the past decade, for good or ill, a second time. It was déjà vu that wouldn't quit for ten long years.

413

K.V. goes on to say that in "the rerun" you'd be:

...betting on the wrong horse again, marrying the wrong person again, getting the clap again. You name it!
Only when people got back to when the timequake hit did they stop being robots of their pasts. As the old science fiction writer Kilgore Trout said: "Only when free will kicked back in could they stop running obstacle courses of their own construction."

Amen on "obstacle courses of their own construction"! (*The Terminator* meets Franz Kafka!)

Trout didn't mind writing it [a certain short story] again. Rerun or not, he could tune out the crock of shit being alive was as long as he was scribbling, head down, with a ballpoint pen on a legal pad.

A-fucking-men!

The moral at the end of the only love story Kilgore Trout ever wrote is this: "Men are jerks. Women are psychotic."

But holy shit that sounds familiar!

Trout: "Listen, if it isn't a timequake dragging us through knothole after knothole, it's something else just as mean and powerful."

Ditto!
But the point being, I suppose: Here I am again on the run (a rerun) and fearful on this little island in the same house and it's again carnival time and the Oscars will soon roll around again (this Sunday) and I'm a mess again and so forth, so the premise of K.V.'s tale sort of strikes where I live. Plus, in writing this book, this nonfiction book, this memoir, I am of course creating my own timequake in reliving the same shit again.
So there's a double whammy effect.

Trout: "Wake up! For God's sake, wake up, wake up! Free will! Free will!"

When I'm finished writing this, will free will kick back in? (See this chapter's epigraph for my view on that.)
Speaking of free will, I may be losing control of this narrative, as if I ever did have control, as if I was ever more than just peripherally involved.

This chapter was supposed to be about something else completely. It was supposed to be about the three weeks during which I believed I would soon be dead. I was going to talk about my fear, not of death but of dying. I was going to talk about Mom's death, and how I tried to help, and how I wondered if she knew I was there right at the end, and if that was at all a comfort. And I was going to talk about some of the thoughts I had the night Mom died, and of which I am ashamed.

I was going to explain why the fear of dying alone resulted in my not blowing holes with my Browning 12 and S & W .38 in my next door neighbor Barry's house and of my not expelling Lisa from my life by her hair. How I preferred to have someone, even her, by my bedside when I was near death, even knowing she had faked everything and would be faking everything while I was dying. How I preferred having the devil there with me rather than being alone and wretched like my father was when he died, sprawled in the filth of his living room with the Christmas card I'd sent him unopened on the floor, and his body desecrated by his goddamn cats.

I was going to talk more about all my dis-eases and terminal loneliness and my dark shit, whatever it is, and repeat something I said earlier about the fragility of body and soul, and how closely the two are connected.

I also had a note to somehow work in how there are only two worthwhile pursuits in life, pursuits that keep you hanging in, body and soul, these pursuits being art and science – relationships with other human beings don't seem to cut it – and somehow as a Meanwhile I wanted to lay in a warning about science.

Trout: "Science never cheered up anyone. The truth about the human situation is just too awful."

The point I wanted to make is that you should be careful with science since even pure science and profound rushes of insight like $E=MC^2$ (a secret of the universe) can have awful repercussions for humankind, while nothing in art can be harmful. The reason for this is that science is lacking in something on some level, although I'm not sure what I mean by that. (That K.V. says these same things in his writings is one of the reasons I like reading him when I'm stressed and depressed. I guess it's comforting to know that although I may be stressed and depressed, nuts, maybe, I'm not alone.)

There's a joke I'm fond of that makes the point about science being lacking in something. It goes like this:

A scientist invents a way of creating life, of breathing life into dirt with a cosmic ray he's developed. He says to God, "Hey, God, I can breath life into dirt! We scientists don't need you anymore!"

God says, "Let me see."

The scientist sets up his equipment, a complex array of tubes and gauges and dials and a chamber where his cosmic ray gets focused just right. He picks up a handful of dirt and goes to put it in the chamber, where life will be breathed into it.

"No, no," God says. "Get your own dirt."

One person I've told that joke to is Stephon Alexander, the physicist who seeks to understand God through looking into first causes and playing jazz music on the saxophone. Stephon laughed his ass off.

Kilgore's Creed: "You were sick, but now you're well again, and there's work to do."

"Kilgore" is Kilgore Trout, of course, the fictional character K.V. uses in many of his books as an alter-ego. K.V. treats Trout very badly, puts him through all sorts of hell, in order to see how Trout handles it. If you're going to write a book (not *someday*): Put your characters through all sorts of hell to see how they handle it. (I think K.V. gives this advice somewhere as well. So be it. None of my advice is at all original.)

The above, Kilgore's Creed, is what Trout tells everyone when the timequake, the rerun, runs it's course and we all have free will again. Trout, in spite of everything K.V. puts him through, in spite of the hopelessness he feels down in his bones, is giving it a shot.

We have to love him for that, as K.V. loves him.

CHAPTER TEN

She lays it on with a trowel.

William Congreve

The summer of 2005.

I was up at Montauk, my former home, in a rented cottage. A battery of tests indicated that aside from the TB, the consumption, I had Lyme disease, babisiosis (a tick-borne virus worse than Lyme disease), and another illness that I can't pronounce, any one of which, much less all three, saps your strength and lays you low in just about every way you can be laid low. One of my doctors said he didn't understand how it was that I was upright in his office at that moment. And I couldn't treat two of three of the new ones because the antibiotics conflicted with the TB meds, which I had to take for a total of eight months, until December.

A complete immune system breakdown.

During this time Lisa was down at Pavones, finishing the spec house we were partners in, plus still fucking my next-door neighbor Barry. Aside from the power of her pussy, Lisa's business acumen was a great source of pride for her, which she sharpened in researching Costa Rica land-buying practices, as real estate prices in paradise were rising almost monthly. One time shortly after our New York trip and my tuberculosis diagnoses, she returned from a Golfito run saying she'd gotten a ride back from Esteban Mora; he had shown her a parcel he "owned" just up the road in Pilon. The parcel, Lisa said, was spectacular, and maybe worthy of our investing in.

Right. Let's get involved in a land deal with the family that murdered an American in order to steal his land, had probably considered murdering me, and is well-known for its various forms of extortion and swindling. Although I was still on surface-friendly terms with the three Moras (Gerardo, Mayela and Esteban), as Lisa well knew, this was motivated by my information-gathering obsession regarding not only Max's murder but the continuing local intrigues, plus my spying for The Waterman Who Would Be King, from whom the Moras had expropriated most of the land they "owned." And from Lisa's description of Esteban's parcel, it was almost certainly Dannyland.

Plus, the idea of our investing in anything *together* again was absurd, although Lisa, with her continuing self-gaslighting, didn't know that. Of the "couple" that we constituted, she was the delusional one.

Some quick psychobabble that may actually be valid: Doc Stout and others have pointed out that sociopaths often target people of higher than average... virtue. By which I simply mean that my borderline obsessive abhorrence of deceit of all sorts – closely related to my need to know the truth about *everything* – and my going out of my way in exposing it is not new to this narrative. Suffice to say that I've walked the walk (and paid some prices for it). Lisa knew this right from the get-go.

She would show my self-righteous ass a thing or two about deceit of all sorts and my need to know everything!

She'd fool a deceit-obsessed writer writing about *her*!

You wanna talk about a domination game?

Holy shit: The Sociopath Heavyweight Championship of the World!

Here's an email I got from Lisa while she was fucking my next door neighbor Barry, plus, as it would turn out, "anything that moves" (to quote a former victim of her gaslighting):

> > I read something 2 days ago about people who have life
> > changing experiences that are not based at all in reality.
> > The author wrote (NYTimes) that the people
> > reimagine the experience and that every time they do
> > that, they have a serious physisiological (sic) response
> > and their blood pressure goes up and all that, and that
> > makes them all the more convinced that they are right,
> > that what they believe is true. And I think maybe that's
> > part of all this, that you think about me being with
> > another man, and that of course upsets you, and
> > because you're so upset, you (subconsciously) believe
> > you are more and more right.

Now it was my *blood pressure* that caused my delusions!

No, no way I could make up this shit.

More ridiculousness: I mentioned that Lisa's New Year's Day whopper about having "accidentally" put her birth control pills in storage would have a payoff if I didn't challenge her on it, right? Six months later, with me at Montauk, she at Big Turkeys, here comes the payoff. I call Lisa and tell her I'm going to her storage area (where I also had some stuff). I transcribed this one, hence the quotes:

"Where are your birth control pills in there? I'll grab them and bring them down when I come back."

Not thinking before speaking: "I *thought* they were in there. I thought they might've fallen into a box…" Here she shuts up.

Me: "Why do you say you *thought* they were in there?"

"Huh?"

"It sounds like you know they're not there and I haven't even looked."

"What's this all about?"

"What box do you figure they're in?"

"I'm not going to play this fucking game!"

Here she hangs up on me.

There are no birth control pills in her storage, of course. I look in the boxes and bags she put in there the previous winter and even the ones from the previous summer. I take the trouble to do this because I know there will be still another payoff, if I'm again patient.

I'm way ahead of Lisa on everything.

It's sort of fun. Right: In the morbid sense.

CHAPTER ELEVEN

The life of every man is a diary in which he means to write one story, and writes another; and his humblest hour is when he compares the volume as it is with what he vowed to make it.

Sir J.M. Barrie

When I first started writing this narrative three years ago (almost to the day, today being March 5, 2006)* my theory was that the story of my *Zero* book deal/demented editor/turncoat book agent, that fiasco, would provide the essential conflict, while my relationship with Lisa would balance that out since with Lisa I'd finally got what I wanted, and what Mom wanted for me, i.e., someone to love in this world. I'd work in a lot of surfing and life in paradise too. The movie deals would be a bit of subplot comic relief, since at the time I figured How bad could they go?†

The expression *living in a dream world* comes to mind. Point being: If you're going to write a book (etc.), when you start you are invariably living in a dream world about how it's going to turn out. But you have to believe it will turn out the way you figure it will; otherwise you'll be too paralyzed with self-doubt to start the fucker. In other words, keep the living-in-a-dream-world observation in mind while simultaneously not keeping it in mind.

Speaking of dream worlds, or of *nightmare* worlds, during the world of last summer (2005), recovering from all my diseases and beset with terminal loneliness and my own dark shit, whatever it was, I felt like I was *dying*, more so than when I was sure I was dying. I'd somehow make it to

---

* Tonight is Oscar night. In a ridiculous attempt at exercising my free will (rerun avoidance), I don't intend to watch. Oh. And today is another anniversary: it was exactly a year ago that I got the chest x-ray/cancer bulletin. I'm considering throwing a party tonight. A theme party of some sort, possibly.

† Bush and his criminal empire-building wars would be good, timing-wise, I figured, but I wasn't sure how. **
    ** That tens of thousands of people would die in Bush's criminal empire-building wars and that somehow, anyhow, I could perceive this as good, shows how cold-hearted writers can be, even ones who more or less claim to be pure of heart, like me. What was that Robert Penn Warren quote I use in Part One? "…if you're pure of heart you don't go into the book-writing business in the first place." A-fucking-men!

the beach, sometimes even for a surf go-out. My Montauk friends would say I looked better, had gained a little weight, and maybe so, but my... my spirit... was more than sapped. It was like it... had poofed out.

Hold on. *Poofed out.* Wasn't I supposed to be writing my goofball comedy about the universe poofing out and The Meaning of Life?

Sort of.

What does that mean?

I was sort of writing it.

How do you *sort of* write something?

To resurrect one of my explanations of how Hollywood works: It doesn't matter.

In the midst of sort of writing my goofball comedy about The Meaning of Life I called New Crime and hemmed and hawed about being sick and then, getting disgusted with myself, owned up. I told the woman executive – the original one who in 2001 had still been nice when I threatened her boss, John Cusack, and whom I liked and still like very much – everything. *Everything* meaning about how the love of my life was a full-blown sociopath and about this book and how I had to finish it or my head would explode, words to that effect. I told her I needed to suspend writing (sort of writing) my adaptation in order to finish this book.

Keep in mind that they'd already coughed up my whole first draft fee, start up and hand-in money, months ago when I'd more or less extorted it from them for forgetting about my sorry ass.

Talk about thin ice...

New Crime conferred and called me right back, didn't make me wait and sweat, God bless them, and told me not to worry. Take as much time as I need to write my book and heal myself and then we'd get back to the adaptation and I almost wept with relief. I mean for me to disappoint the only people who had treated me fairly (and after I'd more or less extorted money from them) would have been too much on top of everything else.

This was more than six months ago and they still haven't hassled me, although I'd said I only needed a couple of months to finish this book and heal myself.

A couple of months?

Talk about denial and living in dream worlds *and* thin ice...

CHAPTER TWELVE

Leaving can sometimes be the best way to never go away.
Cathy N. Davidson

Here's how that summer went and why I allowed Lisa to be at my house still fucking my next door neighbor Barry in my upstairs office bed, plus fucking whomever else she was fucking, plus gaslighting whomever she was gaslighting: Momentum.

Momentum explains that summer. When you're as sick and sapped and fucked up as I was, momentum rules. Whatever's going on, you just let it keep going on.

If you're sleeping you try to keep on sleeping.

If you're lying on the couch you keep on lying on the couch.

If you make it to the beach and you're sitting there on the sand, you just keep on sitting there on the sand.

Whatever.

Lisa was both the exception to the momentum rule and the best example of it. How it went: I left Pavones in late May, went up to Montauk, telling Lisa I'd get better medical treatment there, when the real reason I went was to get away from her. It was fuck the uncertainty principle – finding an ending to all this – and whatever dark shit and other sick puppy shit that was going on with me. Enough! But the momentum factor prevented me from throwing Lisa out of my house, by her hair or otherwise, as it prevented me from resurrecting and carrying out my O.K. Corral extravaganza. Between finishing the spec house we were partners in and worrying about my dogs and my house being untended, I just let her and my next door neighbor Barry and everything slide. Momentum.

I would just have to live with the fucked-up things she would do while living on her own at the home I built in paradise. I'd get her out of there when I felt better.

A Meanwhile. When I left in late May, Danny Fowlie arrived in Costa Rica to begin the recapture of his Pavones empire, having gotten permission from the federal parole people to travel. He arrived in San José the night before I flew out, planning on driving down to Pavones the next day. Danny had brought an entourage and had secured a local government spook for physical protection, a bodyguard. That he would be assassinated while in-country was a possibility. Given the astronomical rise in the value of his more than 6,000 acres of prime coastal property (now worth in the tens of millions), most of which had been (according to Danny) illegally misappropriated while he was in the clink, the list of shitball motherfuckers who had motive to wax The Waterman Who Would Be King's ass was... if the phrase *all but endless* made sense, I'd use it. It was the same list of people I had problems with, come to think of it, plus a few more.

We had breakfast that morning. Danny seemed fit and raring to go, ready for his historic return to the place he had created. Said he was worried about me, my health, and that I didn't look good. I'd be all right, I said, I lied. But, shit, I wanted to go with him and see how it would go down at the end of the road – on top of the Kipling-esque element there was a Cargo Cult vibe as well[*] – but my need to get away from Lisa was urgent.

Although we'd conferred by phone weekly since the previous summer when I visited him in California, it was good to see Danny again, and talk some story with him. I told him to visit my house, see what I'd created; Lisa was expecting him. I didn't tell him about Lisa, what she was and so forth, and that it was all over between us but the final poofing out, although I was concerned that, for whatever reason, she'd subject Danny to her PM campaign against me.

I wished Danny the best, said I'd be in touch from Montauk, and flew the down south coop later that day.

As June became July, Lisa's plan to return to the states for a visit resulted in my return to Pavones for that month, notwithstanding my momentum problem. I missed my pups, missed the wave, and the chance to be in my home without Lisa was a circumstance I'd literally dreamed about. Lisa had invaded my life barely two months after the completion of construction in 2002; I had no images of homelife that were not illusory or ugly. Plus, wherever Lisa was, I wanted to be elsewhere, preferably on a different continent.

We collided in San José on July 6th, me coming, Lisa going.

---

[*] As the story goes: Back in the mid-1980s when Danny bolted to go on the run from the law, his final gesture was to dump out his airplane window a few thousand dollars in small local currency, which fluttered down onto the Big Turkeys campesinos as if from heaven. Danny denies the story and I tend to believe him, but it has nevertheless made it into local lore. Hence the Cargo Cult vibe.

CHAPTER THIRTEEN

*I've often felt that those times when you can [write] or make love
with great energy occur when your best and worst motives are
working in cooperation for once.*

Norman Mailer

July 6th, San José, Lisa going, me coming.

It would have been nice had we collided at the Balmoral, rather than at the El Presidente (right across the walk street, so close!), for nostalgia and symmetry's sake, since so much of our history lay at the Balmoral: our initial lust-consummation after our first kiss, the airport kiss that, Lisa claimed, "changed my life;" the incident when Lisa claimed she was out shopping all morning with only the room key on her; her "switching taxis" to get there in the course of the worst moment of *my* life, and so forth. The Balmoral was *our* place.

During this collision, in the midst of a bout of crazed fornicating, Lisa begged me to go get a whore to join us: "I want to watch you fuck another woman like this." I can use quotes here because I surreptitiously audio-taped the sex and the conversation leading up to it.

But by God Lisa was crazed, out of her mind, not only with lust but with something else as well. Triumph. See, with Lisa's "Gotcha!" semi-rapes of my sorry ass the only sort of physical union we'd had for many weeks, now with my resurrected Sex God status, my crazed fornicating, I was back in the fold where sex is power, my passion testimony to her dominance.

But my crazed fornicating was fueled by resurfaced rage, not passion. Not only rage, but the sure knowledge, knowledge that Lisa did not share, that this would be the last time. This knowledge, I'm thinking now these months later, set free in me, or rather conjured up in me, that which ruled Lisa but which was buried deep inside me. Something deep and dark and mindless and wild and yet cold -- I crossed briefly that night to the place Lisa lived.

It was now reciprocal. Lisa meant nothing to me; if there is less than that, then it was that. But I was doing the dominating, not she, and the correctness and symmetry of that aroused me, physically sick and spiritually sapped though I was.

I have no recollection of my thoughts, my inner life, during our crazed fornicating; I extrapolate, theorize here. On the tape: I said little as Lisa went on and on mid-fuck about nothing and hence about everything; a feral grunt, a mumbled agreement as I banged and heaved; I wasn't listening. And then Lisa was gone from under me, although we were far from finished with the fornicating, and she was jumping around naked on the bed blabbing, blabbing, go get a whore, please, blah blah, so ecstatic that I was back in the fold and I watched her – I do remember this – with interest both detached and intense, her thick dark mane a dreadlock tangle of furry snakes and she was like some wicked foxy witch from your wildest sicko porno fantasy, glistening with sweat and female juices, eyes glowing in the semi-dark of the El Presidente, and I was idly wondering what new shit would be revealed even as I could hardly wait to resume the fornicating.

Nothing, no new shit, was revealed. I knew it all. So I thought. Over. So over. So I thought.

Over. (So I thought.) Endings. Again, symmetry: An incident from the very beginning comes to mind now as I write about this false ending; it did not consciously occur to me as I fornicated with Lisa that night. It was there, though, this incident, the recollection of it, and had been there constantly during our relationship as the initial sign of what I was in for. I've been wondering when it would surface, structure its way in to this. It will now, I realize.

Lisa had just arrived at my little end of the road paradise for her first visit and it was the first or second day at my home after we flew down from San José after our initial lust consummation at the Balmoral and we were going at it on my big bed. It was daylight, I recall, and in the midst of our going at it, and with an intensity that had to come from that deep and dark and wild yet cold inner place where she lives, Lisa cried out, *"God, I love to fuck!!!"*

Italics, exclamation marks (how many?)… I try capitalizing… technique…

Writerly conventions fail, utterly, to convey the depth of her disclosure, the wanton truthfulness of it. How to describe how a wolf sounds, let alone interpret its baying at the moon? Lisa's exhortation was not meant for my ears, although it was not an accidental admission, a blurt, like so many to come. She was baying at the moon.

I struggle here with words. More than usual. I move them around until they sound right, look right, flow right, but all they impart is an impression of an impression, spectral shadows on the cave wall thrown by firelight; that allusion comes to mind. I have not connected with the real stuff of what I thought or felt or even did or saw that night, let alone what was going on with Lisa. (Is this whole narrative like this? Like my tinnitus, my ear ringing, is it so loud and yet so forlornly chimerical as to be inaccessible to all but my sorry ass?)

But I'll try this: I believe there is that deep and dark and mindless and wild and yet cold place where Lisa lives in all of us, in the best of us, a place where we can do anything and if *God I love to fuck!!!* is what moves us, we do that and we do it with *no limits*. It was my fascination with this, my being *drawn* to this, as much as anything that led me so far astray and caused me to hang in for so much obsession and pain. Yes, I wanted to *know everything*, find an *ending*, all that, but this was the real deal, the sick puppy shit, the dark shit that had grabbed me and held me for so long.

And I purged it, got it out of my system, that night at the El Presidente, the last time I fucked Lisa.

PART SEVEN
Butterfly Effects

CHAPTER ONE

It circulated for five years, through the halls of fifteen publishers,
and finally ended up with Vanguard Press, which, as you can
see, is rather deep into the alphabet.

Patrick Dennis

As I write from this little island it's March 15, 2006. The Ides of March. Supposed to be bad luck or some such, right? Julius and Brutus, *et tu Brute* and so forth, a knife in the back courtesy of a friend, and... hold on... and it was a *surprise*? How could Caesar not see *that* shit coming? I guess I'm not the only one not paying attention.

But what I'm getting at: I have exactly one month to finish this book, my ticket back stateside being for April 15, and my passport expires a few days later, on the 23rd, so I really can't miss that flight. I suspect that if I showed up at customs back at The Fatherland with an expired passport it would be The Enemy Combatant Line for my sorry ass. But still, why the self-imposed deadline for this book?

Symmetry. Finish it here on this little island where it started. Started contemporaneously with Bush's criminal empire-building war, the second one, the one after Afghanistan and the one before the next one, probably Iran. Christ. The lies and hypocrisies plus the greed-driven death and misery and horror while I've been writing this, living it, my little problems. But the lies and hypocrisies plus the greed-driven death and misery and horror are not what's important.

What's important is that I believe I've found a publisher for this book. (I know it must seem obvious to you that I found a publisher, but bear with this weird nouveau post-modern or post-post modern or deconstructionist or whatever it is shit.) A UK outfit called Humdrumming. Small, very "independent," run by a bunch of writers and other lunatics, even some actors.

Actors. Whoa.

But this has been my plan all along. Find a UK publisher, get this book in print, then use the edition to get a U.S. deal, maybe with a mid-size house with some balls (and which will overlook my persona non grata status and all the potential lawsuits because they smell money), plus some pizzazz and distribution clout. My reasoning in going the UK-first route is this: *Nothing stinks like a pile of unpublished writing.*

This was my runner up as a chapter epigraph (from Sylvia Plath), and holy shit is it the truth. If you're going to write a book, actually fucking *do it*, don't visit a publisher first, their offices, not that they'd let you in. You do go in there and it's like some sort of writer's version of The Holocaust: Manuscripts everywhere, manuscripts stacked up like the corpses in those godawful old death camp newsreels; manuscripts as door stops, manuscripts jammed between the air conditioner and the window sash to keep the foul air in; manuscripts peeking out from other manuscripts, two manuscripts – maybe a Civil War anthology and a cookbook – riffled together like decks of playing cards shuffled but not squared; manuscripts on the door-sill with muddy boot prints on the title pages; manuscripts massively unread but all somehow soiled, and the shitball motherfucker behind the desk, if you can see him over another teetering pile, looks up from a John Grisham or Dan Brown paperback and gestures at a pile of manuscripts on the floor shaped vaguely like a chair, offering you a seat, saying with an accent from *Stalag 17,* "You haf a manuscript mit you? Ahhh. Put it over... zere."

You find yourself at a publisher's office, don't go in the bathroom, maybe see some poor sap's obsession and pain in there, the first chapter half gone, the pages having been torn off one by one, if you get my drift.

And listen: These are the manuscripts that made it past the mailroom, the lucky ones. I talk about Writer Hell, right? Where Bob Woodward is going to go? Writer Hell is a publisher's mailroom. Think *dumpsters* brimming with obsession and pain, cackling, demented goons with Rosemary's Baby's eyes glancing at return addresses, the cackling rising to hysteria (at a manuscript submission from Peoria), then, maybe using actual pitchforks skewering and over-the-shouldering manuscripts into the dumpsters, the cackling now harmonizing with the beep beep beep of a garbage truck in reverse, come to haul the stinking mass of manuscripts away...

...or maybe they have their own oven, a manuscript crematorium, right on the premises...

I exaggerate only slightly.

Publishers are demons, there's no doubt about it. Another epigraph possibility (William James).

But why the UK? Aren't publishers all the same? Isn't a shitball motherfucker a shitball motherfucker, notwithstanding he says tom-aaah-to and I say tom-ayyy-to? Sure, but as far as I know, at least I'm not persona non grata in UK publishing, not yet, on top of everything else. Plus, the Brits don't like us over here, with our mega-conglomerate publishing houses and our Hollywood pretensions and our George W. Fucking Bush and so forth, so with this anti-everything-Yank narrative I might actually do some reverse petard-hoisting with the UK motherfuckers, if you can wrap your mind around that convoluted allusion. I mean, right?

You have to live in *some* hope to get through the day.

But yes: Get this fucker in *print*.

There's even some bizarre symmetry in how I hooked up with this outfit, and this will bring us back to last summer (2005), which I need to do anyway. See, some lunatics in Canada came up with a stage version of *Cosmic Banditos*. A play.

I shit you not. My goofball comedy about The Meaning of Life ran for ten days at an arts festival in Vancouver. And it was a hit! They were rolling in the aisles, apparently.

The mind boggles.

Aside from the mind boggling, one result was that hearing about this at Montauk I briefly felt better about myself, maybe ten minutes worth of that, but you take what you can get. The other thing was that the play was rave-reviewed by some nutcase up there, a smart, funny, literate nutcase. I emailed him with a Thank You and one thing led to another and it turned out he's hooked up with this UK Humdrumming outfit. He read Parts One through Five of this fucking thing and boom! it looks like we have a deal. In fact, things are going so smoothly – *swimmingly*, as they say across the pond – that I'm waiting for the boom-lowering. Speaking of booms.

We'll see how it goes. Like with the editing, for example.

Editing. Editors. Publishers. Last summer. Montauk. Me. Sick and sapped. A writer friend connected me with his publisher, a small, regional one that was impressed by my track record (and being small and regional didn't know I'm persona non grata) and wanted to read this, so I sent Parts One through Four. I got a quick initial response. Having read the first few chapters of Part One, the head person there, the only person there since it was a one-woman show, emailed saying she likes it… but…

…but looking at all my Word files and extrapolating to how long this book will be, she says, "Your book should come in at about three-hundred or so pages." Says this having only read the first few chapters.

A question: Didn't the words *I don't have to read your book to know how long it should be* sink in, plus my *attitude* about that? You know, my view of *demented* editors? I mean it's one thing to think what she was thinking, but how the fuck could she *say it to me*?

I let her read the whole thing. She wants to publish it. I even let her do some editing on Part One. All the while I'm thinking Sayo-fucking-A-nara, Jack. But I let her jump through hoops and get excited so then I could say, Nahhh.

No slack cutting. I am *not in the mood*.

CHAPTER TWO

I feel so miserable without you, it's almost like having you here.
Stephen Bishop

Imagine this. Montauk, August of 2005, my little rental cottage. I'm slumped slug-like on the couch in front of the tube, the consumption and Lyme disease and the other tick-borne microbes pulsing, plus I've been working on the nonfiction book you are now reading since 4 AM and hence I'm also beset by my after-writing throes. So add some profound fatigue and loss of essence to the mix. Plus terminal you-know-what, which lingered even after the purging of my dark shit at the El Presidente. I'm not drooling, not exactly, but that's only due to the cant of my head being such that the drool pool collecting in the hollow of my cheek has not yet overflowed from my slack mouth.

CNN. Rumsfeld is holding a press conference and he's saying that the media in their reporting of the war in Iraq do not have the *perspective* to point out that the United States, having rid Iraq of a monstrous dictator – our goal all along – now only wishes to give the Iraqi people democracy. Christ. A double doozey/whammy/whopper. Rumsfeld rambles on, saying *the spreading of democracy* has always been the goal of United States foreign policy, plus ridding the world of monstrous dictators. Rumsfeld, unable to work up moral outrage or indignation as he goes on about the media's lack of perspective, is sad. In fact, he actually says this, says he's *sad* at the lack of media perspective.

The spreading of democracy. Although due to my condition I'm barely paying attention, I notice that none of the media asks Rumsfeld to name even one genuine democracy the United States has supported in the last hundred years, as opposed to subverting or outright overthrowing genuine democracies. I'm able to notice this failure on the media's part because it's not necessary to pay attention to do so. It's only necessary to be alive on planet earth.

But yes, it's *sad*, the media's lack of perspective.

And the monstrous dictator he got rid of? Perspective? From 1983 – 84, as Reagan's Middle East Envoy, Rumsfeld's primary mission was to cement relations with Saddam Hussein, the monstrous dictator, and one way he did so was to assure the monstrous dictator that poison gas components (and anthrax spores) would continue to flow via U.S. corporations, along with helicopters, so the monstrous dictator could continue dropping poison gas on other human beings. No, none of the media points out any of this – nor do they point out that if Rumsfeld were to be tried at a Nuremberg-type venue and if there really were *rule of law* in this sorry-ass world he would undoubtedly be found guilty and hanged by the neck until dead for actively aiding and abetting genocide – notwithstanding that, presumably, they all have been alive on planet earth.[*]

Yes, it's sad, though, the lack of media perspective.

As I click off CNN – enough media perspective for today – and get up from the couch and weave my way over to my little office to check emails for bad news, I may have thought of Georgie O., that perennial optimist. (Memory fails.) I'm actively drooling now. My double vision kicks in so I have to cover one eye to read the email from my would-be new editor saying how long this book should be without reading it, after she'd just read about a past demented editor saying the same thing about my last book. Since I haven't yet hatched my plan of revenge, all I come up with as a reaction to the email is a moan.

While I'm staring mindlessly at the computer screen with the email on it the phone rings. The phone is in the living room, where I just witnessed Rumsfeld's sadness at the lack of media perspective. So I have to somehow make it back there. I do. There are two phones on the coffee table. I cover one eye. Now there's only one phone. Good.

It's Lisa. She's back from Costa Rica. She's at her storage area. Says this: "I found the birth control pills. They were in a box marked 'Toiletries.'"

There is actually a victory here in that I saw this coming back in June when Lisa didn't think before speaking on the phone from paradise and in effect admitted to lying about accidentally putting the b.c. pills in her storage. See, I knew she'd eventually "find" the pills in her storage. I even have this prediction in my notes on the call: "Lisa will 'find' the b.c. pills." This was why I'd searched her storage area so thoroughly, although that was a formality. I knew Lisa would "find" the b.c. pills because of the resulting double-duty: One, this would prove she wasn't lying about accidentally putting the pills in storage, plus, Two, it would prove I've lost my mind,

---

[*]   A good place for a reminder: The documents and other public-record proofs that make these assertions (plus the above observation about U.S. foreign policy and democracy subversion) inarguable are archived on the adjunct website.

since the pills were right there in a clearly marked box.*

Hold on. In our imagining of this ridiculous sequence we need to do a flashback, to what we imagine I'm remembering as Lisa tells me she found the b.c. pills in her storage.

Flashback three months, to May, just before I went up to Montauk from Big Turkeys to get away from Lisa, telling her I'll get better medical treatment in the States. My passport wallet comes up missing. I just had it the day before, up in my office. Lisa and I search the office, look everywhere. Christ. *Everything* is in there, my passport and credit cards, Costa Rica bank book, driver's license, even the *copy* of my passport. You name it. I'm freaked. Third World country with no I.D. whatsoever. (I'd be back to Enemy Combatant status.) We search the office for a half hour, scour it. I look everywhere ten times, one of *those* deals when you can't find something and are going nuts. I'm already fucked up and now I'm more fucked up. I hardly sleep that night, even with Lisa's angst pus removal massage, the last of that bullshit, as it will turn out.

The next afternoon I'm in my office crunched up under my desk futzing with my desktop computer terminal, meanwhile still freaking out about what I have to do to get my replacement I.D. I'm maybe wondering about the accommodations at Guantanamo Bay. (Memory fails.) Then, Lisa's voice, Lisa saying, "Look what I found."

"What?"

"Look what I found!"

My passport wallet. Lisa points at my desk. "It was right there." Right there on my desk in plain view. I'm so shaky I go and sit on the office bed, the one Lisa fucks Barry on. I'm vibrating. Lisa sits down by me and puts her hand on my shoulder. "You've been sick for so long," she says gently. Which explains my not seeing my passport wallet right there in plain sight.

I've been sick for so long. Explains my delusions. Explains everything.

It actually does.

Lisa thinks I'm vibrating because I think I'm losing my mind. The reason I'm vibrating is because I really, *really* want to strangle her. Right then and

---

* A bit of perception management failure on Lisa's part: She never asked me if I found the b.c. pills after the call in June (before I went to her storage), and I never brought up the subject again. So, if they were there all the time, why would she say *she* found them? Wouldn't she say, "I guess you found them back in June, since they were in a clearly marked box"? But my point here is that if you're going to lie about *everything*, you really have to stay on your tippy-toes. What you really need is a chart listing all the lies you've told and how they interconnect with other lies and other things you've said or not said. Sort of a family tree of lies.**

** Bush and his gang would have to go one step further, maybe have a Lie Room, like the War Room in *Doctor Strangelove*. You know, with The Big Board, to keep track of their lies – instead of the flight path of a B-52 bent on ending life on earth.***

*** There's symmetry in the above allusion to *Strangelove*: Bush's lies could likewise result in ending life on earth.

434

there, get it over with. Christ, I'm thinking, I could really do it.

In case it hasn't dawned on you: If my passport wallet was sitting right there in plain sight why didn't Lisa herself find it yesterday when she helped me search the office for a half hour or when we both searched it again this morning? Two possibilities: Either she's losing her mind also – some real couple's togetherness – or she didn't think before gaslighting me.

But again, in her twisted way Lisa couldn't lose here. If I accuse her of what she did – hiding my passport wallet to drive me insane – she can say, "Now Allan thinks I hid his passport wallet to drive him insane!" It truly is a motif: Do something too horrendous to be believable then, when I bust her on it, use my busting her on it to prove I'm insane.

I don't strangle Lisa. I don't do or say anything. I just continue vibrating for a while. Momentum.

Back to the scene at Montauk. I've just flashed-back to the passport wallet maneuver after Lisa called saying she found the b.c. pills after getting the email from my would-be new editor after witnessing Rumsfeld's sadness.

My state of mind is what it is.

A couple of hours after her lunatic call from storage, Lisa shows up. It's late August and we haven't seen each other since our early July collision at the El Presidente in San José. We're to work out our finances. My hope of somehow busting Lisa outright on some piece of treachery (catching her in the fuckfesting-act, say) and my dark shit and my sick puppy shit are over and done with. Everything for us both has been over and done with since the morning after the night of fornicating at the El Presidente when Lisa rifled my stuff and found the whirring tape recorder and smashed it and threw it in the toilet in outrage. (I'd already taken out the fornication tape; the current one had our morning's pleasantries on it.)

Her outrage was interesting since my planting tape recorders and Lisa finding them was another motif in our *I Love Lucy From Hell* relationship. I'd plant a recorder, in the house or in a hotel room or wherever, she'd find it and grin and say Didn't catch me, did you? then shrug and give me an angst pus-removal massage or make a jazzy home made pizza. Yes, a motif, a minor quirk.

But Christ, what a couple of sick puppies.

Lisa's outrage that morning at the El Presidente was based on her rush of insight when she found the recorder that I hadn't been back in the fold with my wild man fornicating after all. I was as far from being back in the fold as you can get.

Sitting on my porch at Montauk, we go over the expenses and calculate that Lisa owes me $3,000. I'm so relieved to get her out of my life that I tell her to forget it. I just want her to leave. In a week or so she's going back to Pavones to finish the spec house; we have buyers lined up via my website.

I ask how long she'll be down there. I need to know this so I can delay my return to my home until after she's left, presumably to come back to the States to get on with her fucked-up life, find someone else to torture (she'd already started in again on her ex-boyfriend, as a warm up), whatever.

Lisa says something vague about her travel plans and I have a bad rush of insight. Really bad.

You're not thinking of staying down there are you? I want to know. To *live* there?

I haven't decided yet, Lisa says.

I'm dizzy. The double vision kicks back in. You can't do that, live at the tiny pueblo that's my home, I say, although I know she can.

Don't get all upset, Lisa says. I'll probably move back to New York in October or so.

She's lying. I know without doubt she's lying. Listen, I say. Listen, Lisa. Stay out of my house.

Lisa gets up to leave. I tell her: Stay out of my house and away from my dogs.

Lisa, standing by the porch steps, is staring at me. With my double vision, I'm staring back at two images of Lisa staring at me. Suddenly her two faces scrunch up, eyes slitted, teeth slightly bared, as if she's squatting in the throes of big time constipation. This lasts a few seconds then Lisa's two faces relax and return to normal and she shrugs and goes to her car and drives away. Both of her.

What was that all about?

Lisa was trying to cry. Leave me with the image of a broken-hearted, misunderstood and mistreated love I've lost forever because of my delusions. She was trying to squeeze out some tears via one of her Academy Award-winning actress moments.

But the muse had up and bolted, failed her.

All she could muster was constipation.

CHAPTER THREE

Cynic, n. A blackguard whose faulty vision sees things as they are, not as they ought to be.

Ambrose Bierce

Lisa was en route to the paradise called Big Turkeys when hurricane Katrina hit the Gulf Coast on August 29, 2005 and Bush left zero doubt, except to the dumbest of the dumbest-ass motherfuckers on the planet, that his "war on terror" is a complete, utter crock of shit, and his arrogance or stupidity or some combination of the two is such that he doesn't even *try* to hide it.

The media, of course, failed to mention this, because the media stand by the essential truths of Bush's claimed motives in everything he does. Like Bob Woodward – the personification of the media and of Orwell's optimism – they don't question *anything* about motives, although, unlike Woodward, they *might* nitpick about methods, the execution of those motives. The media didn't even have the respect, the lack of contempt, for the collective world intelligence – your intelligence – to point out that the natural disaster of Katrina was indistinguishable from a terrorist act: someone blowing up the levee that protected New Orleans to flood the city, or, indeed, a nuclear or biological threat or other threat that would necessitate the evacuation of that city, or any city. The media did not mention the obvious parallels with a terrorist attack because the implications would go to the administration's *motives*, its real agenda in the "war on terror," i.e., seizing oil reserves, empire-building, and world domination. Bush had made no plans whatsoever to protect the American people in case of terrorist attack or any disaster because – although he claims his number one priority is protecting the American people – in reality *he doesn't give a flying fuck about protecting the American people.*[*]

If you don't understand this... fuck this *not necessarily* shit. You are a fool. (That I'm a fool is inarguable, I admit, but a separate subject.)

But right: That Bush doesn't give a flying fuck about protecting the

---

[*] When Bush was asked in a press conference his views on Roe vs. Wade his answer reportedly was, "I don't care how they get out of New Orleans."

American people – and your possible status as a fool – isn't what's important. What's important is that while this new horror was transpiring on the Gulf Coast, Lisa invaded my home in paradise at the end of the road at the bottom of Central America. On September 4th, Marcos my caretaker informed me by phone that Lisa had been living in my house for four days, and then he wanted to know if that was all right?

All right? No it's not fucking *all right*!

I had told Marcos and Kim – my new age surf bro who was working with Lisa on our spec house – by phone, and emailed Kim, and not only told Lisa verbally just before her constipation moment but also emailed her, that under no circumstances was she to be in my house.

Marcos said she showed up and claimed I'd changed my mind and she could stay in my house.

Get her out of my fucking house!

"Sí, sí, lo siento," Marcos said. Okay, I'm sorry. I asked Marcos who's been to my house while she's been there. Marcos, nervous because he fucked up, told me one of Danny Fowlie's friends, some guy named John, plus another guy had visited her.

Get her out of my fucking house!

I called Kim and asked why he didn't say anything to Lisa about being in my house. Kim said this: "You said it would be all right if she stayed there."

"What the fuck are you talking about?"

"Well… that's what you said." (I transcribed the call, hence the quotes.)

"To who?" (Should have been *whom*, but I was cranky and not thinking grammatically.)

"Me… you know… you told me that."

The motherfucker was lying again, like he did last January about not hearing Lisa say I'm not allowed to drink. "Kim," I said, "I emailed you telling you she's not to stay at my house. Plus I told you on the phone." (My emails to Kim and Lisa are archived on the adjunct website.)

"… I don't read my emails."

He doesn't read his emails? We've emailed back and forth many times. Email is how the asshole communicates from the end of the road to the outside world. What the fuck?

I briefly wondered if Lisa was fucking Kim. *Kim*? No, her contempt for the wimp was real, not perception management, as it was with Barry. Barry. Besides, she had Barry's uncommitted dick right next door; Barry, though a dimwit, at least was not a wimp. No, she just had Kim cowed, so he was lying for her. Again.

"Kim," I said, "you read your emails, I know you do, plus I couldn't have been clearer on the phone."

"Allan, you're putting out a lot of negative energy."

"Stop it with that bullshit."

"You have friends here. We all love you." There was a "but" here, left unsaid, about my delusions. "Sassy and I…"

I hung up on the fucker. A half hour later I was so aggravated I called him back. Got his voice mail, the outgoing message ending with that dumb-ass "Always create peace" crapola.

I didn't create any peace with the message I left.

CHAPTER FOUR

Home is the place where, when you have to go there, they have to take you in.

Robert Frost

I returned to my home in paradise on October 1st, 2005 to find Lisa had stolen a desk from my office, a big *cachimbo* beauty I'd had made by a local carpenter; it was so big and heavy she had to use a truck to haul it away, Marcos told me. I wondered what else was missing based on her four-day invasion of my home, plus who she'd fucked in my office bed besides Barry.

Barry. The bottle of expensive, piña colada-flavored sex oil, which was about half full when I last saw it, was now all but empty; hardly one fuckfest left. That stuff costs like ten bucks. (At least it wasn't left out on the night table.)

I had a big trunk in my office, crammed with documents, old screenplays, hand-written journal stuff going back to the Dalton investigation, plus diskettes and back up CDs of my desktop files. It was padlocked and I'd stashed the key behind a photograph of my father in his thirties, looking like a Greek god from lifting weights, which was hanging above the trunk. The key did not fit the padlock. I sawed the lock off, getting a bad feeling as I did so. A stack of backup diskettes and CDs was missing, the ones labeled "Can't", meaning the backups to this book. Lisa had sawed the lock off and replaced it with another; we had a box of identical padlocks in the bodega. Another motif was Lisa peeking at my writing or outright swiping backups. While we were in New York "trying to work things out" (the Doc Bruce fiasco) she'd lifted a backup diskette of my journal notes, right out of my laptop. I hadn't said anything, knowing it would just be more ammunition about my absentmindedness.

That little sucker of a diskette must have been fun reading.

But okay. I had to think about this. The CDs, the main ones that backed up everything, which I'd made at the end of my July paradise visit (three copies, two of which I kept with me), were password protected, as were the daily backup diskettes. Right. I'd made two others without password protection, brought one with me and left one in the locked trunk. This was in case something happened to me. I'd talked to my website guy, John, whom I'd come to be close with, about the "event of my death," by assassination or just keeling over from my various diseases; how I wanted this book, whatever was done of it, put up on my site. I was obsessed with this; the idea that I'd croak and this narrative would never be read was my worst nightmare, having replaced the one about being in love with someone who is *dishonest*. (I could have told him the password but I was crazed at the thought that he'd somehow lose it or even that we'd somehow die simultaneously. Yes, I was crazed about this.)

The end result of my thinking was that Lisa had this book up to the end of Part Four, along with my copious notes on how the rest of it would go. She had the text right up until I fantasize about putting the shotgun to the back of her head, pulling the trigger and then burying her with Fang.

Talk about fun reading.

Whatever. Fuck it.

But with Lisa's invasion and thefts I was starting to perceive not only Pavones itself, but the home I'd built there, as being *soiled*.

Lisa had moved her act to a rented house up near the true end of the road at Punta Banco, had bought her own car – now she could actually describe her ride as "*my* car" – a late model white Trooper. She'd made over a hundred grand via the investments I'd shared, with more to come when we sold the spec house to one of the buyers from my website. She was flush and I knew she wasn't going anywhere. I knew she was going to live at the place I'd brought her to, and that she was planning on working her way up in the scheme of things, in the pecking order, maybe to some sort of *queen* status. I knew that since she'd not improve in her water skills – in two years of daily surf sessions she'd barely advanced beyond intermediate beginner – she'd have to employ other methods to do this. (There are a couple of genuinely hot female surfers at the end of the road, which no doubt aggravates the hell out of her.) As I quickly discovered, she had already used other methods, or method, singular, in this goal, the predictable one.

"Lisa's been screwing everyone in sight," a long time *gringa* resident I'll call Cathy told me. (When I whipped out an index card and pen she asked to remain anonymous, so I'll not describe her further.) Cathy apologized for doubting me in my previous claims of Lisa's rampant infidelities. Like virtually all my friends, she'd been subjected to Lisa's gaslighting about my delusions.

I asked Cathy who she knows about for sure.

"Dan Fowlie's friend John, for one."

"How do you know?"

"They tried to keep it secret when John was here since John's married, but it was so obvious."

Cathy described how Lisa and John were inseparable for a week, stayed at the same cabinas, went for walks in the rain forest and so forth. "The two of them were here with some other people one afternoon playing footsie under this table, thinking no one would notice." This sounded familiar: By Lisa's own account, she and the New Year's Eve Guy had played footsie under the table when they first met. I couldn't picture Lisa playing footsie with someone and not figuring a way to fuck him.

Who else?

"Keith."

Keith. A local resident and sort of a friend of mine. Married, of course.

"How do you know?"

"Keith was over here one night. We had a few beers and he told me." Keith told Cathy he was at La Piña (of karaoke night fame) one night and ran into Lisa and she took him home. "And I was in the mood to get laid that night," Keith had said, according to Cathy. Keith's wife was in San José at the time.

I briefly described election night with Clay and the vaudeville scenes with Barry. Cathy nodded, grinned. "Sure, why not Clay and Barry?" Although Lisa denied "socializing" at all with Barry over the summer, Marcos had told me that one of his in-laws who works at La Piña saw them one night having drinks in the back.

"That reminds me," Cathy said. She described how one afternoon she was having a beer with Marcos at the cantina and Marcos told her that "a guy from Pilon" (the next hamlet up the road, where Max got whacked) had been up to my house while Lisa was living there by herself. A guy with dreadlocks, he'd told her. Marcos wouldn't name the guy, got evasive when Cathy asked about his identity.

"Do you think she's been fucking Kim?" Cathy inquired, wincing at the thought. Sassy, Kim's wife, had been in the States working all summer. Cathy and I looked at each other, contemplating a Lisa/Kim flesh pile, and then we both said, more or less in unison, "Nahh." Cathy: "Too much of a wimp." We both laughed.

"You were right, Allan," Cathy said. "Lisa's a pig." It was nice hearing a female, a Pavones female, say this. That I was able to laugh was also a positive, sort of a milestone on my road to being less fucked up. And it appeared that Lisa's perception management campaign was starting to collapse. She'd self-destruct soon enough, due to her not being able to help herself; her sex-as-tool M.O. would result in some big time petard hoisting.

Cathy: "Eventually, the women here, the wives and girlfriends, will run her out of town."

I'd deal with Lisa being here until she was run out of town, I was thinking. Soiled or not, completely fucked-up or not, this little end-of-the-road piece of paradise with its point surf perfection was still my home.

CHAPTER FIVE

You only have power over people as long as you don't take everything away from them. But when you've robbed a man of everything he's no longer in your power – he's free again.
Aleksandr Solzhenitsyn

It's now a week into my return, a couple of days after my conversation with Cathy, her revelation that Lisa has been screwing everyone in sight. I've been reclusive, mostly holed up at my house with my pups, sweating over Part Five of this, surfing when I work up the energy. I'm still sick; aside from the TB itself, the slew of TB meds are laying me low, plus the untreated Lyme disease and the rest of the repercussions of my immune system breakdown.

I've seen Lisa twice, once in passing on the road – she waved, I did not – and once from a distance down by The Point as she was putting her surfboard on her car. I've seen the Trooper at the spec house we're partners in, which is about a hundred yards from my house. Barry has been around but not in my presence. I haven't seen Kim, nor do I want to. Alex and Amy were friendly when I spoke to them at Alex's surf shop but eye contact was sparse. Lisa had been working on them, especially Amy, I assumed, who shrugged *So what?* when I reminded her of an inarguable lie Lisa told her about me.

There's a bit of a swell so I go down to Sawmills, my favorite local wave; my favorite wave on the planet. It's a semi-secret spot, a long left-hander unknown to outsiders without connections. On the shore in the nook of the point lies the cement foundation of the old sawmill Danny built and which was burned down by squatters in 1988 after Danny went on the run. The remains of outbuildings and of Danny's three-story manse, itself hardly more than ruins now, complete the picture of an era long gone and fading from memory. Technically and for the moment, Logan the Nutcase controls the land overlooking this perfect wave. Logan, who wants to run me out of town or worse, controls the land but cannot stop me from surfing the wave. No one can own a wave, or control it.

I arrive to find one car and the usual two grazing horses in the clearing behind the beach. The car is Lisa's white Trooper. I park and walk the few yards to water's edge. There is only one human being anywhere in sight, Lisa sitting her board maybe 150 yards from where I stand. Birds warble. A distant cow lows, perhaps.

Seeing Lisa out surfing at Sawmills is as much an assault on my dignity as her invasion of my home, the theft of my desk and of this narrative. This wave is a gift I gave her and now I wish more than anything that I could take it back. As with all else I gave her, she betrayed the gift of this wave. She shared it, its existence, with a cantina bum, a "land buyer" she was interested in last spring, an outsider who has no right to know about this wave except through personal exploration. She brought him here, gave him this wave, which I had given her. She will do this again, assault my dignity in this way. Of that there is no doubt.

Lisa takes a wave, surfs it poorly, does not cut back where the middle section flattens, and stalls and falls off her board. I'm thinking she does not deserve this wave, not on any level of deserving. Lisa climbs onto her board and across the water we look at each other, for the moment the only two human beings on this wild and distant coast, this piece of paradise.

I don't surf Sawmills this morning. I go to the pueblo and paddle out at the cantina. I surprise myself. Sick and sapped as I am I find my rhythm and have a fine session. I hang ten toes several times, solid tens, the most difficult longboard feat and which very few surfers can or ever do. I'm 57 years old.

I paddle in to see Barry's car parked at the cantina. I don't care about Barry any more, don't care what he did with Lisa or where he did it. He is a non-person to me, as are many of the other residents of this place where I live.

I'm making breakthroughs.

I have the wave, I have the home I built.

With time I will regain my dignity.

When I get home my pups, Honey, Cho Cho, Aleeza, and Tigre are at the gate barking and grinning in welcome. The afternoon I first got back I wandered my property with my pups, wandered it for an hour, noticing how the fruit trees were coming along, how much thicker the hibiscus hedge had gotten from the rains since July. I trimmed the banana and plantain trees, found some ripe bananas and ate one. I walked the fence line, checking for breaks in the chicken wire. I believe the chicken wire keeps out the snakes; my great fear is that one of my pups will get bit by a terciopelo. As I walked the fence on the south side that day I noticed that below the only break in the hedge the stack of tiles Barry used to invade my home and fuck my girlfriend is still there. This was a week ago.

On the day I speak of I was up well before dawn to work on this narrative, as I do every day no matter where I am, then I went down to Sawmills and saw Lisa out surfing, then I surfed in front of the cantina, as described. I napped in my porch hammock after my session.

Now, late in the afternoon, I call Danny in California. I have some news for him about Mark Sherman, my neighbor who bulldozed my property while I was in the States thinking I was dying. Sherman also bulldozed some of Danny's land, damaging the rain forest watershed, so Danny and I are working together to stop him from wreaking further havoc on the environment. After Danny's visit in June the Costa Rican government banned him from entering the country again, citing a law that allows them to bar entry to anyone who might upset the domestic tranquility. Danny is sure that Sherman and/or Logan are behind this maneuver, through bribes or mendacious testimony or whatever, hoping to prevent Danny from pursuing court action against them. Danny has never been accused of breaking any laws in Costa Rica so something like this must be going on. The Waterman Who Would Be King is therefore more dependent on me than ever, at least as his presence at his former empire.

Aside from the Marc Sherman matter, which is getting nasty, I recently sabotaged a sale of one of Danny's former parcels by taking the greenhorn gringo buyer aside and giving him a Pavones mini-history lesson, pointing out that the seller was a violence-prone squatter turned real estate broker whose land title was undoubtedly bogus. The day after the deal-killing I started getting threatening phone calls.

Danny is appreciative of my efforts on his behalf and recommends that I keep my head down – advice I've heard before.

As the conversation winds down I bring up Danny's friend John, saying I have reason to believe he had sex with Lisa. I'm thinking Danny should know about this since if it's true John's loyalty towards Danny becomes questionable. Although I've never met John, that he had sex with my girlfriend would be an affront to Danny, since John without doubt knows of my putting my ass on the line for Danny.

Danny says he didn't think anything happened during his and John's short visit in June. John had returned without Danny, though, and had visited Lisa at my house last month during Lisa's four-day invasion. Danny thinks about it. "It was obvious to everyone that Lisa had a thing for John."

Here I recall that Danny had previously told me how Lisa did one of her weeping routines in front of him when she told him how much she loves me and worries about me. This in the course of a few days during which she also made it obvious that she had "a thing" for one of Danny's entourage. I don't say anything but I wonder if Danny has reflected on the implications of this blatant two-facedness.

Danny tells me that John is married with kids and wants to bring his family down, build a house. Yes, I say to Danny, this would further explain John's keeping secret his screwing around, even from him, especially from him.

Danny hems and haws here, getting uncomfortable with the drift. Then he says this, perhaps to change the subject: "I heard that Lisa's been screwing around with the Mora kid, whatsisname's son."

"Gerardo Mora?"

"Right. The squatter who killed Max Dalton. His kid."

"You mean Esteban? Esteban Mora?"

"Right. Esteban."

CHAPTER SIX

Story turning points are based on action or revelation. There is no other way.

Robert McKee

Although I didn't transcribe it immediately, I believe my conversation with Danny, where I use quotes, is exactly accurate as written. As is my habit, I had a notepad in front of me but I was unable to deal with writing anything for a few minutes.

I was on the porch when Danny and I spoke and went into my office when we hung up. I sat at my desk for a while, looking out at the Sweet Gulf and thinking. Just to my right as I sat there were two photographs on the wall above the trunk Lisa broke into, the one of my father in his thirties looking like a god, the other of Mom at about age 20. I may or may not have looked at Mom's photograph that day as I sat there, but I thought of her, I'm quite sure. I always think of Mom when I need help or advice or sometimes just in problem-solving. Now that I'm alone I have no reason not to talk to her aloud, even if only to say, "Please help, Mom," or "I know you're there, Mom." I don't mean *there* literally, like she's watching from heaven or some such, but there because I'm thinking of her. When someone who has passed away is in a living person's thoughts, that person lives too, in a sense. Even now, because you're reading about Mom and therefore thinking about her, she is a little bit alive. Not as alive as when I'm talking to her, certainly. It's a spectrum kind of thing that I don't fully understand. (If you will, look at the photograph of Mom at the end of this book; it's the one from my wall. Please do this now, just for a moment... Mom is beautiful, isn't she?)

Odd how the mind works. My first full thought when Danny said, "Right. Esteban" was of a small incident from many months back. Small but odd enough that I have mentioned it here, albeit in an aside, in a footnote (page 220). Here it is again:

A while back Mora's son Esteban – who I occasionally run into surfing – out of the blue asked me to whom I have left my land in my will. What the fuck was with that?

The incident happened so long ago that I had to estimate when by extrapolating from when I wrote the chapter in which the footnote appears. Luckily, the first words in that chapter define the time of the writing: "Second week of February, 2004." I thought about it and came up with October or November of 2003 as when Esteban asked me who gets my land in my will.

What the fuck was with that? I asked myself.

As I sat in my office last October I had a semi-dark moment as I came up with an answer to the question – my real dark moment would occur in a few days and would indeed have to do with Esteban Mora. See, at the time of the incident I at first wondered if it was some sort of veiled threat, maybe having to do with my Max Dalton investigation. But this made no sense. I'd been back at Pavones for two years, the Dalton matter was way in the past, had never come up, and I was on more than surface-friendly terms with the Moras. I'd listed their land on my website; there was even a photo of Lisa walking the beach at Pilon with Gerardo. As I say, though, my relationship with the family was a false one. I had no intention of helping these people sell land. I wanted them at ease so they'd tell me things. I wanted to *know everything.*

The only person on the planet who knew what I was up to with the Moras was Lisa. But the conclusion I came to was not that Lisa had put my life at risk by telling Esteban about my motives, although in retrospect it's a given. My conclusion at the time came through knowing about Esteban, and the Latin-male mentality, of which he is an extreme example. Esteban is a ladies' man, has a major rep as such, and although he's recently gotten doughy and dissipated from alcohol and drug abuse, back in 2003 he was lean and handsome and, as with many sociopaths, charming, even charismatic – until you got to know him and if you were paying attention while doing so. (The photograph that opens this section is of Esteban, with a block of pot, circa 2002.) Father and son, aside from having murdered an aging American plus their own blood relative to steal land, have committed well-known acts of fraud and mayhem to control other parcels. The family is crazed about land, owning it, controlling it, selling it. As I say in Part Three, they covet the shebang plus.

Sitting in my office thinking about Esteban, here's the conclusion I came to: he was fucking Lisa and therefore figured if Lisa inherited my land holdings and my house – maybe the nicest house in the province – he could somehow get his hands on it, all of it or part of it. This is the Mora mentality, to some extent the Latin mentality. If you're fucking a woman you control her. So Esteban's question was really about Lisa. Had I left my land to her?

I recalled that aside from his participation in the Dalton murder there was a rumor that Esteban had sold land with bogus titles to two *gringos* who had paid cash, then they were never heard from again in Costa Rica. And Gerardo, dear old dad, had recently boasted that he'd used a machete to whack off the hand of a squatter who was recalcitrant in leaving a parcel Gerardo controlled and Gerardo was getting impatient with the legal eviction. And there was plenty more, unsubstantiated rumors, yes, but I knew more than enough not to discount them.

Although Esteban's query back in 2003 was so rude and so out of whack that I saw fit to write about it here, I had answered truthfully. I said, "To relatives in the states." (Meaning Ellen and my cousin and her kids.) Had he asked three or four months later, after I briefly made Lisa my sole heir to prove my love, and had I answered Esteban truthfully, it occurred to me that Esteban might have killed me, or tried to.

This was my semi-dark moment.

And other things fit. Lisa's many excuses to go to Golfito solo... her "I gave it a shot" blurt when a spur-of-the-moment trip made no sense and I nixed it...the Moras kept an apartment in Golfito and back around this time Esteban was staying there while doing a welding job... how around the time that Esteban had moved out of the family *finca* Lisa quit going there for "Spanish lessons" from Mayela or tortilla baking or whatever.

...Marcos had said that a guy from Pilon with dreadlocks visited my house when Lisa was there alone. Esteban often wears his hair in braids that look like dreadlocks. Esteban now lives in Pilon.

But I was getting ahead of myself. Danny's revelation was second-hand; I'd have to go to the source of his information. On the phone I had asked Danny who his source was and at first he didn't want to tell me, saying we'd talk about it when we next met. No, no, I said, I need to know *now*. Danny relented and gave me the name of a female expat I'd run into in passing at the cantina a few days previously. Danny asked that I keep his name out of this, citing his reputation and how dangerous it was for him in Pavones.

Sitting at my desk looking out at the Sweet Gulf that day, I wondered how long Danny had known about Lisa and Esteban. I wondered why he hadn't told me immediately upon hearing that my girlfriend, whom he assumed had my love and trust, was fucking a land thief, a fraud, a colluder in murder and a sociopath who, aside from his father Gerardo, was maybe the most dangerous person within 50 miles.

Yes, I was thinking, it was dangerous down here for The Waterman Who Would Be King. Dangerous enough that he had employed an armed bodyguard on his short visit.

Me, I was in the middle of the shit as much as he was.

Where was *my* bodyguard?

It was a lonely feeling.

CHAPTER SEVEN

By the pricking of my thumbs,
Something wicked this way comes.

William Shakespeare

Danny's source was a long-time gringa expat named Jean, whom I only knew very casually. She owned land in nearby Cocal, I recalled. Cocal was the Mora's turf, where they had their *finca*, something like twenty acres they were trying to sell for big bucks, and which was less than ten minutes from my house. Danny told me that Jean had recently rented a place near the pueblo; he didn't, wouldn't, say exactly where. Said he didn't know.

I put off looking for Jean, not sure why. I was still sick and sapped and I was very weary of things piling up. My agoraphobia was active, the momentum factor too. I rationalized my procrastination by figuring I'd run into Jean again and maybe it would be better if it seemed I was bringing up the Esteban/Lisa matter in passing, like it was no big deal. Right.

Perhaps I didn't want to know. Perhaps I knew that the information I now sought went beyond my need to know things just for the sake of knowing. Perhaps I knew that my time was running out at the place I called home. I theorize.

No one knows shit about why he does anything.

From my office and the adjacent porch I had a partial view of the spec house Lisa and I were partners in. For the months of construction Lisa had been giving the workers – the Ramirez brothers – a ride home to Pilon each afternoon, passing by the little dirt road to Esteban's ranchos, some five miles from my property and just a few hundred yards from the bothers' house. Sometimes she'd come back late from the drive, saying she'd hung out with the Ramirez family or had taken a walk to look at their land or whatever. She always had a reason when she was late, and supplied details.

But okay. Eventually it was time to do this, talk to Jean. On October 13th, four days after my conversation with Danny, I asked someone who was friendly with her if he knew where Jean was staying. I was directed to a little dirt road up behind The Point, not far from the locale of the first fatality in the squatter wars, when a mob stormed a gringo's property and the caretaker opened up with his shotgun. There's a little stone monument at the spot where the man, Hugo Vargas, died in 1991. A little piece of Big Turkeys history.*

I found the road easily enough, then was directed to Jean's new rental house by a guy I knew, Ruey, who had been helping her move in and was now leaving. I found Jean alone in the house, which was on a hill on the edge of the rain forest.

It was awkward at first, showing up with the questions I had. As I say, Jean and I were no more than passing acquaintances. I did not take notes, fearing I'd spook her. I stopped on the road after our meeting and wrote down some specifics, then the rest when I got home. Here's how my hour with Jean went, the relevant stuff:

About age 50, Jean had the sort of world-weary and yet somehow cheerful slant I'd seen before in expats who are looking for something better, not quite finding it, and then moving on. As I would come to realize, Jean had been through some shit in her life, including a bout with cancer, and had toughed it all out. A ballsy woman.

I kept preliminary chitchat to a minimum, quickly sensing Jean would see through it. I wanted to be completely up front with her and let the chips fall; I soon asked what she knew about my girlfriend Lisa and Esteban Mora.

Jean smiled and said, "You've been talking to Danny."

This put me in an awkward position. I'd told Danny I'd keep his name out of this. Dispiriting as it was that Danny didn't want to be involved in my problem – I'd been hanging *my* ass out for *him* – I wanted to keep my word. So I just shrugged and smiled and said that I like Danny.

"Danny speaks very highly of you," Jean said, then added that Danny said I can be trusted and if Danny trusted me so could she, she figured. I kept my trap shut, not denying I'd spoken to him on the matter in question. A compromise.

"Let's have some tea and we'll talk," Jean said. I already liked her.

As Jean made tea we talked about Danny, with whom Jean was close, and for whom Jean was also "a presence" down south. She knew the Moras well, had bought land from them. She knew who and what they were, and had been subjected to their treachery. She, like me, had taken some chances in helping Danny.

"I saw you and Esteban at the cantina the other day," Jean said from the stove. I'd run into him a couple days after my return. "Esteban acting like

---

* Speaking of history, the guy who owns the land is a surfer I know from Long Island. In 1979, during my pot smuggling days, he helped me unload a planeload of Jamaican purple bud at the East Hampton airport. The world of the end-of-the-road surfer/expat is a small one.

you're some long-lost brother. I literally got nauseous." As usual, Esteban had been effusive in his greeting. There was a natural segue here and I used it, saying, "So tell me about Lisa and Esteban."

Jean went to the couch, had a sip of tea and got to it. Described how she was at Danny's in California soon after Danny's Costa Rica visit in June. A group was watching a video Danny had made of the trip and there was a short clip of Lisa at my house. Jean had called out in surprise, "That's Esteban's girlfriend!"

Watching the tape were Danny, his friend John and another guy from the entourage, Chris. Jean told me that John and Chris were unsurprised by the revelation and started in with "sly male comments" about Lisa. Jean didn't remember the specifics and had left the room in disgust, not wanting to hear the male posturing.

This was how Danny learned about Lisa and Esteban.

I digressed for a moment, saying I thought Lisa and John had been screwing around, maybe during the time Lisa and I were still technically together. Jean nodded, recalling how Chris said he'd seen the two of them emerging from a jungle walk looking "very pleased with themselves."

"Freshly fucked?"

"That's what Chris meant, yes."

And John had been to my house. How many had Lisa fucked in my bed?

"Back in June I didn't even know Lisa was your wife."

"She was my girlfriend, not my wife," I said. "The love of my life." I added the last bit with a minimum of irony. I was running low on irony.

"I'm so sorry." Jean told me that in her interactions with Lisa over the last couple of years Lisa had never mentioned me. She always "behaved like she was single."

"How do you know about Lisa and Esteban?" This of course was the big question.

"I'm getting scared." Like everyone, Jean was afraid of the Moras.

I knew this was coming at some point and was ready for it. I told Jean I was writing a book about my life down south, among other things, and that she had my word as a person and a journalist that I'd not identify her as the source of any information she supplied. Jean had read *Zero* and liked it very much. And I had Danny's trust, which counted a lot.[*]

Jean took a breath and nodded. She then began a detailed history of her life down south, working backwards from the present. At first I was disconcerted, not understanding how any of it had anything to do with

---

[*] Later, by phone after I came to this island, Jean would tell me to go ahead and use her name if I wanted. She said, "The hell with it. What are they (the Moras) going to do to me?" Courageous, and a great boon to this narrative, it's veracity. Thank you, Jean.

Lisa and Esteban. As I would come to realize over our many talks, she was trying to pinpoint a time and place by reviewing chronology. It was her way of getting the facts right.

"Okay. I was working on my cottage, the one I'd bought from the Moras above their finca, and I was talking to Esteban's brother David. Right. We were at their finca. David told me that Esteban was screwing 'la gringa flaca, Lisa.'"

"When was this?"

"I was working on my cottage so it had to be October of 2003."

This exactly fit with when Esteban came up with his bizarre question about my will, which was no longer bizarre. I described this, the question, and my theory of why Esteban had asked it. Jean nodded vehemently, saying I had it right. She knew Esteban well, his attitude towards women especially. He had tried to seduce Jean, then Jean's 16 year-old daughter. He had been completely obvious about his designs on her daughter, as if there was no problem.

"Esteban's an animal," Jean said. "He has that dangerous charisma that turns on certain types of women." She laughed. "But not this woman."

I find certain Tico men very sexy. Lisa's journal; still another entry that got my attention. The expression *birds of a feather* comes to mind, aside from, once again, the wanton female baboon allusion.

That David, Esteban's brother, had known about Lisa and Esteban reminded me of another incident, long dormant in my memory. I'm at the Mora's *finca*, by my car, just leaving. Gerardo is saying good-bye. He looks at me and says, "Lisa es una mujer muy especial." Lisa is a very special woman. Here he turns away, and he turns away because he is *smirking*. Like he can't help himself from smirking and doesn't want me to see. But I saw.

If David knew Esteban was fucking Lisa, Gerardo knew. The whole family knew, of course, all of them in the hopes that Esteban's Lisa-fucking would somehow pay off. Although I could not pinpoint exactly when the incident with Gerardo took place, it was prior to Esteban's question about my will; weeks prior, or months. I had brought Lisa down to live with me around the first of April, 2003 and had soon introduced her to the Moras, including Esteban.

Do you think I have two boyfriends?

Do you think I have a local boyfriend?

Esteban Mora was her second, her local, boyfriend, aside from the San José one, from the beginning, maybe *right* from the beginning of her coming to live with me. Plus Barry, plus others on the side.

I asked Jean if she could remember anything else.

"This was all a long time ago," Jean said, and apologized for not remembering more. "I didn't think much about it at the time because I didn't know Lisa was your wife."

I reminded Jean that Lisa was not my wife.

At least there was that, I was thinking.

CHAPTER EIGHT

For me writing is a horseback ride into heaven and hell and back.

Thomas Sanchez

Jean would remember more. How in late 2004 at the cantina Esteban had indicated Lisa, who was nearby, and said to Jean, "I've had that." How once at the beach at the Salea River mouth in Pilon, Jean had seen Lisa and Esteban together, playing "touchy feely." Jean couldn't remember exactly when this was, but by doing another personal history routine came up with early 2004, maybe more recently than that.

That Lisa was on the beach with Esteban at Salea, at another semi-secret surf spot I had given her – aside from being a godawful assault on my dignity – reminded me of another incident, which I also thought strange at the time, but now was explained.

It was the spring or summer of 2004 and Lisa and I had just returned from a good session in front of the cantina. Lisa said she wanted to surf more and thought she'd go down to Salea and see how it was breaking. The wind had come up and it would be blown out at Salea, as it now was at the cantina. Lisa wanted to check it anyway. She didn't suggest I come with her, which was fine. I was surfed out, aside from knowing that the surf would be poor.

Never before or since that day has Lisa ever done a second go-out on any given day; she doesn't have the stoke or the stamina for multiple sessions. Plus she knew that with the wind up it couldn't have been worth the trip. I'm sure she went to see Esteban, who lived right at the break. She *gave it a shot* and this time it worked.

These added revelations, plus more, came later, after my bolt to this island, Jean and I speaking by phone when Jean was back in the states, at Danny's in California. But I didn't need more revelations. I *knew*. And my genuinely dark moment came the next morning after I'd slept, more or less slept, on what Jean had told me. I went right upstairs to the office. I did not take a piss or put on the coffee or say good morning to my pups. I went right to the trunk Lisa had broken into. I did this because of the work my subconscious had done while I was sleeping. It had put some things together and when I awoke I had a rush of insight.

It wasn't there. I knew without a doubt I'd put it in the trunk when I left in late July, but it wasn't there. I searched the office, just in case, and the bodega and the bedroom, where I kept some papers. It was nowhere in the house.

I speak of the hard copy of my Max Dalton investigation, which I had printed up in February of 2004 so Lisa could read it. She had taken the hard copy along with the backup CDs and diskettes of this narrative. This is where I had my dark moment, the second of three. And this is where things get complex and strange and where some words are required to explain what was going on with me, with Lisa, and with the book you are reading right now.

And to explain why I didn't see it all coming.

CHAPTER NINE

If you are killed because you are a writer, that's the maximum expression of respect, you know.

Mario Vargas Llosa

Back in early 2005, about a year ago as I write and six months prior to the events I describe, I made the decision to cut the Max Dalton investigation from this book, for this reason: I felt that no matter how the narrative eventually ended – and at that time I was still searching for an ending, hanging in with Lisa hoping one would loom, either through some sort of confrontation (the blown one at airport comes to mind again) or something else, some dramatic event, I knew not what... but no matter how it would eventually end I could not see how the Dalton affair would be relevant. No matter that it was interesting and said some things about where I lived and my obsessions and so forth – when all was said and done, it would just lie there. I felt that it must be cut.

So that section, Part Three, the Dalton stuff, was gone, a non-factor in my thinking about this book and about Lisa as well. For months it was forgotten. Thing is, though, it didn't occur to me that Lisa didn't know this. She had read Part Three when I considered it included, herself saying that if it were made public we'd certainly have to leave Pavones to avoid the revenge of the Moras, which would be a given. She read Part Three and saw the implications of it while she was fucking Esteban Mora. (Her reading and her reaction are described page 223). That Lisa not only told Esteban about the Dalton section but took it from my trunk to give it to him was the rush of insight I experienced that morning when I couldn't find the hard copy, and which resulted in my dark moment. Ask yourself this: Why would she take the hard copy? She'd already read it, and she is not in it. Plus it was on the CD. So she must have taken the hard copy for someone else to read. But who? Who else but Esteban Mora, whose English is good enough that he could see it for what it is, a major threat to the financial, if

458

not legal, future of himself and his family.*

Who would buy land from the Moras after reading that?

Let's Put Ourselves In Lisa's Place. We have Parts One through Four of this book plus notes about how the rest will go, right? Further, our worst nightmare is the truth, the truth of our behavior, the truth of what we are. *The truth is our worst nightmare.* So depending on the degree of our denial, our arrogance about our ability to lie our way out of anything, we may realize that this book will *ruin our life*.

Here's where it gets difficult to Put Ourselves In Lisa's Place. We have to assume that in getting what we want there are *no limits* to behavior, to deceit and treachery. This is hard to imagine unless we are like her, unless we are that way. This is why she has been able to fool so many people, myself included. People cannot believe anyone could *be* like that, be it a woman living down the little dirt road from us in paradise or a president of the United States.

See if we can come up with an explanation other than this: Lisa took the hard copy to give it to Esteban Mora, hoping Esteban, maybe in concert with Gerardo, would kill me to prevent this book's Part Three from ruining the Mora's land-selling schemes, Lisa's motive being to avoid her life being ruined by the public revelation of the truth of what she is.

Lisa wanted me dead.

---

* The uncertainty principle rears here in a complex and profound way. The crucial turning point of Lisa giving the Dalton hard copy to Esteban Mora exists *outside of* the events of the story, in the sense that this event would not have occurred without the telling. In other words, the very existence of the story, i.e., the telling of it, profoundly changed the story. To put it a slightly different way: There's nice symmetry in the exposé-axe falling on the Moras due to Lisa's treachery with Esteban (without this treachery the Dalton section would not be included in this book). If you really think about this, the weird circularity of it, it gets downright dizzying.

CHAPTER TEN

We will now discuss in a little more detail the struggle for existence.

Charles Darwin

Same day. October 14th, 2005.

By mid-morning I'd gone over everything a dozen times, thought about it all from every angle, then did so again. I searched the house once more for the Dalton hard copy. But Christ I wanted to find it. I did not find it. I could not see why Lisa would take it other than to give it to Esteban Mora.

But still…

I re-examined history, Lisa's escalating betrayals, culminating in her attempts to make me believe I've lost my mind, the last of which being the passport wallet disappearance. (Although her "finding" the b.c. pills was more recent, that one was more a defensive tactic, against another lie exposure.) Transparent as that maneuver was, transparent as all her gaslighting was, how was it essentially different from physical violence?

Violence.

Given Lisa's prodigious verbal assertions and love note/letter/email authorship (plus sexy post-its and calligraphic quatrains in the margins of books I may get around to reading), one particular passage from *Without Conscience* sounds familiar. See if you agree, as a nutcase sociopath boasts about her loveless relationships with men, which were motivated solely by sex.

> "(I made) promises of undying love, endless devotion and oaths that no one else on earth would ever touch me. It was the game I played with men. And I played it best with Bert… I was writing letters to Bert telling him how much I loved him, that he was the only man on earth for me… 'I love you, Bert, why aren't you here, I need you, you're the only man for me…'
>
> I mixed a drink and wrote my hollow words of love to Bert as I sank into a bubble bath… Minutes later Jason knocked at the door, and as I

flew down the stairs to meet him, thoughts of Bert flew as well."*

Change the "Bert"s to "Allan"s and the only thing that's off here is the bubble bath – I don't have a tub in my house at Big Turkeys.

I somewhat redundantly refer to the above sociopath as a *nutcase* because the woman relates her wayward sexual history as an explanation of why she shot her three children: the juxtaposition of rampant sexual infidelity to a casual view of violence might ring a bell, an alarm bell, regarding Lisa, the love of my life, no?

And here Lisa wouldn't even have to do the violent deed; she need only perception-manage another sociopath.

But still…

I booted up and scanned Parts One through Four. The way I work is to rewrite as I go, each writing session preceded by a rewrite of the couple or so thousand words that precede the blank page. And some days I'll spend rewriting from the beginning. The point being that I knew Parts One through Four well. I knew what was there but I reviewed it all anyway, Putting Myself In Lisa's Place, which I had never done before.

Part One. Christ. That last chapter, where I come to the conclusion that Lisa is at heart "a good and honest person." What a victory that was for her! I recalled how she'd given Part One to friends at Montauk. The self-congratulatory smirking she must have done.

The rest, Parts Two and Four… I don't think she'll be giving those sections to friends at Montauk.

Part Three, the Dalton section. I tried to see Part Three as Esteban and Gerardo would. How Would That Go? How would it go with Lisa telling them how so many people that come to Pavones have read *Zero*, how it affected them, "changed their lives." How it would be the same with this book. How the Dalton exposé would ruin everything for the family.

Again, who would buy land from the Moras after reading that?

She'd lay it on thick all right. Lisa had had more than a month since her invasion of my home in early September, her stealing the CDs and the hard copy. Plenty of time to work on Esteban Mora.

But still…

With all my enemies, if done right, killing me would be risk free. I had multiple bull's eyes on my back all right.

But still…

But didn't she just keep escalating the treachery? Where would she stop? *Why* would she stop?

No limits. We know without doubt that with Lisa there are *no limits*.

---

* This is the same woman who bragged about "salting the mine," which is another Lisa-hallmark.

But still...

Why hadn't they already done it? I'd been back a couple of weeks. How much planning would it take?

Marcos had told me that Lisa was taking a surf trip up the coast with my fucking bro Kim and his kid, who Lisa says is a whacko. She wouldn't want to be here when it went down, would she? She'd want to be elsewhere and have witnesses.

My mind was on the run.

On the run.

I'd run into Esteban at the cantina last week. Right. How had it gone? Was there a look in his eye, a wry smile, like he knew something I didn't, as he greeted me as a long-lost brother? The smile, yes, I remembered it well, but was I imagining that look in his eye?

I checked my weapons, the Browning 12, the .38, my little .22 semi-automatic rifle, 15 shot magazine, hollow points, a deadly weapon if not a stopper like the Browning. I talked to my pups, told them to be vigilant, and please don't eat any meat thrown over the fence. Shit. Wouldn't that be the first move, kill my dogs? Maybe not. No. That would put me on alert.

If something went down, it would come out of nowhere.

Another thought: Was I making more out of this than there was to provide an *ending* to this? Seeing escalation because I needed it?

In my narratives if not in my life, everything tends to work out for the best.

Was that a truth or a self-fulfilling prophecy or maybe just bullshit?

Is this real life or is it *nonfiction*?

CHAPTER ELEVEN

Where I am, I don't know, I'll never know, in the silence you don't know, you must go on, I can't go on, I'll go on.

Samuel Beckett

But Christ I needed a surf.

In waiting for a wave, in sitting out there between sets, bad thoughts, obsessive thoughts, will surface, but while actually riding, while standing up and searching for that rhythm, no matter how awful the day I'm having my mind is clean and clear and blank and therefore content. I have never, not ever, had a conscious thought, good, bad or indifferent, while in the act of riding a wave. I needed that purity, that vacuum.

For the first time in my life I armed myself for a trip to the beach.

I surf in front of the cantina for an hour and when I come back Lisa's Trooper is at the spec house, Casa Tigre, named for Tigre, my pup who died while I've been on this island. I stop and kill the engine. I'm feeling better after the waves I rode. My head is clear. By God what would I do, where would I be, without wave riding?

I need to speak to Lisa about Esteban Mora. I know if I play it right, she will tell me everything. She can't help herself with her mouth. I think about how to do this. Okay. I get out of the car and go to Casa Tigre. I haven't spoken to Lisa since I told her to stay out of my house and she tried to cry on my porch at Montauk, but could not cry. And neither have I seen her close up since then. What will she look like to me now?

Lisa is doing something at the kitchen sink. She turns and I look at her face. I ask myself something, although not in actual words: How could I ever have thought that face attractive, let alone beautiful?

Lisa is surprised to see me there, right at the door, six feet away. There is a moment during which nothing happens, a suspended moment. I remain very calm and non-confrontational. I look around at the house this woman and I are partners in, as if I'm interested in the progress of its completion. I nod, although I have noticed nothing.

"Who was at my house those four days when you stayed there?" I ask, and my voice is casual. When Lisa doesn't answer: "I think I have a right to know."

"No one." Lying, of course.

"How about John? Danny's friend."

Lisa makes a big gesture of confusion, of not knowing who John is. That she would do this, deny knowing John, re-confirms that she was screwing him. "John," I say patiently. "Hung out with Danny's other friend, Chris. Marcos said he came to the house."

"Oh, right," Lisa says, as if a minor detail has come back to her. "John came up to the house once. Chris was with him." Chris was with him?

"Why did he come to my house?"

"Looking for you." A whopper. I've never met John, so John would have no reason to look for me, and anyway, John, through Danny and through anyone in the pueblo, would have known I was in the States recovering from all my diseases. I let it lie, though, not wanting to get confrontational yet.

"You get along okay with John?" An innocent question, the way I say it.

A shrug. "Not particularly." Except for hanging out with him for a week and having an obvious "thing" for him and playing footsie with him under the table and fucking him in the jungle. But let's get to it. My turn to lie.

"I just saw Esteban Mora at the cantina."

Lisa looks away at this, actually turns her body away from me, saying, "How *is* Esteban?" She's looking out the window at a tree or something. Trust me that Lisa herself just told me that she has been fucking Esteban Mora.

"He was drunk and coked up and talking a lot of shit." This is spur-of-the-moment, and smart. Lisa will not know what Esteban said and get nervous and maybe fuck up again. "Has Esteban been to my house?"

"No." She still will not look at me. She's lying. He's the guy with the dreadlocks from Pilon Marcos saw come to my house. Marcos would not name him to me because like everyone else he's afraid of the Moras.

"When was the last time you saw him?"

"That time he gave me a ride back from Golfito." I'm remembering that day last spring, when Lisa suggested we invest in Esteban's land in Pilon, now knowing she fucked him that day, either in Golfito or at his rancho when they got back or maybe up at his land in the bush overlooking the Sweet Gulf. I know this through remembering her description of the ride back, how she was as detail-rich as she's ever been, wandering around the kitchen and breezing it up about Esteban's Rover, how it has the best suspension system for the bad roads here, how Esteban drives *so fast* but since his Rover has the *best* suspension system the car just *glides* over the potholes and ruts and then Lisa was going on about how his land has these amazing *trees* and such a view of the Sweet Gulf, and on and on and wandering around as she went on and on, and why I didn't know about the two of them right then and there last spring is beyond me since I already knew by then that with Lisa there are *no limits*; and then with her suggestion that day that we invest with Esteban was more proof that with Lisa's treachery, with her deep need to dominate me and humiliate me, there are *no limits*.

But the day I speak of, October 14th, 2005, in Casa Tigre, as soon as Lisa said "That time he gave me a ride back from Golfito," she immediately turned from the window and still without looking at my eyes bolted past me and out the door, yelling out, "I'm not going to do this!" and she was trotting down the walkway and into the sleeping cabina.

Lisa was worried about what Esteban might have just told me when he was drunk and coked up and talking a lot of shit at the cantina. *Really* worried about it. Lisa didn't know I'd made that up, that I hadn't just seen Esteban drunk and coked up and talking a lot of shit at the cantina.

Esteban. Fuck *this*. I needed to find that fucker. Right now.

CHAPTER TWELVE

Words are loaded pistols.

Jean-Paul Sartre

I don't remember the drive to Pilon except that the rattletrap Ranger stalled in Cocal, near the little schoolhouse. I thought of Kim, most likely, as I did whenever the Ranger stalled, how Kim had had two months since late June to see to the fixing of my other car, the Explorer, for which he was being paid, and how I'd emailed him to make sure he did it, so I'd have a reliable car to drive when I returned. But in two months he did not do it. He *doesn't read his emails*, not about fixing my car or about keeping Lisa out of my house. And he doesn't listen while talking on the phone either, since I'd also told him these things from Montauk.

So now I'm driving a rattletrap that stalls on the way to Pilon to find Esteban Mora. Christ. Everyone here is either fucking Lisa or being gaslit or cowed by her, as with Kim and his *negative energy* and his *always create peace* horseshit. God I hate that new age horseshit. I hate it because it does not *mean* anything. How do you *create peace*? How about putting this on your fucking voicemail message: *Always speak the truth*.

Over that last bridge now, one that Danny built back in the day before it all got ugly, and I turn left toward the ocean down the little dirt track to Esteban's ranchos and right away there's deep standing water. It's the height of the rainy season and everything is very green and wet and the ground is soft. I go 4 x 4 and the water is briefly up to the door and the Ranger sideslips but doesn't stall again. It's maybe a quarter mile of slippery going past a couple squatter shacks to Esteban's ranchos at the dead end, and I'm just a few hundred yards from where Max Dalton and Alvaro Aguilar were killed by gunshots by Esteban's father in 1997, with Esteban's collusion. Pilon is squatter central and this is the heart of it.

I stop 30 or so yards from Esteban's gate; there is too much mud to go further and getting stuck here would be bad. I don't cut the engine, fearing it will not start again. Other than the Ranger's misfiring rumble it's quiet. I don't see Esteban's Rover or any car or anyone, just Esteban's ranchos and the bush surrounding them, but the Rover could be parked behind one of his ranchos.

My .38 is under a towel on the seat. I stick it under my belt behind my back and get out and walk through the mud to the gate and call out the fucker's name.

Esteban's German shepherd, on a tether by his sleeping rancho – where Esteban has been fucking Lisa – is looking at me but doesn't bark. I wonder if he recognizes the Ranger from Lisa's visits.

I have very little in my mind as a plan except to ask the fucker how long he's been fucking Lisa. Then I'll see how it goes. I'm calm and alert, not thinking in words.

Esteban is not there.

There is a light drizzle falling from the heavy overcast as I get back in the Ranger and manage to turn around without bogging. Halfway back to the main dirt road there's a kid walking his bike in the mud. I stop and look at him. He's twelve or thirteen, maybe a squatter kid I've seen surfing at Salea. He grins and asks me if I'm looking for Esteban: "Buscas Esteban?"

Yes, I say. "Sabes donde esta el?" Do you know where he is?

"No," he says, "Tal vez Golfito." Maybe in Golfito.

There are no recent signs that another car has passed this way; Esteban's is the only car that regularly uses this little dirt track. "Reconoces este carro?" I'm asking if he recognizes my car. I'm maybe thinking of the German shepherd not barking because he knew the Ranger.

The kid nods yes.

"La gringa pasa por aquí en este carro, verdad?" I gesture back toward Esteban's ranchos. I want to know if the American woman comes this way in the Ranger. The kid nods, says, "La flaca." The slim one. He flutters his hands around his head to indicate a lot of hair, Lisa's thick mane.

"Y en el ortro carro también?"

"El verde, si."

He's telling me that Lisa has also been here in our other car, my other car, the green one, the Explorer. I'm smiling to put him at ease but he suddenly continues on, slogging fast through the mud, maybe realizing he's said too much about La Flaca.

I now capitalize *La Flaca* because, as Jean would later tell me, La Flaca is Lisa's nickname with the Moras. *La Flaca*. The Slim One. *El Chivo*. One with horns. Nicknames down south are reserved for people who are well known and are distinguishable in some way and are often talked about.

When I drive up my little private road that is also my next door neighbor Barry's private road I see that Lisa's Trooper is still at Casa Tigre. I stop and get out and go to the house again. Lisa is on a ladder doing something with a light fixture and at first doesn't know I'm there. When she senses my presence she says that she's not going to speak to me.

I tell her I just need to know one thing and it's very simple. As before I'm calm and non-threatening. As Lisa comes down the ladder I say this: "I just

467

need to know what you told Esteban about me."

"I didn't have sex with anyone in your house."

"I'm not talking about sex." In fact, even in our scene before I didn't say anything about sex or sex in my house. This is a change of subject, a misdirection, from my question of what she told Esteban about me. Lisa is afraid to lie in answer to my simple question because she doesn't know what Esteban said when he was drunk and coked up and talking a lot of shit at the cantina.

Now Lisa is standing a few feet away. I can see she wants to bolt again but I'm in the doorway, casually blocking her way. "I need to know if you're trying to get me hurt," I say and I'm completely calm, as if asking about the light fixture she was working on. "Or worse."

Lisa tries to go around me and I take a small step and block her way, the first aggressive move I've made. I ask very calmly again what she's been telling Esteban and the Moras about me and if she is trying to do me harm.

"I did not have sex with Esteban in your house." She doesn't look at me as she says this and I let her pass and leave.

She did not have sex with Esteban in my house.

Not knowing what Esteban might have told me, this was Lisa's best response to my asking if she's trying to get me killed.

She had answered my question very clearly, as I knew she would.

CHAPTER THIRTEEN

In Russia they have a system where they all pull together. I know Texas, and down here you're on your own.

Joel Coen & Ethan Coen, screenwriters

An hour or so after dark Alex and Amy visit me at my house. When the dogs start barking and I see car lights I go outside, my .38 in my hand but held behind me. When I realize it's Alex's Toyota I go back in the house, put the weapon under a t-shirt on the couch, turn off CNN, which is playing without sound so I can hear outside noises, and go back out to greet them.

I'm glad they came. I've been pacing and talking to myself and to Mom since the events of the morning and need to talk to someone. It's this need, I will realize in a few minutes, that prevents me from seeing what's going on with their visit. It's my weakness that in times of stress and in my need to trust someone, I sometimes don't see things clearly. What's going on and what I don't see is that Lisa sent my friends Alex and Amy to spy on me, after lying to them about what happened between us earlier.

As I lead them inside Alex quickly says they've come to borrow my DVD of *Bowling For Columbine*. I just assume he's being truthful but he's lying. I say sure and tell them to sit down. They do so, Amy on the couch almost on top of the .38. I did not think of that when I put the weapon there. I excuse myself and remove it from behind her and put it on a chair, still wrapped in the t-shirt but it's obvious what it is. Their seeing I have a pistol on the couch needs explanation and this is what sets me off. I first ask if they've seen Lisa today and they both say no and they're lying but I don't realize this because I'm too busy being a dumb ass who needs to trust someone.

I tell them everything, starting with Lisa's invasion of my home last month, to which Amy interrupts and says it could have been a misunderstanding. I explain why that's not possible and she shrugs. I'm forgetting things, like how Amy read the Marc letter and thought Lisa had erased the Holiday Inn tape because of an embarrassing fart. I'm forgetting that Amy is Lisa's number one gaslighting victim, aside from myself.

So I just roll on and tell them everything, all I've told you here and I'm methodical and logical from going over it all so many times. I remind them about Lisa's weeping routines and her swearing fidelity and undying love for me as she tried to make them think and me think I'm delusional and now we know she's been fucking Esteban Mora since 2003.

"Maybe their affair will come out in the open," Amy says.

I just look at her.

"Esteban seems a nice guy." This is Alex.

These are exact words. They were burned into my memory by their very nonsensicalness. Amy's line is such nonsense, so disorienting, that I can't deal with it so I look at Alex, trying to figure the meaning of his. Alex has been living locally for well over a decade and knows that Gerardo Mora killed Max – it's common knowledge now – and that Esteban is his father's son, a thief and a drug dealer and a perpetrator of land fraud and a colluder in murder and rotten to the bone. Why would he say that Esteban *seems a nice guy*?

Alex and Amy said these things because it was all they could think of as a way of supporting Lisa, since they had supported her before and were now on a mission on her behalf. Once people take a side in anything, be it in a matter of a friend being delusional about his mate's infidelities or in a matter of a bogus war on terror, new information is processed in such a way as to support the side already taken. This is the way of human beings and a major reason why people believe untruths, which in turn is the main reason why the world is so fucked-up. I know this, have known it for a long time, simply by being alive on planet earth and paying a little attention while doing so. But yet I don't realize what's going on with my friends' visit that night. I don't realize it because I myself am not properly processing new information, needing more than anything right then to trust someone.

Alex and Amy stayed a while longer but I don't remember much about what was said. My mind was elsewhere, busy blocking the truth of their visit. But as they were at the door leaving and as I handed Amy the *Bowling For Columbine* DVD and some others Amy said this: "We ran into Lisa on the way up here and she said you'd have this (meaning the DVD)."

I properly processed this new information, though, and suddenly knew what had been going on. Amy's was a classic blurt. She and Alex both said they hadn't seen Lisa that day. Amy forgot about that when she said they ran into Lisa on the way over. As with people who are lying, Amy wanted to throw in a little truth, *salt the mine*, as the sociopath who shot her children calls it, and as Lisa so often does. A very little truth in this case, since Alex and Amy did not run into Lisa on the way to my house. They "ran into her" when she came to them for a gaslighting session, Lisa probably claiming I had threatened her or some such and that she was worried about *her* safety, a classic example of perception management, claiming the opposite of the truth, which was that my safety was at risk. *Then* Alex and Amy came to my house, to see what they could find out about my paranoiac state, if I was a danger to Lisa.

As I watched them leave, thinking about Amy's blurt, I also made a calculation: In the thousand-plus days I'd lived in my house, Alex and Amy never once paid a visit without being invited first, let alone after dark. This was an aspect of living there I liked; people didn't just drop by, especially after dark; it just wasn't done.

After a thousand days, the one time Alex and Amy did drop by was right after my confrontation with Lisa wherein Lisa confirmed her greatest treachery, and now knew that I knew about it. The *first thing* Lisa would do after that scene would be to go to someone who believes her lies and enlist them against me. It's her way. So my friends lied to me and betrayed me.

It was either that or a one-in-a-thousand coincidence.

I stood in my doorway watching Alex's Toyota's lights flicker through the hibiscus hedge as he drove off and then it was dark as pitch out there. I don't recall specifically but the howlers were probably still bellowing in the bush, as they do for a while after sundown.

There was a carved wood sign by the door where I was standing so you could see it as you're leaving my house. It reads, "Cuidado, es una selva afuera."

Careful, it's a jungle out there.

CHAPTER FOURTEEN

The snotgreen sea. The scrotumtightening sea.

James Joyce

Not only did Amy contradict her and Alex's assurances that they had not seen Lisa that day, and not only was it one-in-a-thousand that they just happened to stop by that night, and not only was it guaranteed that Lisa would go to them after our scenes at Casa Tigre, and not only was their nonsense about Esteban Mora a giveaway, but Amy said something else that confirmed they'd been subjected to more of Lisa's lies. When I was describing the scenes with Lisa, Amy said this: "You're always accusing Lisa of having sex with people in your house."

I asked her where she got that.

"You told us."

"When?"

"...Just now."

"No I didn't." I hadn't said anything of the sort.

Amy knew she'd fucked up. I could see it in her eyes. Lisa had told her that lie earlier, in her gaslighting session. I hadn't mentioned sex at all in my scenes with Lisa or with Alex and Amy. But *Lisa* had, in her misdirection at Casa Tigre.

So now I even knew the tack Lisa had taken with my friends. My delusions were now focused on her having had sex with people, plural, in my house, which I had never accused her of, and which I now realized she definitely had done; it wasn't just Barry. She was yet again using what she did, the too-awful-to-be-true betrayals, or rather my knowing about them, or even my not knowing about them but Lisa claiming I made the accusation anyway, as evidence of my mental instability.

That my friends had lied to me and betrayed me was dispiriting in the extreme, but knowing Lisa, how hard she'd been working on Amy, I wanted to give them a chance to own up, to put this right. Next morning I loaded my surfboard in the rattletrap Ranger, put the .38 on the seat under the towel in case of ambush and went to see them at their oceanfront house just past The Point on the south side of El Rio Claro.

Here's another weakness I harbor: If human beings are given a fair and non-confrontational chance to do so, I always think they will own up. This was part of my hanging in with Lisa, at least in the beginning; I thought she'd eventually see herself for what she is and own up and ask for forgiveness and another chance. No matter how often I'm disappointed, I persist in believing that human beings will eventually do the right thing. (I mean: *Don't they know they're going to die someday?*) Problem is, they never do.

And so it went with Alex and Amy. I could not have been mellower, gentler, in explaining that I knew Lisa, knew she'd come to them the day before, probably saying she was worried about her safety or some such, but given the Esteban Mora revelation, the various confirmations of it, I needed to clear the air with the two of them, my friends, because I needed some support. I then suggested that Lisa had sent them up to my house and I understood why they would do that, but please let's clear the air on this, and would they please just tell the truth?

I was then thinking, Don't disappoint me, kids.

"Absolutely not!" was Alex's blurt. He did not say this in anger, but his vehemence was startling; he almost shouted. He also paused beforehand – there was a two, maybe three second gap between my query and his answer, a long time, during which Alex was making a crisis decision.

To lie, to further his lie, or not?

Alex then went on to assure me their visit was to borrow the *Bowling For Columbine* DVD. He was sitting on his patio step as he went on and on with his assurances, Amy standing behind him. Uninterested in Alex now, I was examining Amy; Amy who had done something dishonest in her past, perpetrated an infidelity of some sort, and felt guilty about it and would never do anything like that again, ever. She'd told me this in the context of Lisa claiming that I would not forgive her for her cheating with her ex-boyfriend and lying about it in the beginning of our relationship, Amy saying that I have to put the past behind me.

This was Amy's weakness, you see, which Lisa worked on, repeating to Amy that I was unforgiving for her early "mistakes." It wasn't that at all, of course. It was Lisa's continuing treachery, escalating treachery, that was the problem. But since Amy had made a decision about right and wrong and about how the world works, she would not listen, would not properly process new information. Amy saw herself as guilty of an indiscretion and wanted to be forgiven, so she was supporting Lisa on what she thought was the same issue. This was Lisa's play and she had played it well, although with Amy it was fish in a barrel time.

But in my attempt to explain this, looking into Amy's eyes was like looking into the eyes of a mannequin. And so it is with uncomfortable truths, whether they expose a lie repeated over and over by a sociopath in paradise or a lie of a government that repeats over and over that it only wants to *spread democracy* -- if the lie is repeated often enough and if what you are willing to believe is based on your need to feel comfortable, you believe the lie. Someone tries to point out obvious truths and he finds himself looking into your eyes and they are the eyes of a mannequin.

Perception Management Commandment 6: *With Big Lies, to offset their intrinsic transparency, simply repeat them over and over. This technique works every time.*

We only want to spread democracy…
You've ruined me for other men…
And rid the world of monstrous dictators…
It's us against the world…

On the road toward the Rio Claro bridge I'm doing a slow burn over Alex and Amy's failure to own up, anger replacing my understanding and sympathy for why they deceived me. The Rattletrap Ranger stalls on the bridge. Fucking Kim. He doesn't read his emails. Not about fixing cars or keeping sociopaths out of my house.

Asshole. But I'm thinking of Alex here, not Kim. Alex who is my age and went along with his young and pretty if vapid wife's state of denial and her support of Lisa's lies; Alex knows better. But Alex as much as anyone here is absorbed in the local pecking order issues and probably wants to see me fall anyway, for my little bit of acclaim. The Germans have a word for it, when you want to see a friend fall: *schadenfreude.*

I park under the big avocado tree near the cantina. I need a go-out, need some waves. I walk to the seawall and look out at the sea.

Kim is surfing near the river mouth.

*Ass*hole.

Easy. I need to ease up, clear my head.

I paddle out. I'm off. Don't find that rhythm. I come in.

I shower at the cantina and am rounding the corner just as a car pulls up, a boxy 4 x 4, a Rover with heavily tinted windows.

Esteban. Esteban's fucking car.

I'm standing right by the driver's side, two feet away, staring into the opaque of the window, my own reflection there. Come on out, motherfucker, let me see you. Seconds go by. I think of my .38 in the Ranger a few yards away. What is he waiting for? The door finally opens. *Barry.* Barry climbs out. It's Barry's Trooper, not Esteban's Rover. He sat in there not wanting to come out with me standing in his face.

Christ. I thought it was a shitball motherfucker who fucked my girlfriend and now wants to kill me but I was wrong. It's only a shitball motherfucker who fucked my girlfriend.

"Barry!" I'm grinning like the dumb-ass fucked-up fool that I am with all this shit, grinning big to see how Barry handles it. Barry turns his head away from me and looks into the cantina, visibly shaken, can't make eye contact, doesn't know what to make of this. Half a head taller, this big dumb ass non-person still cannot look at me.

"What's up, Barry?" I say, my shit-head grin frozen and sarcastic as he mumbles something and bolts into the cantina.

Asshole. This shitball motherfucker doesn't even surf.

On the way home the rattletrap Ranger stalls twice, the second time by the Rio Higo bridge, just past Logan the Nutcase's Sawmills construction project. Logan has gotten into trouble lately for his blatant muni-bribing, and shut down the construction. Now he's back at it. He probably bribed his way out of the bribery trouble. He'll be fine, no doubt, weather the shit storm just fine.

Should I call Danny with the bad news?

Danny. Danny knew since June that Esteban Mora was fucking Lisa. He knew for three full months and didn't tell me. And hold on. He only did tell me in order to change the subject from his friend John fucking Lisa. Had that subject not come up he never would have told me.

Let's go over this, see how it worked.

Had Danny not shot a short video clip of Lisa at my house, Jean would not have yelled out, "That's Esteban's girlfriend!" and Danny wouldn't have known about Lisa and Esteban in the first place and so would not have been able to tell me.

But hold on. I'm thinking the chain of causation therefore really starts with Lisa fucking John, since Lisa fucking John was the reason Danny wanted to change the subject, as above.

But hold on. The chain of causation really starts in 1998, when I first saw Lisa in the beach lot at Montauk in her little MG and I was smitten but too intimidated to speak to her because of the negativity, the *negative energy*, in my life at that time, best exemplified by the Cat Woman Incident. Hold on. Had the Cat Woman Incident not happened, I might have been less intimidated and spoken to Lisa that day, maybe beaten her future ex-boyfriend to the Lisa-punch, which would have changed everything. So maybe Cat Woman is involved in all this too. (A question: *Should* Cat Woman be on the list of women I've had sex with?)

But hold on. What I'm *really* thinking of with all this is The Butterfly Effect. A butterfly flaps its little wings in Tibet (maybe in the garden of a monastery where the monks are not allowed to speak, for further symmetry) and next thing you've got a hurricane wreaking havoc somewhere in the tropics.

I'm thinking too much, no?

And the rattletrap Ranger keeps stalling.

CHAPTER FIFTEEN

My words fly up, my thoughts remain below:
Words without thoughts never to heaven go.

William Shakespeare

The rattletrap Ranger brought me home that day, barely, like a broken-down horse in need of the barn. The expression *rode hard and put up wet* comes to mind, regarding us both, man and car.

I entered my house and sat on the living room floor, which was my way of gathering my pups for a chat. When I'd sit on the floor they'd gather and swarm, whining and grinning and licking and sniffing, tails a-blur everywhere, and Aleeza would be unable to contain herself and she'd bark at high pitch and everyone would get jealous of everyone else in the doggy frenzy to be loved most. Moments like this I'd think of Fang, and grieve a bit.

And so it went that day as I told my pups I was leaving and might not see them for a while. When I said this I was lying to two of them, to Aleeza and to Cho Cho, whom I knew I would not see again. I'd send for Tigre and of course for Honey, have them shipped to wherever I eventually ended up, maybe the States but I was also thinking about Mexico. Four was too much, though. Just too much.

I'd see that they were well-cared for.

Maria Louisa, my maid, was there that day and she came into the living room and saw me on the floor with my pups and saw that I was in tears and she knew I was leaving and so she started crying. She'd seen this coming and she knew why it had come, why I needed to leave. Although Lisa had spent a lot of time with Maria Louisa and had gaslit her about me, this simple campesina, unlike my sophisticated gringo friends, was not fooled.

I hugged Maria Louisa and told her that her job was safe, that I'd keep her on even with the house empty, and when it was sold the new owner would keep her on also, I guaranteed that, but she wouldn't stop crying and I went along with her on this, with the real emotion I was being touched by.

Around sundown I spoke at length to Marcos, telling him his job was safe as well, and that when the house was sold and my pups taken care of and two of them shipped out safe and sound, he'd get $1,000 plus my motorcycle; I'd also send $300 for Maria Louisa as a little thank you for everything.

There were other details to see to, which I did, but 36 hours later I was in a taxi out of there, bound for Golfito, the puddle jumper to San José, and then a big jet to the island from which I now write.

As I passed the Mora *finca* and then Esteban's little dirt track in Pilon that day it was a strange and disquieting replay of my leaving in 1998 after the Dalton investigation, when I was likewise concerned about the Mora family and what they might have been planning due to my being a writer of nonfiction.

This time was different, though, in that my involvement in events was more direct and personal and complex; I was not just an observer and a chronicler of the treachery but a victim. And it was different this time in that in leaving the little paradise at the end of the road at the bottom of Central America it was not over yet. I still had another dark moment to go through, my darkest. It would occur up in San José before I could get out of the country and it would have to do with who and what I am.

CHAPTER SIXTEEN

Four legs good, two legs bad.

George Orwell

Since my arrival on this island back in October I've been speaking by phone to Danny Fowlie's friend Jean, the lady who had the first-hand knowledge of Lisa's fucking Esteban Mora since 2003. I told her that the count of Lisa's fuckbuddies – known fuckbuddies – at the end of the road was now eight. I told her about the female baboon allusion and that it appeared Lisa was taking it literally; she was working her way through the whole troop.

"Oh, boy. That reminds me," Jean said.

"What?"

"I probably shouldn't tell you this."

I laughed, thinking that at this point no news could shock or dismay me. I was wrong.

"Esteban Mora had sex with a cow."

"A *cow*?"

"That's what he told me."

"He *told* you?" I was back to mindlessly repeating paradise bulletins.

"He was trying to seduce me, get me to go to Mexico with him."

"I don't get it about the cow."

"I guess he thought it would turn me on."

I don't bring up Esteban's having sex with a cow to raise still further the coefficient of sordidness here, nor to further paint a picture of a soiled paradise; God knows there's enough of that. But in trying to understand how people like Lisa and Esteban *get through the day*, a question arises, given that Lisa and Esteban have a problem in common: What's with all the blurts?

A possible answer: Sociopaths – by whatever definition you care to use – sometimes forget how fucked up they are. It just slips their minds. This is natural and predictable since on top of the daily challenge of keeping their lies and deceptions and treacheries straight, they have to remember what constitutes acceptable behavior in the normal world around them.

Talk about a *tough job*!

Sometimes they forget stuff:

Esteban must know that in the normal world having sex with a cow is a no-no, right?

But hey: *He forgot.*

Esteban's dad, Gerardo, must know that revealing to a journalist that he is running a murder investigation wherein he himself is the prime suspect is a no-no, right?

But hey: *He forgot.*

Lisa must know that... so many choices here... that telling the man who has ruined her for other men that the first thing she thinks about when she meets another man is whether she'd like to have sex with him is a no-no, right?

But hey: *She forgot.*

George W. Bush's PM team must know that... so many choices here as well... that threatening others with war crimes prosecution for the destruction of oil wells while your own forces go about bombing civilian restaurants (to cut the head off the serpent) and destroying civilian infrastructures and torturing human beings and then threatening to cut off aid to anyone who doesn't exempt you from war crimes prosecution is a no-no, right?

But hey: *They forgot.*

There's nothing wrong with any of *them*!

Me being me, after my conversation with Jean I came up with the following mental images: Esteban gets up one morning and has sex with a cow. That afternoon he has sex with Lisa. I have sex with Lisa that night. Since there was no surf that day and Esteban didn't bathe, *I've* now had sex with a cow, if you get my bodily-fluid drift.

I'm thinking too much again, no?

CHAPTER SEVENTEEN

We do on stage things that are supposed to happen off. Which is a kind of integrity, if you look at every exit as an entrance somewhere else.

Tom Stoppard

I couldn't get out of Costa Rica right away due to a legal commitment. I had to be in San José on October 24th to sign papers with Francisco, Lisa's and my lawyer. So I had a week to kill in-country. I rented a car and took a drive to the northern Pacific coast to see if I could find Lisa's San José fuckbuddy, the guy from the Fleabag Hotel Incident, "David Peter."

Based on my theory that David Peter was a legal resident of Costa Rica, I'd had the spooky colluder in Max's murder, Fajardo, use his government-document connections to amass some dossiers. Farjardo came up with a sheaf of possibilities, all David Peter somethings, complete with photos plus biographical details. One guy jumped out at me: Lean, moustache, about the right age (mid-40s) – I'd caught just the barest glimpse of him at the fleabag hotel. The guy in the dossier was "an investor" from Fort Lauderdale, Florida, close to but not exactly "a commodities broker" from Miami, as Lisa described him in her detail-rich blathering.

I drove six hours to David Peter's business and residence to find he was not there; he was not currently in-country. Maybe I'd be back. I'd try to come back.

Although *No one knows shit*, etc, I have a theory of why I went to this trouble, and it was more than my need to know everything for the simple sake of knowing. I believe I also needed to show Lisa, via this narrative, that she had not gotten away with *anything*. I wanted her to know that I *knew it all* and that with me she was out of her league in smarts and in twistedness too. (The uncertainty principle rears again, as the tale is affected by the telling.) My twistedness, however, was of a very different sort from hers, as different as you can get.

But the *arrogance* of her in believing she could play her domination game with me! Yes, I'd caved, caved mightily, and, unlike Logan the Nutcase, she had succeeded in running me out of town, out of my paradise, out of my home, but… but in the end, in the ending, no, I would not suffer *that* shit well.

To put it another way: No matter how this tale, this nonfiction book, ends, the *real ending* is its very existence.

Can you wrap your mind around that?

To put it still another way: Imagine that for Lisa, for all of them, perception really *is* truth.

CHAPTER EIGHTEEN

I want to hear all about Anna Livia. Well, you know Anna Livia?
Yes, of course, we all know Anna Livia. Tell me all. Tell me now.

James Joyce

Lisa would have her *no limits* revenge for everything I know, for knowing who and what she is, and God knows I should have seen it coming.

On February 22, some six weeks ago here on this island I got an email from Danny Fowlie that stunned me to the core. Out of the blue Fowlie was accusing me of stealing his land, of being a fraud and a thief. The details of Fowlie's accusations are so absurd, so over the top in their falsity, that I'll not detail them here. (Aside from what you know from this narrative, his misinformation, his lies, and the speciousness of his twisted logic are obvious from our correspondences, which are archived on my website.) I immediately called Jean, now in Florida, and asked her if she had any idea what happened to precipitate this current fucked-up turn of events. She said she did:

"Lisa's been emailing Dan."

"Since when?"

"For a couple weeks at least. I remember on Valentine's Day Dan had me read one of her emails." Jean had been at Fowlie's in California in mid-February and at Fowlie's invitation had read a long, detail-rich Lisa-email, sent from Costa Rica. Chatty, describing her life, Jean recalled an anecdote about Lisa's day getting a Costa Rican driver's license; something about her "bony ass" was mentioned, how it hurt from sitting on hard DMV seats. Fowlie had remarked what a good writer Lisa is.

Lisa and Fowlie were now pen pals; more emails were subsequently exchanged. Jean hadn't read them but soon after Valentine's Day, Fowlie told Jean that he thought Lisa was "the victim" in her relationship with me, and that I'd not been honest in my land dealings with Lisa. Lisa also told Fowlie that I'd been dishonest in my dealings with *him*. From the Fowlie email of February 22:

> I think I will start communicating with her [Lisa]; she

> may have something to say about your real intention
> surrounding this property and the rip off...

Fowlie is lying when he says he *will start* communicating with Lisa. As we know from Jean, he'd been in contact with Lisa for at least a week. From a Fowlie email a couple weeks later:

> I did later contact her [Lisa] as I told you I would, to
> inquire on how much property you were talking about
> [the land I'd bought with Lisa], and found that there
> was more than you told me on several purchases.

That Lisa would work on Fowlie, the ultimate male member of the troop, the silverback baboon, as it were, was a maneuver I should have seen coming. In Lisa's domination game – the same game played by the shitball motherfuckers who run this sorry-ass world – this would be a given. As is pointed out by Doc Stout and others, *domination is the game of all sociopaths.*

Lisa, of course, had a major obstacle to overcome. Not only did Fowlie know of her treachery, he had provided me with its most horrendous example: the Esteban Mora revelation. (That for three months he hadn't told me was the tip off that treachery would eventually come from his direction.) So Lisa had to play it just right, and she obviously had. In a stroke of PM genius, she *used* her betrayals.

From a Fowlie email:

> You know Lisa is a free spirit and not really ready to
> settle down with one man – unless he is perfect in her
> eyes. You weren't.

And Fowlie would reveal in more detail what Lisa told him. On the phone he came up with this blurt: "Lisa told me that yes, she went out on you, but you knew she was a free spirit from the start."

Yes, she went out on me. Now, finally, it's from *la boca de la yequa*, the mare's mouth, no?

But *free spirit*? You want to talk about a euphemism? With Lisa's admission to screwing everything in sight when she was with me – the man who had ruined her for other men and on and on – plus with her detail-rich pen pal intimacies, Fowlie's 72 year-old mind must have run amok with Lisa-pussy fantasies.

And something relatively rare had transpired. Fowlie had *reprocessed* everything he knew about Lisa and her deceit and treachery, and everything he knew about me and my respect and loyalty, to fit with his new agenda: Copping some Lisa-pussy. He had betrayed me for the *possibility* of copping some Lisa-pussy.

Copping Lisa-pussy.

Symmetry.

I can now picture how it went during Fowlie's Pavones visit in June. I had been told that Lisa hung out with Fowlie and his entourage "constantly." Aside from her "thing" for John, I have no doubt that she subtly – or maybe not-so-subtly – flirted with Fowlie, giving the 72-year-old (who'd been in jail for 18 years) some subtle – or maybe not-so-subtle – thoughts about this fine, much younger piece of ass.

As it turned out, Fowlie had lied to me about virtually everything. He accepted my $10,000 gift (more dumb-ass unmotivated kindness) then used my sorry ass, letting me put it on the line for him in his desperate scramble to reclaim the empire he legally had no claim to.[*]

And there was more behind this deception than Lisa's desire to supplant me as Fowlie's confidant, his trusted ally, and all that that would imply for her business future at Pavones (she recently bought a 60-acre parcel, raising well over $600,000 to do so). Lisa learned that I'd found a buyer for my house in late January and needed to block the sale, if possible. Why? My house, worth about $400k, was my weak point. As long as I still owned it I was vulnerable to retribution, from the Moras or Logan or... or aside from Lisa herself, the list is... long. She must have figured that I would not likely publish this book until my house was gone and the money safely out of the country. (She was correct.)

And indeed Fowlie tried to block the sale. That this was impossible (for multiple reasons) is not the point. That Fowlie would *try* to do this after all I had done for him, and given that he well knew of my need to extricate myself from Costa Rica, in part due to my helping him, was a betrayal surpassed only by Lisa's own.[†]

And somehow it gets worse.

Fowlie was one of only a handful of people who knew where I've been since October. Although I doubted the Moras would try to reach out and have me murdered on this island, it was not an impossibility (nor was it

---

[*] I was later able to procure the documents proving that Fowlie had legally signed over his holdings to Alan Nelson, who in turn had the right to sell.[**]

[**] Lisa managed to compound her treachery by telling Nelson – Fowlie's deadly enemy – that I backed Fowlie with a large cash contribution to his war chest after I sold my house (meanwhile telling Fowlie I had ripped him off in the selling of my house): She lied to both sides of the land conflict in an attempt to turn everyone against me. (She perpetrated both lies around Valentine's Day – there's further symmetry here, I think.)

[†] I've archived on the adjunct website all the emails I refer to in this chapter – Fowlie's and Lisa's to me, and my responses, plus my land surveys and paperwork with Fowlie proving I did not misrepresent anything, plus the documents proving Fowlie lied about the legal status of his land. Fowlie's having alerted me to Lisa's treachery with Esteban Mora is also verified. It's all there, if you doubt me.

impossible that Lisa herself would seek a way to get it done, possibly using connections the Moras would supply her); keeping my whereabouts secret as I write this narrative is a precaution I've taken instinctively. Fowlie well knew this, and well knew the power of the Moras, as well as their cold-blooded relentlessness in getting what they want, i.e., stealing land and selling it. (They'd of course murdered Max and their own cousin for land.) Fowlie and I spoke of this back in early November after I came here and I told him of my location and plan to finish this narrative. He agreed I was in potential danger even on this island, outside of Costa Rica. He promised not to tell a soul where I was and that I was writing this narrative.

I say all this as prelude to what Fowlie did next: He told Lisa (and hence the Moras) that I was working on this narrative and that I assumed I was in danger because of the revelations about the Dalton murder. And he also did this:

He told Lisa where I am.

I no longer brood about the hopelessness of it all, nor on most days do I choose to be beset with terminal loneliness. No, fuck *that*. My final word on The Waterman Who Would Be King:

He should rot in hell along with the rest of them.

CHAPTER NINETEEN

Now, here, you see, it takes all the running you can do, to keep in the same place. If you want to get somewhere else, you must run at least twice as fast as that!

Lewis Carroll

On October 23rd, a week after my bolt from my home in paradise and three days after my failed attempt to find Lisa's fuckbuddy, the San José one, "David Peter," I was in San José in a 4-star hotel called the Del Rey, which is world famous as a whorehouse (prostitution is legal in Costa Rica).

Lisa and I had gone to the Del Rey about a year and a half previously, to the bar downstairs, looking for a whore to do a threesome with (this was well before our collision at the el Presidente, when Lisa begged me to go get a whore). The Del Rey bar in full swing is a sight. Whores all over the place, like a hundred whores, some of which whores being quite beautiful, in the morbid sense. We didn't pick up a whore that night — I didn't have the heart for it. As I've said, I'm not into whores, sexually. I don't know if Lisa would have agreed to grab a whore and go back to our room at the Balmoral that night had I not said Let's get out of here after a few minutes at the bar. Maybe, maybe not. She was pretty bright-eyed, looking around at all the whores and she being the only non-whore in the place. I say non-whore in the sense of *not getting paid* to fuck a lot of guys.

I know: Christ this is all so *sordid*.

But a question: Why was I staying at a whorehouse if I'm not into whores? Because of the armed security downstairs.

I came up with a couple of things over the four days I was at the Del Rey. I thought of how I'd dedicate this book. As you may have realized by now, the dedication is tinged with irony, based on it being sly and misleading, although in no way is it a deceit. On a certain level, it may be the truest dedication you've ever come across.

While hiding out at the Del Rey I also came up with the cover design of this book, pictured it quite clearly. The opening epigraph from Gene Fowler is of course the inspiration. *Writing is easy. You just stare at the blank page until your forehead bleeds.*

Another question: What could be going on in a person's mind that would result in his forehead bleeding?

The answer, for me, is this: *Obsession and pain.*

We're back to that one.

Let me tell you something. When you're writing *sordid* stuff as I am now, and when the sordid stuff is your life, your forehead *really* bleeds. And writing about a whorehouse you were staying at because the armed security made you feel safer than at a normal hotel doesn't do much to stem the flow either.

Although the security was my reason for being at the Del Rey, I thought it unlikely that the Moras would try to kill me in San José, or even had I stayed at Pavones, at least not prior to this book's public appearance and the repercussions regarding their land-selling became obvious. I put it at around a one-in-four chance that I was in any current danger. My reasoning was simply in knowing the Moras. To some extent they are ignorant campesinos; not stupid, just ignorant. Ignorant of the potential power of words, of truth. Even with Lisa's haranguing about this book, the damage it would do them, they'd probably not go to the trouble of trying to kill me. For all Lisa's ego and arrogance and sociopathic persuasiveness, I doubted that the Moras would take her or even the Dalton hard copy seriously. With no chance to get their hands on my land, Lisa was now just another piece of *gringa* ass – to Esteban, anyway. One among many.

Also, I did not leave Pavones out of fear of the Moras. This is not courage I speak of. I did not care if they killed me, or tried to. I truly felt this way about it: Fuck it. No. I left because I could not stand being there any longer. It was no longer my home.

But still, I took some simple precautions, like carrying a firearm and staying at a hotel with armed security and not being on the hotel phone list – when I checked into the Del Rey I made it clear I didn't want my name on the list. This way if someone called asking for me they'd be told that there was no such person at the hotel. If the Moras were looking for me in San José – and Lisa knew I had to be there to sign papers – they, or Lisa on their behalf, would certainly try to locate me by calling the hotels I might stay at.

Thing was, though, on the 24th, which was the day after I checked in, I got a call. It was a female voice, a *gringa*, asking for "Rich." First thing I thought of: How many guys staying at a whorehouse tell a female, i.e., their wife, girlfriend, secretary, or any female except a whore – and the voice was that of a *gringa*, therefore not a whore – where they are? The phone voice was muffled, maybe disguised; it could have been Lisa or a girlfriend she'd enlisted to help look for me.

I immediately went to a pay phone and called the hotel and asked for myself by name. The dumb-ass desk operator not only rang the call through but told me my room number. I went to the hotel desk. *Ass*hole. Before I tore him a new one, I told the operator that I'd just gotten a call, a *gringa*, and did she ask for me by name or room number?

By name, the guy said, and he said my name.

A *gringa* asks for me by name and then when I answer wants "Rich"? Just to be sure, I asked the name of the person who'd been in the room before me. It was not a "Rich." It was Lisa behind that call all right. If it was a friend on the phone, one of her gaslit buddies, Lisa had probably told her she was worried about *her* safety, that routine or something similar, and needed to know where I was. She'd gone to a lot of trouble; the Del Rey would have been far down on the list of hotels she'd think of. Lisa knows I'm not into whores.

There were three guys at the front desk at this 4-star hotel and I tore them all new assholes: "You're running a fucking *whorehouse* and you don't know enough to take it seriously when someone says remove his fucking *name* from the phone list?!"

They knew they'd fucked up all right and more so when I suggested at high volume that they stay alert for a gang of Ticos storming in with machine pistols. That one turned some *puta* heads in the lobby.

With Lisa going to so much trouble to find me, I considered my situation slightly more serious. But again: *Fuck it.* I did change rooms, though.

I was stuck in San José after signing the papers with Francisco because Hurricane Wilma had just roared through South Florida and fucked up Miami, where I had to go first to get to this island, and my flight had been cancelled. (The Butterfly Effect, maybe literally.) I wouldn't be able to get out of there until the 27th. Two more nights in that fucking whorehouse – I had not yet touched whore one. I would, though, that very night, October 25th, and for reasons I cannot explain.

I hit the street just after dark, needing a walk and something other than the Del Rey's room service food. I'd go down to Chelles, a local joint Lisa and I had often frequented, *our* restaurant, which was on the same block as the Balmoral, *our* hotel. Chelles door is always open and as I went to turn into the place I made a sharp sudden left and kept on going down the street.

Sitting at a front table was Lisa, leaning forward in deep conversation with someone, a guy I know.

CHAPTER TWENTY

You shan't evade
These rhymes I've made.

Gaius Valerias Catullus

Kim. Lisa and Kim were alone together in San José.

They hadn't seen me so I crossed the street and stood behind a newspaper kiosk and watched them through the door. Although they weren't doing any touchy-feely shit, I knew immediately that they were fuckbuddies. I just *knew*.

Marcos had been telling me he thought they were, based on their comings and goings at my house all summer while I was at Montauk, how they'd make border runs for construction materials and get back late, once after 10 PM, hours after any supply stores were open. Kim's wife Sassy was back now but had been in the States for months. Still and all, I'd told Marcos I just could not picture it.

I find something sexy in half the men I meet. Lisa's journal again. She'd even managed to find something sexy in Kim, whom she'd denigrated from day one, even branding him a rip-off for "forgetting about" money he owed me. (This was a version of her "us against the world" act, i.e., I couldn't trust anyone but her.)

And Sassy was Lisa's "best friend."

What a piece of work the love of my life was. I mean I could sure pick 'em, no?

Kim had called me on my cell a couple of days after my bolt from Pavones with some bullshit question about a water pump that was in the bodega, had prefaced the query with "I don't know where you are but..." and I now realized he was trying to locate me for Lisa. I'd evaded the question and told him how fucked up it was that he had lied for Lisa and also hadn't fixed my car while I was in the States. Kim had immediately gone into his *negative energy* spiel, how I was putting out too much of it, saying again that I had *friends who loved me*. Yes, Kim, I had a whiz-bang helluvan *extended family* down here in paradise, didn't I?

How long had this been going on? Kim's lying for Lisa went all the way back to January, eight months ago, when Lisa came back on New Year's Eve to try to "work things out" with me. But fuck: The border runs. All last spring, too, while Lisa and I were still living together, Lisa and Kim would make runs together to buy construction materials, sometimes getting back late, as Marcos had pointed out. They'd knock off a piece at a border flophouse while they were at it.* Talk about right in my face. And *I just could not picture it.*

How did she juggle all these guys, with no one knowing about anyone else, let alone me knowing? They were all married, for one thing, and would keep their traps shut.

But hold on. Lisa knew I was in San José, and knew this was my block as much as hers. Didn't she figure I might stop by Chelles and see her with this asshole?

That phone call yesterday. I'd had my name removed from the hotel list right after that call. She'd called again today, found me not registered at the hotel and figured I'd checked out and left San José. There's good news here, though. Lisa hadn't been trying to pinpoint my location for the Moras; she wanted to know if it was safe for her and Kim to be out and about. No, I was not likely in danger from the Moras, at least not for now, especially with Lisa in San José too.

With Kim.

I found myself cackling at this shit.

No limits.

In watching the two of them I felt a sense of empowerment. And I had to see where this went, how they interacted, where they'd go. I waited.

Twenty minutes go by and they exit Chelles and turn right, toward the bus stop a couple of blocks away. They're across the street so I stay in the shadow of the kiosk and watch as they walk half a block then Lisa stops, touching Kim's arm. She gabs for a bit, Kim nodding, then the two turn around and walk back the other way; Lisa changed her mind about something. She is of course completely in charge.

The street is crowded so I follow them from no more than 20 yards as they pass Chelles and continue up the block. They stop for a moment in front of the Balmoral and then Lisa goes into the hotel, Kim waiting outside. Maybe 30 seconds pass then he follows her in.

Here's what all that was about: Kim, being a cheapskate, stays at some fleabag joint on the outskirts of San José. When they first left Chelles's the two were going there (probably via bus), then Lisa changed her mind, saying fuck the inconvenience, they'll go to her hotel, the Balmoral, just a block away. But since the staff knows her so well she went in first so it

---

* I would even find out what flophouse they used. This story is archived on the adjunct website in the Cut Chapters section.

wouldn't look like she's doing what she's doing, i.e., fucking some guy. Why else go in separately?

I wait outside Lisa's hotel, *our* hotel, giving them ten minutes to get naked, get started, then I follow them in.

CHAPTER TWENTY-ONE

In following him, I follow but myself.

William Shakespeare

I use the house phone to find out which room Lisa is in, then take the stairs up so there would be no elevator door-opening surprises. Hers is right next to the stairwell. Just looking at the number, 322, from 10 feet away I'm feeling strange, a sense of unreality.

I've waited so long for this moment, fantasizing and dreaming of it for going on two years, through all the lunatic shit, the obsession and pain, the death of love, the sick puppy shit and the dark shit...

...bust her with some uncommitted dick...

...my fantasy and my need...

... grab her by the throat and demand to know *how she gets through the day...*

...I'm right at the door now and yes I can hear it, Lisa's little ah ah ah ah anthem, not raucous and crazed with lust (and triumph) like the last time *I* fucked her, but they've just got started and maybe it will get better...

...no, it will not get better... because I'm going through that door...

...except... except this isn't right... this isn't how it's supposed to be...

...I should have caught them back in the spring or early summer when we were still a couple and Lisa was protesting her innocence... undying love... how I'd ruined her for other men...

...I should have caught them in my bed or at the border flophouse...

...*ruined her for other men...*

...this isn't how it's supposed to be...

...no, this isn't right...

...*negative energy...*

...you're putting out too much *negative energy, Allan...*

...you have *friends who love you, Allan...*

...always *create peace...*

...*kill Kim...*

...I don't care that Kim is fucking Lisa or when it started or where he did it...

...I don't care about any of that...

...I want to kill Kim for...

...for being *full of shit*...

...ah ah ah ah ah ah...

...Lisa is not even in there...

...she does not exist...

...there is only Kim and I want to kill him for being...

...full of shit...

...ah ah ah ah ah ah...

...not for being a sociopath, like Lisa, but just...

...full of *shit*...

...I'll go through the door...

...ah ah ah ah ah...

...*full of shit*...

...*full of shit*...

...I'm sitting by the door now, room 322, the Balmoral, *our* place, slumped there, back to the wall, feeling dizzy and sick and sapped and fatigued and...

...not at all right... what I'm feeling now is not at *all* right...

...I'm just some fucking fool in a hotel hallway with his back to the wall...

...this is my life?...

...a sordid life...

...this is me...

...is there any more to it than that?...

...*why is the world so fucked up?*...

...a dark moment...

CHAPTER TWENTY-TWO

A protagonist can only be as strong as the forces of antagonism arrayed against him.

Robert McKee

How to explain What I Did Next?

How to explain why I got up from my slump with my back to the wall at the Balmoral and left and went back to the Del Rey and found a whore at the bar and brought her to my room and asked her about her life in Nicaragua and about her two year-old son at home and listened to her tale and then fucked her?

As I say, I'm not into whores.

Art is the imposing of a pattern on experience, and our aesthetic enjoyment is the recognition of the pattern.

Alfred North Whitehead

Mom Goes to the Beach

January 16th, 2001 was the day of Mom's last birthday before she died. Mom was in a wheelchair now – her bones were too fragile from the tumors for her to be hoofing around, even on a walker. The doctors were afraid that if she fell she'd just sort of shatter.

Mom hadn't been out of the house in a while, not even to go to the cancer clinic just down the street. She had made the decision to go the hospice route, which meant no more chemo or radiation treatments. Going the hospice route is essentially giving up on life, or at least the possibility of an extended one.

Although Mom denied it up and down, I believe a part of this decision was a financial one. See, the way it works in the U.S. of A is that when an old person still feels like there's hope and is continuing treatment, Medicare won't pay for certain things, like pain medication – for which, toward the end, Mom was spending about $4,000 a month. You give up and go the hospice route, Medicare pays for your pain medication. Medicare's motive here is to persuade old folks to give up as soon as possible, to save government money on expensive stuff like chemo and radiation treatments.

Mom's concern was that she was going through my inheritance with all the money she was spending on pain medication. Mom never said this to me, knowing I'd flip. I found out by overhearing words to this effect one day when Mom was talking to Ellen.

Although arguments with Mom were unheard of, Mom and I argued about her quitting treatments and going the hospice route. During these arguments Mom lied, which was also unheard of. Mom denied that the inheritance issue had anything to do with her decision. Said it was a relief, really, to quit the treatments. No more bullshit from the doctors about possible remissions and so forth. When I said I'd overheard her tell Ellen another story, Mom said she was just confused that day with Ellen and didn't know what she was talking about.

But the point being that Mom was on hospice care and hadn't been out for a while. Mom's doctor had strongly recommended against Mom going anywhere; the fear of falling issue. Now it's January 16th, 2001, Mom's birthday, and I tell Mom we're going to the beach. Mom's eyes light up, not only because she loves the beach as much as I do but because she loves going against her doctor's orders. She gets this look like a kid who's about to get away with something.

So I bundle up Mom, wheel her out to the car, put her in the passenger's seat, pile Honey in, and we go to the beach. It's mid-winter and the beach is deserted. Blue skies, bluer sea. Beautiful. Problem is, I can't wheel Mom across the sand down to the water; that just won't work. I find a beach access for cars. It's got a chain and lock across it. There's a lifeguard station nearby so I go there. There's a lone cop inside, not a lifeguard. He's not a beach cop, which is sort of a semi-cop, but a full-blown cop in full cop regalia. As soon as the cop swivels around in his cop-chair and shoots me a cop-look, I know I'm in for trouble. Think central casting for a cop you know is going to give you trouble.

I tell the cop I'd like to take a ride on the beach and could he maybe unlock the chain across the access? He asks to see my beach-driving permit. I don't have one. I can tell this pleases him. Sorry, he says, not meaning it. I say I have Mom in the car and it's her birthday and she's sick and I want to take her down to the beach. I know this isn't going to work, but I give it a shot.

The cop stares at me, frowning, then gets up and goes to the window and looks out. Sees Mom and Honey in the car. Looks at me for a bit. He doesn't have the key to the chain, he says. Okay, I say, Thanks anyway. I go to leave. He says Wait a minute. Calls someone. They don't have the key and the guy who does is off that day. The cop calls someone else and gets the guy's home number but no one is home. He makes some other calls. No one knows where the key is. The cop hangs up and sits there shaking his head and frowning. I tell him Thanks anyway and go to leave. He says Wait a minute. He calls the fire department and they send an emergency vehicle, one of those big red and white jobs with a mini-hospital inside and the Jaws of Life and a crew of uniformed guys. The thing comes roaring up with its lights flashing. The cop talks to the head guy and then they get out a bolt cutter and sever the chain across the beach access.

Mom and Honey and I drive down to the beach and have a fine time.

The point being, though: Sometimes people will surprise you. I mean in a good way.

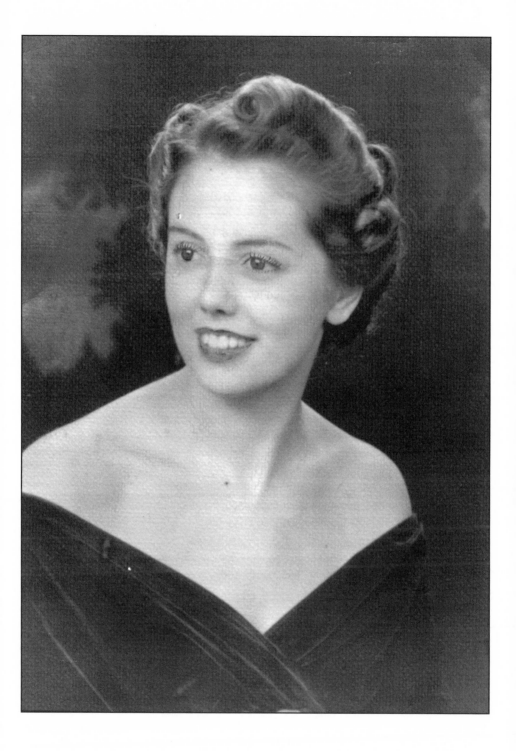

Final Author's Note

The people and events described in this book are real, i.e.: not *made up*; except as noted, names have not been changed. Further, virtually all the crucial assertions I make regarding events in my personal life, world affairs, and so forth are substantiated in various ways on my website – way too much material to add as an appendix to this book. There are additional photographs, Acknowledgements, A (Long) Note on Veracity, a Cut Chapters section, story updates, some of my related writings; all sorts of stuff. Go to www.cantyougetalongwithanyone.com (or www.cygawa.com).

I have gone to great lengths to prove I'm not lying about anything - at least not anything important.*

At cygawa.com or banditobooks.com (my publishing company's website) you can subscribe to my (free) eZine; find out how things have been going since the events of the book.

If you either don't have access to the World Wide Web or *can't stand* the motherfucker – in a sense I would respect you for either of these circumstances – what can I say?

It is, after all, an imperfect world we live in.

---

* I made an error in chronology in the Hollywood through-line. The error, and why I didn't correct it, is explained on the website. (If you noticed it: Good for you and thanks for paying such close attention. I didn't notice it for 2 years.)

Also by Allan Weisbecker

In Search of Captain Zero

Cosmic Banditos

Websites:
www.banditobooks.com
www.cygawa.com